GLENN GOULD

The Performer in the Work

GLENN GOULD

THE PERFORMER
IN THE WORK

A Study in
Performance Practice

KEVIN BAZZANA

CLARENDON PRESS · OXFORD

1997

Oxford University Press, Great Clarendon Street, Oxford OX2 6DP

Oxford New York

Athens Auckland Bangkok Bogota Bombay Buenos Aires
Calcutta Cape Town Dar es Salaam Delhi Florence Hong Kong Istanbul
Karachi Kuala Lumpur Madras Madrid Melbourne Mexico City
Nairobi Paris Singapore Taipei Tokyo Toronto Warsaw

and associated companies in
Berlin Ibadan

Oxford is a trade mark of Oxford University Press

Published in the United States
by Oxford University Press Inc., New York

British Library Cataloguing in Publication Data

Data available

Library of Congress Cataloging-in-Publication Data
Bazzana, Kevin.
Glenn Gould: the performer in the work: a study in performance practice / Kevin Bazzana.
p.   cm.
Includes bibliographical references
1. Gould, Glenn—Criticism and interpretation.   2. Gould, Glenn—Performances.
3. Gould, Glenn—Views on performance practice.   4. Performance practice
(Music)—20th century.   5. Piano music—Interpretation (Phrasing, dynamics, etc.)   I. Title.
ML417.G68B39   1997   786.2'092—dc21   97—12606
ISBN 0–19–816656–7

1 3 5 7 9 10 8 6 4 2

Typeset by Seton Music Graphics
Printed in Great Britain
on acid-free paper by Bookcraft Ltd.,
Midsomer Norton, Somerset

in memory of my mother, Jean Bazzana,
and in memory of Simon and Mysha—my friends

PREFACE AND ACKNOWLEDGEMENTS

My first contribution to Gould studies was to hunch over a coffee table and mimic for friends the strange sight I had seen on Canadian television the night before. It was early October 1982, and I had been listening for a week to radio bulletins about a Canadian pianist, previously unknown to me, who had suffered a massive stroke and died a few days later, at the age of 50. That week I listened with growing interest to broadcasts of Gould recordings, and watched his film of the Goldberg Variations on TV. Like many, I was immediately impressed by his virtuosity at the keyboard, captivated by his intensity as a communicator, and intrigued by his eccentric personality. I soon began buying Gould recordings, beginning with his best-selling second recording of the Goldberg Variations, released a few days before he was stricken; later I read Geoffrey Payzant's monograph *Glenn Gould: Music and Mind* and began following the growing posthumous Gould literature.

It was not long before I began contributing to that literature myself. In 1987, while an undergraduate at the University of Victoria, I published my first article on Gould, and from the beginning I consciously (if circuitously) worked towards the book-length study that is finally published here. Through the next decade, I continued to explore Gould's work, contributing articles, reviews, and reports to a variety of magazines, journals, and encyclopedias; writing liner notes for Gould CDs; giving lectures; doing research among the Gould papers at the National Library of Canada in Ottawa; and, most recently, editing a journal for the Glenn Gould Foundation. My work expanded in several directions over the years: I continued to work on specific Gould-related topics, keeping pace with the dissemination of his work and the growth of serious international interest in him, but I also found myself increasingly drawn to other, broader topics and literatures (musical and otherwise) as I pursued the implications of his work and saw it in ever-new, ever-wider contexts. My studies culminated in a Ph.D. dissertation, titled 'Glenn Gould: A Study in Performance Practice', for the University of California at Berkeley, which I began in the autumn of 1992 and filed in the autumn of 1996, and which formed the basis for this book.

This is a work of criticism, not a reference book: for all its scholarly foundations, it remains, ultimately, my own personal confrontation with Gould's work. It is, moreover, a study focused on Gould as a pianist and interpreter of music. It is surprising to note, at this late date, that Gould the performer has been somewhat slighted as a subject for sustained critical attention. There are close to three dozen books about him (including those currently in preparation), and among them one can find much material on his life, musical upbringing, career, image, reception, psychology, personal eccentricities, physiology, philosophy, aesthetic ideas, working methods, radio documentaries, television and film work, writings, letters, compositions, film scores, posthumous effects, discography, and place in Canadian culture and thought, among other topics, yet there is exactly one book that deals seriously and at length with Gould the performer, and it was published in German in 1991. It is certainly evidence of the cultish side of Gould reception that his work away from the piano is held in exaggerated esteem without there being a comprehensive accounting of his more obvious achievements as a pianist. Rectifying this glaring gap is one principal aim of this book.

But if this book is focused on Gould the performer, it is by no means narrow: the topics that properly fall under this rubric are many and varied, and there is a wide range of relevant, stimulating literature, from musical and non-musical fields. My aim is not so much to dissect the mechanics of Gould's virtuoso piano technique, but to study him more broadly as an interpreter of musical works, to examine his pianistic style and his thoughts on matters of music and performance. The two-part structure of the book reflects my effort to assess details of performance practice as well as the premises and ideas that informed them. And though I insist on keeping my attention on Gould the performer, the book does ultimately place him within a variety of musical, aesthetic, intellectual, and historical contexts.

Gould was a controversial figure, and continues to provoke wildly disparate commentary. I have tried to be as balanced as possible in assessing and contextualizing him, but I would never pretend that my work existed in a critical vacuum: I do not write book-length studies of artists I do not admire greatly. With an artist like Gould, one is always tempted to dismiss or defend; his extreme stances provoke no less extreme reactions in his listeners. There are, I know, many who will reject the very idea of this book, the idea of treating an idiosyncratic modern performer in scholarly terms and in such detail; there are others—rabid Gould fans—who will recoil at the critical treatment their hero often receives in these pages. I certainly want to make the case that Gould does merit and repay scholarly attention, that he was at least as important as some other musicians who were primarily performers and who have inspired significant bodies of serious secondary literature: Casals, Furtwängler, Horowitz, Klemperer, Leschetizky, Menuhin, Paganini, Schnabel, Segovia, Toscanini. . . I want to show that Gould's work offers many opportunities for legitimate scholarship that to date have rarely been exploited, that his work addresses many issues of interest in contemporary music and culture, especially because he always sought to bridge the gap between music in theory and music in practice, between idea and performance, thought and sound.

This book is, predictably, indebted to countless individuals and institutions with whom I have dealt over the past fifteen years, including many not directly connected with either the dissertation or the book. Though the number is large, I will try to acknowledge them all here, to the extent that my memory and records permit. I can only apologize abjectly for any omissions.

Many friends, colleagues, professors, acquaintances, and even occasional strangers have aided my work, by copying recordings, broadcasts, films, and writings, some of them unreleased or unpublished; providing me with bits of information or critical insight; permitting me to work on Gould topics for academic credit; accompanying me to conferences; opening doors, making introductions, promoting my work, and directing me to promising sources; or simply providing encouragement, support, feedback, discussion, and debate that proved fruitful. For such help over the years (whether they remember it or not), I am grateful to the following persons: William Aide; Charles Barber; Brian Berryman; Noël Bisson; Damjana Bratuz; Greg Caisley; Darla Crispin; Jim Curtis; Jennifer Griesbach; Jens Hagestedt; Tal Hebdon; Bruce Hill and Stephanie Martin; Walter Homburger; Dale Innes; Abbie Jones and Scott Pauley; Eric Jorgensen; Pamela Kamatani; William Kinderman; Gordana Lazarevich; Jörgen Lundmark; Don Miller and Mary Mouat; Junichi Miyazawa; Bruno Monsaingeon; Carl Morey; Marguerite Mousseau; Janet Munsil; Jean-Jacques Nattiez; Ardina Nehring; Ruth Oppenheim; the late Peter Ostwald and Lise Deschamps Ostwald; Geoffrey Payzant; Alan Penty, Pam Slyth, and Joe Slyth; Piero Rattalino; Neil Reimer; Ken Rinker; Erich Schwandt; and Leslie Wyber.

The generous financial support I received as an undergraduate and graduate student in music proved invaluable. The University of Victoria twice earned an undergraduate's gratitude by looking kindly upon applications for funds normally reserved for graduate students or professors; the results were a Graduate Students Society Travel Grant that helped me to attend a Gould conference in Montreal in 1987, and a travel grant from the Social Sciences and Humanities Research Council of Canada (a grant administered by the university) that permitted me to lecture at a Gould conference in Amsterdam in 1988. I also thank the staffs in the Music and Audio and Interlibrary Loan departments at the McPherson Library, University of Victoria, for assistance in the later stages of my work. I am grateful to the University of California at Berkeley for a Humanities Graduate Research Grant, which permitted me to spend two crucial weeks, in the summer of 1992, among the Gould papers at the National Library of Canada in Ottawa.

Cornelis Hofmann, as President of the Glenn Gould Society in Groningen, the Netherlands—an organization now sadly inactive—was an important early supporter of my work, and eagerly published my first writings on Gould. At his invitation, and with his financial assistance, I lectured at conferences in Amsterdam (1988) and Groningen (1992). I thank him heartily for all his support. For inviting or permitting me to give lectures on Gould, I am further grateful to the Pacific Northwest chapter of the American Musicological Society; and Rick Kool, of the Royal British Columbia Museum in Victoria.

Fred Maroth, President of Music and Arts Programs of America, Inc., commissioned me to write liner notes for six Gould CDs released in 1990 and 1991, and in so doing introduced me to important, previously unpublished concert and broadcast performances, as well as spoken commentary by Gould; these proved invaluable even years later. I am grateful to Fred and to his wife Elena for much encouragement and hospitality.

I thank Joel Flegler, editor and publisher of *Fanfare*, and Robert Silverman, former editor of the *Piano Quarterly*, for giving me excuses to familiarize myself with new Gould books and recordings by writing reviews.

I have appreciated, over the years, the support and encouragement of the Estate of Glenn Gould, and its executor, Stephen Posen. He granted me permission to use National Library materials by mail (1987) and in person (1992). For this book, he granted me permission to quote from unpublished Gould writings and to reproduce National Library materials as photographic plates, and supported the idea of the supplementary CD.

I have also appreciated the support of the Glenn Gould Foundation in Toronto, in particular John Peter Lee Roberts, its Founding President, and Vincent Tovell, one of its Directors. I also owe a large debt to John Miller, the Foundation's Administrator. In 1992, he invited me to speak at a conference in Toronto, where I was able to preview the contents of this book. In 1994, he sought my input on future Foundation projects, the result being the creation in 1995 of a new, international Friends of Glenn Gould society with its own twice-yearly journal, *GlennGould*. Editing this journal has brought me into contact with more people, more published and unpublished Gould writings, and many other materials and bits of information that were very beneficial to me in the later stages of my work.

I am grateful to several offices of Sony Classical for acts of kindness over the years: Sony Classical in New York provided review copies of Gould CDs and videotapes in the autumn of 1992; Patrick Suttles of Sony Classical in Belgium arranged and financially supported my lectures in Groningen and Brussels in 1992; Faye Perkins, head of Sony Classical in Canada, invited me to participate in various Gould events in Toronto in the autumn of 1996; and Michelle Errante in New York provided complimentary prints of Gould photographs. Faye Perkins, moreover, saw how much the supplementary CD would enhance the value and self-sufficiency of this book, and agreed to produce it on very friendly terms. And Brenda Dainard, of Sony Music Special Products in Toronto, took charge of the production of the CD.

The Music Division of the National Library of Canada has provided invaluable assistance to me over the years, by telephone, fax, and post as well as on site. I am grateful to the Music Division's Director, Timothy Maloney, the late Stephen Willis, Gilles St-Laurent, Barbara Norman, and Richard Green, but most especially to Cheryl Gillard: her assistance in the summer of 1992 saved me precious time and allowed me to reap maximum benefit from a too-short research trip, and her continued, long-distance help, on behalf of *GlennGould* as well as my personal work, is everywhere apparent in this book. Finally, I am grateful to Helmut Kallmann, founder of the Music Division, for much encouragement and support, and for providing me with some valuable in-house Library material.

I am grateful to the Department of Music at Berkeley for permitting me to pursue what is not universally considered a valid subject for a scholarly dissertation, and for other kindnesses during my time as a doctoral student. I am grateful to Joseph Kerman for permitting me to give a colloquium on Gould in the autumn of 1992, and to John Thow and Donald Davidson for reading, approving, and commenting on the finished dissertation. My biggest debt of gratitude is to my dissertation adviser, Richard Taruskin, who was enormously influential on the tone, structure, contents, and argument of the final text. There have, inevitably, been significant revisions in the transition from dissertation to book, and there are some personal indulgences in the present text for which I alone am responsible, but I can guarantee the reader that if he finds something here that stands out or impresses it is undoubtedly something that still bears Taruskin's fingerprints.

Oxford University Press, first in Canada and later in England, moved quickly to read, accept, and comment on my dissertation, and to begin the production process. They also proved accommodating to my ideas in terms of the supplementary CD, musical examples and illustrations, textual revisions, promotion, and other aspects of production. Oxford has permitted me to produce an attractive and (I hope) accessible book without sacrificing the integrity of my vision of the subject. I am grateful in particular to Euan White at Oxford in Toronto, who quickly and enthusiastically passed my typescript on to England; to Bruce Phillips, Oxford's Editor of Music Books; to Helen Foster, Assistant Editor of Music Books; to desk-editor Janet Moth; and to copy-editor Mary Worthington.

For supplying the photo reproductions from Gould's manuscripts and scores used in Plates 1–2 and 6–8, I am grateful to the Music Division of the National Library of Canada, and for permission to reproduce them I am grateful to Stephen Posen (for the Estate of Glenn Gould). For permission to reproduce the page of score in Plate 1, I am further grateful to the C. F. Peters Corporation in New York. For supplying and permitting me to reproduce the Don Hunstein photograph in Plate 3, I am grateful to Michelle Errante of Sony Classical in New York. For supplying the photo reproductions of the Scriabin score in Plates 4–5, I am grateful to Photographic Services, the University of Victoria, and for permission to reproduce them I am grateful to Dover Publications, Inc.

Finally, I am grateful to my family, and particularly my late mother, Jean Bazzana, for much encouragement and financial assistance throughout my music studies and work on Gould. I owe an enormous debt of gratitude to my partner, Sharon Bristow, without whose unconditional love and support, not to mention infinite patience and understanding, this book would probably never have seen the light of day. She spent three years seeing me through those times (approximately twice weekly) when I was tempted to abandon my dissertation entirely, then through months of seemingly endless text revisions and production details for the book—in all, a long, laborious, and not exactly lucrative process. It is really to her that the dedication of this book properly belongs, and it is only at her insistence that it is formally dedicated to those close to me who offered loving support for my work but, sadly, did not live to see it completed.

K.B.

Brentwood Bay, BC, Canada
June 1997

CONTENTS

CONTENTS OF CD

All tracks are drawn from Gould's studio recordings for Columbia/CBS, and all appear on CD in Sony Classical's Glenn Gould Edition.

LIST OF PLATES

Between pages 170 and 171

1. Handel, Suite for Harpsichord in A major/Prelude, in Gould's Peters edition of the score (NLC Scores 28/5, 6)
2. Handel, Suite for Harpsichord in A major/Prelude, 1–7, from Gould's autograph manuscript of his arrangement, final draft (NLC 27/6/1, 1)
3. Gould in the recording studio, March 1963 (photograph by Don Hunstein)
4–5. Scriabin, *Two Pieces* ('Désir' and 'Caresse dansée'), Op. 57
6. Sibelius, Sonatine in F sharp minor, Op. 67 No. 1/I, 47–72; Gould's copy of the score, marked with his instructions for 'acoustic choreography' (NLC Scores 44/2, 4)
7. Sibelius, *Kyllikki*, Op. 41/II, 1–29; Gould's copy of the score, marked with his instructions for 'acoustic choreography' (NLC Scores 43/5, 8)
8. Sibelius, Sonatine in F sharp minor, Op. 67 No. 1/III, 38–54; Gould's copy of the score, marked with his instructions for 'acoustic choreography' (NLC Scores 44/2, 10)

LIST OF MUSICAL EXAMPLES

LIST OF TABLES

LIST OF FIGURES

NOTES ON FORMAT

Books, book chapters, articles, interviews, letters, films, commentaries for radio and television broadcasts, sources from the National Library of Canada (NLC), and so on are cited in short form in footnotes; a full citation for each item is given in the bibliography. Where an author's name alone is given in a footnote, only one item by that author appears in the bibliography; where no author's name is given, the author is Glenn Gould. All individual items under Gould's name—published and unpublished, titled and untitled, written and spoken—are listed chronologically by original date of writing (the original date is given in brackets where it differs from the date of publication or broadcast); published collections of Gould writings, however, are listed by publication date. With unpublished writings, a note on its nature and provenance is included. Gould writings that appear in *The Glenn Gould Reader* and other published collections are cited as such and are not listed separately, though original dates and sources may be given in the text or footnotes where relevant; writings by other authors published in collections are, however, cited separately. Interviews with Gould published in print or as recordings, including those later interviews which he alone scripted, are listed under the name of the interviewer. Recorded or broadcast texts never published in written form, and so not paginated, are cited only generally.

The bibliography includes only items cited in the text and footnotes, in the particular versions, translations, and editions used; it is not a complete list of the sources I consulted in writing this book, nor is it intended as a general Gould bibliography. (Such bibliographies are available in Angilette, 197–218; Canning, 215–20; Friedrich, 422–6; Matheis, 123–32; Payzant, *GGMM* 158, 173–5; Payzant *et al.*, 543–5; Stegemann, 417–36; the NLC's *Descriptive Catalogue*, 13–50, 223–53; and the collection *Glenn Gould: Variations*, 307–9.) The bibliography does not include Gould's compositions, arrangements, and sketches, or the videotapes, acetate discs, and annotated scores and books in the NLC.

Sources in languages other than English are quoted in the text in my own English translation; the original quote appears in a footnote. Among these sources are some Gould writings and interviews that appeared in print only in translation, and for which the original English text no longer exists or was not available to me.

When quoting from Gould's letters and drafts, and from unpublished sources in the NLC, I occasionally standardize spelling, punctuation, and capitalization, where Gould's errors in these respects are not pertinent.

❦

This book makes constant reference to pieces of music and to Gould performances, and a musical example or CD excerpt could not be included for every such reference; to make complete use of the book, therefore, the reader should have access to relevant scores and Gould recordings. I have tried to limit musical examples to those cases in which graphic representation of a Gould performance is required to make a point. In examples showing both the original score and the Gould version of an excerpt, the Gould version is so labelled; in all other examples, only the Gould version is shown. (In other words, where a caption for an example simply identifies the musical excerpt, the reader may assume the phrase 'Gould's performance of'.) It should be noted that my intention in a musical example is not necessarily to represent accurately the music as it might appear in an Urtext edition, or to record as completely as possible every detail of Gould's performance; I indicate only as much information as I think necessary for the reader to understand the point I want to make. I have not included musical examples for excerpts that appear on the supplementary CD, which includes Gould performances of works and movements discussed in detail or given special emphasis in the text. Individual tracks of the CD are cited thus: 'CD $\boxed{10}$'.

In references to musical works, upper-case roman numerals refer to movements, arabic numerals to bar numbers. The letter 'r' after a bar number refers to that bar on repetition. If reference is made to a bar as played both initially and in a repeat, both will be cited (for example, 'IV, 15, 15r').

With virginal music by Gibbons and Byrd, the bar numbers and spelling of titles used here conform to those in the series *Musica Britannica*, vols. xx and xxvii–xxviii, with the following exception: for the pavans and galliards in vol. xxvii, 100–4 and 114–18, I borrow the titles 'First Pavan and Galliard' and 'Sixth Pavan and Galliard' from Byrd's collection *My Ladye Nevells Booke;* all of Gould's preserved performances of these pieces are so labelled. Piano sonatas by Haydn are cited here as they are in Gould's various recordings: according to the numbering in Hoboken XVI.

'Sonata' means 'sonata for solo piano', and 'concerto' means 'concerto for solo piano with orchestra', unless otherwise specified.

❦

I refer to specific recorded, filmed, broadcast, and live Gould performances casually in the text, but provide a list of performances cited on pages 269–76. Most of these performances appear in Sony Classical's Glenn Gould Edition (GGE) and Glenn Gould Collection (GGC), the former a comprehensive edition on CD of his recordings, the latter a selection on videotape and laserdisc of his film and television work. Those performances in my list that do appear in these two series are simply mentioned as such; I provide discographic details only for unreleased performances available in the NLC or elsewhere, and for performances released on LP, CD, or videotape by companies other than Sony Classical, including the Canadian Broadcasting Corporation (CBC), the National Film Board of Canada (NFB), INA/Éditions du Léonard, and various pirate labels. (More detailed information on Gould's recordings is available in Canning, and in the smaller discographies published in Cott, 139–59; Friedrich, 355–421; Hagestedt, 201–7; Kazdin, 174–218; Payzant, *GGMM* 177–83; Payzant *et al.*, 543–4; Stegemann, 437–505; and the NLC's *Descriptive Catalogue*, 83–126, 255–80. Canning's catalogue, incidentally, while it cites releases of Gould recordings up to 1991, was published too early to include Sony Classical's Edition and Collection, but most of the catalogue numbers for these two series are included in Stegemann's discography.) My references to performances do not follow a consistent format: such data as year and medium are given only where relevant, but enough information is provided for the reader to locate more information in my list of performances cited, or in Canning and other published sources.

Where my reference to a recording conflicts in some detail with the data in Canning, it may be assumed to be a correction. My corrections and additions to Canning were taken from the NLC's *Descriptive Catalogue*, Stegemann, Canning's own appendices to Friedrich, documents in the NLC, and the liner notes for Sony Classical's Edition and Collection.

Where I refer to the year of a recorded performance, I mean the year it was made, rather than the year it was released. Where a recording was put together over a period of years, I specify the time span: for example, I refer to Gould's recording of Beethoven's 'Tempest' Sonata, made at different points between 1960 and 1971, as his '1960–71 recording'. Where I do not specify a particular performance from among several possibilities, the reader may assume that any of Gould's preserved performances of the work in question will serve to make my point.

I use the term 'television programme' to refer to the programmes that Gould made for the CBC from the 1950s to 1970s, and the four programmes he made with Humphrey Burton for the BBC in 1966, even though some of these have been shown at film festivals and have been released commercially. I use the term 'film' to refer to the two NFB films from 1959, to Bruno Monsaingeon's 1974 series (even though originally shown on French television), and to Monsaingeon's Bach series (even though shot on videotape). I use the term 'studio recording' (or simply 'recording') to refer to all preserved performances that were not made before an audience or a camera.

All Gould performances are on the piano unless otherwise specified.

It should be noted that I take seriously Gould's claim that he was a *recording* artist for whom the ethics, standards, and criteria of the concert hall were irrelevant. When assessing his studio, film, or broadcast performances, or his piano playing generally, I have ignored issues like 'integrity' as they apply to the concert hall. Thus when, for example, I note Gould's control of dynamics in his piano recording of Wagner's *Siegfried Idyll*, I am not concerned with whether or not, or to what degree, the performance was spliced together from different takes. I have treated his preserved performances as finished musical products, without regard for the circumstances of their production. This position, consistent with Gould's own aesthetic, is, I believe, necessary to a proper assessment of his work as a performer.

❦

The Gould items in the NLC fall under the general heading 'The Glenn Gould Papers' and the general catalogue number 'MUS 109' (formerly '1979–20'); I do not repeat this information throughout my NLC citations.

Written materials in the NLC's Gould collection are housed in files within boxes, and are cited here as follows: 'NLC 10/10, 1–10', meaning 'box no. 10, file no. 10, pp. 1–10'. Sometimes there is more than one document in a file: thus, '10/10/10, 1–10' means 'box no. 10, file no. 10, document no. 10, pp. 1–10'. The letters 'r' and 'v', for 'recto' and 'verso', are added to page numbers where necessary. I use the NLC's pagination wherever it conflicts with Gould's.

Unpublished and untitled sources held only in the NLC are cited in footnotes by NLC filing number. These sources, including spoken commentaries (some in the form of a conversation) for films and broadcasts, and drafts of unpublished writings, lectures, and letters, appear in the bibliography as follows: 'Gould, Glenn, NLC 10/10/10' (an explanation of the source is included). In both footnotes and bibliography, I include only those specific NLC documents I have cited, not all the related copies and drafts that may also exist in the NLC, all of which have their own cataloguing numbers.

Gould's annotated scores are filed in a separate series of boxes, and are cited here as follows: 'NLC Scores 10/10, 1', meaning 'scores, box no. 10, score no. 10, p. 1'. Books that Gould annotated, of which there are 143, are filed by number at the NLC as 'B1' through 'B143', and are cited as such here ('NLC B10'). Those of Gould's scores and books that were not annotated are listed in the NLC, but are no longer held there; they are none the less mentioned where relevant. (It should be noted that the scores and books recovered after Gould's death are by no means a complete record of the music and literature with which he was acquainted.) Acetate discs and videotapes held among the Gould papers are cited here simply by number ('NLC acetate no. 10'; 'NLC videotape no. 10').

❧

Tempos for performances are cited as follows: '♩ = 60' (meaning 'M.M. 60'). I have quantified tempos by using a stopwatch to time a significant passage (the number of bars depending on the rhythmic context) and then calculating the resulting metronome reading, which thus represents an average for that passage. This method generally works well given the relative continuity of tempo in many Gould performances, but in those cases where he takes enough rhythmic liberty to render an average tempo marking somewhat academic, I have added 'c.' before the marking. Metronome markings within the text and tables are (unless otherwise specified) taken from the opening of the work or movement in question, and may be assumed to establish the general character for the whole of that work or movement, even where the opening tempo is not literally maintained throughout. Metronome markings in musical examples apply to the specific excerpts shown.

The terms 'soprano', 'alto', 'tenor', and 'bass' are used to denote the component voices of a musical texture. In a texture of more or less than four voices, an inner voice is labelled according to the approximate register it occupies on the keyboard, and its relationship to the soprano and bass voices.

Where pitch classes are referred to casually (this is apparent by the context), capital letters are used: C, B♭, F♯, E♮. Specific pitches are identified according to the Helmholtz system (middle C = c').

ABBREVIATIONS

The following abbreviations are used throughout the introductory matter, text, footnotes, and bibliography:

BBC British Broadcasting Corporation
CBC Canadian Broadcasting Corporation
GGC Sony Classical, Glenn Gould Collection
GGE Sony Classical, Glenn Gould Edition
GGF Gould, Glenn, *A Glenn Gould Fantasy*
GGR Gould, Glenn, *The Glenn Gould Reader*
GGSL Gould, Glenn, *Glenn Gould: Selected Letters*
NFB National Film Board of Canada
NLC National Library of Canada
Payzant, *GGMM* Geoffrey Payzant, *Glenn Gould: Music and Mind*
WTC I, and *WTC* II J. S. Bach, *The Well-Tempered Clavier*, Books I and II

INTRODUCTION

THE CANADIAN PIANIST, broadcaster, writer, and composer Glenn Herbert Gould was born in Toronto on 25 September 1932. (The family's original surname, Gold, was changed in 1939 or 1940.[1]) He was found to have perfect pitch at the age of 3, and other unusual musical talents—a photographic memory, gifts for sight-reading and improvisation—soon became apparent. Both his parents were amateur musicians, and until the age of 10 he studied the piano with his mother. In 1940, he began studies at the Toronto (later Royal) Conservatory of Music, and received his Associate diploma in 1946. He studied music theory 1940–7 with Leo Smith, organ 1942–9 with Frederick C. Silvester, and piano 1943–52 with the Chilean-born pianist Alberto Guerrero (1886–1959). He first performed in public on the piano in 1938, on the organ in 1945; he first played with an orchestra at a Conservatory concert in 1946, and made his professional solo-recital and concerto débuts in 1947. By the early 1950s, Gould had acquired a considerable reputation within Canada as a concert artist. In 1950, he began performing on radio, and in 1952 on television, for the CBC, with whom he would work for the next three decades. His first commercial recording was made in 1951 and released in 1953 on the Hallmark label. Between 1953 and 1963, he performed often at the annual summer Shakespeare festival at Stratford, Ontario; from 1961 to 1964, he served as one of its directors of music. Even as a child, and especially in his teens, he was active as a composer, occasionally performing his own works in public; these early works, most in a late-Romantic or twelve-tone idiom, include piano pieces and a bassoon sonata. His only major work is a long, one-movement string quartet, composed 1953–5, published as Opus 1 in 1957, and recorded several times. Once established internationally as a concert and recording artist, he composed only sporadically, completing few works.

In January 1955, Gould made his American début, with recitals in Washington, DC, and New York. His unorthodox programme (Sweelinck, Gibbons, Bach, late Beethoven, Berg, and Webern), distinctive style, idiosyncratic interpretations, and flamboyant platform manner immediately marked him as an iconoclast. The day after his New York début, he was offered a contract with the Columbia Masterworks (later CBS Masterworks) label, for which he recorded exclusively for the rest of his life. His American début recitals, and the popular and critical acclaim that greeted his first recording of Bach's Goldberg Variations, released in 1956, launched his international concert career. For the next nine years, he toured

---

[1] See Beckwith, 'Master Glen Gold'; and Ostwald, 35–6.

throughout North America. In May 1957, he gave a series of concerts in Moscow and Leningrad, and between 1957 and 1959 he made three overseas tours, playing in Berlin, Vienna, Salzburg, Brussels, Stockholm, Florence, Tel Aviv, Jerusalem, Lucerne, and elsewhere. (These were not extensive tours, however, and in fact he earned a lasting international reputation on the basis of remarkably few overseas concerts—less than fifty.) Gould's repertoire immediately attracted attention. He played little early-Romantic or impressionistic music, preferring the Baroque, Classical, late-Romantic, and twentieth-century Austro-German repertoires, along with some more unusual fare (Elizabethan virginal music, transcriptions, contemporary Canadian music); early in his career, he gave a number of Canadian and world premières. His highly individual piano style, interpretative liberties, and published pronouncements made him a controversial musical figure, but he was also widely admired, by audiences, colleagues, and critics, for his technical virtuosity, probing intellect, command of musical architecture, rhythmic dynamism, precise fingerwork, and extreme clarity of part-playing. Though idiosyncratic, Gould was to some degree influential, and many pianists of the generation that grew up with his concerts and recordings (Zoltán Kocsis, Ivo Pogorelich, Andras Schiff, Peter Serkin, and others) have acknowledged a debt to him. His repertoire inspired other pianists to explore beyond the confines of traditional nineteenth-century concert fare, which was conspicuously absent from his own recitals and recordings. ('Ever since Gould,' said the pianist Christopher Sager, 'every young pianist feels obliged to include some "intellectual" pieces in his recital.'[2]) His insistence on interpretative freedom also inspired some later musicians, as did his 'classical' approach to the piano, especially in the music of Bach and moderns.[3]

By 1963, Gould's concert activity had fallen off sharply, and at the age of 31, after a recital in Los Angeles on 10 April 1964, he retired permanently from the concert stage, citing temperamental, moral, and musical objections to live performance and announcing his intention to pursue a musical career solely through the electronic and print media. He went on to make dozens of studio recordings, and became a prolific performer and commentator in films and broadcasts. He made a series of four programmes for British television (*Conversations with Glenn Gould*, 1966), a series of four films for French television (*Chemins de la musique*, 1974)

---

[2] Kostelanetz, 136.

[3] Opinions as to Gould's influence vary, however. Lipman, 91, writes that 'Gould's playing has been largely without influence on colleagues and the countless piano students of his generation. Even where he might be thought at first glance to have had such an influence—in the tendency toward drier and clearer performances of Bach—the trend was present and gaining strength long before him and stemmed more from general musicological and technological considerations than from the work of any one person.' This last point is certainly indisputable—it is validated throughout Philip, for example—but that Gould set an especially influential example seems no less clear. Lipman further notes that where Gould's interpretations conspicuously failed to set an example for others was (perhaps inevitably) precisely where they were 'totally and startlingly original'. He cites the notorious 1962 performance of Brahms's D minor concerto, but recordings of Mozart and Beethoven, among others, might also be mentioned.

and a series of three films for German and Canadian television (*Glenn Gould Plays Bach*, 1979–81), in addition to many series and individual programmes for CBC radio and television. Gould had published some writings since the early 1950s, but after 1964 their number increased significantly, as he worked out ideas about music and related issues in liner notes, in articles in a variety of periodicals, in interviews (many of them scripted), and, for a brief period in the mid-1960s, in public lectures. These would often prove as controversial as his performances. (Around the time of his death, he was considering giving up performance in the near future to devote himself to writing.) Gould's radio work in the 1960s and 1970s extended beyond recitals and talk-and-play shows to the creation of 'contrapuntal radio documentaries', evocative collages of human voices, sound effects, and music that were not only explorations of a given subject or theme but (as Gould insisted) musical compositions in themselves. He also composed and arranged music for two feature films: *Slaughterhouse-Five* (1972) and *The Wars* (1982).

Towards the end of his life, Gould claimed to have largely exhausted the keyboard literature that interested him, and indeed one senses in his final piano recordings that he was tying up loose ends. In the autumn of 1982, he embarked on what might have been an important new career as a recording conductor, with a chamber-orchestra performance—as unusual as any of his piano performances—of Wagner's *Siegfried Idyll*. On 27 September 1982, shortly after celebrating his fiftieth birthday, and coinciding with the release of a new digital recording of the Goldberg Variations, Gould suffered a massive stroke; he died in Toronto on 4 October.

The surge of publicity surrounding his sudden death focused international attention on Gould, and led to a reassessment of his work. In the years since, the critical attention accorded him has grown exponentially, in quantity, geographical scope, and intellectual range. His impact has grown increasingly international. Indeed, he is taken much more seriously as an artist and thinker in Japan, in Russia, in Western and Eastern Europe, and elsewhere than in the United States, England, or even Canada, where his status as a national hero often obscures the real nature of his work. Gould himself complained, in his concert days, that while in Europe critics wrote about his musical interpretations, in North America they wrote more about his platform mannerisms and personal quirks;[4] it remains true that his idiosyncrasies sit less well with the musical establishment in the English-speaking world. But one encounters everywhere a wide range of opinions about Gould. Many musicians, especially those whose work is most directly challenged by his ideas (pianists, musicologists, historical performers), dismiss him, sometimes vehemently; he is more easily accepted by composers, conductors, and performers

---

[4] See Payzant, *GGMM* 17.

on other instruments. Professional critics and reviewers have always been divided as to his achievement; he has been called a genius and a charlatan. Among his admirers have been some impressive names, both musical and otherwise: Igor Stravinsky, Aaron Copland, Roland Barthes, Samuel Beckett. He has always enjoyed a large and passionate following among non-musicians, who respond intuitively to his intensity as performer and communicator. Perhaps inevitably, given his eccentricities, he has also acquired a cult following; in fact, he already complained of being plagued by fanatical admirers during his concert days.[5]

The clearest signs of increasing interest in Gould have been the posthumous efforts to collect and disseminate his work. While he lived, he was known, at least outside of Canada, almost exclusively as a concert and recording artist; the work in other media that occupied so much of his time after 1964 was much less known, scattered in a wide variety of sources, many not easily accessible. His films and broadcasts were shown infrequently, most only in Canada; his writings and interviews appeared on record jackets or in long-forgotten issues of magazines; his early compositions and recordings went out of print. This diffuseness diluted Gould's impact on the public, while the popular venues in which his work was concentrated did not encourage serious attention. But since 1982, his work has been made readily available almost in its entirety, and appreciation of its range and implications has grown. He has become, posthumously, a significant presence in contemporary music, and one of the most important cultural figures Canada has ever produced.

The central repository for Gould's legacy is now the Glenn Gould Papers, housed in the Music Division of the NLC in Ottawa. The collection was created in October 1983, when the NLC purchased more than 200 boxes full of Gould's personal and professional effects from his estate, and was officially opened to the public in January 1988. The NLC sponsored an exhibit of Gould effects at Expo '86 in Vancouver, and a major exhibit in Ottawa from April to September 1988, which was subsequently shown in seven Canadian cities and in Tokyo. A small Gould exhibit from the NLC shown at the Centre Culturel Canadien in Paris in 1986 was enormously popular, and later toured Rome, Bern, Belgrade, Bonn, Brussels, Amsterdam, Stockholm, and Oslo. In the autumn of 1996, the NLC began posting a detailed catalogue, archival documents, miscellaneous news and information, and other Gould materials on a World Wide Web site.

Many of Gould's studio recordings for Columbia/CBS, digitally remastered, were rereleased on CD throughout the 1980s and 1990s. Some very early studio recordings that he made before 1955 for other companies, including Hallmark and Radio Canada International, were also rereleased, and in 1993 the CBC began releasing some of his broadcast performances from the 1950s. Pirate editions of

---

[5] See Bester, 153. On Gould's cult following, see Fulford; and Kazdin, 77–83.

Gould performances occasionally appeared during his lifetime, but during the 1980s and early 1990s, many rare Gould performances (live and broadcast) were released by more than a dozen small labels around the world. None of these releases was sanctioned by Gould's estate, and some are of poor sonic and artistic quality, yet they contain much significant work that had never been widely disseminated in Gould's lifetime: documents of famous recitals and concerto appearances; important repertoire that he did not record commercially; significant variant interpretations of works he did record commercially; and concerto and chamber-music collaborations with major colleagues. In 1992, Sony Classical, which acquired CBS Masterworks in the 1980s, undertook a comprehensive Glenn Gould Edition, including his 'official' studio recordings, some never before released, as well as some of the above-mentioned live and broadcast performances that have appeared in posthumous pirate editions. As of June 1997, the Edition comprised eight volumes and more than seventy CDs. Films and radio and television programmes featuring Gould—those already mentioned and others from the NFB and elsewhere—have been revived since his death, on television and at Gould events around the world. Some are now available commercially, and like the posthumous CDs they significantly augment his commercial discography. In 1992, Sony Classical began release of the Glenn Gould Collection, a series of videotapes and laserdiscs containing a generous sampling of his film and television work, eventually running to sixteen volumes by 1994. Gould's 'contrapuntal radio documentaries' have been rebroadcast, and in 1992 the CBC released on CD the three documentaries that make up his 'Solitude Trilogy': *The Idea of North* (1967), *The Latecomers* (1969), and *The Quiet in the Land* (1977).

Most of Gould's published writings were collected in 1984 in *The Glenn Gould Reader*, and Gould writings have also appeared in French, German, Japanese, and other foreign editions (some more complete than the *Reader*). The publication in 1992 of *Glenn Gould: Selected Letters* offered further insights into his life and work, including his thoughts on issues that he did not address in published writings. Some of Gould's early compositions have enjoyed a minor revival since his death, particularly the expansive, neo-Romantic string quartet, which has been widely performed at Gould events and elsewhere in Canada and abroad. A 1992 Sony Classical CD, *Glenn Gould: The Composer*, includes recordings of the quartet and a handful of other early works. In 1995, the music publisher Schott began a new edition of previously unpublished Gould compositions and arrangements; as of early 1997, some of the piano pieces and the bassoon sonata have appeared.

An important source of study and dissemination of Gould's work was the Glenn Gould Society in Groningen, the Netherlands. Founded on 1 October 1982—by macabre coincidence, just days before Gould's death—the Society sold books and recordings, sponsored two conferences as well as smaller events, and published a twice-yearly *Bulletin*, containing a wide range of original and reprinted articles. Eighteen numbers of the *Bulletin* had appeared by the autumn of 1992, from which time the Society has been inactive. Since 1983 there has been a Glenn Gould Foundation in Toronto. It aims to disseminate Gould's work and ideas, and has been involved in broadcasts, publications, exhibitions, and conferences in Canada and abroad. Since 1987, it has awarded a triennial Glenn Gould Prize in music and communication. (Laureates to date have been R. Murray Schafer, Yehudi Menuhin, Oscar Peterson, and Toru Takemitsu.) In 1995, the Foundation formed its own international society, the Friends of Glenn Gould, and began publishing its own twice-yearly journal, *GlennGould*, which includes previously unpublished primary sources as well as new and translated critical studies.

There has been enough interest in Gould's work to spawn four conferences. The first, held 13–15 October 1987 at the University of Quebec at Montreal, featured sixteen lectures in English and French, divided into four workshops that explored Gould as pianist, philosopher, creative interpreter, and media communicator. The proceedings of the conference were published in 1988 as *Glenn Gould, pluriel*. A smaller symposium was held 13–15 May 1988 in Amsterdam, part of a month-long 'manifestation' that also included performances and presentations of films and television programmes. In recognition of the tenth anniversary of Gould's death, two conferences were held in the autumn of 1992, one 23–7 September in Toronto, the other 2–4 October in Groningen. The Toronto conference featured numerous lectures and presentations, and amounted to a survey of recent approaches to Gould's work. Taking as a general theme 'Music and Communication in the Twenty-First Century', it showed how some of his ideas and predictions about technology are being realized today by composers, performers, and technicians. The smaller Groningen conference featured a series of short lectures, and both events included performances of works by Gould, films, and the launching of books and recordings. In addition to full-fledged conferences, many smaller Gould events—film presentations, lectures, performances—have been held since 1982, in Ottawa, Montreal, Quebec City, Victoria, New York, San Francisco, Berlin, Paris, Tokyo, and elsewhere.

Gould's posthumous impact has been remarkable, perhaps unprecedented for a recently deceased performing musician. (Indeed, the Gould reception history would itself make a fascinating study.) He has received countless tributes, awards, and honours of every kind, but has also inspired original musical compositions, transcriptions of the Goldberg Variations, novels, plays, poems, works of art, portraits, sculptures, radio and television programmes, and even a feature film (the Canadian production *Thirty-two Short Films About Glenn Gould*, directed by François Girard and released in 1993 to considerable international acclaim). Many of the posthumous tributes cannot be viewed without a sense of irony, however.

The International Bach Piano Competition, held in Toronto in May 1985 and dedicated to Gould's memory, was justly criticized in view of his life-long aversion to competitions and concerts and to the nineteenth-century virtuoso repertoire associated with them. The Toronto conference included a number of public celebrations of the sort that Gould shunned; one wonders what he might have thought of a parade in his honour, a city park in his name, a plaque in front of his apartment building. During the conference a Glenn Gould Studio was inaugurated at the CBC's new broadcasting centre—again a somewhat inappropriate tribute, since the facility is designed for the recording and broadcasting of live public performances.

There are clearly cultish and sentimental elements in such attention, but Gould has also been studied increasingly seriously since his death. During his lifetime he inspired much written commentary because of his provocative performances and views, though this literature consists mainly of concert and record reviews and articles in newspapers and popular magazines. Detailed analysis of his ideas and interpretations was rare until 1978, when there appeared a monograph that counts as the first significant work of Gould scholarship: *Glenn Gould: Music and Mind*, by Geoffrey Payzant. The first lengthy study to take Gould seriously as an artist, it has had a seminal impact, laying a foundation for many later writers (myself included). With the widespread posthumous dissemination of Gould's work, there has been a virtual explosion of secondary literature, from throughout the world, including countless periodical articles and reviews, special issues of magazines, and more than two dozen monographs, theses, and anthologies. The range of this literature says much about Gould's broad and multi-faceted appeal. There is hagiography and propaganda as well as criticism and scholarship. He has been the subject of gossip and chat on the Internet but has also been cited by musicologists and philosophers. He has been written about in *Rolling Stone* and *Vanity Fair* as well as such scholarly periodicals as the *Canadian Journal of Political and Social Theory*, the *Musical Quarterly*, *Music Perception*, the *Journal of Aesthetics and Art Criticism*, *Analyse musicale*, *La nouvelle revue de psychanalyse*, and the *Neue Zeitschrift für Musik*. The posthumous literature is a wide-ranging one: biography (most notably Otto Friedrich's), psycho-biography (most notably Peter Ostwald's even studies in physiology; collections of anecdote, reminiscence, appreciation, homage, even coffee-table books of photographs; chapters in books on pianists; works of bibliography, including a book-length discography and a descriptive catalogue of the NLC's Gould papers; general studies (many indebted to Payzant) of the Gould *œuvre*, of the Gould aesthetic, of Gould as performer, thinker, broadcaster, writer; detailed studies of Gould's compositions; studies of the implications of Gould's ideas in terms of the sociology of music, the philosophy of music and music education, even ethics and theology; close study of Gould performances and performance practices (most notably Jens Hagestedt's), in addition to reviews of recordings; studies of Gould's relationship to recording technology; semiological analysis by French and French Canadian musicologists on subjects ranging from his aesthetic ideas to his organ playing to his physical mannerisms at the keyboard; studies and critiques of Gould's posthumous reception; even an interactive hypermedia computer programme and a CD-ROM. By 1992 the posthumous literature was vast enough that a writer like Michael Stegemann could justifiably feel the need to summarize it in a comprehensive life-and-works study. And the growth of that literature, five years later, shows no signs of abating: as I write this I can think of a half-dozen new Gould books of various kinds in various states of preparation, to say nothing of periodical issues and articles. There is no question that Gould has led, to date, an extraordinary posthumous 'life', and it should prove intriguing to follow its developments into the next century.

PART I

PREMISSES

1

Aesthetics and Repertoire

THE MOST BASIC premiss of Gould's aesthetic was that music is primarily mental and only secondarily physical—that sound is a medium for the transmission of music but not a necessary, defining aspect of music itself. For Gould a musical work was an abstract entity that could be fully comprehended in the mind in the absence of performance, without even the recollection of sounds or of physical means of production. A musical work thus existed beyond the sensory experience of it. Such a premiss may at first seem odd: Gould was, after all, first and foremost a performer, not a theorist, and much of his thinking about music took place in the context of performance. His work brought him constantly into contact with physical aspects of music-making; indeed, he took a more active interest than most classical musicians in such practical matters as the mechanics of his body, the action of his piano, and the techniques of recording. And he certainly cared about how his performances sounded. But there is really no contradiction here. To think about music in abstract terms is not necessarily to ignore music as sound; it is merely to make the physical aspect of music subservient to the conceptual. The hands serve the mind, not the reverse. Such a premiss is in fact commonplace: it places Gould within a particular tradition in the history of music aesthetics, a tradition with a long history and a substantial literature, and including performers of many different historical periods and intellectual backgrounds. What set Gould apart is that, unlike most performers, he did not reconcile his abstract view of music with conventional views on matters of performance. Instead, he permitted his view to influence his musical opinions and activities in unusually direct and idiosyncratic ways, and it was this willingness to adjust practice to accommodate theory that was the source for many of his controversial ideas and interpretations. Ultimately, it is to Gould's abstraction, however commonplace it might at first seem, that we owe much of what is most interesting, characteristic, and provocative about his work.

Gould had no formal education in music aesthetics or philosophy (he did not finish high school), nor did he undertake systematic study or sustained writing in such subjects in later life. His aesthetic premisses are sometimes stated, more often strongly implied, in his writings and interviews, but can be inferred most reliably from his musical practices; moreover, those premisses were largely consistent throughout his career, from at least his teens, even if his comments on aesthetic matters became more frequent after his retirement from concert life in 1964. The Gould aesthetic was first analysed in depth by Geoffrey Payzant, who used the term 'idealism' to describe his abstract view of music.[1] The term is apt, particularly as Gould often expressed his philosophy as an opposition to a materialistic view of music that might best be called 'empiricism'. What Payzant calls idealism is more commonly labelled 'Platonism' in the literature on the philosophy of music, but then Gould's idealism had affinities with any number of related, overlapping philosophies, variously labelled, all allied in distinguishing musical works from musical performances. Many characteristic comments by Gould ('one does not play the piano with one's fingers, one plays the piano with one's mind'[2]) recall, for instance, the 'mentalist' aesthetics of Benedetto Croce and R. G. Collingwood. For Croce, the work of art itself 'is always *internal*'; the aesthetic fact is wholly mental, to be separated from the external phenomenon of artistic practice; a musical work exists whether or not we 'stretch out our hands to touch the notes of the piano'.[3] For Collingwood, too, the work of art is an imaginary object: 'Music does not consist of heard notes,' he writes; it is 'not something audible, but something which may exist solely in the musician's head'; the external craft of performance is again separate, secondary.[4] Even if Gould did not (or could not) relate his ideas to a broader philosophical literature, his aesthetic can be profitably assessed in this context. In fact, he offers a revealing example of the practical consequences of an aesthetic position that is usually only discussed in theoretical terms. As much as, say, the historical performance movement, the implications of which have recently been discussed by philosophers of music, Gould's approach to performance often raises basic issues in aesthetics.

Gould's idealism can be placed within the history of Romantic aesthetics from Kant's *Critique of Judgement* forward, yet it is also a conspicuously modern point of view: there is much in the Gould aesthetic that recalls the premises of twentieth-century formalism and structuralism. (Indeed, he provides a sort of test case suggesting that the distinctions between Romanticism and modernism may not be more interesting than the similarities.) Gould's ideas certainly ally him with the aesthetics of absolute music, the tradition that famously included Eduard Hanslick's treatise *On the Musically Beautiful*, first published in 1854. His idealism led him insistently to privilege musical structure over sonority, in terms strongly reminiscent of Hanslick, though I know of no evidence that he was ever consciously

---

[1] See Payzant, *GGMM* 6, 73–88, which includes relevant citations from Gould's writings; see also Payzant, 'The Glenn Gould Outtakes', 300–6.

[2] Dubal, 183.

[3] Croce, 50–1.

[4] Collingwood, 141, 151.

influenced by, or even familiar with, Hanslick's writings, to say nothing of Kant and the larger idealist tradition. Like Hanslick, Gould did not take an idealist position in order to deny or eliminate sensuous pleasure, emotion, or other consequences of the physical production and reception of music; he did not deny 'feeling' in music, and no one, to my knowledge, has ever suggested that his playing was inexpressive—quite the contrary. Rather, he sought to assert the primacy of the ideal aspects of music over the physical, and so to make the latter subject to the control of the former. As Hanslick puts it, even though music originates in sensation, its immediate effect is on the imagination, to which the effects of sound and feeling are necessarily secondary.[5] The true meaning of music, therefore, lies in the ideal, rather than phenomenal, sphere—in its essence rather than its appearance. For Hanslick, 'the composed piece, regardless of whether it is performed or not, is the completed artwork', an avowed 'antimaterialist' view in which music is anterior to sound. 'Composing', he writes, 'is a work of mind upon material compatible with mind,' and music is, of all the arts, 'the most ideal because of its nonphysical material'.[6]

For Hanslick the content of music was its form, not the feelings aroused by performance; he famously defined the content of music as 'tönend bewegte Formen' (translated by Payzant as 'tonally moving forms').[7] His references to 'purely musical ideas', 'specifically musical beauty', and the like are to a meaning inherent in musical structure, independent of performance or verbal explanation.[8] This same bias runs throughout Gould's work: his idealism made 'structure' a primary criterion of value. His constant claim, in writings and interviews, that his performance practices had a 'structural' motivation reflected a desire that interpretative decisions be determined by 'purely musical' observations, rather than by instrumental sonorities and effects, considerations of physical technique, emotional qualities, allegorical or programmatic associations, specific occasions and venues, an audience, or other performance-related factors. Gould was concerned with musical expression but was *motivated* by musical structure: matters of expression were dictated by matters of structure. (Many performers of earlier generations had precisely the opposite priorities.) To be motivated by structure was, for Gould, to control one's work intellectually, to submit sound and expression to the control of reason. Not surprisingly, this aesthetic position was analogous to a more general trait of Gould's psychology, one very clear in the biographical literature: the submission of instincts, impulses, and emotions to rational control.

---

[5] See Hanslick, 5–6.

[6] Ibid., 48, 52, 31, 51.

[7] Ibid., 29; see 95–102 for Payzant's explanation of his translation of this crucial phrase, and see also Payzant, 'Hanslick, Sams, Gay, and "*Tönend Bewegte Formen*" '.

[8] Hanslick, 10, 28.

Gould's idealism was of a relatively pure sort, to judge from the literature on the subject, in which musical idealism (or Platonism) appears in a variety of pure and modified forms.[9] Many writers, for example, have modified the purely abstract view of music by arguing that the history of production is an aesthetic attribute that helps define and evaluate a musical work—that a work is 'temporally bound', and cannot be considered purely as a musical structure isolated from its historical context. To such writers, it matters that Brahms's first piano sonata was written after Beethoven's 'Hammerklavier': the influence of the Beethoven work is a defining attribute of the Brahms. But Gould seems to have treated authorship, date of composition, and the like as accidental, rather than essential, properties of works. His writings do not avoid historical issues, but his musical philosophy and practices were basically devoid of historical method. He approached pieces of music as self-sufficient structures the historical trappings of which were perhaps interesting but not constitutive. It is not surprising that his knowledge of music history was spotty, dated, and prone to clichés and conventional categories and binarisms; the least convincing of his writings are those which attempt a historical perspective. He drew on music history where it helped to rationalize his aesthetic positions, but conspicuously ignored or distorted it where it did not. In this sense, his priorities were in accord with those of modern formalists and structuralists, who took an 'immanent' view of texts, and were more interested in the form than the evolution of ideas. Moreover, he rejected the quite common view that authorship and historical context should contribute to the evaluation of a work. As he wrote in 1966, 'The determination of the value of a work of art according to the information available about it is a most delinquent form of aesthetic appraisal.'[10] On several occasions, he offered a hypothetical example of a newly discovered work that is evaluated differently depending on the perceived composer and date of composition.[11] The point of his example was to reject the idea that what is most 'progressive' in music necessarily has the greatest aesthetic or moral value—a position less modern than post-modern (a point to which I will return). But in making this point Gould also implied that a work's identity derived from its structure alone, and thus stood outside time. It is common in the literature on aesthetics for

[9] One convenient point of entry to this subject is through the debate between Jerrold Levinson and Peter Kivy. In his 1980 essay 'What a Musical Work Is', Levinson offered three main grounds for modifying a purely Platonist view of music, and Kivy, in three separate essays, challenged each of those grounds in turn. In each case, Kivy's defence of a more pure form of Platonism has the incidental effect of throwing light on Gould's aesthetic. See Levinson, *Music, Art, and Metaphysics*, 63–88, 215–63, for the original 1980 essay and his 1990 reply to critics, 'What a Music Work Is, Again'. Kivy's three essays—'Platonism in Music: A Kind of Defense' (1983), 'Platonism in Music: Another Kind of Defense' (1983), and 'Orchestrating Platonsim' (1988)—are reprinted consecutively in *The Fine Art of Repetition*, 35–94.

[10] *GGR* 341.

[11] See *GGR* 94, 341–2; and 'Forgery and Imitation in the Creative Process', 4–5. There have been real-life cases of this sort, perhaps the most notorious being the Sinfonia Concertante for winds, K. 297b, the critical fortunes of which have risen and fallen over the years depending on whether or not Mozart was believed to have been the composer.

a writer to ask what is the status of two indentical sound structures composed by different people. For Gould, clearly, they were the same work with the same value: a forgery and an original had the same status and value to the extent that they were truly identical. In this sense, his aesthetic was allied with Nelson Goodman's view of music as an 'allographic' art, in which those factors which could separate a forgery from an original are not those which identify or confer value on a work.[12]

The idealist issue most often discussed by Gould, and the one which truly places him in the purist camp, was that of performance means—that is, instrumentation. For many, a musical work is a structure of performed sounds, and some who hold this position, like Goodman and Jerrold Levinson, have gone as far as to insist that a transcription of a work is necessarily a new work—an extreme position, to be sure, and much criticized.[13] There is an obvious historical bias to such a position: composers were much less strict about instrumentation before the late eighteenth century. Tchaikovsky, a composer who played no part in Gould's canon, wrote in an 1878 letter: 'I never compose in the abstract, the musical thought never appears otherwise than in a suitable external form. In this way I invent the musical idea and the instrumentation simultaneously.'[14] It was just such inseparability of idea and sound that Gould generally disdained in music. He professed to be, to a large degree, 'instrumentally indifferent',[15] and believed that a transcription that preserved the integrity of a work's structure succeeded in preserving the work. Indeed, transcribability seems to have been an important and value-laden factor in his assessment of music. For him the best composers were those who thought in terms of structure preceding, and to some degree standing apart from, instrumentation, and works he considered to be most readily transcribable were those he considered models of an idealistic orientation, to be highly valued as such.

This meant, above all, Bach: for Gould, the transcribability of Bach's music was proof of the composer's idealism. Bach's 'magnificent indifference to specific sonority' was the subject of the first of his Bach films with Bruno Monsaingeon, *The Question of Instrument* (1979), and was one to which he returned often throughout his career.[16] Gould tended to focus his attention on one side of Bach's art, that represented by fugues, which could most easily be adapted to an idealist outlook. Indeed, idealism as an aesthetic value operated even within the Bach *œuvre*. Those works most idiomatically suited to given instruments—toccatas, organ preludes, fantasias, concertos for solo keyboard—were precisely those which he tended to denigrate; even the Goldberg Variations, a work with which he was

---

[12] Goodman, 113.

[13] See ibid., 206; and Levinson, *Music, Art, and Metaphysics*, 87–8, 232–5.

[14] Quoted in ibid., 246 n.

[15] Mach, 102.

[16] See *GGF; GGR* 17, 21–2, 31, 201, 433; *GGSL* 110, 183; Page; and Payzant's discussion of transcribability in *GGMM* 84–8.

closely associated throughout his career, was not spared criticism by this standard.[17]
Those works most susceptible to transcription formed the standard against which
others were judged. Gould's image of Bach was, in outline, not far removed from
that of Forkel, one of the founders of the Romantic aesthetic programme. His
tendency to denigrate Bach's early works (the toccatas and early fugues), his relative
lack of interest in the vocal music (and in the composer as Lutheran, text setter,
and tone painter), and his tendency to derive his image of Bach overwhelmingly
from the mature instrumental music, recall the basic prejudices of Forkel's 1802
biography. It was through the instrumental (especially keyboard) music that Bach
first appealed to early Romantic proponents of absolute music, and as Jörg
Zimmerman observes, 'it is remarkable just how enduring the normative basis of
the discourse on Bach as it was established by Forkel has remained'.[18] The historical evidence does not suggest that Bach was as cavalier about instrumental sonority
as Gould suggested, and Bach's own frequent transcribing—for Gould indicative of
idealism—reflects if anything different prevailing standards about musical works,
musical notation, and performance, not to mention the practical pressures under
which Bach worked. But Gould's view was, typically, more aesthetic than historical:
he argued from the nature of the music as he saw it. His preferences among Bach's
works form a classic example of what Imre Lakatos called 'monster-barring', the
excluding of 'difficult' examples. Idealism was the bar.

Typical was his view of *The Art of Fugue* as a model of Bach's idealism. His
comments on this work's 'lofty disdain' for specific instrumentation, on its withdrawal 'into an idealized world of uncompromised invention', are commonplaces
with a long history.[19] *The Art of Fugue*, written and originally published in open
score, has often been seen as a purely theoretical, didactic, mystical work of
Augenmusik, indifferent to performance, and has been transcribed many times for
various ensembles. But as Christoph Wolff observes, the familiar picture of the
work as esoterica—as *musica sui generis*—'is more in accord with a certain ideology,
idolization, and speculation than with reality', a reality revealed by a better
understanding of the sources.[20] Gustav Leonhardt's 1952 monograph on *The Art of
Fugue* was already able to summarize an extensive literature, dating back at least to
the 1920s, showing that the work is unequivocally for keyboard, not merely
speculative.[21] (Open-score notation is common in early keyboard music.) Having
performed, recorded, or broadcast most of the fugues at various points in his
career, Gould was aware that they are keyboard-playable. But, significantly, the

[17]   See Friedrich, 312; and Page.
[18]   Zimmerman, 355–6.
[19]   *GGSL* 110; *GGR* 17.
[20]   C. Wolff, 239.
[21]   See Leonhardt, 1, 59.

idealism that he claimed for *The Art of Fugue* he also claimed for other works like *The Well-Tempered Clavier* that are designated for keyboard (if not *which* keyboard). Such works do not impose their 'keyboardness' on the performer; though keyboard-playable, they are not idiomatic keyboard music, because they do not rely on effects native to a particular keyboard instrument. Not surprisingly, Gould would use arguments about idealism to rationalize the playing of Bach on the modern piano.

In fact, implications of Gould's idealism are apparent in many of his musical activities. For example, he insisted that playing the piano limited him as a musician, and, from an early age, he would spend many (perhaps most) of his working hours pursuing musical matters away from the piano.[22] He also spoke of reducing his contact with the piano as much as possible, in order to preserve an ideal view of music only minimally compromised by the necessities of the medium. Gould always analysed and memorized a work completely before beginning to play it at the piano, a method that had been instilled in him by Alberto Guerrero from at least the age of 12.[23] He wrote in a 1962 letter that 'a work learned in analytical terms and only secondly at the instrument will leave you permanently a stronger sense of its structure and its internal workings'—and by implication, with a more informed performance.[24] Gould expressed such views from the very beginning of his career (he said in 1959, for example, that 'fingers give nauseating interpretive ideas'), though in a recorded interview in 1968 he noted that, in the years since his retirement from concert life, his view of music had grown increasingly idealized, and that he thought less and less in terms of the piano or the performance occasion.[25] In 1974, he said that 'the degree to which you can minimize [the piano's] effect is the degree to which you can reach out for the ideal', and in 1980, near the end of his life, he said: 'I suppose premise number one is to try to forget that I'm playing the piano. I don't want to be aware that anything specifically pianistic is being done in order to bring out whatever structural design I have in mind.'[26]

In performance, Gould apparently relied more on an analytical image of the music than on tactile imagery or muscle memory, and he was, from his youth, conspicuously lax in one area in which the tactile approach to learning a piece is manifested: the working out of fingerings. (The Gould scores preserved in the NLC, which are generally annotated with little but editing markings, confirm his later recollections on this matter.[27]) He claimed that he practised as much as

---

[22] See Beckwith, 'Glenn Gould, the Early Years', 61; and Mach, 107–8.

[23] See Cott, 40; and Harris, 52.

[24] *GGSL* 52.

[25] Tovell; McClure.

[26] Cott, 40–1; Aikin, 25. In 'Bach Series/Program 1/Draft 2', 15–17, in a 1979 discussion with Bruno Monsaingeon of his recording of the first movement of Beethoven's Sonata in A flat major, Op. 26, Gould makes it clear that he keenly resented those occasions on which the piano demanded certain interpretative compromises.

[27] See Aikin, 27; and Dubal, 180–1.

possible in his head, and that when learning a piece he delayed turning to the piano as long as possible, to ensure that his image of the work was not derived from the instrument; he even claimed to play better after being away from the piano for a considerable period of time.[28] Given his technical virtuosity, his claim that he rarely practised has been dismissed as pure legend by some, notably Jacques Drillon, though this need not be a controversial point. Some performers (Paderewski, Serkin, Richter) have always had to practise constantly throughout their careers to keep in performing condition, while others (Kreisler, Gieseking), by whatever fluke of psychology or physiology, apparently required very little technical maintenance, at least as adults; the evidence does suggest that Gould belonged in the latter group. But even those adult performers who need hardly practise invariably practised like fiends in their youth (Kreisler admitted as much), and in this respect Gould was no different. In any event, his technique may have been low-maintenance, but was not maintenance-free. When he played Webern's *Variations*, Op. 27, at a recital in Moscow on 12 May 1957, he cheekily apologized to the audience because 'I haven't practised it in two years'; it showed. And in his few forays into nineteenth-century virtuoso repertoire, one occasionally notices technical flaws and limitations of just the sort that practise would have cleared up. (See his performance of the storm movement in the Beethoven-Liszt *Pastoral* Symphony.)

Gould's compositions also reflected his idealism. He noted in 1959 that he tended to conceive his music more abstractly than instrumentally,[29] and there is considerable evidence to this effect among his papers in the NLC, including piano music written in four-stave open score. His String Quartet, Op. 1, which is hardly idiomatic for the ensemble, seems to have been intended as a work of 'pure music'. He admitted that he knew little of string technique and was really thinking 'in terms of blank instrumentation'; his later liner notes on the work suggest that it was more an exercise in motivic and harmonic development than a real piece for strings.[30]

It is in the matter of repertoire that Gould's idealism was perhaps most influential. He never formulated a generally applicable theory on the nature of music, or claimed to; his theoretical views were inseparable from his chosen repertoire. Ernst Krenek was citing a commonplace of the literature when he wrote in 1937 that 'all theories of musical aesthetics have tended to be apologies, intellectual systems designed to defend a certain musical style', valid only 'on the basis of assumptions which are exactly those it is setting out to prove and defend'.[31] Gould's aesthetic was no different: it privileged certain periods, styles, genres, composers,

[28] See Aikin, 28; Dubal, 180–3; Harris, 52; and *Non, je ne suis pas du tout un excentrique*, 131.
[29] Tovell.
[30] Ibid.; *GGR* 227–34.
[31] Krenek, *Exploring Music*, 134.

and works. Idealism was an aesthetic value that determined the most sympathetic repertoire. While his writings and comments imply that all music could to some degree be thought of in idealist terms, it is clear that for him the best music was that which could most easily be defended by an idealist—that which could be considered most complete apart from performance, in which transcription was most viable an option, in which sound quality *per se* was not a constitutive factor, in which matters of structural cohesion (like motivic relationships) did not depend on particular tone colours or performance practices. (Judgements on such matters can be problematic, of course.) Gould's idealism, in short, was as much a practical programme as a general theory. A similar relationship between idealism and repertoire is immediately obvious in the work of Hanslick. His disingenuous claim that his thesis 'contains no hint of partisanship' because it applied equally well to Bach, Mozart, Beethoven, and Schumann, shows clearly just how ingrained the bias towards the 'classical' Austro-German canon was in his thinking.[32] The aesthetic that purports to prove the superiority of this particular canon is in fact derived from it. In general, Gould's aesthetic was sympathetic to Hanslick's premises and repertoire, and to the circular reasoning that linked them. Like Hanslick, his aesthetic was based largely on instrumental music. He shared the bias of Hanslick (and Schopenhauer, Schoenberg, and many others) against texts, titles, and programmes; his interest in opera, for example, was almost exclusively musical, not literary or theatrical, and he showed little interest in the textual and allegorical concerns of pre-Romantic aesthetics.[33]

Notwithstanding Gould's interest in some unusual corners of the keyboard literature, the vast majority of his preserved performances feature works by composers in the Austro-German tradition: C. P. E. Bach, J. S. Bach, Beethoven, Berg, Brahms, Handel, Haydn, Hindemith, Krenek, Mahler, Mendelssohn, Mozart, Schoenberg, Schubert, Schumann, Strauss, Wagner, Weber, Webern. And with composers from other traditions (English, French, Russian, Scandinavian, Canadian), he tended to prefer works that adhered to Austro-German procedures and forms—contrapuntal works, for example, or sonatas. Two composers have long been recognized as staples of his repertoire, as models of his musical values, and as major influences on his aesthetic ideas, interpretations, and performance style: Bach and Schoenberg.[34] Both composers were important to him from his early youth, and formed axes around which other musical preferences clustered: Bach was the centre of an interest in formal counterpoint of the Renaissance and

---

[32] Hanslick, 38.

[33] See Hanslick, 6, 14–27; Schoenberg, 141–5; and Schopenhauer, i. 263–4, and ii. 448–50. On Gould's approach to opera, see Burton, iv; and Tovell.

[34] As early as 1962, the assumption that Gould was interested in little besides Baroque and twelve-tone music was already widespread enough that he was concerned to refute it: see Asbell, 92.

Baroque periods, Schoenberg the centre of an interest in structurally dense music of the twentieth century. But there was much overlap: Bach was as much a model for structural density as Schoenberg was for counterpoint, and both were models of an idealistic attitude towards music. And it was in light of the values that Gould perceived as common to Bach and Schoenberg that the other music prominent in his repertoire—virginal music, Viennese Classical music, music of the late nineteenth and early twentieth centuries—was analysed, judged, and performed.

If Bach's music was statistically the more central to Gould's repertoire, and more influential on his performance practices, Schoenberg, with whose music and ideas he became acquainted in his teens through Guerrero, may actually have been intellectually more crucial. Gould's Bach was not a figure that the eighteenth century would have recognized; his interest was not in a historical perspective on Bach, and in fact his historical knowledge on the subject was conventional, not extending much beyond the musicological perspective of the 1950s, and prone to many clichés of early Bach scholarship (Spitta, Schweitzer, etc.). Gould's was, rather, a modernist's Bach, a legacy of early twentieth-century conceptions of Bach that were themselves deeply indebted to nineteenth-century German Romanticism. Like Schoenberg and his followers, Gould took an idealistic view of music and projected it back onto Bach, and from him to subsequent Austro-German music, making Bach the fountainhead of a musical tradition. In essence, the figure so influential on Gould's thinking and performing was Bach seen through the eyes of Schoenberg.

Of course, idealistic comments about music were common enough before Schoenberg, from many performers and theorists, and it is common to assume that some separation of structure from sonority was taken for granted in the thinking of many composers, especially before around 1830—the time of Berlioz, Chopin, Schumann, Liszt—when tone colour first became a truly constitutive aspect of musical form. Beethoven's famous quip about not caring for the needs of a 'wretched fiddle' when seized by an idea, and Brahms's remark that he could hear a better performance of *Don Giovanni* at home (that is, in his head) than in the theatre, could easily be multiplied; even the great orchestrator Richard Strauss wrote the occasional low F♯ for violins, instructing the players to 'think the note'. Charles Ives put the matter bluntly when he famously wrote, 'My God! What has sound got to do with music! . . . That music must be heard, is not essential—what it *sounds* like may not be what it *is*.'[35] But the idealist's separation of work from performance was perhaps never more pronounced and influential than in the work of Schoenberg. He told Dika Newlin in 1940, 'Music need not be performed any more than books need to be read aloud, for its logic is perfectly represented on the

---

[35] Ives, 168–9. Ives's father had expressed the same idea to him: 'Don't pay too much attention to the sounds. If you do, you may miss the music' (quoted in Perry, 57).

printed page; and the performer, for all his intolerable arrogance, is totally unnecessary except as his interpretations make the music understandable to an audience unfortunate enough not to be able to read it in print.'[36] A musical thought does not require sounds; tone colour should serve to articulate structure; instrumental limitations constrain composers—such views are expressed throughout Schoenberg's writings. Gould was clearly influenced by the writings of not only Schoenberg, but of such followers as Webern, Krenek, Theodor W. Adorno, and René Leibowitz, in which Schoenberg's views are often restated with greater polemical force.[37] (Gould also had a long-standing personal relationship with Krenek.[38]) Adorno's essay on Schoenberg in his book *Prisms* takes tension between substance and sound as a basic theme; for Adorno, Schoenberg's music was primarily for the mind, the intellect, and did not depend on tone colour or even performance—was, in fact, even suspicious or impatient with pure sound. Gould's own comments on Schoenberg reveal a similar bias. He wrote in 1966, 'Schoenberg does not write *against* the piano, but neither can he be accused of writing *for* it. There is not one phrase in his keyboard output which reveals the least indebtedness to the percussive sonorities exploited in an overwhelming percentage of contemporary keyboard music.'[39]

Gould was also deeply influenced, both in terms of theory and practice, by the pianist Rosalyn Tureck. The unique, highly articulated style of Bach playing that she developed very obviously influenced Gould's style, as he acknowledged, and he may well have known the writings and interviews in which Tureck explicitly reveals an idealist orientation, at least when it came to the music of Bach. Indeed, for all her claims to historical performance and musicological research, Tureck reveals premisses no less modern in orientation than Schoenberg's: her concern for structure rather than colour has less to do with Baroque aesthetics and performance practice than with Romantic and modern ideas about music. In 1960, in a passage that might have been written by Schoenberg or Adorno or Gould, she wrote:

In Bach's music, the form and structure is of so abstract a nature on every level that it is not dependent on its costume of sonorities. Insistence on the employment of instruments of the seventeenth and early eighteenth centuries reduces the work of so universal a genius to a period piece. Only a pedantic attitude can be satisfied with insistence on prescribed sound for this type of music. In Bach everything that the music is comes first, the sonorities are an accessory.[40]

---

[36] Newlin, 164.

[37] To take one example, Gould's critiques of Stravinsky—especially the idea of Stravinsky as a superficial poseur—borrowed heavily from the polemics of Krenek, Adorno, and others. Cf. e.g. his comments in *GGR* 180–2 with the interpretation of Stravinsky developed in Adorno, *Philosophy of Modern Music*, 135–217; and Adorno, *Quasi una Fantasia*, 145–75.

[38] See *GGR* 189; *GGSL* 217–19; Krenek, 'Glenn Gould'; and Stewart, 279.

[39] *GGR* 123.

[40] Tureck, *An Introduction to the Performance of Bach*, i. 11; see also Tureck, 'Bach in the Twentieth Century'. For Gould's comments on his debt to Tureck, see Cott, 62–5; Mach, 103–4; and M. Meyer, 'Interview', 16.

(Payzant has further noted the influence of Artur Schnabel on Gould's idealism, an influence Gould also acknowledged.[41])

Bound up with the idealism of Schoenberg and his followers were polemics on behalf of such values as 'logic', 'reason', 'unity', 'order', and 'organization', expressed specifically as a preference for motivic development and other means of structural integration. Schoenberg's own writings are rife with justifications of his own music on the basis of its 'logic', noting that, in twelve-tone music especially, everything is 'thematic', nothing 'decorative', and in this respect again his followers were if anything more polemical. Adorno praised Schoenberg's music for being 'totally composed', 'structural down to the last tone', 'substantial at every moment'. Most important, everything in Schoenberg's music is 'developed logically', the outward form totally determined by the 'latent structure' of the music—by the nature and potential of the given musical material.[42] Carl Dahlhaus, discussing the premises of such thinking, draws on Jacques Handschin's distinction between 'on the one hand the "architectonic" aspect of form, the clarity achieved by the repetition of sections, and on the other hand the "logical" aspect, the development of themes and motifs whose distribution over a whole movement imparts an inner coherence to the musical process'.[43]

Admiration for 'logical' music, in this sense, and with it a disdain for the improvisatory, is apparent throughout Gould's writings, from as early as his first important essay, 'A Consideration of Anton Webern' (1954). Indeed, in an unpublished writing probably dating from c.1964, he suggests that the issue of logic is one of the most important in all music.[44] Some form of the logical/ architectonic distinction was apparent when, in a 1976 interview with Monsaingeon, he acknowledged his tendency to analyse all music by the formal standards of Schoenberg's 'developing variation', and stated his preference for works (like Bach's fugues) concerned 'with the evolution of one idea or of one complex of specific thematic ideas', rather than works (like Mozart's sonatas) that conform to 'a previously established formal scheme'.[45] When he claimed, with characteristic polemical exaggeration, that he had 'a century-long blind spot approximately demarcated by The Art of the Fugue on one side and Tristan on the other— everything in between [being] at best an occasion for admiration rather than love', he was, not coincidentally, siding with the music in which the 'logical' aspect of form is most manifest, and distancing himself from the music—that of the so-

[41] See Payzant, GGMM 77–80.
[42] Adorno, Prisms, 157, 152, 156, 154.
[43] Dahlhaus, Schoenberg and the New Music, 222.
[44] See NLC 18/5, 1.
[45] Le dernier puritain, 153 ('avec l'évolution d'une idée ou d'un complexe d'idées thématiques spécifiques'; 'un schéma formel préalablement établi').

called 'High Classical' period—for which the term 'architectonic' was coined.[46] Gould's liner notes for his own string quartet show that his intention was to see how rigorously he could make a single four-note motive serve as a basis for an extended musical structure. He placed his quartet (composed 1953–5) within the motivic tradition of Schoenberg and Webern; indeed, his comments strikingly recall Webern's own boast, in a 1939 essay on his Op. 28 string quartet, that a single succession of four pitches was the basis for the entire structure.[47] Gould's written and spoken analyses reveal a very Schoenbergian fondness for music that demonstrates unity through the intensive development of a relatively small amount of thematic material.[48] And as we will see throughout subsequent chapters, such values as unity, coherence, consistency, and parallelism, all by-products of this admiration for musical logic, inform many details of Gould's performances.

Idealism and musical logic were, for Schoenberg and his followers, aesthetic values not only taken as a prescriptive for new music, but also projected back onto earlier music. Schoenberg did so most famously in his influential 1947 article 'Brahms the Progressive' (which is as much a treatise on the principle of developing variation as a study of Brahms), but Bach too was drawn into the same tradition. The 'rational total organization of the total musical material' made possible by dodecaphony (the phrase is Adorno's) was posited as the culmination of an evolution in Austro-German music that began with Bach, and in light of which the music of that tradition was properly assessed.[49] As Friedrich Blume observed, Philipp Spitta, in the 1870s, was already appropriating Bach as a paragon of the composer of absolute music, placing him at the head of a tradition culminating in Brahms and Hanslick. 'As he saw it,' writes Blume, 'Bach had to be adapted to the purity of the Classical ideal.'[50] Schoenberg placed himself within this tradition, and saw in Bach the wellspring of his own music. That dodecaphony (as opposed to Stravinsky's or Hindemith's neo-Classicism) was the true heir of Bach was a commonplace of his school to which Gould was sympathetic. Bach, in contrast to Handel, was for Schoenberg the founder of 'the art of development through

---

[46]   GGR 37.

[47]   See GGR 227–34; and Tovell. Cf. Webern, 752–6.

[48]   It would perhaps be more accurate to say that Gould admired a balance between unity and variation, between logic and expressiveness, for he never admired the sort of unity that derives automatically from system-driven music, like that of the total serialists of the 1950s. In fact, he stressed that his fondness for Schoenberg's twelve-tone works was based on the aesthetic quality of the music, and professed to no special admiration for the twelve-tone system itself, the basic premisses of which he described, on different occasions, as 'childish', 'arbitrary', 'artificial', 'high-handed', 'naïve', and so on. (See e.g. his comments in GGR 116–17, 127; and Burton, iii. See also his remarks on Schoenberg from a 1975 CBC television programme, in GGC xvi.) The sensitivity to reproaches of intellectuality apparent in Schoenberg's work had a counterpart in Gould's defensiveness about charges of coolness, intellectuality, and detachment, and in his occasional polemics against music (like that of Stravinsky and Boulez) that he considered to be focused purely on matters of 'technique': see e.g. Asbell, 92; GGR 324; Contrepoint à la ligne, 295; and 'Forgery and Imitation in the Creative Process', 6–8.

[49]   Adorno, Philosophy of Modern Music, 53.

[50]   Blume, 66. A copy of this book is among the Gould effects in the NLC.

motivic variation', of 'producing everything from one thing and of relating figures by transformation'.[51] Adorno's vocabulary was more reminiscent of Gould's: he saw in Bach's musical structures an 'essence' that lay behind the 'sensuous appearance'; structure was 'concealed beneath the surface of sound'.[52] Moreover, for Adorno, following Schoenberg and Webern, Bach's greatness as a fugue writer, especially in *The Art of Fugue*, lay less in his contrapuntal manipulations than in his developing variation of the material.[53] The Bach arrangements (or 'recompositions') of Schoenberg and Webern were intended to make this very point, in fact—to underscore the motivic developments in the music. As Joseph N. Straus has shown, projecting backwards into history the quintessentially modern value of 'motivicization', as in these arrangements, was the central 'analytical misreading' of earlier music made by Schoenberg and his followers.[54]

Gould's own comments, and his markings in his copy of Adorno's essay 'Bach Defended against his Devotees', make clear his allegiance to these ideas. (He also often used these ideas, as did Adorno, to argue against the premisses of the historical performance movement.) His own interpretations of Bach's works often strikingly recall the 'analytical misreadings' of the Schoenberg school. In Monsaingeon's 1980 film *An Art of the Fugue*, he refers to the Fugue in E major from *WTC* II as a perfect embodiment of the principle of developing variation, and his verbal analysis and subsequent performance of the fugue are as much concerned with motivic development as with contrapuntal artifice.[55] Moreover, he uses this fugue to link the two issues of idealism and musical logic. For him, the absence of idiomatic keyboard writing (the fugue mimics choral style) is a direct result of structural density: 'And maybe because [Bach] wasn't trying to cater to an instrument in any way, there's a sense that there isn't a wasted note, there isn't an artificial or superficial note. Everything is material to the material, everything absolutely grows out of the original subject, out of the original six notes which started it all.'

Gould's analysis includes the usual contrapuntal developments of the principal subject (stretto, stretto diminution), as well as transformations of the subject itself (reharmonization in the relative minor in bars 16–17, filling-in of the crucial interval of the third in bars 23–6); he also discusses the contrapuntal developments (notably stretto) of various counter-subjects. But he also proposes more subtle motivic relationships between subject and counter-subjects, and internal transfor-

[51] Schoenberg, 171, 173.

[52] Adorno, *Prisms*, 144, 145.

[53] See Adorno, *Prisms*, 139; and Adorno, *Philosophy of Modern Music*, 94. The same point has been made about Beethoven's *Grosse Fuge*, another contrapuntal work hailed as 'modern' by some 20th-cent. musicians, including Stravinsky, Boulez, Kerman, and Gould (see *GGR* 458).

[54] See Adorno, *Prisms*, 146; and Straus, 21–54, 70–3. See also Dahlhaus, *Schoenberg and the New Music*, 181–92, on the analytical nature of these arrangements.

[55] The bulk of Gould's spoken analysis of the fugue is transcribed in Friedrich, 154–7, which is the source for the quotations that follow.

Ex. 1.1. Motivic relationships proposed by Gould in Bach, *WTC* II, Fugue in E major (1980 film)

mations of counter-subject material. He suggests, for example, that the bulk of the first counter-subject (bass, bars 3–4) 'is just the transposition of the subject with a little bit of ornamentation'; that the counter-subject introduced in the tenor in bar 16 can be considered a permutation of the ornamental figure with which the original subject ends in bars 2–3 ('even that doesn't go to waste entirely'); and that the counter-subject introduced in the bass in bar 23 might also be derived from the head motive of the subject, now expanding its range from a fourth to a fifth. (These motivic relationships are shown in Ex. 1.1*a–c*.) Gould further shows how the five-note scale in the first counter-subject (bass, bar 3) is extended later in the fugue, first to six notes (soprano, bar 29), then to seven notes (tenor, bar 31), finally to eight notes (soprano, bars 35–6), forming a complete E major scale that enhances the sense of fulfilment at the point of tonal and thematic recapitulation (see Ex. 1.1*d*). His analysis, ultimately, makes a case for an extreme economy of material in this piece, recalling Schoenberg's definition of fugue as 'a composition with maximum self-sufficiency of content'.[56] In its premisses—even, perhaps, in its occasional over-eagerness—the analysis certainly recalls Schoenberg's own analyses of developing variation in earlier music.

Gould's debt to the Schoenberg aesthetic is also apparent in his occasional recompositions, for like many Romantic performers and editors (though much less frequently than some) he was willing to amend a musical score in the service of his own structural values. His 1969 CBC radio broadcast of Mozart's Sonata in B flat major, K. 333, offers one example. In the rondo-form third movement, there are three parallel spots that serve a transitional function: bars 36–40, 105–11, and 179–83. The first and second of these transitions lead into returns of the opening theme in the tonic key; the third appears in the middle of a cadenza. According to Mozart's score, the structural functions of these passages are not synchronized with the musical material: the first and third passages end with an arpeggiated dominant seventh chord, while the second ends with a chromatic scale. Gould obviously believed that the first two passages, sharing exactly the same structural function, should be alike in terms of musical material, and that the cadenza was the proper place for a departure from the pattern. He therefore replaced the arpeggio in bars 39–40 with the same chromatic scale as in bars 110–11, saving the arpeggio for bars 182–3 only. In Gould's version, the rondo is a little more exact, the cadenza a little more unique. For Mozart, variety was the point, for Gould, typically, consistency and clarity of structural function.[57] He made another significant amendment in Bach's Toccata in F sharp minor: he dropped fourteen bars (113–26). In so doing, he cut by about two-thirds a long sequential passage, excessive sequencing being one feature of improvisatory works that he deplored.[58] (Schoenberg also complained of such passages, especially in the music of Handel.) Since bar 127 begins with the same dominant seventh chord on F♯ that begins bar 113, this long passage offered him a rare opportunity to amend such a 'flaw' without creating an awkward seam.

[56]   Schoenberg, 297.

[57]   This recomposition does not appear in either his 1965–70 recording or his 1967 CBC television performance of K. 333. It may have occurred to him only at the time of the 1969 radio broadcast, by which time he had probably finished with the third movement in the recording studio.

[58]   See e.g. *GGR* 16, on Bach's early toccata fugues. Gould equated frequent sequencing with failure of inspiration in his spoken commentary on Mozart's Fantasia in C minor, K. 475, in a CBC radio recital of 29 Nov. 1966. In a 1976 published conversation with Monsaingeon, he proposed a revision of a sequential passage that he considered weak, from the second movement of Mozart's Concerto in E flat major, K. 482 (a work he never played); the revision appears in *Le dernier puritain*, 149–51.

Ex. 1.2. Beethoven, Concerto No. 3 in C minor/I, cadenza (1959 recording)

In Beethoven's cadenza for the first movement of his Concerto No. 3 in C minor, Gould made a significant revision that suggests a Schoenbergian privileging of the 'thematic', in the scalar passage for the right hand alone near the end of the cadenza. In a draft of an undated letter in the NLC, he noted in this case his 'disinclination to see the right-hand chromatic scale go unoccupied . . . [when it] seems to me to cry out for a 6–4 chord'.[59] In providing that 6–4 chord support, he rewrote the cadential trill, but gave the passage greater significance by incorporating the principal theme of the movement in the bass (see Ex. 1.2). Also, the repeated tones C and G that he added in the bass under the trill were intended to make the passage seem still more 'cogent' by anticipating the timpani strokes— repetitions of the fourth G–C—that immediately follow the cadenza. This example, like the previous, validates the observation of Canadian composer R. Murray Schafer that Gould, when taking up works that he considered flawed in some way, would try 'to locate their deficiencies in order to attempt repairs in his recording of them'.[60]

[59]   NLC 32/47/20, 1.
[60]   Pacsu *et al.*, 50.

Gould sometimes changed notes in a score to reinforce such values as unity, consistency, and clarity, by creating a parallelism, increasing motivic density, making explicit a musical relationship, or otherwise tightening the structure. There are countless small-scale examples among his recordings. Where a composer presents a particular figure in several guises, for example, Gould tended to choose one option and use it consistently. In both his recorded and filmed performances of the Allemande of Bach's Partita No. 4 in D major, he renders consistently an inconsistently notated turn figure at parallel spots in bars 10, 12, 45, and 47. In the 1962–3 studio recording, he takes the unique version of the turn in bar 45 and applies it to the other three spots; in the 1979 film version, he makes the turn in bar 45 conform to the triplet pattern of the other turns. In other words, the profile of the turn itself was less important to him than the consistent use of it in places that are otherwise parallel.

Such changes to the score—and they are not limited to performances of early music—certainly emphasize the Schoenbergian bias in Gould's thinking, but they do not necessarily amount to improvements. In Ex. 1.3, from Gibbons's 'Pavan: Lord Salisbury', Gould creates a new motivic parallelism. The change from g♯ to d' in the tenor voice on the seventh beat of bar 10 now brings the tenor motive exactly into line with the soprano and tenor motives in the next bar, making an exact threefold imitation.[61] The density of motivic content is certainly increased, though Gibbons seems to have quite deliberately denied the motive that Gould insists upon. His amendments in Ex. 1.4, from the Toccata of Bach's Partita No. 6 in E minor, must surely be considered impoverishments. In both his 1956–7 and 1974 performances, he adds notes in several places that resolve explicitly melodic lines and registers that Bach intended to cut off abruptly and leave hanging, making audible what is only implied. The explicitness of Gould's version, particularly in 1974, is certainly characteristic, but hardly improves upon the dramatic shifts of register that Bach built into the music.

The most striking example of Schoenbergian recomposition in Gould's *œuvre* is found in his 1972 recording of the Prelude from Handel's Suite for Harpsichord in A major, in which he imposed an organic structure on an improvisatory work (see CD ⏹). In this Prelude, the performer is expected to realize the solid chords marked 'arpeggio', usually with more or less simple rolling of plain chords up and down in the given space of time.[62] (See Plate 1 for the original Prelude, as it appears in Gould's own score.) Gould, however, composed a version in which the

---

[61] This revision appears only in Gould's 1974 film performance of the pavan.

[62] Largely conventional solutions are suggested by the editor in the edition of the Prelude that Gould used—Händel, *Kompositionen für Klavier*, i (Suites nos. 1–8), ed. Adolf Ruthardt (New York, London, and Frankfurt: C. F. Peters, [n.d.]), 7, preserved as NLC Scores 28/5. Cf. also the conventional solutions suggested in Beyschlag, 111–14. A draft for Gould's recomposition of the Prelude is in NLC 28/5; the fair copy is in NLC 27/6/1. A facsimile reproduction of Gould's complete arrangement appears in *GlennGould*, 2 (1996), 20–3.

Ex. 1.3. Gibbons, 'Pavan: Lord Salisbury' (1974 film)

Ex. 1.4. Bach, Partita No. 6 in E minor (1956–7 recording and 1974 film)/Toccata

arpeggios are no longer merely ornamental, but participate in a motivic dialogue that develops ideas presented in the opening bars. (See Plate 2 for the first page of the arrangement in Gould's autograph, and see Ex. 1.5 for some of his motivic developments.[63]) He takes the motives of bars 1–2—the mordent and octave leap

---

[63]   The bar numbers that follow correspond to those of the original score in Gould's Peters edition (see Plate 1). Gould, in his autograph, broke up many of the bars, some of which are of four semibreves' length. In Ex. 1.5, solid barlines correspond to those in the original score; dotted barlines indicate the additional barlines in Gould's autograph. All excerpts begin at the beginning of the indicated bars. The excerpts preserve Gould's notation faithfully, with one exception: in the third part of bar 14, I indicate an F♯ where Gould wrote a clearly erroneous F♮.

Ex. 1.5. Excerpts from Gould's arrangement of the Prelude from Handel's Suite for Harpsichord in A major, showing some of his developments of motives from bars 1–2

in the bass (*x*), the ascending and descending scales (*y*), and the decorated triad (*z*)—and uses them often within or in place of the indicated arpeggiated chords, creating a more unified network of recurring motives, and with it a denser contrapuntal texture. In bar 3, for example, he does not play an arpeggiated A major chord of a semibreve's length on the downbeat, as marked by Handel; instead, he repeats the opening mordent and octave leap (*x*) in the bass, and in the right hand imitates motives *y* and *z*, offering a kind of stretto version of bars 1–2. In place of the chord on the downbeat of bar 4 and the chords written in bar 5, he plays right-hand figures that again develop motives *y* and *z*. He incorporates motives *y* and *z* into bar 10. He introduces a broken figure in the alto voice in bar 12 that is based on motive *z*, and develops it in the bars that follow. He increases the amount of ornamental accented dissonance in bars 12–14, developing an idea Handel uses only on the downbeats of those bars. And throughout the Prelude, he adds coun-terpoint and spells out many left-hand harmonies in a linear fashion. Moreover, he saturates the motivic texture enough that even conventional figuration begins to appear thematic: plain arpeggiated chords, for example, like those in bars 4–5, sound in this context like developments of motive *z*.

Gould generally preserves the improvisatory character of the Prelude through florid figuration and flexibility of rhythm, and his motivic developments are certainly less rigorous and less intrusive than those in Schoenberg's recompositions of Handel, Bach, and others. He did not alter the basic structure of the Prelude, and confined his recomposition to those passages in which the performer is expected to participate anyway. None the less, he clearly sought, like Schoenberg, to apply the standards of structural integration—of developing variation—that he perceived in the music of Bach to the 'weaker' music of Handel. Schoenberg, who became enraged at the automatic pairing of Handel with Bach, compared the 'empty, meaningless, étude-like broken chord figures' in Handel to the richer transitional and subordinate sections in Bach, and with his 'free arrangement' of a concerto by M. G. Monn, he spoke of replacing sequences and filler 'with real *substance*', and so remedying 'the defects of the Handelian style'.[64] Gould's response to Handel in this Prelude shows the influence of some basic Schoenbergian prin-ciples: making thematic what is merely ornamental filler, developing the given material, and so increasing the overall unity and cohesiveness of the composition.

The values that made Bach and Schoenberg—and Schoenberg's Bach—para-digmatic for Gould affected his other repertoire choices. An idealist premiss is apparent in many of his comments on repertoire (his view of Schoenberg's piano music was mentioned above), and he tended to divide composers into two camps according to their perceived sympathy with his standards. He was by no means immune to or uninterested in factors like beauty, emotional power, and profundity, but an admiration for idealism and musical logic did act as a kind of barrier: he admired *Bach*'s beauty, emotional power, and profundity, but not Chopin's or Liszt's or Rachmaninov's. Gibbons, whom he repeatedly called his favourite com-poser, was, he wrote in 1970, 'an artist of such intractable commitment that, in the keyboard field at least, his works work better in one's memory, or on paper,

---

[64]   Schoenberg, 117–18; the comments on the Monn concerto, from a 1933 letter to Pablo Casals, are quoted in Haskell, 77.

than they ever can through the intercession of a sounding board'; his music was 'of such incredible, other-worldly beauty that it simply transcends all such mundane considerations [as instrumentation]'.[65] He admired many composers, from Sweelinck to the later Beethoven to Webern, for similar reasons; he even praised the 'abstract' thinking in such late-Romantic works as the *Vorspiel* to Wagner's *Die Meistersinger* and Richard Strauss's *Metamorphosen*, making it clear that for him idealism was a point of praise.[66]

From early in his career, Gould favoured densely worked out, complicated, rigorous music—'constructed' music, in Schoenberg's sense—in which the pervasive development of musical materials created, on the one hand, a sense of constant variation, and on the other, overall unity; he admired many disparate composers for this reason. Contrapuntal ingenuity, harmonic sophistication, and motivic development were recurring features in his favourite works, which included fugues and other contrapuntal forms, ground-bass variations, some late-Classical sonata forms, works exhibiting developing variation, and twelve-tone music. By contrast, he was less interested in musical forms that depended upon the dramatic interplay of contrasting elements (like solo concertos and many sonatas), upon the techniques and sound qualities of specific instruments, upon virtuosity or improvisation, upon the circumstances of the live concert situation, or upon the demands of a text, programme, ritual, or other external stimulus. He always found a rationalization for the various significant exceptions to this rule: with Wagner and Strauss, a degree of 'abstraction'; with Scriabin, a propensity for extramusical ideas that transcended the piano; with a middle-period Beethoven work like the WoO 80 variations, a tight passacaglia structure that 'excused' the stormy rhetoric. Gould's Austro-German bias (like Hanslick's) was matched by a relative disdain for Italian music, especially Italian opera, and he admitted to a 'general francophobia' in a 1974 letter.[67] (His thinking was always prone to such simplistic binarisms as German–Italian and North–South, and he lacked—purposefully, it seems—the sophisticated grasp of historical issues that might have corrected them.) He was relatively uninterested in idiomatic keyboard music of many types: Couperin and Scarlatti, Debussy and Ravel, and those early modern composers (Bartók, Stravinsky, Prokofiev) who exploited the percussive possibilities of the piano. He was most notoriously disparaging about early-Romantic piano music: Schubert, Chopin, Schumann, Mendelssohn, Liszt. On many occasions he expressed a disdain for such 'resolutely and ostentatiously pianistic' music, which, in his view, was determined 'to flatter the resources of the keyboard' at the expense of the

---

[65] *GGR* 13; 'CBC Radio Script from 1978', 16.

[66] 'Transcribing Wagner', 55; *GGR* 455.

[67] *GGSL* 216. Cf. the negative view of Italian music in Hanslick, 64–5, 82, with Gould's comments in Tovell and quoted in Friedrich, 141, 175.

musical values he preferred.[68] He accused these composers of 'fall[ing] into the trap of the instrument and forget[ting] the abstract world outside of it'.[69]

It is not surprising that when Gould did turn to Romantic repertoire, he showed the greatest affinity for the music he could most easily rationalize, music in which he could perceive such cherished values as contrapuntal development and intimacy of expression, music that was relatively discreet in its use of the piano's tonal resources—Brahms's Intermezzi, for example, or the Sibelius Sonatines (I would include his piano version of the *Siegfried Idyll*, too). This was music in which technical virtuosity was not really an aesthetic factor, introspective music perhaps better suited to the privacy of the recording studio than the concert hall. It was the Romantic music that Gould played best, with the most sensitivity, insight, colour, and personal expression. When it came to larger and more extrovert Romantic fare—Beethoven's 'Appassionata', the Beethoven-Liszt symphonies, Chopin's B minor sonata, Brahms's Rhapsodies, Scriabin's Fifth Sonata, Ravel's *La Valse*, works by Bizet, Grieg, Strauss—his playing could still be probing, interesting, and attractive in many respects, but could also be quite ordinary, even dull, and certainly no better than that of acknowledged specialists in such repertoire. It is not that he was physically unable to play it; his technical prowess has never been questioned, and he could hurl out thundering octaves when the occasion demanded. But it is also true that his technical accomplishments were more about precision, clarity, control, dexterity, speed, and strength than virtuoso showmanship. He seems to have been simply bored by the particular challenges of most Romantic music. He clearly did not understand the function of Chopin's virtuoso filigree, and so could not sustain or convey any enthusiasm for it. And what was a champion of Sibelius, Hindemith, and Krenek to do with a direction like 'con una ebbrezza fantastica' in Scriabin's Fifth Sonata? It is no surprise that his Chopin had less colour than Rubinstein's, his Scriabin less explosive drama than Horowitz's.

His performances of such works were often of indifferent success because he felt the need to 'correct' the music by controlling what he perceived as their excesses or indulgences; some of his most experimental (and some of his least successful) performances amounted to 'corrections' of this sort. When he played uncongenial Romantic works, not to mention other uncharacteristic repertoire like toccatas and fantasias, it was often with sobriety and restraint in terms of expressive nuance, tone colour, virtuosity. He might use relative continuity of rhythm and dynamics, bring out latent counterpoint at the expense of singing melody—anything in order to restrict the element of sensuous play and force upon the music a more controlled, analytical performing style. Yet, there was often a great deal of sensuous

    [68] CBC radio broadcast commentary, 23 July 1970. See also *GGR* 453; 'Mostly Music', 7–9; and Tovell.

    [69] *Non, je ne suis pas du tout un excentrique*, 130 ('ils sont pris au piège de l'instrument et oublient le monde abstrait qui lui est extérieur').

play in his performances of 'abstract' music of which he had a higher opinion. His Bach playing was often much freer than that of many earlier Romantic pianists, who tended to play Bach reverently, literally, dryly. Gould's Bach sarabandes were more beautiful, more colourful, more expressive, more 'Romantic', even more 'pianistic' than his Chopin sonata. This may seem paradoxical, but is in fact consistent with his strong tendency towards rationalization, in both his musical and personal lives. Apparently, he could 'let loose' in performance only with music whose structure met his standards of idealism and logic, music that he could first justify rationally. There is an old cliché (with some merit, I think) that Bach's music is so well constructed that no performance can ruin it, and Gould seems to have held this view. In music (like Bach's) that passed muster, that was 'immune' to performance, he felt free creatively at the keyboard; in music (like Chopin's) that did not, that was closely tied to the instrument, he was more cautious, refusing to indulge himself pianistically, unwilling to underscore what he perceived as an already too strong emphasis on tone colour and idiomatic effect. The resulting tendency to 'romanticize' Bach and 'classicize' Chopin did more service to Bach than Chopin, to be sure, but it revealed much about Gould's aesthetic premisses and musical values.

2

The Role of the Performer

The Work, the Score, and the Performer as Creator

GOULD'S IDEALISM, however commonplace in principle, was directly responsible for his unusual freedom in realizing works in performance. Believing that a musical work existed apart from performance, he considered the profile of the music in performance—how the music *sounded*—to be a function of a specific interpretation, not an integral part of the work. Contrapuntal balances, rhythmic nuances, dynamic levels, articulation, tone colour, instrumentation—even where specified by the composer—were all subject to the performer's will without compromising the identity or status of the work. (This was a matter of principle, and did not depend on how precise the music's notation was.) In other words, for Gould 'the work' was not equivalent to 'the score', in the conventional sense of 'everything on the printed page', including both the notes and the supplementary words and symbols intended to shape the profile of the work in performance.[1] He was in accord with a theoretical position put forward by Nelson Goodman, that only what can be considered notation (that is, what can be specified quantitatively) can be considered to define a work—in essence, pitches and rhythms.[2] Goodman denies that there can be 'correct' renderings of, say, dynamics because these cannot (in the present Western system, at least) be fixed quantitatively—cannot be part of the notation. Goodman's view demands a distinction between the identity and the aesthetic character of a musical work: if only what is notational in a score defines the work, then its aesthetic character can vary substantially without its identity changing. It is a controversial position, much criticized in the literature on aesthetics and rare among practising performers. Most writers and musicians, it is fair to say, believe that a work must possess certain fixed aesthetic properties, conveyed through prescriptive performance directions, if it is to retain its identity and make sense; for most it is disturbing, absurd, even potential chaos to suggest that a piece might be played either andante or allegro, piano or forte, *dolce* or *maestoso*. But Gould seems to have been willing to entertain just such possibilities. Like Goodman, he put all non-notational directions into the

---

[1] In his copy of *Prisms*, Gould flagged Adorno's comments to this effect, with which he was obviously sympathetic ('The musical score is never identical with the work . . .'); see NLC B1, 144.

[2] Goodman explains his five qualifications for notationality in *Languages of Art*, 127–73.

category of the composer's suggestions for performance, not as firm prescriptions, and pursued the implications and possibilities of this position with unusual vigour, often far exceeding conventional boundaries of interpretative licence. When he casually rejected the assumption that a performer had an obligation to comply fully with a score, he in fact rejected values that have guided classical-music practice for the last two centuries.

Gould's attitude towards the score is one of many cases in which Baroque music served as a general model. Put simply, he treated all scores as if they had been written by Bach, as collections of pitches and rhythms with no firm guidelines as to how they were to be realized in performance. And he granted himself the liberty of a Baroque performer without limiting himself to the early music most amenable to creative interpretation. In so doing, he extended the performer's business back into areas generally considered the province of composition. He took over from the composer (or at least, gave himself the option of doing so) at a late stage in the compositional process, the stage at which the basic notation of a work begins to acquire tempo and dynamic markings, slurs, accents, and so on. (He did occasionally take liberties with the pitches and rhythms, too.) One has to look to Baroque or Romantic practice to find analogies in classical music to Gould's position, but one finds contemporary analogies in other fields, as he was probably aware. His attitude towards the musical text, while controversial in classical music, is commonplace in jazz and popular music, of course, and is strongly entrenched in the theatre. Theatre directors frequently treat all scripts as though they had been written by Shakespeare, as collections of words for which the director alone decides on performance directions. The pioneering director, designer, and theorist Edward Gordon Craig wrote in 1905 that to a director an author's stage directions are, in a word, 'worthless'—are, indeed, 'an offence to the men of the theatre'. The staging of a dramatic text was for Craig entirely the province of the director, and the author's stage directions 'are not to be considered by him'.[3] (He cites Shakespeare's bare-bones scripts as models in the matter of stage directions.) Today, many directors still black out whatever stage directions may exist in a script and base their interpretation solely on the dialogue, without regard for the author's views on the interpretation of lines, blocking, and *mise en scène;* often the author's ideas are not even entertained. In his treatment of musical texts, Gould sometimes called to mind his contemporaries in the theatre more than his colleagues in classical music.

The rationale for his attitude towards musical texts may be found in his obsession with 'structure', which he cited to justify many of his performance practices. Ever the idealist, he seems to have equated musical meaning with musical structure, and structure was to be found in the work's notation—its pitches and

---

[3] The quoted phrases are taken from the discussion of stage directions in Craig, 149–55. Craig did not, however, advocate tampering with the text itself: see 150–1, 281–5.

rhythms—rather than its performance markings. (Nicholas Cook writes that Schoenberg, too, thought of music 'in terms of its meaning rather than its effect, that is to say in terms of productionally conceived structures to be communicated through sound, rather than in terms of intended effects to be created by appropriate musical means'.[4]) When preparing a performance, Gould seems first to have interpreted the work on the basis of its notation alone, then to have developed the performance means—the tempo, dynamics, phrasing—necessary to convey that interpretation. He seems not to have taken a composer's performance markings as guides to interpreting a musical structure, and where his interpretation conflicted with those markings he did not hesitate to change them. His approach did not, incidentally, imply anything about quality or degree of musical expression; it did not imply a lack of concern for expressive performance; it implied only that expression was subservient to structure.

Gould frequently challenged the standard of correctness that is taken for granted in conventional classical performance and criticism, and is stated or implied in much of the literature on music aesthetics. Roman Ingarden, for example, asserts that if 'a particular performance contains tempi, dynamics, and melodic lines differing from those proper to the work, this is simply a false performance'[5]— a perfectly commonplace modern attitude, even if it does consign much of what we call 'Romantic' performance to the dustbin. Jerrold Levinson, too, assumes a standard of correctness in assessing performances, a standard that includes historical factors as well as all of the markings in a score, and his relativism (like Ingarden's) exists only within strict limits. (Recall that for Levinson a transcription of a work is a separate work.) He writes that

there can be good performances that, though somewhat incorrect, achieve certain worthwhile ends or results from some defensible listener perspective, without completely undermining the character of the music involved. Glenn Gould's Bach Partita renditions are not, perhaps, in matter of instrumentation and phrasing, strictly correct performances of those works, but they answer to appropriate and even historically grounded musical interests (e.g., clarity of counterpoint and voice-leading, inwardness of expression), and they do so without *inordinately* traducing the sort of sound, performance means, and emotional domain envisaged by the composer. Many would agree with me that their musical virtues make them, as a matter of fact, *outstandingly* good performances of Bach's Partitas, even though, paradoxically, they flirt with not being performances of them at all.[6]

Levinson goes on to contrast these Gould performances with Walter Carlos's Moog-synthesizer performances of Bach's Brandenburg Concertos, which are 'distorted and transmogrified', 'caricatures', even 'nonperformances', because they

---

[4] Cook, 181.
[5] Ingarden, 21.
[6] Levinson, *Music, Art, and Metaphysics*, 384.

alter too radically the aesthetic character of the works to properly be considered performances of them. The choice of examples here is revealing of the conservatism of Levinson's position. Gould's Partita recordings (made between 1956 and 1963) are among his less idiosyncratic performances; there are many more recordings, including Bach recordings, in which he offers what by Levinson's standards are 'nonperformances'. Moreover, Gould's avowed sympathy with the premisses of the 'Switched-On Bach' phenomenon, precisely on the basis of his claim of Bach's idealism, shows that 'correctness', in Levinson's sense, was not a goal he necessarily sought, even when he happened not to be 'inordinately traducing' conventional bounds of interpretative licence.[7]

Because he did not assume that the aesthetic merit of a performance depended necessarily on its 'correctness', he did not attempt to make definitive statements about works; rather, he conceived of a performance as one necessarily provisional variation on the work, seen through the prism of the performer's point of view. By extension, he felt that the susceptibility of works to variant interpretations extended well beyond the truism that no two interpretations are alike. For Gould, the performer's role was creative. As he said in a 1980 interview, 'I refuse to conceive of the recreative act as being essentially different from the creative act'.[8] In fact, for him there was really no such thing as a 'recreative act' at all. The performer had no choice but to enter the creative process and make his own decisions about the aesthetic profile of the work; to enter that process should, indeed, be his main reason for performing a work. It goes without saying, of course, that a performer cannot avoid interpreting the music he plays, but Gould, characteristically, acknowledged this situation openly and pursued its implications, sometimes to extremes.

For many writers on interpretation, the performer's contribution is limited to necessary gaps or indeterminacies in the score—that is, to only those nuances which the composer is unable to specify. It is a commonplace that musical scores in the Western tradition are 'under-determined', in the sense that they can only approximately indicate the profile of the work in performance, and even performances that attempt to observe all of a composer's markings necessarily differ in subtle ways. According to this line of argument, a multiplicity of interpretations is permitted within strict interpretative limits, the prescriptive function of all markings in the score being assumed. Pluralism is thus not a programme for what the performer should do, but an observation of what the performer necessarily does. As many writers have observed, the character and properties of a musical work can change, or be perceived differently, over time. The meaning of a work differs in various eras and traditions; even what count as gaps or indeterminacies in the score

[7] See GGR 433.
[8] Aikin, 30.

are not necessarily fixed for all time. Thus Ingarden notes that the musical work 'endures in historical time but undergoes gradual change', and Renée Cox prefers 'to think of a work not as something fixed and closed' but as 'fluctuating' and 'dynamic'.[9] Stephen Davies goes as far as asserting that even a performance observing conventional limits counts as creative:

It is because the score of a work under-determines the sound of a performance of that work that performance is essentially (and not merely incidentally) creative. The creative element in performance is not something added on to the performance after accuracy has been achieved; rather, the artist's creativity is integral to the faithful realization of the work in performance.[10]

In other words, 'The creative role of the performer, rather than involving a departure from the concern to realize faithfully the composer's intentions, is integral to the execution of that concern.'[11] (A similar argument has been made in the context of literature by such reader-response critics as Wolfgang Iser.) Yet for Davies, too, that creativity is limited to 'subtleties of attack, decay, dynamics, tone and so on which cannot be captured in any notation that composers are likely to use'. He does not defend interpretative licence in a performer beyond what is unavoidable by definition. The argument from gaps or indeterminacies in the score ultimately assumes the authority of the total score, and does not permit the performer to intervene actively in the music where the composer's markings are clear and unequivocal.

For Gould, however, creative performance was a more self-consciously intrusive act, not a necessary by-product of the performer's function; faithfulness to the score was not a given. His views on where and to what degree the performer may properly assert himself set him apart from many of his contemporaries among performers, but also from the majority of music critics and philosophers. Highly radical or personal interpretations, in most of the literature, are dealt with as mere aberrations, to be neutralized, marginalized, not permitted to influence basic aesthetic positions. By Ingarden's standard, many of Gould's most interesting performances are simply 'false'. Gould hardly approached the 'anything-goes' attitude often feared in the literature, yet his œuvre does contain enough 'aberrant' interpretations to imply a serious challenge to conventional assumptions about what constitutes proper behaviour on the part of a classical performer. He was always pushing boundaries, wondering 'how far to go too far', and some of his interpretations do approach the extreme hypothetical cases (andante movements played allegro, and so on) that some writers introduce to argue against too much creative licence.

---

[9] Ingarden, 151; Cox, 'A Defence of Musical Idealism', 136.
[10] Davies, 'Transcription, Authenticity and Performance', 224.
[11] Davies, 'Authenticity in Musical Performance', 48.

The creativity that Gould advocated is, incidentally, as common in the theatre as it is rare in classical performance, to the point that there is much concern and discussion about excessive licence on the part of directors and performers. Directors with a respectful, subordinate attitude towards authors and texts, once common, have grown increasingly rare, especially since the Second World War; by comparison, the trend in music performance since the Romantic era has been basically the reverse. In the theatre, the Gouldian interpreter, for better or worse, is the rule, not the exception; creative interpretation is simply how interpretation is done. Much twentieth-century theory concerning theatrical interpretation—Craig, Artaud, Brecht, Grotowski, Kott, to mention only a few major names—has sought to justify the creative manipulation of dramatic texts to serve the personal interpretation of the director and reflect the issues and values of his times. (In this respect, modern operatic performance is more an adjunct of theatre than of music.) Such issues as fidelity to the text, the intentions of the author, and historical performance practice exercise a much less inhibiting influence in theatre than they do in music. (Occasional attempts at historical performance in the theatre, most of them in the plays of Shakespeare, generally have the self-conscious air of quaint experiments never intended to be widely imitated.) The title of Jan Kott's influential book *Shakespeare Our Contemporary* might serve as a motto for much twentieth-century theatre, for making a playwright 'our contemporary' in some respect has been perhaps the most common rationale for mounting a new production of a dramatic work—the more so the older and more 'classic' is the work. Indeed, the most personal and radical interpretations of classic plays (the Shakespeare productions of Orson Welles and Peter Brook, for example) are among the most admired and influential in modern theatre history. Gould's thinking about interpretation, again, often resonates provocatively in this context.

Jean-Jacques Nattiez proposes another analogy. He has suggested that Gould, in insisting on a creative role for the performer, 'seems to me to draw on a sound semiological conception of the musical work: in the chain from the composer to the listener, there is no communication, strictly speaking, but a series of constructions'.[12] The semiological view that the 'esthesic process and the poietic process'— that is, the processes of reception and creation—'do not necessarily correspond' is a general observation about all music,[13] but in Gould's case that view became a licence for creative liberty, not a cue to search harder for the 'true' meaning or 'correct' interpretation of a work. As Stanley Fish puts it, in the context of literary criticism, 'Interpretation is not the art of construing but the art of constructing. Interpreters do not decode poems; they make them.'[14] The performer who seeks to

[12] Nattiez, 'The Language of Music in the Twenty-First Century', 29.
[13] Nattiez, *Music and Discourse*, 17.
[14] Fish, 327.

disappear into the work is frequently complimented, but in Gould's view the performer should, rather, impose his own values and prejudices onto the work—should, in a sense, create his own new work based on the existing score.

An obvious corollary of this position was a rejection of the idea (still occasionally defended) that the work or score or some hypothetical performance represents an ideal to which the performer should strive. As Gould put it in a 1978 essay, the quest for that 'one optimum performance'—the quest for 'Beethoven's Beethoven or Mozart's Mozart'—is not only logically impossible, but simply 'boring', especially if the implication is that that ideal performance should be 'duplicated again and again'.[15] He was more liberal: a musical work was by definition too open to interpretative renewal for any ideal profile, real or hypothetical, to be available to the performer. This was a position that he did not grudgingly acknowledge, but rather took pleasure in testing.

Gould's transcription of the *Vorspiel* from Wagner's *Die Meistersinger*, which he recorded in 1973, offers a typical example of his personal prejudices at work on a given score (see CD 2). In this performance his primary goal was to bring out Wagner's rich chromatic counterpoint, even where it meant undercutting to a significant degree the piece's martial character.[16] As a result, in the first half of the *Vorspiel* (bars 1–121), which in Wagner's score is marked as mostly loud, march-like, and rhythmically strict, Gould sharply reduces many of the dynamics, and is also quite free rhythmically. By reducing the basic dynamic level, he allows himself to use subtle dynamic fluctuations to clarify the contrapuntal texture. In bars 14–27, where the opening march theme continues in the subdominant key, he reduces Wagner's fortissimo marking to about mezzo-piano, diminishing even to piano by about bar 20. The passage beginning at bar 27, marked *meno f* in the strings and forte and *ausdrucksvoll* in the winds, he again plays at about mezzo-piano, diminishing to piano. With the upright march theme beginning at bar 40, he observes the *sehr gehalten* marking but not the dynamics: he allows the volume to increase gradually through this section, reaching the indicated forte only at about bar 48. In the passage beginning at bar 59, he again sharply reduces the dynamics: *immer ff* becomes piano, diminishing to pianissimo. (He makes a significant crescendo at the climax of this section, around bars 71–85, though he never reaches the indicated fortissimo, and diminishes to piano again by the time he reaches the deceptive V–vi cadence at bar 89.) In the transitional bars 89–96, he significantly underplays the numerous forte and fortissimo markings, never playing louder than mezzo-piano. He reduces forte markings at bars 107, 111, and 113, too, but does observe Wagner's crescendo markings beginning at bar 115, in order

---

[15] 'Sviatoslav Richter', 12. Payzant, *GGMM* 67–8, discusses the 'non-repetitiveness of musical performance', which he considers one of Gould's most basic tenets.

[16] Gould makes this contrapuntal bias clear in 'Transcribing Wagner', 55.

to build up tension into the double bar (bar 122), at which point the final minutes of contrapuntal peroration begin. (In this closing section, the contrapuntal clarity afforded by over-dubbing permits him to observe the written dynamics to a greater degree.) Even where Gould's playing does approach the loudness indicated by Wagner, there is still a sense of holding back: he never plays with the percussive bluster that we might expect in a piano transcription of march-like orchestral music. By the standards he has set for himself, the interpretation does succeed; at times, indeed, the counterpoint in his transcription is more transparent than in any orchestral performance. But his dynamic and rhythmic liberties also greatly alter the expressive character of at least the first half of the piece: a swaggering march becomes frequently languid and poignant; upright textures dissolve into a molten flow of polyphony. One aspect of the work is isolated and set in high relief, as though Gould had set out to reveal the Wagner of *Tristan* within *Die Meistersinger*.[17]

As this example suggests, Gould did not believe that an interpretation must be consistent with the standards that the composer seems to have set, a limit on interpretation common in literary criticism. There have been many efforts to clarify the limits of interpretative licence, even from writers (Barthes, Booth, Culler, Eco, Fish) who insist on pluralism in interpretation. Roland Barthes refuted the parody of his *nouvelle critique* as permitting the critic to say 'anything at all', and Umberto Eco, particularly, is concerned,

if not about the meanings that a text encourages, at least about those that a text discourages. . . . We can thus accept a sort of Popper-like principle according to which if there are not rules that help to ascertain which interpretations are the 'best ones,' there is at least a rule for ascertaining which ones are 'bad.' This rule says that the internal coherence of a text must be taken as the parameter for its interpretations.[18]

Now, Gould did not, of course, play pieces backwards or upside down, and, exceptions notwithstanding, he generally did not rewrite the pitches or rhythms of a work, so one can immediately rule out the idea that he observed no limits on interpretation. But he also clearly rejected the particular standard of coherence that Eco proposes. For Gould (as for many, once again, in the theatre), the point of an interpretation may be precisely to illuminate only one aspect of the work, even if at the expense of others, or to hold the work to an interpretative standard that is not consistent with all of its parts. (Amendments to performance markings in the score are usually required for such interpretations to work.) The result can be a tension between the aims of the interpretation and the work itself, but a tension that can prove refreshing, revealing, fertile, as in the *Meistersinger* Prelude. This attitude is a

---

[17] *Tristan und Isolde*, which made a tremendous impact on the 15-year-old Gould, seems to have remained for him the model of Wagner's art, an art of luxuriantly unfolding chromatic counterpoint; see *GGR* 37, 76–7.

[18] Eco, *The Limits of Interpretation*, 45, 60. For examples of 'bad' interpretation in this sense, see Eco *et al.*, 45–66.

polemical extension of the commonplace, expressed by Göran Hermerén, that if you want to play a musical work 'you cannot play it in general, you have to play it in a particular way'.[19] Or as Fish puts it, 'while relativism is a position one can entertain, it is not a position one can occupy'; one is always limited by one's 'own beliefs and assumptions'.[20]

This is not to suggest that all or even most Gould performances involved radical rethinkings of works, though comments to that effect are common enough in the Gould literature. Just as Fish is less extreme and more 'responsible' as a practising critic than as a theorist on interpretation, so Gould insisted on principles of interpretative freedom that he did not feel bound to exercise to extremes on every occasion. It is not literally true that every single Gould performance of a work differs radically from every other. He repeated interpretations no less than any other performer during his concert career, and some of these interpretations were repeated in the recordings and broadcasts he made at the same time. Even after he quit performing in public, he would sometimes use the occasion of a CBC radio or television broadcast to publicize an interpretation that he had just recorded or was about to record in the studio. And there is the occasional work like the Fugue in B flat minor from *WTC* II, which, notwithstanding some changes of articulation and dynamics, he played with an almost identical tempo and character in five performances in different media made over a period of twenty-six years. (See Table 2.1 for this and other similar examples.) The degree of Gould's personal imposition onto the music varied from performance to performance, but he never abandoned the principle of the performer as creator. Though he could usually be counted on to 'do something' with the more familiar warhorses of the repertoire, his interpretations are difficult to predict: he might play a well-known work relatively 'straight' while tinkering with a piece unfamiliar enough that most of his listeners would not appreciate what he had done. One senses that he took nothing for granted in performance, and that where he did perform a work more or less as written he made a conscious decision to do so from among potential options. In a 1964 lecture to the graduating class at the Royal Conservatory of Music in Toronto, he stressed the importance of 'the inner ear of the imagination' in music, the 'vast background of immense possibilities' from which 'all creative ideas come'.[21] The performer should constantly maintain an awareness of that which does not exist, of potential, in order to counteract the inhibitions of learned systems and to discover new possibilities. Gould made explicit the pedagogical implications of this principle, suggesting that performers, including students, avoid too much outside influence before formulating their own view of a piece. 'Stop listening to each

[19] Hermerén, 24.
[20] Fish, 319.
[21] *GGR* 7.

TABLE 2.1 Comparable interpretations in different Gould performances

Composer	Work	Performance	Compare with
C. P. E. Bach	'Württemburg' Sonata No. 1 in A minor	1968 recording	1968 CBC radio
J. S. Bach	Brandenburg Concerto No. 5 in D major	1962 Baltimore concert	1962 CBC television
J. S. Bach	Clavier Concerto No. 7 in G minor	1967 recording	1967 CBC television
J. S. Bach	WTC II, Fugues in C major, C minor, D minor, and E flat major	1966 CBC radio	1966–7 studio recordings
J. S. Bach	WTC II, Fugue in B flat minor	1954 CBC radio	1963 CBC television, 1970 CBC television, 1971 recording, and 1980 film
Beethoven	Sonata in E flat major, Op. 31 No. 3	1967 recording	1967 CBC radio
Beethoven	Sonata in F sharp major, Op. 78	1968 recording	1968 CBC radio
Beethoven	Thirty-two Variations on an Original Theme in C minor, WoO 80	1966 recording	1967 CBC television
Hindemith	Sonata No. 1 in A major	1966 recording	1966 CBC radio
Hindemith	Sonata No. 3 in B flat major	1966–7 recording	1968 CBC radio
Mozart	Sonatas K. 284, 309, 310, 333, 570, Fantasia in C minor, K. 475	1966–74 recordings	1966–9 CBC radio
Mozart	Sonata in C major, K. 330	1958 recording	1959 Salzburg concert
Scarlatti	Sonatas in D major, L. 463, and G major, L. 486	1968 recording	1968 CBC radio
Scriabin	Sonata No. 3 in F sharp minor, Op. 23	1968 recording	1968 CBC radio
Scriabin	Sonata No. 5, Op. 53	1969 CBC radio	1970 recording
Scriabin	Two Pieces ('Désir' and 'Caresse dansée'), Op. 57	1972 recording	1974 CBC television, 1974 film
Webern	Variations, Op. 27	1954 CBC radio	1957 Moscow concert, 1964 CBC television, and 1974 film

other' was his hypothetical advice to students in a 1980 interview. 'Listening to your peers before you've formulated your own concept, or *instead* of formulating it, seems to determine a lot of what passes for continuity in the piano-playing tradition, and I think that that kind of listening is an exercise guaranteed to make it very difficult for performers to assert whatever it is that makes them valuable as individuals.' There is a freshness in many of Gould's performance choices that suggests that he took his own advice seriously. He said in the same interview that it was inconsistent for a performer to undertake his own, necessarily personal, analysis and interpretation of a musical structure and then attempt to reconcile them with received conventions of performance. New points of view demand new performance practices, even if it means departing from the score.[22]

Gould did sometimes permit an unusual and self-consciously extreme degree of variation in alternative performances of the same piece, especially when taking up a work anew after a prolonged absence from it; in such cases, he tended to use the occasion to interpret the work in a new light. He made this a career principle, one derived in part from the fact of recording. Recording, he claimed, allows the performer to take a 'composerly' attitude towards a work, to live intensely with it for a time and then put it out of the mind, perhaps for years or decades, until there was a need or desire to take it up again. This approach is conducive to producing radically different interpretations at different times, and it contrasts with that of the concert artist, who must keep many works permanently in his repertoire in a more or less ready state. Gould once again took this principle far beyond the normal bounds observed by other artists who revisit repertoire, and a few of his alternate interpretations are extreme enough to provoke comparisons with jazz or popular-music performance. He spoke of trying to forget entirely the premises and constraints imposed by his initial interpretation when he approached a work anew. He told Humphrey Burton in 1966, 'What I forget is not the work, not the notes, but I forget the particular relationship to the work.'[23] He felt that each major public encounter with a work should be a new and pointed exploration of some particular interpretative option that it offered; indeed, that was for him the only legitimate reason to revisit a work of which one has already published a perfor-mance. (Table 2.2 lists some of the works of which he published more than one performance, years apart and in strongly diverging interpretations.)

Gould was interested not only in revealing what was present or implicit within the music, but also, on occasion, in seeing what the music could be made to do. Some of his interpretations stray into what Eco, in the context of literature, calls 'overinterpretation', though for Gould, unlike Eco, such a concept clearly had no negative connotations. Gould's position is better expressed by Jonathan Culler, for whom the 'excess of wonder' with which Eco characterizes overinterpretation is

a quality to be cultivated rather than shunned . . . like most intellectual activities, inter-pretation is interesting only when it is extreme. Moderate interpretation, which articulates a consensus, though it may have value in some circumstances, is of little interest . . . if critics are going to spend their time working out and proposing interpretations, then they should apply as much interpretive pressure as they can, should carry their thinking as far as it can go. Many 'extreme' interpretations, like many moderate interpretations, will no doubt have

<hr />

[22] Aikin, 28, 30.

[23] Burton, i. In Monsaingeon, *Chemins de la musique*, i, Gould compares this approach to the soap-opera actor's daily learning and forgetting of lines. See also *GGR* 335–6.

TABLE 2.2 Diverging interpretations in different Gould performances

Composer	Work	Performance	Compare with
J. S. Bach	*The Art of Fugue*, Contrapunctus 1	1957 Moscow concert	1959 film, 1962 recording (organ), 1979 film
J. S. Bach	French Overture in B minor	1969 CBC radio	1971–3 recording
J. S. Bach	Goldberg Variations	1955 recording	1981 recording
J. S. Bach	Partita No. 6 in E minor	1956–7 recording	1974 film
J. S. Bach	Sinfonias (various)	1955 CBC radio	1957 Moscow concert, 1963–4 recording
J. S. Bach	*WTC* II, Fugue in C sharp major	1966–7 recording	1970 CBC television
J. S. Bach	*WTC* II, Fugue in E flat major	1954 CBC radio	1963 CBC television, 1966–7 recording
J. S. Bach	*WTC* II, Fugue in E major	1952 CBC radio	1957 recording, 1969 recording, 1970 CBC television, 1980 film
J. S. Bach	*WTC* II, Fugue in F sharp minor	1954 CBC radio	1957 recording, 1969 recording, 1970 CBC television
J. S. Bach	Prelude in B flat minor	1954 CBC radio	1971 recording
Beethoven	Bagatelles, Op. 126	1952 CBC radio	1974 recording (both complete), 1967 CBC radio (Nos. 1, 2, 5 only), 1970 CBC television (No. 3 only)
Beethoven	*Six Variations on an Original Theme in F major*, Op. 34	1952 CBC radio	1960–7 recording, 1970 CBC television
Beethoven	Sonata in D minor, Op. 31 No. 2 ('Tempest')	1960 CBC television	1967 CBC television, 1960–71 recording
Berg	Sonata, Op. 1	1951 recording	1952 CBC radio, 1957 Moscow cocnert, 1958 Stockholm concert, 1969 CBC radio, 1974 CBC television, 1974 film
Gibbons	'Italian Ground'	1968 recording	1968 CBC radio
Gibbons	'Pavan: Lord Salisbury'	1951 CBC radio	1956 CBC radio, 1968 recording, 1968 CBC radio, 1974 film
Haydn	Sonata No. 49 in E flat major	1958 recording	1981 recording
Mozart	Sonata in C major, K. 330	1958 recording	1981 recording
Prokofiev	Sonata No. 7 in B flat major, Op. 83	1962 CBC television	1967 recording
Schoenberg	Suite, Op. 25/Intermezzo	1952 CBC radio	1959 Salzburg concert, 1964 recording, 1974 film, 1975 CBC television

Note: In Burton, i, Gould offers a hypothetical example: he suggests that the first movement of Beethoven's Sonata in C Minor, Op. 10 No. 1, which he recorded in 1964 at a very fast tempo ($\rfloor$. = 106), could be performed convincingly at a much slower tempo ($\rfloor$. = *c.* 70), and he plays the opening of the movement at both tempos. I have not had access to two late Gould studio recordings that are said to differ dramatically from his much earlier performances of the same works: Bach's Italian Concerto (1981; cf. 1952 CBC radio and 1959 recording); and Beethoven's Concerto No. 2 in B flat major, Op. 19, of which Gould conducted the first two movements with pianist Jon Klibonoff and the Hamilton Philharmonic (1982; cf. 1951 Toronto concert, 1957 Leningrad concert, 1957 recording, and 1958 Stockholm concert). On the latter performance, unreleased as of this writing, see Friedrich, 281–3; and Silverman, 147–8.

little impact, because they are judged unpersuasive or redundant or irrelevant or boring, but if they are extreme, they have a better chance, it seems to me, of bringing to light connections or implications not previously noticed or reflected on than if they strive to remain 'sound' or moderate.[24]

The position Culler describes captures some of the apparently willful naïveté, even arbitrariness, with which Gould made interpretative experiments to see what they would yield, a procedure that Culler observes in Barthes's work: using overinterpretation as a way of making new and personal discoveries about a text.

Perhaps inevitably, the term 'deconstruction' has been applied to Gould's work, though somewhat casually, referring either to his fondness for subverting conventional expectations or to his analytical mindset.[25] To be sure, there are some points of agreement between Gould and deconstruction: both seek to defamiliarize canonical texts; both are profoundly ahistorical; both seek out alternative possible structures within a work, structures that the work does not demand or suggest, but that it also does not resist or refute. But whether we consider the more radical deconstruction of Jacques Derrida or the somewhat 'softer' deconstructive criticism of many of his Anglo-American followers, the term is not strictly appropriate to Gould's interpretations. (Indeed, it is difficult to see how the term might apply at all to music performance, given the crucial differences between music and language in terms of denotation and connotation.) Gould did not, for example, share the deconstructionist's fondness for exploding the binary oppositions common to structuralism; binarisms were, in fact, common in his perceptions of composers, styles, and forms. Unlike deconstructionists, Gould did not reject 'organicism'; in fact, 'organic unity' was a value he prized highly. And despite occasional critical comments to the effect, Gould's interpretations, as a rule, hardly approach the 'unlimited semiosis' of much deconstruction, the infinite postponement of the fixing of meaning. (As many Gould interpretations are 'correct' as are extreme enough to demand special analysis.) Gould's interpretative strategies do not suggest an analogy to deconstruction's aim of subverting the apparent coherence of texts by exposing their internal contradictions, what Barbara Johnson calls 'the careful teasing out of warring forces of signification within the text'.[26] Rather, Gould's interpretations, even—especially—the most extreme ones, always take a strong stand, usually a stand that he makes explicit, often in a written or spoken text. In other words, Gould the performer does not deconstruct ideologies; he imposes them. The purpose of his extreme interpretations is generally to make a particular point of view, a particular meaning, very clear. He may not have viewed the mean-

---

[24] Culler, 'In Defence of Overinterpretation', 122–3, 110.

[25] For references to deconstruction in the Gould literature, see e.g. Hagestedt, 97–102; M. Meyer, 'Das Sprechklavier'; and Rivest, 103.

[26] Quoted in Culler, *On Deconstruction*, 213.

ing of a particular interpretation as comprehensive or permanently valid, but his concern was still with presenting a valid (or at least plausible) interpretation intended to impart some meaning to the work, not to show its inability to hold meaning. In this sense, Gould was very much a structuralist rather than post-structuralist: he sought unity of meaning, not dispersion, even if that unity was not necessarily the composer's.

One of his most extreme interpretations, the first movement of Mozart's Sonata in A major, K. 331 (see CD ③), has been discussed in terms of deconstruction, but in fact offers perhaps his most unyielding effort to impose new meaning onto a given score. In his reading of this theme-and-variations movement, at least two sections—the theme and Var. 5—depart drastically from the performance markings in the score, and as a result the dramatic profile of the movement is fundamentally different from that suggested by the composer. Gould took Mozart's conventional set of ornamental variations and fashioned a wholly new structure out of it, but a structure involving no rewriting of the movement's notation. He conveys his dramatic reinterpretation of the movement largely (though not entirely) through the tempo relationships between the various sections. Both Mozart's and Gould's versions of the movement achieve a balance of opposing forces, but in totally different ways: Mozart balances off concluding slow and fast variations against a basically moderate movement; Gould offers continuous motion from slow to fast, with the extreme slowness of the theme compensating for the absence of a later slow variation. Here are Gould's tempos:

Theme ('andante grazioso'; 6/8)	$\dotted\quarternote$ = 20
Var. 1 (6/8)	$\dotted\quarternote$ = 29
Var. 2 (6/8)	$\dotted\quarternote$ = 31
Var. 3 (6/8)	$\dotted\quarternote$ = 33
Var. 4 (6/8)	$\dotted\quarternote$ = 47
Var. 5 ('adagio'; 6/8)	$\eighthnote$ = 97
Var. 6 ('allegro'; C)	$\quarternote$ = 167

In Gould's scheme, the music moves from a condition of near immobility in ever-faster increments towards the concluding 'allegro'; the suppression of repeats throughout, and a slight gradual increase in basic dynamic level, contribute to the feeling of continuous forward motion. In explaining his conception of the movement to Bruno Monsaingeon, he invoked, characteristically, some of the structural values of modern music. He said that he wanted to subject the theme 'to a Webern-like scrutiny in which its basic elements would be isolated from each other and the continuity of the theme deliberately undermined. The idea was that each successive variation would contribute to the restoration of that continuity and, in the absorption of that task, would be less visible as an ornamental, decorative element.'[27] To Burton, Gould invoked the name of Webern again, referring to the 'apostrophes' with which he divides the theme into a series of component cells.[28] As Jens Hagestedt observes, the theme as Gould plays it is not merely slow but in slow motion, and the distinction is relevant: he undermines the theme as a 'tune'— it moves forward too slowly to be perceived as an integral, lyrical entity—presenting it instead as a collection of discrete musical facts; he offers an exploded view of its contents, precisely what slow motion offers in a film.[29]

The 'restoration' of continuity in the movement takes the form of a gradual restoration of order at that surface level at which it is dissolved in the theme. This Gould expresses not only through the increases in tempo, but through a gradual move away from the extremely detached phrasing of the theme towards less extreme articulation and more conventional units of phrase. By Var. 6, he has restored a performance practice that is much closer to conventional standards than that in his rendering of the theme. The result of the performance is precisely that the aspect of ornamentation is made 'less visible': the theme is so exploded that its relationship to the ornamental variations that follow is unusually distant; moreover, the accumulating momentum of the performance undermines the basically static nature of ornamental variations. The source for this interpretation might once again be found in Schoenbergian values. Just as he sought to 'improve' Handel's A major Prelude by making it more substantial motivically, here he sought to 'improve' the structure of the movement by undermining an ornamental process and imposing a single evolving trajectory onto a series of related but self-contained events. (This is more *re*construction than deconstruction.) Leonard B. Meyer, in fact, used just this movement to make the distinction between 'additive' and 'processive' structures. Like most Baroque and early-Classical sets of ornamental variations, it is inherently 'flat', a 'kind of active steady-state', as opposed to the more 'goal-directed' processes in sets by Beethoven, Schumann, and other later composers.[30] It was just such 'additive' structures that Gould generally disdained, and his performance of this movement might be heard as his attempt to 'correct' such a structure by imposing a sense of cumulation that mimics a more processive manner of organization.

Var. 5, the point of greatest tension between Mozart and Gould, offers the most surprising by-product of this performance, since it (unlike the theme) betrays no

---

[27] *GGR* 40–1.

[28] Burton, ii.

[29] See Hagestedt, 96–7. It is interesting to note that the closest precedent for Gould's tempo in the theme is in Max Reger's *Variationen und Fuge für Orchester über ein Thema von Mozart*, Op. 132 (1914). Reger marks the theme at ♪ = 120, but the 1951 recording with Eduard van Beinum conducting the Amsterdam Concertgebouw Orchestra (Decca Gold Label Series DL 9565), opens at a tempo of ♩. = c.30. There is no evidence that Gould knew this work or recording, however.

[30] See L. B. Meyer, *Music, the Arts, and Ideas,* 309–10.

internal musical tensions or incongruities in its conversion from an adagio to a modest allegro. The harmonic rhythm never seems rushed (as one might expect); the treble figuration and bass pedal tones are, of course, faster, but never absurdly so; and perhaps most surprisingly, this particular set of notes seems to accommodate Gould's *buffa* interpretation as easily as Mozart's *cantabile* one. In short, it is difficult to fault Gould's reading of Var. 5 except on the grounds that it conflicts with Mozart's—a situation that is certainly disturbing to conventional notions of fidelity in performance. Gould may not show that the work is incapable of holding meaning, but he does at least show that it has difficulty insisting on a single tempo marking. If this is a sort of musical deconstruction, it is only in the loose sense advocated by Fred Mauk, for whom the performer, when making performance choices, 'should focus on the factors that arise as a consequence of the obvious distance that exists between score and performance, and between score and composer'. It is an 'insurrectionist' approach to interpretation: 'the performer is one who constructs his own "work" from the notations that the composer has left'.[31] Deconstruction or not, this performance of K. 331 counts as one of Gould's furthest outposts as an interpreter, yet nothing in it is inconsistent with his basic view of the performer as a creator.

Gould and Romanticism

Gould's aesthetic of performance was to some extent a throwback to Romantic notions about the performer's relationship to the text, just as his views on the nature of music had roots in the Romantic aesthetic of absolute music. His temperament and premises recall attitudes towards score and performance more common among Romantic than post-war musicians, even though he considered the label 'Romantic' to be derogatory, and was in many stylistic respects an avowed *anti*-Romantic. There were some interesting contradictions in his comments on the subject; in his concert days especially he often acknowledged a strong Romantic streak, one that his early recordings of Beethoven, Brahms, and Strauss confirmed. He called himself 'very much a romantic', even 'an arch-romantic', in a 1959 interview, going as far as praising Tchaikovsky as 'a great composer, one it is now fashionable to dislike on all sorts of grounds such as sentimentality'; he referred to himself as an 'uncurable romantic' when discussing his recording of Brahms's Intermezzi in a 1961 letter.[32] A Romantic streak is certainly apparent throughout his career, notably his passion for late-Romantic repertoire, though he often rationalized this impulse in later life. Still, certain of his basic positions were undeniably Romantic, whether he acknowledged them as such or not. His insistence on

[31] Mauk, 143.
[32] Braithwaite, 28; *GGSL* 41.

imposing his own standards and those of his times onto older music—what Hermann Danuser calls the 'actualizing mode' of interpretation—certainly allies him with Romantic musicians.[33] Some critics, observing Gould's interpretative liberties, have occasionally compared him to the most eccentric of Romantic performers, like Vladimir de Pachmann. It is revealing that most of the musicians about whom Gould spoke and wrote admiringly—Casals, Furtwängler, Mengelberg, Menuhin, Richter, Rubinstein, Schnabel, Schwarzkopf, Stokowski—were performers whom he considered Romantic in temperament, and he admired the greater degree of individuality characteristic of musical performers in the early years of the twentieth century.[34] For the most part, he differed significantly from these musicians in terms of repertoire and style, yet he admired them because they made a strong personal contribution to the music they played, allowing their own tastes and prejudices to dictate their interpretations. What he wrote of one of his colleagues reflects a more general premiss: 'What Sviatoslav Richter does, in fact, is insert, between the listener and the composer, his own enormously powerful personality as a kind of conduit—and, as he does this, we gain the impression that we're discovering the work anew, and very often from quite a different perspective than that to which we're accustomed.'[35] Even in a 1961 lecture to an audience of children, he made individuality his highest priority: the performer must be true to himself first, before the composer or the audience.[36] By accepting this premiss, and exploring its implications more than perhaps any other performer of his generation, Gould was, for all his outward departures from Romantic style, the ultimate Romantic.

He was, moreover, vocal in his opposition to the 'literalist' Toscanini: 'I never found in him those transcendent moments that I found with Furtwängler, Mengelberg and Stokowski.'[37] The performer who affected modesty towards the printed score was, in other words, shirking his proper role as a performer. Indeed, among pianists he seems to have preferred the more overtly Romantic personalities to those of his predecessors (Gieseking, Lhévinne, Rachmaninov) widely admired for a lack of mannerism and idiosyncrasy, and for deference towards the composer. Gould also seems to have been comparatively less interested in many of his contemporaries of a more 'modern' temperament who came to prominence in the years after the Second World War, and whose playing adopted a more 'classical' profile that in some respects resembled his own. (Perhaps most influential were Rudolf Serkin and his pupils.)

[33] See Danuser, 17, on the 'aktualisierender Modus', and 20–3 on Gould.
[34] See Colgrass, 11.
[35] 'Sviatoslav Richter', 12.
[36] See 'A Piano Lesson with Glenn Gould', 6, 9–10.
[37] Colgrass, 11. See also *GGR* 263.

Given that 'classical' style of playing, it may at first seem odd to speak of Gould in the context of Romanticism. As we will see in later chapters, his playing incorporated features that he developed especially for Baroque music and that, no less than contemporary historical performance style, owed some debt to the values of pre-war neo-Classicism: contrapuntal transparency, fast and relatively steady tempos, terraced dynamics, clean articulation, modesty in terms of expressive nuance. The influence of such neo-Classical values as clarity, balance, economy, precision, sobriety, discretion, and formalism is unmistakable throughout Gould's performances. Moreover, for him as much as the neo-Classicists, the paragon of these values was Bach, who was his most important model for performance practice in all repertoire. He applied many of the same stylistic traits he used in Bach in a wide variety of repertoire, from Byrd to Mozart to Brahms to Schoenberg, often with provocative results. When he praised Alexis Weissenberg in a 1977 CBC radio broadcast, he was in fact making a statement about the values that informed his own playing:

I think one of the things that makes Weissenberg's performance of romantic music so extraordinary is that, unlike almost any other pianists who essay this repertoire, he performs it with an essentially classical technical attitude. The Bach-like precision of his rhythm, the Mozartean clarity of line, the almost harpsichordally registered dynamic relationships in which fortissimos and pianissimos are graded as precisely as one could wish in a Clementi sonatina—all these attributes are normally associated with the interpretation of 18th-century rather than 19th-century music.[38]

Gould's idea of 'classical', like his conception of Bach, was, of course, strongly indebted to Romantic aesthetics (as was neo-Classicism, for that matter). The binarism Classical–Romantic, which recurs in his thinking, is a commonplace that one can trace throughout the nineteenth-century Bach literature. Indeed, the perception of Bach as a composer of 'classical' profile had consequences for performance from the very beginning of the Romantic era. Glen Carruthers has discussed what he terms the 'objective' school of Romantic piano playing, typical of the early Romantic era and already by mid-century subject to criticism by Liszt, A. B. Marx, and others.[39] This style featured a literalistic adherence to the score, uniformity of dynamics and articulation, a dry staccato touch, and a pedantic attitude that admitted little expressive nuance; the similarities to the later neo-Classical *retour à Bach* are obvious. Gould's Bach, or his playing generally, could hardly be called dry or pedantic, yet it clearly had more in common with the 'objective' approach than that of the more subjective Romantic pianists. Comparison has also been made between Gould and other less overtly Romantic pianists who

[38]   'Arts National No. 3/Draft 2', 2–3.
[39]   See Carruthers, 19, 34–44.

achieved renown in the 1950s and 1960s, and it is just, as far as it goes: Gould was one among many pianists after the Second World War who reacted against the type of Romantic playing represented by, say, Arthur Rubinstein.

But however much his practices suggest 'objective' or neo-Classical models, Gould was, significantly, highly critical where he encountered the neo-Classical insistence on literalism in interpretation. He frequently deplored the model of Stravinsky as both composer and performer, and was uninterested in just that twentieth-century music that could be considered truly anti-Romantic in spirit: Stravinsky, Bartók, Prokofiev. Joseph Roddy's often-quoted 1960 *New Yorker* profile, titled 'Apollonian', stressed just this 'classical' aspect of Gould's aesthetic, and the 'apollonian' analogy has been repeated often since. Yet in a 1962 interview, Gould rejected the notion that, given his repertoire and style, he represented a new 'cool' school of piano playing—at least, if one meant by 'cool' a detachment of the performer from the music.[40] The 'classical' profile of his particular style seemed less important to him than the more Romantic notion that the performer should impose himself onto the music, and he rejected the claims to 'fidelity' and 'objectivity' that were typical of neo-Classicism. Gould's Bach style may, as he claimed, have been in part a reaction against the Romantic style represented by Wanda Landowska and others, and may outwardly have been indebted to a more 'classical' model: Rosalyn Tureck. Yet, in terms of the performer's relationship to the music, Gould was in fact temperamentally closer to Landowska than to his own contemporaries, including the more scholarly and historically aware Tureck. When Landowska insisted that she would refuse to allow Rameau himself to influence her interpretation of his 'Dauphine', she was insisting on a degree of creative authority for the performer that was fundamental for Gould.[41] The Romantic nature of Gould's aesthetic of performance was, paradoxically, inspired to a great degree by that very interest in Bach. The relative openness of Bach's scores, he said, 'in contra-distinction to music of the late 19th century, for example, where a very detailed notational style and a very specific instrumental predilection was built in to the creative concept', creates a 'curious combination of structural precision and improvisatory options [that] encourages one to invest it with aspects of one's own personality'.[42] And as Will Crutchfield has observed, the tendency to impose one's own personal style on all music of all periods, rather than to use a different style for each composer, is certainly more characteristic of Romantic than modern performance.[43] Gould the performer, in short, reconciled a modern, neo-Classical playing style with a bygone Romantic tradition of creative and highly individual interpretation.

[40] See Asbell, 92.
[41] See Landowska, 407.
[42] *GGSL* 183.
[43] Crutchfield, 22–3.

Moreover, Gould's playing betrays more actual Romantic performance practices than he was willing to admit. In subsequent chapters I discuss some aspects of his style that suggest a revival of Romantic practices bypassed by most of his contemporaries: 'melodic rubato' (the expressive dislocation of melody and bass lines); a fascination with bringing out inner voices; the casual breaking of vertical sonorities; florid continuo playing. Gould's creative rendering of the arpeggios in his performances of Bach's Chromatic Fantasy has much more in common with Landowska's famous example than with the literalism advocated in most modern editions and performances. (The Chromatic Fantasy was a favourite Bach work among Romantic performers, from at least the time of Mendelssohn, Clara Schumann, and Liszt, precisely because of the degree of creative participation that it demanded from the performer.) Gould's fondness for making piano transcriptions also had few counterparts among his contemporaries, though, of course, many among his predecessors. The sometimes startling extremes of tempo and expression in many Gould performances are also more characteristic of Romantic predecessors like Wagner and Furtwängler, or neo-Romantic contemporaries like Bernstein. Wagner, in his 1869 essay 'About Conducting', wrote:

In a certain subtle sense one may say that the pure Adagio can not be taken slow enough: here must reign a rapt confidence in the eloquent persuasiveness of tone-speech pure and simple; here the *languor* of emotion becomes an ecstasy; what the Allegro expressed by a change of figuration, is spoken here by infinite variety of modulated tone; the faintest change of harmony surprises us, the most remote progressions are prepared for and awaited on the tiptoe of suspense.[44]

To hear Gould draw out the *Siegfried Idyll*—breathtakingly—for twenty-four minutes is to hear, a hundred years later, precisely the languorous adagio that Wagner so desired. The Romantic precept that Richard Taruskin claimed for Furtwängler easily applies to Gould: 'anything is all right if it is enough so'.[45]

As the examples in Chapter 1 already showed, Gould had no moral or musical qualms about amending scores, and as Taruskin has noted a 'fluid, easily crossed boundary between the performing and composing roles' was characteristic of pre-modern performance.[46] The critical response to his performances suggests that he allowed himself a degree of licence unusual by post-war standards, yet by the standards of the Romantic era, even of some recent historical performers, his amendments were often tame. (Even the so-called 'purists' among Romantic performers and editors, like Clara Schumann, were hardly literalists.) Gould's attitude towards the score did evolve through his career; as he noted, his creative tampering became more substantial and idiosyncratic after he gave up playing concerts in

[44] Wagner, 314.
[45] Taruskin, 242.
[46] Ibid. 10.

1964.[47] But even where his amendments were conservative, they were always revealing of his musical priorities. He did not, for example, improvise melodic variations, as Romantic performers at least as early as Chopin were fond of doing, and as many historical performers do today. Rather, he generally made planned textual changes that, by his standards, enhanced the unity or clarity of the musical structure; he clearly considered such amendments improvements. And not surprisingly, he was, like many Romantic performers, relatively uninterested in the choice of edition, a matter considered crucial by most modern performers. The scores preserved in the NLC, though not a complete record of the music he studied, suggest no interest in the matter of the editorial reliability of a score; he seems to have acquired the first score available whenever he needed to learn a piece or record splicing notes. Any score that offered the basic notation of a piece sufficed, since he viewed tempo, dynamics, articulation, ornamentation, fingering, and the like as the business of the performer whether or not a composer's markings existed. (He was, though, occasionally prey to editions in which the notes themselves were questionable.) Where variants existed between editions he owned, he chose between them on the basis of musical preference alone, not necessarily siding with the later or more authoritative edition.

Like many Romantic performers, editors, and arrangers, he was fond of making the implicit explicit, especially in Baroque music, by adding bass support to unaccompanied melodic figuration, or adding chords to make a harmonic sequence explicit.[48] He often added his own harmonic support in Bach's music, generally in textures that resemble those in which continuo figuration is often provided; there are examples throughout his performances of Bach's violin and viola da gamba sonatas. In the Preludes to the English Suites Nos. 2, 4, and 5, he added some implied harmonies where only bass notes were written, in each case enhancing the forcefulness of 'tutti' sections in movements that mimic concerto grosso form. He was generally free with notation and texture in Elizabethan and Baroque music, adding octaves or extra tones to chords, restriking sustained notes, occasionally ignoring an indicated *tierce de Picardie*. Such behaviour is hardly controversial, though he was occasionally extreme, as in the second movement of Bach's A major violin sonata (see Ex. 2.1). In the score, the left hand in bars 74–90 is given a pedal-point on the bass octave E–e, to be held throughout these seventeen bars; of course, on either harpsichord or piano, this note would quickly die away to silence and would normally be restruck several times. The violin part at this point has a

---

[47] See *Non, je ne suis pas du tout un excentrique*, 135–6. Cf. e.g. his recordings of Bach's Partitas, made between 1956 and 1963, with his recordings of the French and English Suites, and his film performances of the Partitas Nos. 4 and 6, from the 1970s.

[48] For an example of each, see, respectively, Bach's Brandenburg Concerto No. 5 (1962 CBC television), 139–43, 195–7; and Bach's Viola da Gamba Sonata in G major/II, 97–104.

Ex. 2.1. Gould's added bass line in Bach, Violin Sonata No. 2 in A major/II

sequence of triple-stop chords obviously intended to be realized as arpeggios. Gould took his cue from the violin part, and filled in the tied bass notes with rhythmically varied, arpeggiated chords that add some counterpoint and spell out the harmonies, losing the pedal-point entirely, not to mention stealing some thunder from the violinist.

More controversial, though no less Romantic, was Gould's willingness to make such amendments in post-Baroque music. In his recording of Mozart's C minor concerto, K. 491, he added some chords (see the second movement, bars 9–12), and filled out some textures with melodically independent material (see the first movement, bars 190–4, where he incorporated the ascending line of the second violin part into the solo part). This concerto, like others Mozart wrote for his own use, includes some solo passages that are only sketched, and which the soloist must flesh out by analogy with surrounding material (in the first movement, see bars 261–2 and 467–70). In these cases, Gould's response was notably florid and contrapuntal. There are also places in the first movement in which he enlivened static bass lines, or added a bass line to support melodic figuration (see bars 243–4, 258–60, 323–4, 355–62, 385, and 464–6).[49] There are small-scale examples of such rewriting in other of his Mozart performances, even in Beethoven, and pianistic demands dictated certain liberties with the score in his transcriptions of music by Wagner and Ravel.

---

[49] See Gould's comments on this concerto in *GGR* 130; see also Cott, 54–6, for an uncharacteristic appeal to historical criteria in defending his performance.

It was characteristic of Gould to side with the Romantic tradition of anachronism and individuality when he wrote his own cadenzas for Beethoven's Piano Concerto No. 1 in C major. Like Hummel, Brahms, Busoni, Schnabel, Britten—even Beethoven himself, in the third and largest cadenza he wrote, in middle age, for this early concerto—he did not concern himself with stylistic consistency when writing a cadenza. In the liner notes for his 1958 recording of the work, he explicitly sides with nineteenth-century composers 'who undertook to produce cadenzas for various older works without forgoing their customary vocabulary'. Like a Romantic performer or editor, he used the cadenzas as opportunities to make a personal contribution to the work. The cadenza for the first movement is particularly Gouldian: a 'rather Regerian' triple fugue on the principal themes of the movement, which are exposed separately and then combined, 'in an idiom considerably more chromatic than that of early Beethoven'.[50] The fugal texture satisfied Gould's fondness for formal counterpoint and late-Romantic tonality, as well as his disdain for the glittery virtuosity usually heard in a cadenza. Moreover, the fugal cadenza amounts to an intense new development of the musical material, and so in some sense satisfied the criterion of structural integration that he thought was absent in most cadenzas. Finally, as Helmut Kallmann notes, the cadenza is much more strict rhythmically than most, and so preserves rhythmic continuity with the movement proper, again satisfying one of Gould's usual priorities.[51] And yet, there is something disingenuous about Gould's rationalizations for his cadenzas, and not only because they are, in their own way, very difficult technically. He deplored conventional virtuoso cadenzas because they drew attention to the soloist at the expense of the work, yet his own cadenzas are so odd that they end up drawing even more attention to the soloist, at even greater expense to the work, than would any conventional cadenza. For all his modernist rationalizations, Gould's very decision to impose these cadenzas in so anachronistic a context could not have been more Romantic.

The Composer's Intentions, 'Authenticity', and the Historical Performance Movement

Gould was rarely forthcoming about his intellectual debts to Romantic aesthetics; he may not even have been aware of them. But he was always explicit about maintaining the creative authority of the performer. He did not, for example, justify interpretative licence by appealing to a composer's intentions; on the contrary, he

---

[50]   *GGR* 69. Gould also refers to his 'vastly inappropriate cadenzas which are in the general harmonic idiom of Max Reger' in an unpublished 1958 letter: NLC 31/5/21. The cadenzas were composed in 1954 and published in 1958, but have long been out of print. The cadenza for the first movement was, however, reprinted in Aikin, 30–2.

[51]   See Kallmann, 53.

insisted that the performer was not bound by them even where they are known. (Thus he simply bypassed as irrelevant the whole argument over whether a composer's intentions can truly be determined.) He maintained this view with greater conviction later in his career, but it was apparent in his thinking while he was still a concert artist. In a 1962 interview, he was asked whether the performer was responsible to the composer or to himself. He replied:

There are a few performers in the happy position of feeling that the way they feel the music is the way the composer felt the music. But sometimes I wonder why we fuss so much about fidelity to a tradition of the composer's generation, and not the performer's—for instance, trying to play Beethoven as Beethoven is supposed to have played it. . . . There are many times when I am quite sure Mozart would not approve of what I do to his music. The performer has to have faith that he is doing, even blindly, the right thing, that he may be finding interpretive possibilities not wholly realized even by the composer. This is quite possible. There are examples today of contemporary composers—I'd rather not name them—who are the world's worst interpreters of their own music.[52]

When asked by an interviewer in 1980 if he felt that Beethoven would approve of his interpretations of his music, Gould's response was blunt: 'I don't really know, nor do I very much care.'[53] To recall the famous words of Wimsatt and Beardsley, writing of the so-called 'intentional fallacy', he did not believe in 'consulting the oracle';[54] he did not believe that a composer's interpretation of his work is privileged. Thus he rejected hermeneutic positions advanced by literary theorists like E. D. Hirsch and M. H. Abrams and by some writers on the subject of historical performance, who insist that the authority of an interpretation depends upon a work's having a fixed, determinate meaning, one generally situated in the intentions or interpretations of the author.[55] So for Gould, as for Roland Barthes, the author was dead and had no bearing on one's reading of his work.[56] This position does not of itself mark Gould as a radical: it is shared by structuralists and post-structuralists alike, and by many musicians and writers with perfectly conventional notions about performance. And Taruskin's writings on the historical performance movement include enough testimony from composers to make one wary of assuming the authority of their own comments and performances.[57] But Gould was unusually extreme: he rejected the authority of the composer's intentions regardless of how widely one interprets that concept, or, to use Randall R. Dipert's terms,

---

[52] Asbell, 93. One of those 'contemporary composers' was undoubtedly Stravinsky.

[53] Mach, 106.

[54] Wimsatt and Beardsley, 487.

[55] To use the distinction made in Hirsch, 8, Gould seemed to deny that one could discover a musical text's unequivocal 'meaning' (i.e. 'what the author meant'), and instead preferred to explore a text's possible 'significance' (i.e. the text's relationship to 'a person, or a conception, or a situation, or indeed anything imaginable').

[56] See Barthes's 1968 essay 'The Death of the Author', reprinted in *The Rustle of Language*, 49–55.

[57] See Taruskin, 53–5, 97–8.

what level of intentions one considers. He was willing to adjust a minor slur or dynamic marking but also to reinterpret the entire aesthetic character of a work. Even what Dipert calls 'high-level intentions' (the purposes behind a work's conception, the effects it aims to produce in the listener, the formal relationships it poses) were, in Gould's view, subject to the performer's liberty.[58] Like Pierre Boulez, he sought 'amnesia' when it came to interpreting a piece: he wanted to rediscover it afresh.[59]

It is impossible, of course, to test how Gould would have reacted to, say, a Bach recording of the Goldberg Variations, but there is evidence from his contacts with contemporary composers to suggest that he was as good as his word when it came to rejecting a composer's intentions. The Canadian composer Oskar Morawetz has spoken of meeting with Gould in 1966 while the pianist was preparing to record Morawetz's *Fantasy in D*. Gould initially refused to meet the composer, then agreed to but insisted that he would change nothing in his interpretation. During their meeting, Gould, characteristically, insisted on relative equality among contrapuntal voices, despite the composer's own insistence on a more conventional dichotomy of melody and accompaniment. He told Morawetz, 'when you start to tell me which voice is important and which voice isn't, I have the feeling that you don't understand your own music'.[60] The arrogance of Gould's position here is simply an extension of his belief that the work stands alone and can be approached by the performer without regard for the preconceptions of the composer. He would undoubtedly have agreed with Fred Mauk that 'the only good composer is a dead composer'.[61]

Gould was no less free with the work of other living composers whom he knew—for example, Jacques Hétu and Ernst Krenek, both of whom have responded in print to Gould recordings of their music. Hétu's response to Gould's 1967 recording of his *Variations pour piano* goes beyond chronicling the many departures from the score to examining the premisses of Gould's relationship to a score. He notes Gould's tendency to use a musical text as a 'pre-text' to intrude on the composer's territory, and proposes a plausible biographical explanation: 'Personally, I have often thought that Gould might have been a frustrated composer who, consciously or not, channeled a great deal of his creative energy into the often very mannered performances that we know.'[62] Many others have noted Gould's

[58]   Dipert, 'The Composer's Intentions', 207–8.

[59]   Quoted in Nattiez, ' "Fidelity" to Wagner', 89.

[60]   Quoted in Elliott, 'Glenn Gould and the Canadian Composer', 1, 4. See also Ostwald, 94–5. Cf. the comments of the great Romantic pianist Harold Bauer, quoted in Schonberg, 401–2. Bauer believed that a composer's markings were only 'superficially related to the music. . . . Experience has taught me that the average composer's written indications are sometimes, but not always, right, whereas his verbal directions for performance (supplementing those already written) are almost invariably wrong. . . . Personally, although I have sought every opportunity of consulting a composer prior to playing his music in public, it is only very rarely that I have derived any benefit from his suggestions.'

[61]   Mauk, 144.

[62]   Hétu, 24.

'composerly' mindset, his tendency to compose, in a sense, through the act of interpretation. He was not being wholly disingenuous when he referred to himself as a 'composer who plays the piano', and early in his career, especially during his concert years, he spoke often of his desire to withdraw from performing to devote himself to composition.[63] After writing his string quartet in the early 1950s, Gould began many compositions but completed very few, and then only minor ones. He had some evident talent for composition, but many inhibitions that restrained his work, and he never realized his ambition to be a composer. (Gould's biographers have found a sound psychological basis for Hétu's observation.[64]) The creative urge was satisfied elsewhere in Gould's work: in his 'contrapuntal radio documentaries', in his writings, but above all in his performances. Gould made this point in 1966, when he discussed Beethoven's Op. 109 sonata with Humphrey Burton.[65] He spoke of 'recomposing' the sonata, first by analysing it according to modernist standards that would probably not have received the composer's sanction, then by using the analysis as the basis for performance decisions. If Gould had little success as a true composer, it is not surprising that he was that much more intent on revealing a creative voice in his performances.

Obviously, he rejected ethical arguments about fidelity to the composer, whether living or dead. (Such arguments are sometimes advanced in the literature on aesthetics, and have a wide following in common practice.) He rejected the commonplace notion that music should be allowed to 'speak for itself', that a performer should be an unobtrusive vessel through whom the score is realized as exactly as possible. And so he rejected Stravinsky's view that the performer should be a mere 'executant', bound strictly by the letter of the score, a position that was as much moral as aesthetic.[66] Gould's position on the ethics of performance is closer to that expressed in literary criticism by, for example, Stanley Fish, who insists that there is no getting away from interpretation, that the claim to being a passive 'executant' is impossible anyway. As Fish puts it, 'it would seem, finally, that there are no moves that are not moves in the game, and this includes even the move by which one claims no longer to be a player'. In other words, 'interpretation is the only game in town', and the truly ethical stance is to face that reality and to admit openly what one is doing.[67] Thus it is the stance of reading a work

---

[63] Quoted in Skelton, 41. For Gould's comments, from the late 1950s and early 1960s, on his desire to compose, see Asbell, 93; Braithwaite, 28; Carroll; Tovell; and the 1959 NFB production *Glenn Gould: Off the Record.*

[64] See Friedrich, 158–72; and Ostwald, 200–5. The rather cool critical reception Gould's quartet received probably also inhibited his later composing; on this subject, see Elliott, ' "So You Want to Write a String Quartet?" ', 17–18.

[65] See Burton, ii.

[66] See Stravinsky, 125–42. Like Stravinsky, Heinrich Schenker used 'interpretation' as a pejorative term, 'to signify the imposition of a performer's own, personal, idiosyncratic musical ideas on those of the composer' (quoted in Dunsby, 7). Even an *echt*-Romantic performer like Furtwängler bowed to the composer's authority, and used 'creative interpretation' in a pejorative sense: see his 1934 essay 'Principles of Interpretation', in Furtwängler, 8–15.

[67] Fish, 355.

'objectively', of not putting one's personality into one's reading, that is the insidious one. Gould did not think that ethical questions were irrelevant to aesthetics, as we will see, but his position on the interpreter's proper relationship to the score was not, for him, laden with ethical implications.

He rejected, in short, the notion of 'authenticity' in the sense of fidelity to the score, a value-laden term, which, as Taruskin notes, 'always carries its invidious antonym in tow'; Gould sought an authenticity of a more personal nature, the authenticity of post-modernism, what Taruskin defines as 'knowing what you are, and acting in accordance with that knowledge . . . having what Rousseau called a "sentiment of being" that is independent of the values, opinions, and demands of others'.[68] Authenticity, writes Joseph Kerman, is 'a baleful term which has caused endless acrimony—understandably enough, for the word resonates with unearned good vibrations forced by moralists such as Benjamin and Sartre, as well as by those art connoisseurs who evoke it to confound forgery'.[69] Gould in fact challenged conventional moral objections to forgery, as we have already seen, and he was no more concerned with authenticity in the act of realizing a work than he was in defining or identifying it. His work does not offer a reasoned challenge to notions of ethics and authenticity in performance as much as a sidestepping of the whole problem, along with the full acceptance of the practical consequences.

Gould was only being consistent when he rejected the idea that historical performance practices were necessarily binding, for if the composer's own ideas about performance need not confine the performer, neither do the more general practices of the composer's day. Lydia Goehr has written, 'One way to bring music of the past into the present, and then into the sphere of timelessness, was to strip it of its original, local, and extra-musical meanings,' and then 'impose upon the music meanings appropriate for the new aesthetic'.[70] Gould saw such updating as inherent in the performer's work. His approach was what Stan Godlovitch has called 'an abandonment, not so much of taste, but of the historical identity of any music', as against that of the purist who 'will insist that this is to forfeit the music itself, a sentiment deriving from the belief that the identity of a piece is bound up in its setting'.[71] Gould held the view, often expressed in critiques of historical performance, that one necessarily hears only with the ears of one's day, and so a historical performance would necessarily mean something different to a twentieth-century listener even if the specific performance practices could be reproduced absolutely perfectly. He rejected the claims to 'objectivity' in historical performance, and its implicit closure of interpretative possibilities. The principles that

---

[68] Taruskin, 90, 67.
[69] Kerman, 192.
[70] Goehr, 246–7.
[71] Godlovitch, 'Authentic Performance', 266.

guided his recomposition—his 'misreading'—of Handel's A major Prelude guided his performances even where he did not alter the notes themselves. And he did not transcend historical practices only where there were unavoidable gaps in the historical record, as some historical perfomers have claimed to do: the principle did not depend on the state of the evidence.

Naturally, Gould's position challenged the major premisses of the historical performance movement, as he was well aware. The real explosion of interest in historical performance began only near the end of his life, but the movement was important enough in his lifetime that he did occasionally address it directly, clarifying his position on such issues as instrumentation and fidelity to documentary evidence. It is important to clarify his theoretical differences with historical performers, since his playing does share certain similarities with historical performance as practised in the latter part of the twentieth century—a symptom of shared roots. (Indeed, early in his career he was considered to be 'an historically literate interpreter', by the musicological standards of the day.[72]) Taruskin, drawing on a distinction made in 1914 by the English aesthetician T. E. Hulme, has shown that historical performance generally shares the same 'geometrical' values admired in both composition and performance by neo-Classical musicians, as opposed to the 'vital and organic' art characteristic of Romanticism. (Hulme contrasted the naturalism and realism, the very human 'messiness', the 'soft and vital lines' of Romantic art with the 'hard and geometrical' style, the 'stiff lines and cubical shapes', the 'dry hardness', the 'tendency to abstraction' of Classical art; he placed modern art, with its comparatively fixed view of human nature, its detachment, and its stylistic analogies to machine-age life, into the latter category.[73]) Gould, like modern historical performers, held the somewhat discredited view that a 'rational' or 'classical' performing style prevailed before the Romantic era, though in Gould's case it was a view based solely on the music itself, not historical documentation. Moreover, like his model Tureck and many historical performers, Gould considered his performance style to be a reaction against earlier practices, a stripping away of irrelevant accretions of Romanticism—an image that appears often in the literature on historical performance. Later chapters show many similarities in profile between Gould's playing and that of recent historical performers, including his preferences among pianos and piano actions, and offer evidence that he did have some knowledge of historical performance practices, and often applied them

---

[72] This term is used in Schafer, 59, dating from 1958.

[73] See Taruskin, 90–154, esp. 102–43. His point has been reiterated by others—e.g. Dreyfus, Hill, and Leech-Wilkinson. The parenthetical summary and quoted phrases are taken from Hulme, 73–109 (his 1914 lecture 'Modern Art and its Philosophy') and 111–40 (his essay 'Romanticism and Classicism'). In 1925, José Ortega y Gasset, another of Taruskin's sources, contrasted 'the round and soft forms of living bodies' characteristic of Romantic art with the 'geometric patterns' favoured by the modern artist (Ortega y Gasset, 40). Taruskin's 'geometrical' interpretation of modern performance is quantified and validated throughout Philip.

in 'correct' ways. One might also point to the shared aspect of novelty. For many writers on historical performance it is the novelty, more than the historical foundation, that recommends it—its 'passion of the new', 'its spirit of adventure', its 'freeing minds and hands to experience old music newly'.[74] Gould's work, like historical performance, offers what Laurence Dreyfus refers to as 'defamiliarization', the making new of works with long performance histories.[75]

But the distinctions between Gould's aesthetic and that of historical performance are more fundamental than any superficial similarities of style. If, as Kerman suggests, historical performance 'is essentially an attitude of mind rather than a set of techniques applied to an arbitrarily delimited body of early music',[76] then the absence of historical method in Gould, who deplored the 'archeological' mindset of historical performance, must set him apart. Most definitions of historical performance agree on two basic tenets: that historical sounds should be reproduced through the use of historical instruments, and that historical practices should be used in interpreting the notation in a score. Thus the performer has, according to Alejandro Planchart, 'an absolute injunction to try to find out all that can be known about the performance traditions and the sound-world of any piece that is to be performed, and to try to duplicate these as faithfully as possible'.[77] These two tenets generally lead to two consequences that are fundamentally opposed to Gould's aesthetic: an obsession with sound quality *per se*, and a tendency to deal with individual cases in terms of the generic performance practices of the day.

Historical performance, as Taruskin notes, 'renounces all distinction between sound and substance: to realize the sound is in fact to realize the substance, hence the enormous and, be it said, ofttimes exaggerated concern today for the use of authentic period instruments for all periods'.[78] The view expressed by Malcolm Bilson, in a 1980 article, is only an extreme version of a bias apparent in the work and comments of many historical performers: 'I have often heard it stated by scholars and others interested in performance on early instruments that they would rather hear a great artist on the wrong instrument than a mediocre player on the right one. I am no longer willing to accept that statement. Perhaps it is wrong to put the instrument before the artist, but I have begun to feel that it must be done.'[79] It was indeed wrong, according to Gould, to put what amounts to little more than tone colour above every other musical value, for sound quality—in Dipert's terms, the lowest level of the composer's intentions—was only of secondary importance to

---

[74]   Kenyon, 1; Winter, 50; Taruskin, 148.

[75]   See Dreyfus, 306–8.

[76]   Kerman, 210.

[77]   Quoted in Kivy, *The Fine Art of Repetition*, 97.

[78]   Taruskin, 60; see also 75–7, where Taruskin shows the positivist philosophy at the heart of this premiss, invoking the analogy of E. D. Hirsch's literary hermeneutics.

[79]   Bilson, 161.

him. Harry Haskell thus errs when he relates Gould's Bach to contemporary historical performance: Gould's suppression of 'all traces of Romantic pianism', and his use of recording technology to make his piano sound 'more like a harpsichord', suggest an 'implicit recognition that the sound and the spirit of Bach's music were indivisible'.[80] In reality, it was fundamental to Gould's conception of all music that sound and spirit were indeed divisible, and Bach's music provided him with a model of that principle. His and (as he assumed) Bach's idealism provided his most important rationalization for playing Bach's music on the modern piano.

Romantic musicians did not use idealistic notions about absolute music to justify their use of the piano; instead, they considered the piano to be inherently superior to early keyboard instruments, the instrument towards which Bach's music aspired. Spitta, for instance, held that the piano was the real instrument that Bach had in the back of his mind when he composed for the keyboard, a view that persisted well into the twentieth century. Gould rejected the Romantic notion that Bach 'would have' preferred the piano, and did not (as the Romantics did) justify the modern piano in order to apply performance practices derived from idiomatic nineteenth-century piano music. Rather, he argued that the whole question of instrument—of sound quality—in Bach's music was 'a red herring', that the insistence on historical performance in Bach amounted to 'musicological overkill'.[81] There were no right or wrong instruments, to recall Bilson's terms: different instruments offered different options that could be exploited or suppressed in the service of revealing the structure of the music. Thus the modern piano, Gould claimed, permitted subtle dynamic gradations that could greatly enhance contrapuntal transparency in Bach's music, while it also had a tendency towards silky legato, enhanced by the sustaining pedal, that should be suppressed for the same reason.[82]

When Gould restated Adorno's arguments on the distinction between 'essence' and 'sensuous appearance' in Bach's music, it was primarily to argue against the necessity of historical performance. Like Adorno, he claimed to argue from the nature of the music itself. Thus Bach's music, fugues serving as the model, did not need period instruments in order to be communicated as structure, since instrumental colour was not a constitutive factor. And indeed, as many scholars have shown, there is some historical basis for this belief, as the transcribing practices of Renaissance and Baroque musicians partly suggest. (It is indeed ironic that historical performance dictates performance practice in just that early repertoire in which matters of instrumentation and performance were most flexible.) In a passage that Gould flagged in his copy of *Prisms*, Adorno writes:

[80] Haskell, 181.

[81] Page; *GGF*.

[82] See Gould's discussions of this matter in Davis; Johnson; Monsaingeon, *The Question of Instrument*; and Page. He also used idealism to defend the synthesizer as appropriate to Bach's music: see *GGR* 433.

The only objective representation of music is one which shows itself to be adequate to the essence of its object. This, however, is not to be identified—as Hindemith, too, took for granted—with the idea of the historical first rendition. The fact that the coloristic dimension of music had hardly been discovered in Bach's time, and had certainly not yet been liberated as a compositional technique; that composers did not make sharp distinctions between the different types of piano and organ, but rather abandoned the sound in large measure to taste, points in a direction diametrically opposed to the desire to slavishly imitate the customary sounds of the time. Even had Bach been in fact satisfied with the organs and harpsichords of the epoch, with its thin choruses and orchestras, this would in no way prove their adequacy for the intrinsic substance of his music.[83]

This point of view is inconsistent not only with modern historical performance but with neo-Classical positions (those of Stravinsky even more than Hindemith), though it is consistent with Romantic aesthetics.[84] When Gould remarked that Bach cared less about how many singers performed his choruses than how they sang, he was, unconsciously, restating Furtwängler's views on choral polyphony.[85] Gould's argument was primarily aesthetic, even where, as in the case of Bach, there was some historical justification: to the extent that he perceived an idealistic bent in the composer and music, he perceived a lack of relevance in historical performance.

Given his ahistorical bias, it is not surprising that Gould insisted on treating musical works as individuals, rather than as examples of generic types, and this position naturally led him away from historical performance. If he had a good working knowledge of historical performance practices, he also openly contradicted them without qualm wherever a particular work suggested to him a sound reason to do so. Kerman has noted that historical performance, by its very nature, makes interpretation 'a normative matter, not an individual one'.[86] Historical performers, as Adorno famously put it, 'say Bach [but] mean Telemann'[87]—that is, they apply historical performance practices without accounting for the vast difference in quality between Bach's music and the ordinary music of his day. According to Adorno, and to Gould, Bach's music makes greater demands than Telemann's, and offers more options to the interpreter, and so cannot be limited to the performance practices appropriate to Telemann. In Taruskin's words, 'a performance that merely sets out to demonstrate that Bach was Baroque represents preparatory work, not the substance of performance'.[88] (Kerman notes that arguments about historical performance—Gould's being no exception—invariably circle back to Bach: his music simply matters more.[89]) Moreover, historical practice

---

[83]   Adorno, *Prisms*, 143; cf. NLC B1, 143.
[84]   On Stravinsky's neo-Classicism as intellectual ancestor of modern historical performance, see Taruskin, 113–32.
[85]   The comments of Gould and Furtwängler are in Page; and Haskell, 91.
[86]   Kerman, 191.
[87]   Adorno, *Prisms*, 145.
[88]   Taruskin, 60.
[89]   See Kerman, 203.

was hardly monolithic: every era saw a variety of practices, each with its proponents and detractors. Quantz and C. P. E. Bach worked for years in the same
court—often the same room—while disagreeing on many matters of performance
practice.

Gould always supported the image of Bach as standing defiantly outside his
times. He tended to stress how far, in terms of both style and quality, such works
as *The Art of Fugue* stood out from most music of their day, while ignoring or
denigrating the more fashionable elements in Bach's style. The Romantic image of
Bach as an anachronism is a long-standing commonplace, and has been challenged
by recent scholarship showing his interest, even late in life, in the musical fashions
of his day. Yet the image was crucial to the Schoenberg school. Adorno, for example, rejected the 'impotent nostalgia' of the historicist view, in which Bach was
'degraded' to the status of mere church composer, for 'Bach's music is separated
from the general level of his age by an astronomical distance'.[90] However inade-
quate from a scholarly standpoint, this image of Bach served Gould as justification
for analysis and performance by twentieth-century standards. His Bach was an
aesthetic rather than historical figure; it was simply not a product of a historical
perspective, and he resisted correcting it on that basis.

In performance, Gould permitted the individual response to individual structures to overrule historical practice in any case of conflict. Chapter 9, for example,
shows how he would depart intentionally from historical practice where his
harmonic or motivic analysis of a passage argued against a 'correct' reading of an
ornament. Even leaving aside the issue of the quality of the music at hand, the
historical record cannot account for the needs of every individual case. Still, few
critics of historical performance—even the most liberal among them—have been
willing to go as far as Gould when it comes to individuality: Charles Rosen, for
example, considers it self-evident that the belief 'that the performer should use the
work as a vehicle for expressing his own personality' is 'intellectually disrep-
utable'.[91] But if Gould was in a sense the ultimate Romantic, it is simply consistent
that in fundamental ways he was the opposite of a historical performer.

Gould and the Culture of 'Fluctuating Stasis'

If Gould's premises and practices had roots in Romanticism and neo-Classicism,
he was also in many respects a child of his times, a product of intellectual currents
in music and culture during the years of his professional life, especially the 1960s.
He was keenly aware of the place of his thought within contemporary culture, and
made many explicit connections between his work as a performer and ideas that

---

[90]   Adorno, *Prisms*, 135, 145.
[91]   Rosen, 'Should Music Be Played "Wrong"?', 54.

were 'in the air' at the time. His awareness of historical issues was strongest when it came to his own times, and indeed, the atemporality, the absence of historical method, so fundamental to his thinking and playing was grounded in contemporary thought, as he recognized.

Gould's view of music, and the creative role he demanded as a performer, were symptomatic of the same cultural forces that inspired (to take one influential example) Leonard B. Meyer's book *Music, the Arts, and Ideas,* first published in 1967. Meyer's analysis of cultural forces offers an appropriate context for the Gould aesthetic, especially his idea that modern Western culture, since about the First World War, has increasingly given way to a condition of 'fluctuating stasis— a steady-state in which an indefinite number of styles and idioms, techniques and movements, will coexist in each of the arts'.[92] Gould saw post-war musical life in just these terms: as he said in a 1974 film, he saw in the mixing of styles 'the future of music'.[93] This point of view traces back to the beginning of his career, at least to his work in the early 1950s on his string quartet, which he placed explicitly in the context of the prevailing stylistic permissiveness. In a draft for a 1967 radio commentary, in which he discusses his string quartet, he writes, 'As a composer, I'm a maker of grafts, which I suppose is a fancy way of describing an attitude to composition which some would call eclectic and others, less well disposed, derivative.' He goes on to discuss the 'schizophrenic' nature of the quartet, in which Renaissance polyphony, Baroque fugue, Classical sonata-allegro form, and the developing variation of Schoenberg, among other elements, all coexist within 'the most expansive and indulgent harmonic vocabulary ever invented', namely the highly chromatic, contrapuntal, late-Romantic tonal language of Bruckner, Strauss, Mahler, Reger, and the young Schoenberg.[94] Gould never, to my knowledge, used the vocabulary of contemporary post-modernism, but his sympathy with Meyer's analysis of 'fluctuating stasis' can certainly be understood in these terms: Jyrki Uusitalo, in his article 'Postmodernism in Music', shows the trend towards the mixing of styles as characteristic of the post-modern artwork, and Nattiez has convincingly cited Gould's views on the matter as evidence of an incipient post-modernist aesthetic.[95]

As Meyer points out, one of the most important implications of the pluralistic nature of contemporary musical style is the rejection of a teleological view of music history, since all of history has, in a sense, become equally close, equally accessible. The rejection of ideas of 'progress', 'fashion', and the 'avant-garde' recurs frequently in Gould's writings and interviews; it was a point of view crucial to his aesthetic,

[92] L. B. Meyer, *Music, the Arts, and Ideas,* 172. Meyer's book does not appear among Gould's effects in the NLC.
[93] Monsaingeon, *Chemins de la musique,* iii.
[94] 'Draft II (The Art of Glenn Gould)/Part III/ *String Quartet*', 1–2.
[95] See Uusitalo, 271; and Nattiez, 'The Language of Music in the Twenty-First Century', 29–30.

and one that he argued passionately. Writing of Grieg's Sonata in E minor, Op. 7, which he refused to denigrate because it was less 'modern' than (though contemporary with) *Tristan*, he said that the calendar 'is a tyrant; submission to its relentless linearity, a compromise with creativity; the artist's prime responsibility, a quest for that spirit of detachment and anonymity which neutralizes and transcends the competitive intimidation of chronology'.[96] The rejection of musical progress was in fact one important respect in which his thought differed from that of Schoenberg and his disciples, who defended the historical justness, even necessity, of dodecaphony. Gould was emphatic that his admiration for Schoenberg was solely for his achievements as a composer, not for his status as a revolutionary.[97] By the same token, he might also dismiss a composer (like Monteverdi) whose music he did not like, even if that composer was important in terms of the history of style.[98] And he admired composers who remained true to their individual styles in spite of the musical fashions of their day. He made a polemical point of championing both the 'revolutionary' Schoenberg and the 'reactionary' Strauss. Though his affection for Strauss's music was sincere, one suspects that when, in a 1962 article, he called Strauss 'the greatest musical figure who has lived in this century' he was speaking not of Strauss's compositions so much as his implicit stand against the idea of musical progress. In the same article, he concluded:

The great thing about the music of Richard Strauss is that it presents and substantiates an argument which transcends all the dogmatisms of art—all questions of style and taste and idiom—all the frivolous, effete preoccupations of the chronologist. It presents to us an example of the man who makes richer his own time by not being of it; who speaks for all generations by being of none. It is an ultimate argument of individuality—an argument that man can create his own synthesis of time without being bound by the conformities that time imposes.[99]

(He defended Sibelius, Hindemith, and other 'reactionaries' in like terms.) He rejected the concept of a *Zeitgeist* that could validate or invalidate an artistic product: just as historical circumstances did not affect the nature of a work, they did not affect its value. He was especially vociferous in condemning 'the tyranny of stylistic collectivity', the 'combative elements' within the various stylistic 'factions' of his own day, and he himself was never concerned about being or appearing 'contemporaneous'; he was especially critical of the early writings and pronouncements of Boulez, who had contended that only the serial composer could claim relevance.[100]

---

[96] *GGR* 78.
[97] This is one of the principal themes of his 1964 lecture 'Arnold Schoenberg: A Perspective', reprinted in ibid. 107–22.
[98] On Monteverdi, see ibid. 12–13; and *Non, je ne suis pas du tout un excentrique*, 189–91.
[99] *GGR* 85, 92.
[100] Skelton, 46; Colgrass, 10; McClure. On this issue, see also Monsaingeon, *Chemins de la musique*, i; and Moore. On Boulez specifically, see *GGR* 216–20; and Harris, 53–4.

In his 1963 lecture 'Forgery and Imitation in the Creative Process', Gould played down the importance of novelty and invention, even denied the possibility of true originality, in the development of musical language—precisely those aspects stressed in ideologies that cherish musical progress. He discussed such ideas more often in a historical-critical context—in polemics against the idea of musical progress—than in a philosophical one, but his position was still consistent with an idealist (or Platonist) view of music. As Renée Cox wrote in 1984,

There has been a resurgence of interest lately in the idea that works of art in general, and musical works in particular, belong within the category of eternal being rather than that of temporal existence, and thus have being independent of artists' and all other human minds. This entails that what we refer to as the compositional process would be one not of creation but of discovery or selection.[101]

Gould showed himself to be a true idealist when he emphasized the debts that 'original' creative achievements owe to earlier music, and saw more give and take between creation and discovery in the act of composition. In his 1963 lecture, he stressed how music develops through the imitation, ornamentation, development, and transformation of received elements in new contexts. (Schoenberg made a similar point when he referred to dodecaphony as a discovery rather than an invention.) In other essays from the same period, Gould writes (paraphrasing André Malraux on painting) that 'all music is really about other music'; 'All art is really variation upon some other art', so that the genuinely 'original' work of art 'would be unrecognizable'.[102] And he praised eras and cultures in which ideas of originality and individuality were less prized than they have been throughout Western music history. Meyer, likewise, notes that 'the radical changes in ideology which have occurred in the twentieth century have made the pursuit of novelty somewhat incongruous', since 'the Idea of Progress and of dialectical development have given way to a neutral ahistoricism'.[103] Uusitalo, again, makes the same point in explicitly post-modernist terms, and for Nattiez, Gould's atemporality and view of musical creation place him as much among the post-moderns as the Romantics or moderns.[104]

Meyer's analysis of the origins and nature of the ideology of fluctuating stasis sheds light on Gould's aesthetic positions. He traces the pluralism that characterizes contemporary culture back to its roots in larger epistemological changes, including the idea that history and knowledge are not objective facts but rather constructs that necessarily reflect a present-day point of view; the idea of the neutrality of history, that 'all pasts . . . coexist as ever present possibilities upon which the artist,

---

101   Cox, 'Are Musical Works Discovered?', 367.
102   'Anthology of Variation/Draft 1- Part 1', 1; *GGR* 94.
103   L. B. Meyer, *Music, the Arts, and Ideas*, 218; see also 146–9 and 160–1 on the same topic.
104   See Uusitalo, 273; and Nattiez, 'Gould singulier' and 'The Language of Music in the Twenty-First Century'.

writer, or composer may draw'; and the tendency towards formalism that results from seeing no distinction between past and present and so removing the aspect of time from the identity of the work.[105] All of these positions are consistent with Gould's views on the nature of music and the role of the performer, and he approved strongly of artistic practices that confirmed this pluralistic and ahistorical condition.[106]

Meyer believed, in fact, that dealing with relativism and pluralism was one of the central problems of his time, and this has been even more true in the decades since he wrote *Music, the Arts, and Ideas*. The counterpart to this problem in the arts is how to 'move forward' in a static situation in which the concept of an avant-garde has no real meaning. In music circles, it has been common enough in recent decades to hear complaints about the ossified state of conventional performance. As Will Crutchfield writes,

No complaint has been heard more often in recent years than that there is a dearth of really interesting new violinists, pianists, singers, and conductors for the standard repertory. The complaint is valid. In the general run of sober young conservatory graduates and hot (sober) young competition winners whose débuts I regularly hear in New York, cautious correctness is the rule. In the work of the mid-career touring soloists, a deadly sense of get-the-job-done often compounds the lack of a purposeful musical message. Of course there are exceptions; the rule, though, is discouraging.[107]

Gould was well aware of this situation, and it is not an exaggeration to say that his whole approach to performance amounts to a practical attempt to address it. There was a self-consciousness in his relationship to the Western classical canon and to conventional ideas about performance practice, a self-consciousness that implied a search for novelty in a relatively static situation. Many such efforts can be discerned in Western musical practice in recent decades: the constant invention of new compositional styles; the revival of historical performance practices; the merging of foreign and popular styles with 'serious' music; and the search for new repertoire in previously slighted corners of Western music history, as in the revival (especially since Gould's death) of obscure Romantic fare, including salon music. Similar self-conscious efforts have recently been common in fields like theatre and literary criticism: Gould's 'mission' clearly reflected broader cultural conditions. His views on musical works and the interpreter's role recall conceptions of the text and critic

---

[105] On these topics, see L. B. Meyer, *Music, the Arts, and Ideas*, 139–45, 149–51, and 151–3, respectively; the quoted passage is on 193. On 193–208, Meyer discusses the artistic practices that draw on music of the past (paraphrase, borrowing, modelling, etc.).

[106] In Moore, 8–9 he offers the example of Ludwig Diehn, a wealthy amateur musician from Washington, DC, who wrote symphonies in the style of Bruckner and had them privately recorded; he also mentions Diehn in *GGSL* 121. Gould interviewed Diehn for his 1965 CBC radio documentary *Dialogues on the Prospects of Recording*.

[107] Crutchfield, 21. Kerman, 184, also notes that, in terms of performance, 'the situation in "traditional" music has been relatively stagnant, except for an occasional figure like Glenn Gould or Pierre Boulez or Maria Callas'.

in much post-modern literary theory and criticism, especially those strains, like Barthes's *nouvelle critique* of the mid-1960s, contemporary with his own post-concert career. Umberto Eco, from at least the early 1960s, recognized a trend towards openness, ambiguity, and indeterminacy in literary criticism. Writing in the later 1980s, he observed that '[d]uring the last decades we have witnessed a change of paradigm in the theories of textual interpretation', adding, after a survey of reader-response criticism from the 1960s and 1970s, that such an 'insistence on the moment of reading, coming from different directions, seems to reveal a felicitous plot of the *Zeitgeist*'.[108] Susan R. Suleiman wrote in the late 1970s:

> One could adduce many reasons for this shift in perspective. . . Even at first glance, however, it is obvious that the current interest in the interpretation, and more broadly in the reception, of artistic texts—including literary, filmic, pictorial, and musical ones—is part of a general trend in what the French call the human sciences (history, sociology, psychology, linguistics, anthropology) as well as in the traditional humanistic disciplines of philosophy, rhetoric, and aesthetics. The recent evolution of all these disciplines has been toward self-reflexiveness—questioning and making explicit the assumptions that ground the methods of the discipline, and concurrently the investigator's role in delimiting or even in constituting the object of study. Such self-reflexiveness, which has its analogue in the principles of relativity and uncertainty as they emerged in physics early in this century, necessarily shifts the focus of inquiry from the observed—be it defined as text, psyche, society, or language—to the interaction between observed and observer.[109]

Gould's work, no less than such literary trends as reader-response criticism, can be understood in light of this same paradigm shift—not only his aesthetic premises and his specific interpretations, but also his self-conscious, even polemical attitude towards his own field of endeavour.

Gould's way of 'moving forward' was to subject the standard canonic repertoire and conventional classical performance practices to radical personal critique. Some of his more extreme interpretations, especially given the self-consciousness with which he misbehaves, suggest efforts at realigning accepted standards and categories, at persuading listeners to extend accepted boundaries. Many critics have noted this aspect of his playing, observing that his creative intrusions tended to be greatest in those canonical works, like Mozart's and Beethoven's sonatas, with the most deeply entrenched conventions of interpretation and performance. What Gould called the 'deliberate distortion of the text' in his playing generally had the polemical intent of offering fresh hearing precisely where it was most difficult.[110] Stanley Fish has noted how a new interpretative position or paradigm 'announces itself as a break from the old, but in fact it is radically dependent on the old, because it is only in

---

[108] Eco, *The Limits of Interpretation*, 44, 47.
[109] Suleiman, 4.
[110] *Non, je ne suis pas du tout un excentrique*, 193 ('distorsion délibérée du texte').

the context of some differential relationship that it can be perceived as new or, for that matter, perceived at all'.[111] One of Gould's goals was to make this kind of self-consciousness an issue in music, to make his knowing revisions of conventional views obvious as such. He occasionally made it clear that he knew how the pieces he experimented with were 'supposed to go'. In the second of his televised conversations with Burton in 1966, he used the example of Mozart's Sonata in B flat major, K. 333, to contrast 'correct' performance practice with the more 'distorted' angle from which he approached the piece, and which can be heard in his 1967 CBC television performance. As he told Burton in the same programme, in a discussion of Beethoven's Op. 109 sonata, the modern performer had an obligation to recompose canonical works in this way. Such a self-reflexive attitude towards canons and conventions is characteristic of the post-modern artist, critic, or work, and part of Gould's achievement was to have explored the implications this position might have for musical performance.

He revealed his awareness of his historical position in a CBC radio broadcast from 23 July 1970, in which he discussed his performance of some surprising repertoire: Chopin's Sonata No. 3 in B minor. In the accompanying scripted interview, which included a prepared tape segment reviewing musical trends in the decade just ended, Gould situated his decision to take up this uncharacteristic work in the very intellectual milieu that Meyer analyses. Aspects of the musical scene in the 1960s that Gould discussed include the decline of serialism, the persistence of tonality, electronics, the revival of Ives and Mahler, the 'East-meets-West' and 'Switched-On Bach' phenomena, and finally Berio's *Sinfonia*—a 'music of multiple inclusion' backed by no theory, for Gould a work whose pluralistic message summarized the decade. With Chopin's sonata, he acknowledged that his usual priorities in performance were at odds with an appropriate, or at least conventional, Chopin style, most especially his preference for a rhythmic continuity that did not permit the flexibility demanded by Chopin's large-scale works. In the 1950s, he said, he simply left Chopin alone because of his inability to reconcile the music with his own aesthetic. But by 1970, he had drawn inspiration from the freedom and pluralism that had characterized so many aspects of contemporary music, and that he felt could properly be extended to the performance of canonical works. In a cultural climate in which 'every work of art is in fact reduced to its potential as the source of another work of art', one worries less about the 'acceptability' of blatantly anachronistic practices and 'starts wondering about the outcome of certain kinds of aesthetic cross-breeding'. For Gould, the cultural climate, which some derided as chaotic but which he found liberating and inspiring creatively, validated his experiment. The resulting performance of the sonata draws on the same rhythmic

[111] Fish, 349.

premisses as his Baroque and Classical performances: he declines to use conventional tempo shifts to articulate theme groups,[112] and applies his usual practice of exploring inner voices at the expense of the primacy of lyrical melody. Gould ultimately did not consider the results of the experiment to have been particularly successful in this case,[113] and he was right: the performance (perhaps excepting his lean, *moto-perpetuo* finale) is actually rather dull, and certainly offers little insight into Chopin. But it is the urge to make the experiment in the first place that is revealing.

We have already seen how Gould in performance demanded some of the creative licence usually accorded only to composers, and when it came to situating himself within his cultural milieu, he frequently allied himself temperamentally and intellectually with composers more than fellow performers. (There have been few performers willing to follow him very far in his rethinking of the canon.) He was certainly influenced by some trends in music composition in the 1950s and 1960s. He considered the 'contrapuntal radio documentaries' that he made for the CBC in the 1960s and 1970s to be musical compositions by the standards of his day, by analogy with contemporary works, like Stockhausen's *Gesang der Jünglinge* (1956), which draw on unorthodox audio materials. He was aware of the importance of the spoken word in much of the new music of the 1950s and 1960s, and was influenced by Marshall McLuhan's observations on the subject, as he acknowledged.[114] Indeed, in his approval of the idea that not only speech but all sounds were becoming increasingly valid as the stuff of music, Gould often sounded surprisingly like another contemporary devotee of McLuhan: John Cage.

We might also see something of Gould's attitude towards performance in what Eco, in a 1962 essay, calls 'the poetics of the open work'. Eco discusses works by Stockhausen, Berio, Pousseur, and Boulez that are 'open' (literally, unfinished) in the sense that the performer is required to assemble the final form of the work out of a number of given segments; such works, by definition, have no fixed form. But Eco goes on to posit a broader cultural condition in which 'openness' is '*the* fundamental possibility of the contemporary artist or consumer';[115] the explicitly 'open' work merely reflects a more general trend towards openness in the interpretation of art works. Gould did not advocate literally rearranging the parts of a work, of course, but he did advocate openness with aspects of works conventionally considered inviolate, a point of view that once again allies him closely with some trends in

---

[112] In the first movement, note Gould's use of the same tempo for the opening theme (♩ = 89) and the lyrical second theme in the relative major, beginning at bar 41 (♩ = 87). His rhythmic treatment of the major theme groups in the exposition seems to have sufficed to make his polemical point, and he does not maintain a literally strict tempo throughout the whole movement. Philip, 19–20, 57–8, offers examples of the more conventional flexibility of tempo in the first movement from a number of early 20th-cent. recordings.

[113] See *GGR* 453.

[114] See Davis, 280; and *GGR* 74.

[115] Eco, *The Open Work*, 22.

post-modern criticism of his (and our) day. Barthes, for example, writing in 1966, analysed cultural conditions in terms similar to those of Meyer and Eco:

The very definition of the work is changing: it is no longer a historical fact, it is becoming an anthropological fact, since no history can exhaust its meaning. The variety of meanings is not a matter of a relativist approach to human mores; it designates not the tendency that society has to err but a disposition towards openness; the work holds several meanings simultaneously, by its very structure, and not as a result of some infirmity in those who read it. . . . the work proposes, man disposes.[116]

Gould's experiments in performance also reflected the same conditions that encouraged many contemporary composers to cannibalize the past to create new works, even more so than their neo-Classical predecessors. Robert P. Morgan writes,

the extraordinarily fragmentary nature of much contemporary composition, evident, for example, in the widespread use of quotation and in the tendency towards pastiche, betrays the absence of a common core. Though anticipated by Stravinsky (the inevitable concomitant of his historical views) and by still earlier forerunners such as Ives and Satie, only recently has the trend reached epidemic proportions. In composers as disparate as Luciano Berio, Bernd Alois Zimmermann, Lukas Foss, Peter Maxwell Davies, and George Rochberg, we hear bits and pieces of previous music, which have been torn from their original contexts and then reassembled into new, collage-like configurations. Deprived of their original meaning, which was dependent upon a total structural context, these fragments are bestowed with a new meaning in which the pretence of totality and integration is largely abandoned. A purely synthetic context is created where no 'natural' one exists.[117]

Gould's rethinking of canonical works was, in a sense, also an appropriation of the music, not just a realization of it—a bringing to bear of personal, contemporary thinking onto the music. His performances, even the more radical ones, almost never amount to rewritings or arrangements, though some critics have used these terms; yet there is a certain validity in the criticism, which he accepted, that some of his performances merit hyphenated attributions ('Mozart-Gould'). Musicians of his day as different as Cage and Boulez frequently expressed the view that the 'museum' model of music, the entrenched canon of musical 'masterpieces', exercised a crushing influence on contemporary music, including composition. Gould's refusal to be 'correct' in performance, like Boulez's yearning for 'amnesia', reflected a creator's desire to be freed from convention.

But of all the contemporary factors influencing Gould's open aesthetics of performance and his relationship to the classical canon, perhaps the most important was recording technology.[118] He was much concerned with the implications of

[116] Barthes, *Criticism and Truth*, 67, 69.
[117] Morgan, 'Tradition, Anxiety, and the Musical Scene', 72.
[118] The basic Gould manifesto on this subject is his 1966 essay 'The Prospects of Recording', reprinted in *GGR* 331–53. See also Payzant, *GGMM* 21–50, 119–27.

recording in terms of musical composition, performance, and reception. In fact, on the subject of recording his thinking was considerably more up to date, even prophetic, than that of many thinkers of his day. Meyer, for example, like many, rejected the idea that recording technology fundamentally alters important premisses about music; he regarded recording technology as merely a conduit for the dissemination of conventional performances. But Gould pursued the implications of McLuhan's idea, summarized in his famous catchphrase 'the medium is the message', that the content of any medium is less influential than the changes in scale or pace or pattern that the medium itself imposes on human affairs. Though Gould was sometimes critical of McLuhan's trendy vocabulary and some of his specific analyses, including his distinctions between 'hot' and 'cold' media, he appropriated several important ideas from McLuhan about the nature and social implications of electronic media. He insisted that electronic technology affected the basic patterns of professional musical life in many fundamental ways, and he was critical of those musicians who resisted it.

For Gould, the implications of recording extended even to one's conception of what constitutes an integral musical work or performance. In this he was considerably more radical than writers on music aesthetics like Stan Godlovitch, for whom splicing and other features of recorded performances 'compromise performance integrity', at least 'from a traditional perspective'.[119] But as Gould pointed out, the consequences of technology for musical works and performances were negative only where one assumed that concert performance must remain the standard. For him recording had created a separate musical art form with its own imperatives and possibilities, and in which the standards of integrity relevant to the concert hall did not apply. For one thing, though it might seem to fix a historical moment, recording is in fact an inherently atemporal enterprise, because the standards of real time do not apply in the creation of the recorded work. As Gould put it in 1966, 'The inclination of electronic media is to extract their content from historical date'; a recording need not be a picture-postcard of a concert performance.[120] In McLuhan's terms, a recording is a 'modular' or 'cubist' production, a 'labyrinth', to which the 'linear' or 'pre-Einsteinian' conception of time in the concert medium is irrelevant.[121] In short, the atemporal condition in which Gould thought musical works should be considered was, he believed, enhanced by the recording process.

[119] Godlovitch, 'The Integrity of Musical Performance', 580.

[120] GGR 342. Gould uses the picture-postcard analogy in Aikin, 32, 36. On the atemporal nature of the recording process, see Mach, 92; and 'What the Recording Process Means to Me', 36.

[121] McLuhan applied such terms to his own style of writing, and to the electronic media as compared with the traditional book. (The very first sentence of The Gutenberg Galaxy announces that it 'develops a mosaic or field approach to its problems': the parts of the book can be read in any order.) Because of McLuhan's 'mosaic' or 'modular' or 'non-linear' approach, which he also observed in much 20th-cent. literature (Joyce, Dos Passos, Burroughs), his writing is sometimes cited as quintessentially post-modern, something that might be said of the process of recording as opposed to concert performance.

He felt, moreover, that the recording medium had fundamental implications in terms of the role of the performer. Just as Cage, from the 1930s, insisted that electronics had changed the ground rules for composers, Gould insisted that 'recording will forever alter our notions about what is appropriate to the performance of music'.[122] For one thing, he believed that recording permitted the performer to take technical and interpretative risks that would not pay off in a concert situation, and he rejected the commonplace complaint that recording inhibits performers. Johanne Rivest observes, moreover, that recording inherently enlarges the role of the interpreter, relative to those of composer and listener, and increases the amount of attention focused on the interpretation.[123] Gould seems to have recognized this when he claimed, as early as 1959, that he preferred recording to live performance because it was a more truly creative process.[124] (His discography bears him out: the interpretations in his polished studio recordings are invariably more creative (whatever else one may think of them) than those in his preserved concert performances, or even his CBC broadcasts.) Gould provided a practical model for his point of view: one thing we can always say about his performances is that they sound fresh. He went as far as to suggest that recording demands of the performer 'to recreate the work, to transform the act of interpretation into an act of composition'.[125] In other words, the relationship of his ideas about performance to the cultural and intellectual milieu of his day was only strengthened by concurrent developments in the electronic media.

Gould felt, moreover, that the fact of recording made a creative aesthetic imperative for a modern performer of the classical canon. Because so many conventional performances of canonical works are now permanently preserved, performers of such works have the option, even the duty, to be creative. He believed that basic statements about the canonical repertoire had already been made, and repeatedly made the point that one had no reason to record a familiar work again unless one had a significant and distinctive new interpretation of it to offer.[126] It is tempting

[122] GGR 337. Cage, incidentally, differed from Gould in that he preferred to use recording technology as a kind of musical instrument, rather than as a means to fix interpretations.

[123] See Rivest, 5, 34, 43–4.

[124] See Braithwaite, 28.

[125] Quoted in Nattiez, 'The Language of Music in the Twenty-First Century', 28. This attitude may explain some aspects of Gould's discography. For example, he never recorded Beethoven's Sonatas in E flat major, Op. 81a ('Les Adieux'), and in A major, Op. 101, two works that he singled out for special praise (see GGR 37, 45–6, 458–9). The reason may simply have been that he never found the special interpretative point of view that, for him, justified making a new recording. And around 1970, he abandoned the idea of recording a Scriabin sonata cycle after the complete sets of Hilde Somer and Ruth Laredo were released, for similar reasons (see Kazdin, 138; and 'CBC Radio Script from 1978', 10). On the other hand, he devoted considerable amounts of time to recording works of which he had a low opinion (Beethoven's 'Appassionata' Sonata, Chopin's B minor sonata, some later Mozart sonatas) where he did feel that a significant interpretative point was pressing. It is worth mentioning in this regard that there were, apparently, no external constraints upon Gould's choices of repertoire, since both Columbia/CBS and the CBC gave him complete freedom to play what he liked, including works of little commercial viability (see Colgrass, 6, 8; Friedrich, 149; and Kazdin, 156–7).

[126] See GGR 458; Burton, i, ii; McClure; and Monsaingeon, Chemins de la musique, ii. On several of these occasions, Gould also insisted, with understandable defensiveness, that these new interpretations had to have some worthwhile points to make; eccentricity for its own sake did not suffice.

to concede his point: there are, and always will be, scores of conventional readings of Beethoven's Fifth in the record shops, not to mention the concert halls; it is difficult not to despair when confronted with yet one more performance of a familiar piece that simply reminds us how the music 'goes'. Gould here tapped into a curious fact of his historical situation. It is indeed ironic that it is in post-war musical life, in the era of recording, that fidelity to the work is such a prevailing principle. If ever a Romantic era was needed it is now, when recording has released performers from the necessity of perpetuating conventional interpretations. One could have defended the need for such interpretations a hundred years ago, when one would hear a particular piece of music infrequently, and only in concert, yet a hundred years ago highly individual interpretation was much more common. Recording should really liberate rather than inhibit musical interpretation, and if it generally does not, even today, it is because we still have not fully grasped the implications of recording on musical life. But Gould did, and his mission as a kind of one-man Romantic era was the result.

The 'Kit' Concept and the Roles of Composer, Performer, and Listener

Given that Gould demanded a creative role as a musical performer, that his own piano style was highly idiosyncratic and instantly recognizable, that he has been the subject of a posthumous personality cult that he himself helped promote, it comes as a surprise, and an apparent contradiction, to find him insisting on a condition of anonymity as proper to the artist, and prophesying a future in which recording technology increasingly undermines the final authority of the interpreter. Yet he repeatedly made these points throughout his career.[127] In reality there is no contradiction: Gould's belief in the anonymity of the artist was, in fact, a logical extension of his belief in the creative function of interpretation.

Meyer has noted a trend towards 'impersonality' characteristic of the culture of fluctuating stasis, towards the undermining of the importance of the identity and personality of the artist, which have become increasingly irrelevant as factors in appreciation and criticism. This trend is acknowledged in Gould's discussions of one of his most cherished themes: the changing relationships of composer, performer, and listener. He frequently deplored that period in music history, around the later eighteenth century, when these roles became increasingly specialized, splitting into the hierarchy that persists today. He spoke approvingly of his sense that, by at least the 1960s, the old hierarchy was breaking down—that the ancient notions

---

[127] On the subject of anonymity and the artist, see his 1964 article 'Strauss and the Electronic Future' and his 1974 self-interview, reprinted in *GGR* 92–9, 315–28. See also *GGR* 78, 351–3; 'Forgery and Imitation in the Creative Process', 8–9; and 'What the Recording Process Means to Me'.

about the roles of composer, performer, and listener were becoming 'joyfully muddled'—precisely because the artist's identity was becoming increasingly irrelevant to his work.[128] Contemporary composers like Berio, Cage, and Rochberg recognized this situation, and wrote music that explicitly addressed it. And Gould was aware that his point of view had contemporary adherents. In a 1974 film, he compared his view of the hierarchy of roles with that of Cage, claiming as one of Cage's most important points that 'the perceiver' can also be 'a doer', that 'the listener and the maker are intermingled'.[129] (Or as Cage once put it, the composer also has ears.)

This point of view was intimately connected with Gould's championship of recording technology: it was technology, he claimed, that was one of the most important factors contributing to the 'muddling' of the roles of composer, performer, and listener, because it radically altered the relationship to music of all involved with it. This was true in part because it was a team effort, a kind of laboratory situation, but also because it was essentially atemporal. As he said a few months before his death, what is perhaps most important about recording is its unique ability 'to involve the listener in the music or in whatever the substance of the recording happens to be while at the same time separating that listener from all extraneous biographical data—from all concern with its documentation, its preparations, its performances, its post-production processes, and so on'.[130] The condition of privacy implicit in the production and reception of recorded music was crucial for Gould, since it naturally reduced the presence of the performer's ego even as it emphasized the importance of the interpretation. He believed that recording, unlike concert performance, placed more attention on the music and less on the personality of the artist—even, presumably, an artist as idiosyncratic as himself. In this matter, Gould (like Cage) was deeply influenced by McLuhan, who had observed that 'electronic technology . . . would seem to render individualism obsolete'.[131] McLuhan too noted how the conventional specialization of roles was diminished by the electronic media, which encourage 'participation' rather than passive reception. In a 1969 article, Gould acknowledged McLuhan's idea that 'it's a trend of our times to take an interest in the process of production'.[132]

Gould took these ideas to their logical conclusion by advocating the direct participation of the listener in the creative process. He argued not only for a creative performer, but for a

---

[128] CBC radio broadcast commentary, 23 July 1970.

[129] Monsaingeon, *Chemins de la musique*, i.

[130] 'What the Recording Process Means to Me', 36.

[131] McLuhan, *The Gutenberg Galaxy*, 9.

[132] *GGR* 373. Given Gould's debt to McLuhan, it is worth mentioning that they were personally acquainted. They were for a time neighbours in Toronto, they exchanged ideas in conversation and by letter, and Gould interviewed McLuhan for his 1965 CBC radio programme 'Dialogues on the Prospects of Recording'. References to McLuhan, both explicit and implicit, appear throughout Gould's writings and interviews.

creative listener—a listener whose reactions, because of the solitude in which they're bred, are shot full of unique insights. These are insights which will not necessarily duplicate or overlap those of the performer or the producer or the engineers; they're insights which initiate a new link in the chain of events, a new link in the network. It's a link which holds out the possibility that the work we do here [in the recording studio] doesn't necessarily come to an end when the final product is dispatched from the pressing plant, but rather that, from that point on, it will have consequences which we can't begin to measure, ramifications which we can't possibly attempt to quantify, and that, eventually, like a benign boomerang, the ideas which feed on those consequences, the ideas which, out there in the world of the creative listener, begin to take on life of their own, may very well return to nourish and inspire us.[133]

Whether or not Gould agreed with McLuhan's definition of the phonograph as a 'hot' medium (that is, a medium low in audience participation), he was certainly concerned to pursue its potential for interaction.[134] As he envisaged the techno-logical future, the listener would be permitted the same freedom to manipulate the recorded product (that is, the interpreter's work) as the interpreter was permitted to take with the composer's score; the listener, too, would be permitted to impose his personality onto the music. Thus Gould's own stage in the creative process (and notwithstanding his own obsessive control over his recordings) would not neces-sarily be the end product of the creative process, but could be altered by listeners for their own creative purposes.

'Dial twiddling is in its limited way an interpretative act,' Gould wrote in 1966; that is, even the listener of his day, limited by his home stereo equipment largely to adjusting volume, tone, and balance, was still exercising creative options, whether he knew it or not. He saw no reason why the listener's ability to participate creatively should not grow along with technological developments. Indeed, he claimed that it was the listener 'upon whose fuller participation the future of the art of music waits'.[135] He envisaged a time when the listener might be able to splice together segments from different performances of the same work, making necessary adjustments for tempo and so on, to create a more satisfying new performance. The future performer, in turn, might, instead of issuing completed performances, issue 'kits' containing the raw materials (i.e. variant takes) from which the listener could splice together at home his own ideal version of a piece, or as many versions as he liked, making precisely the sorts of interpretative decisions that today are exclusively the province of the performer, producer, and technician.[136] Most

---

[133] 'What the Recording Process Means to Me', 37.

[134] On 'hot' and 'cold' media, and on the phonograph, see McLuhan, *Understanding Media*, 36–45, 241–8. If Gould disagreed with McLuhan's analysis, it would not have been the only time: he also disagreed with McLuhan's definition of radio as a 'hot' medium.

[135] Both quotations, from 'The Prospects of Recording', are in *GGR* 347.

[136] Gould discussed the 'kit' concept on several occasions: see *GGR* 92–3, 347–8; 'Forgery and Imitation in the Creative Process', 8–9; Burton, ii; McClure; Monsaingeon, *Chemins de la musique*, ii; and Payzant, *GGMM* 26, 29–32.

musicians and writers find such implications of recording disturbing, to say the least. Godlovitch, for example, writes that 'performance integrity requires that a performer be fully in a position to take credit for the performance', and is concerned with the moral implications where technology compromises this integrity.[137] And many writers have wondered about the implications for the concept of the musical work of such hypothetical circumstances as a recorded performance of a work that consists of movements played or conducted by different people. But Gould rejected ethical and philosophical objections to the 'kit' concept, as he did to recording generally, and considered them by-products of a persistent but irrelevant model of concert performance. Precisely because he considered the identity of the artist to be increasingly irrelevant to the art work, especially in the milieu of recording, he did not consider the integrity of the recorded work to be undermined regardless of the number of hands involved in the finished product.

Harbingers of the 'kit' concept could be found in Gould's own day, as he undoubtedly knew. John Cage's and Lejaren Hiller's work *HPSCHD* (1967–9), for harpsichords and computer-generated sound tapes, as released on the Nonesuch label, was, according to Hiller, 'the first instance that I know of where the home listener's hi-fi set is integral to the composition'.[138] The harpsichord soloists are clearly separated within the stereo spectrum in this recording, so that the listener is able 'to alter the composite by increasing, decreasing, or eliminating some parts of the whole'—that is, changing the relative density of the parts by manipulating the balance between the left and right channels. A computer print-out sheet included with the recording allows the listener who follows its instructions and manipulates the stereo's controls 'to become a performer'. Gould's earliest pronouncements on the 'kit' concept pre-date this ground-breaking, eminently Cagean recording, but it offers further evidence of the relevance of his ideas to some of the artistic and intellectual currents of his day. Like Cage's compositions and McLuhan's writings, Gould's 'kit' was yet another example of the 'collage' principle so typical of 1960s aesthetics. It was as much a post-modern creation as those 'open' works of Berio and Stockhausen in which, as Eco notes, 'the author seems to hand them on to the performer more or less like the components of a construction kit'.[139] And it was utterly contemporary in its pluralistic rejection of a controlling mainstream: *chacun son stil.*

Though Gould's hypothetical extensions of the 'kit' concept seemed absurd when he made them in the mid-1960s, they have in fact become viable in the years since his death. Today, it is possible for a selection of takes recorded digitally and distributed on CD or DAT to be edited by a dedicated listener into a finished

---

[137] Godlovitch, 'The Integrity of Musical Performance', 579–80.
[138] This comment, and those that follow, are taken from Peter Yates's liner notes to Nonesuch H-71224.
[139] Eco, *The Open Work*, 4.

recording using a home computer with editing software. Moreover, some recent digital recordings are beginning to demand a degree of listener participation. In one recent recording of Handel's *Messiah*—amusingly, a 'historical' performance— each of the three parts of the work appears on a separate CD in the standard performing version, followed by a selection of alternative versions of selections from that part. The liner-note booklet contains a chart showing how the CDs can be programmed to substitute alternative for standard versions, allowing the listener to use this one recording to recreate any of nine documented variant performances from Handel's day. Another recent recording offers a performance of the Brahms violin concerto along with fifteen alternative cadenzas for the first movement, and allows the listener to programme the desired cadenza into his CD player.[140] Both of these recordings demand that the listener create the final product from a collection of raw material. Nattiez produced a CD of Inuit games and songs that 'appealed directly for the intervention of the listener, who could listen to the pieces according to different principles of comparison: by genre, by village, by performer, and so on'.[141] None of these recordings made any grandiose Gouldian claims as to the implications of its technology, but in such cases we can perhaps see Gouldian prophesies being slowly and naturally insinuated into our listening habits as our comfort with the prevailing technology increases. Moreover, as Tod Machover reported in a 1992 lecture, some of the recording technologies currently in development suggest work precisely along the lines that Gould predicted:

Home systems are currently under development which will make music into a much less passive activity that it is at present. One set of techniques would make the Karaoke-style sing-along ever more adaptable to the imperfections or 'personal style' of the particular singer. Within a few years, we are likely to see a home conducting system, which will use simple hand and finger tracking technology to allow the listener to shape the performance of a particular piece of music. With such a device it would be possible for the music lover to shape his or her own 'virtual orchestra' at home—using conducting gestures—or to combine data from existing performances, to produce, for instance, a hybrid Leonard Bernstein/John Williams performance of Beethoven's Ninth.[142]

Machover notes that some future technologies, including musical games, will 'allow the user to experiment with creating musical structures', and he rightly notes (as did Gould) that the implications of such technologies include a transformation of the very idea of 'a musical piece'.

---

[140] The Handel recording, featuring Nicholas McGegan conducting the Philharmonia Baroque Orchestra, was released in 1991 on Harmonia Mundi HMU 907050.52. The Brahms recording, featuring R. Ricci with the Sinfonia of London, conducted by Norman Del Mar, was released in 1992 on Biddulph LAW002.

[141] Nattiez, 'The Language of Music in the Twenty-First Century', 31. *Jeux vocaux des Inuit*, Ocora-Radio-France C559071 (1989).

[142] Machover, 5. The latter option—combining parts of existing recordings to create a new whole—was specifically predicted by Gould: see *GGR* 348; and Burton, ii.

Gould's arguments on such matters were ultimately moral as well as musical. The technological and other factors that were causing a breakdown in the hierarchy of the roles of composer, performer, and listener were, in his view, morally positive, because they reduced the influence of individuality and ego in the creative process. (He invoked by comparison those anonymous Medieval illuminators who served a purpose higher than themselves.[143]) His critique of the ideas of innovation and originality, as opposed to continuity and imitation, was ultimately ethical: such ideas, he observed, were characteristic of societies in which individuality was most highly prized, and with individuality inevitably came the competitive instincts to which he always strenuously objected. His proposed technological remedies for this situation amounted, in Rivest's words, to a desire 'to democratize the musical experience'.[144] Gould's claims on behalf of the anonymity of the artist were not disingenuous in light of his own record as a creative interpreter; rather, they merely extended his views on creativity, on the openness of interpretation, beyond the realm of his own work. The 'kit' concept is thus the ultimate extension of a creative aesthetic of performance.

The semiological analogy that Nattiez has pursued seems especially relevant here. (Recall Gould's own remarks above, on the 'creative listener' forging 'a new link in the chain of events'.) Gould's attitude towards the roles of composer, performer, and listener, no less than Barthes's position on the reader as writer, acknowledges the continuity of the semiological process at every stage. Every interpreter can become a creator, as can every receiver; the interpreter can mould a new 'composition' from the composer's work, but the interpreter's product can in turn become a 'composition' in relation to which the listener can act as an 'interpreter'. As Barthes wrote in 1970, at the beginning of *S/Z*,

the goal of literary work (of literature as work) is to make the reader no longer a consumer, but a producer of the text. Our literature is characterized by the pitiless divorce which the literary institution maintains between the producer of the text and its user, between its owner and its customer, between its author and its reader. This reader is thereby plunged into a kind of idleness—he is intransitive; he is, in short, *serious*: instead of functioning himself, instead of gaining access to the magic of the signifier, to the pleasure of writing, he is left with no more than the poor freedom either to accept or reject the text: reading is nothing more than a *referendum*. Opposite the writerly text, then, is its countervalue, its negative, reactive value: what can be read, but not written: the *readerly*. We call any readerly text a classic text.[145]

---

[143] See Monsaingeon, *Chemins de la musique*, i. McLuhan observed that recording technology contributed to the breaking down of old class distinctions in music ('classical' versus 'popular', 'high-brow' versus 'low-brow'): see *Understanding Media*, 247.

[144] Rivest, 47 ('démocratiser l'expérience musicale').

[145] Barthes, *S/Z*, 4.

In 'From Work to Text', Barthes draws a parallel between the history of music and the history of 'the Text' (as he conceives of it): like Gould, he notes the separation of the roles of interpreter and listener with the rise of the bourgeois public, and notes the tendency for performers to become, to a degree, composers in the sorts of twentieth-century musical works that Eco defines as 'open'; he uses the latter comparison to explain the post-modern view of 'the Text', which 'solicits from the reader a practical collaboration'.[146]

Gould clearly raised some of the same issues in interpretation as do semiology and post-modernism, and came to some similar conclusions within his own field of endeavour. (Like Barthes, he was a structuralist whose idiosyncratic work as interpreter none the less resonated with post-structuralist poetics.) Goehr describes as 'post-modern' a conception of performance in which a musical work's meaning cannot be fixed, in which performances cannot be considered more or less true to works, in which fidelity to the work and its author is simply not an issue.[147] For Nattiez, as we have seen, Gould's conception of the interpreter's role, along with his atemporal vision and fondness for the mixing of styles, reveal a post-modern aesthetic *avant le mot*. And the list of qualities that Uusitalo considers characteristic of a post-modern view of music reads like a summary of Gould's thought: an ahistorical vision; a belief in the musical work as discovered rather than created; the mixing of styles; self-reflexiveness about work as a musician; an opposition to the idea of musical progress; a Platonist view of the nature of music; and a relative lack of interest of the concept of invention.[148] It does not seem rash or hyperbolic to call Gould the first truly post-modern performer of the Western classical canon. Moreover, there is no contradiction in saying so after having revealed his debts to the aesthetic premises and musical practices of Romanticism, early modernism, and neo-Classicism. Some have recently argued that post-modernism is merely a kind of late-late Romanticism, and indeed Gould's smudging of the boundary between creation and interpretation was at once the most post-modern and most Romantic of values. There was as much that was forward-looking as backward-looking in his thought. But there was, ultimately, a consistency in the Gould aesthetic: his eclecticism converged on his insistence that the performer's role was properly creative.

[146] Barthes, *The Rustle of Language*, 63.
[147] See Goehr, 283 (Goehr does not agree with this post-modern position, by the way).
[148] These qualities are reviewed in Uusitalo, 271–4, but are discussed throughout the article.

3

Performance as Discourse

The Performer in the Work

THERE IS THE QUESTION of *whether* a performer should play a creative role, but there is also the question of *why*. To what end does the creative performer impose himself on the work—or, perhaps more accurately, put himself *in* the work? Is it only for the sake of random play that the performer should demand some of the composer's creative authority? I do not mean to underestimate the importance of sheer play in Gould's work (more on that later), but I believe that for him a performance usually served some higher purpose. In many of his performances, he seems not only to realize or interpret the work, but to discourse about it. Sometimes he would explain the intended discourse in spoken or written comments, but often his performances of themselves had a didactic or polemical quality that amounted to a contribution to the secondary literature on the music at hand. Often, indeed, he seems to have performed a work only when he had some distinctive personal comment to make about it, and this tendency became increasingly marked as his career progressed. Gould, in short, set in high relief the commonplace that all performance is, by definition, a kind of exegesis. He held an unusually liberal view of what it means to 'play a piece', of the proper uses of the performance occasion. In fact, his performances and writings constitute an important body of work addressing performance-related issues like analysis and criticism. (In this sense his work can be considered metacritical.) For example, he clearly sought to blur the distinction that Jerrold Levinson has proposed between 'performative' and 'critical' interpretation. For Levinson, the performer is 'more transmitter than explicator', more like a translator of a foreign language than one 'whose mission is inherently exegetical and amplificatory'; he denies that a performed interpretation can embody or 'unambiguously communicate' a critical interpretation, even where it is demonstrably based on a critical interpretation.[1] (His 'transmitter' recalls Stravinsky's 'executant'.) Levinson suggests that while critical interpretations focus on a work as a whole, performances are necessarily limited to presenting only one side of a work at once. But this point of view does not

---

[1] Levinson, 'Performative vs. Critical Interpretation in Music', 37, 57. On 41 n., he refers to Gould as a 'theory-driven' performer, in that his performances often rested on explicit critical foundations.

acknowledge that prejudices and limitations are necessarily imbedded in analysis and criticism no less than in performance. Göran Hermerén, like Levinson, separates performance ('a series of actions') from criticism ('a text about a text'), yet some of the hypothetical 'purposes of interpretation' that he suggests—to illuminate 'a contemporary moral or political problem'; 'to defend the object of interpretation against criticism'—are of precisely the sort that Gould often tried to make directly through performance.[2]

Gould's view of the performer as a creative force with as much authority as the composer calls to mind a commonplace of much literary criticism since the beginnings of the Romantic era, one greatly exalted by post-modernists: that a reader or critic is not parasitic upon the work, but is in fact involved in 'completing' or even 'creating' the work, carrying on from where the author left off and engaging in his own creative literary activity. This idea has been at the heart of much post-war literary criticism. Northrop Frye, for example, wrote in 1957, in the 'Polemical Introduction' of *Anatomy of Criticism,* that 'criticism is a structure of thought and knowledge existing in its own right, with some measure of independence from the art it deals with'.[3] In the *nouvelle critique* of Roland Barthes, likewise, 'the boundaries between creative writing on the one hand and criticism on the other do not really exist'.[4] The reader or critic, no less than the author, enters the 'play' of language and meaning; he becomes a writer himself (whether or not he literally writes anything down); he produces rather than discovers meanings, creates a new text in the process of reading an existing one. (This is what Barthes meant when he wrote of the movement 'from work to text' in the process of reading: the process of interpretation demands the imposition of the interpreter's personality and ideas.[5]) Stanley Fish, too, advocates a model of criticism that offers 'a greatly enhanced sense of the importance of our activities. . . . No longer is the critic the humble servant of texts whose glories exist independently of anything he might do; it is what he does, within the constraints embedded in the literary institution, that brings texts into being and makes them available for analysis and appreciation.'[6] Gould's sympathy with such views is especially obvious in those extreme interpretations (like K. 331) in which he does most stubborn battle with the composer—in which he puts himself into the music and, in effect, constructs a new piece out of the given score. But the principle is apparent throughout his work: speaking about music in the process of playing it.

---

[2] Hermerén, 17, 13.
[3] Frye, 5.
[4] Barthes, *Criticism and Truth,* 21.
[5] See Barthes, *The Rustle of Language,* 56–64.
[6] Fish, 368.

Analysis and Performance

Gould's idealism led him to believe that a performance should be founded on 'analytical' rather than 'tactile' (that is, instrumental) considerations.[7] Like Hanslick, Schoenberg, Adorno, and others in the same tradition, he favoured a type of listening—and by extension, performance—in which structural properties amenable to analysis were given priority over sensual, dramatic, and emotional properties.[8] Gould believed that performance based on analysis of 'structural relations in the work' was possible and appropriate in all of the music he played, whether by the virginalists or the serialists, and he noted on several occasions that his preparation for recording a work involved less physical practising than musical analysis.[9] He felt, moreover, that the analysis of the music should determine the performance practices however unusual the results. In this respect, he differed from most performers and from most writers on analysis and performance. Wallace Berry, for example, writes that to 'draw conclusions for performance is largely to verify the composer's abundant directions', and like Heinrich Schenker, Edward T. Cone, and most other writers on the subject he takes all of the performance markings in a score as given, to which the analysis (with few, usually minor, exceptions) must conform.[10] But Gould did not, in either analysis or performance, assume and set out to strengthen the composer's authority.

'Analysis' here does not necessarily mean the rigorous academic forms of music analysis, and there is no evidence that Gould had the ability or desire to practise analysis in the manner of a professional music theorist. His musical education included a basic grounding in theory, and his teacher Alberto Guerrero insisted on analysis in preparing for a performance, but he never had advanced training in theory or analysis.[11] Moreover, the materials in the NLC, including annotated scores, do not suggest that he worked out analyses on paper, either in prose or graphs, even with works that he analysed in articles, films, and public lectures. In spite of the detail into which his analyses sometimes delved, he seems to have worked them out in his head. There is somewhat more written evidence of his analyses of twelve-tone music—for example, marked scores in the NLC showing row and cell analyses of works by Schoenberg and Webern—though he did agree with Schoenberg that it was not necessary for the performer or listener to know

---

[7] He makes this distinction in Cott, 40.

[8] Dunsby, 6–7, argues that the modern belief in the importance of analysis, of a conceptual understanding of the work, in preparing a performance owes at least as much to Schoenberg as to Schenker.

[9] *GGSL* 52. See also Cott, 38; Dubal; and Harris, 52.

[10] Berry, 110. As Burkhart, 96, notes, Schenker insisted on using the word *Vortrag*, which 'might be more precisely rendered as "execution" ', for 'performance', a preference which can be interpreted as evidence of his respect for the composer's performance markings.

[11] On Guerrero's analytical bent, see Beckwith, 'Shattering a Few Myths', 69; and Harris, 52.

row structure in order to appreciate a twelve-tone piece.[12] From his teens, he was a keen student and composer of twelve-tone music; his skills in analysing tone rows and assessing their harmonic and formal implications are apparent throughout his published commentaries on Schoenberg and later composers.[13]

Gould's analyses, like his performance practices, were highly selective and eclectic, and adapted to the music at hand. They were consistent with his tendency to consider works individually rather than generically: his analyses were responses to individual structures, not demonstrations of an analytical system. They were, moreover, provisional rather than definitive. As his alternative performances sometimes show, he rejected the implication of much literature on analysis and performance that a work offered one ideal, 'correct' analysis on which the performer should draw.[14] But he never specified his analytical principles, or clarified how much theory and analysis he considered useful as a performer. (This is a controversial subject, and it is often bemoaned that formal analysis does not necessarily yield direct and convincing implications for performance.) He seems not to have shared the Schenkerian bias of most writers on analysis and performance, a bias reinforced by Schenker's own intense interest in performance practice; there is no evidence that he ever studied Schenker, and he certainly did not make the sort of detailed reduction graphs that are the primary basis for performance suggestions by Schenker, Berry, and many others. He did share some priorities with formal analysts: revealing motives and contrapuntal lines; making long-range musical relationships explicit; articulating events of background significance. But one cannot ally him with any specific school of analysis. One is forced, rather, to speak more vaguely in trying to capture his analytical orientation, as indeed some writers on analysis and performance have done. John Rink, for example, speaks of a performer's analysis as the 'consideration of the contextual functions inherent in a given pitch or passage, and how to convey them in one's playing', of analysis 'regarded not as rigorous dissection of the music according to theoretical systems but simply as considered study of the score with particular attention to contextual functions and means of projecting them'.[15] Leonard B. Meyer speaks of an 'intuitive and unsystematic' process in which the performer makes 'the relationships and patterns potential in the composer's score clear to the mind and ear of the experienced listener', and he notes that one 'can perceive and comprehend actions and relationships—musical as well as nonmusical—without the explicit conceptualization necessary for explanation'.[16]

[12] See Burton, iii.

[13] Gould's analyses of twelve-tone works by Jacques Hétu and Ernst Krenek received the sanction of the composers: see Bachmann and Zweifel, 38; Hétu, 24; and Krenek, 'Glenn Gould'.

[14] Rink, 322–3, notes a tendency towards absolutes and imperatives in the writings of Berry, Eugene Narmour, and others. Lester, 210–14, makes the same point.

[15] Rink, 320, 323.

[16] L. B. Meyer, *Explaining Music*, 29, 16.

Only such relatively loose definitions capture Gould's informal though none the less unmistakable analytical mindset, and the ways in which his performances can be considered 'analytical' will emerge more clearly from the accumulation of examples.

Notwithstanding his limited formal training, Gould did have a strong intuitive grasp of musical organization at all structural levels, a grasp he expressed more or less clearly in print, but often, as many critics have observed, with unusual precision in performance. Both his writings and performances reveal some basic priorities in his analytical thinking—above all, harmonic structure, whether in modal, tonal, atonal, or twelve-tone music. He had a good understanding of many different harmonic idioms, and throughout his career his published writings invariably showed harmonic relationships to be primary determinants of structure, even in highly contrapuntal music, and a primary consideration for the performer.[17] When, in the early months of 1964, he was invited to give a pair of lectures on the history of the piano sonata, he chose to survey tonal and formal practices in Baroque, Classical, and Romantic music, his main object being 'to survey the structural forces at work in the piano sonata from the harmonic point of view'.[18] Beyond harmony, Gould was also, of course, especially interested in contrapuntal interaction, but also in thematic and motivic development, in music of all periods. His analysis of Sweelinck's 'Fitzwilliam' Fantasia, for example, finds a kind of 'developing variation' in the composer's permutations of the opening theme,[19] and his analysis of Op. 109 includes some ways in which Beethoven continuously develops motives in the context of Classical tonality and form. (Recall, too, his analysis of the E major fugue from WTC II.) And of course, he was interested in the aspect of perpetual variation and development inherent in twelve-tone music.

Indeed, the high standards of musical unity held by the twelve-tone composers he admired influenced him deeply as an analyst. In a 1963 letter, he defended the application 'of the Schoenbergian type of molecular [i.e. motivic] analysis in which every facet of a work has to prove itself of structural necessity', at least in Renaissance and Baroque music (though not Romantic music, necessarily).[20] This openly anachronistic approach to analysis is further evidence of Gould's 'composerly' mind. As Jean-Jacques Nattiez puts it, it is composers, more than performers or musicologists, who tend deliberately to strike 'a *delinquent* stance' when analysing

[17]   Kazdin, 69, notes that Gould, who had perfect pitch, tended to identify sections of musical works in terms of key area.
[18]   'Piano Sonata—Draft 3', 39. The lectures were delivered on 31 January and 4 March at Hunter College in New York, and repeated on 2 February and 8 March at the Gardner Museum in Boston. They drew extensively on his analyses of Bruckner's Eighth Symphony and Beethoven's Sonata in E major, Op. 109, and especially on the unusual tonal events in the first movement of Op. 109. He also briefly discusses this movement in GGR 56; Burton, ii; Cott, 51–2; and in commentary for a 17 June 1964 recital on CBC television.
[19]   On Sweelinck, see 'Anthology of Variation/Draft 1 - Part 1'.
[20]   GGSL 71.

music; thus 'composers draw past works toward the future in reading them in terms of their present', and so 'their analyses are *testimonies*, bearing upon an engaged hearing of works by contemporary artists'.[21] Gould not only tended to assess all music in terms of a modern aesthetic, even if the results were patently 'wrong', but he also acknowledged and defended this 'delinquency'.

His analytical approach to music manifested itself in his performances in a variety of ways, depending on the piece. His playing in general might be considered analytical in that a central priority was clarity—clarity of musical detail but also of musical relationships on the largest scale. Schoenberg wrote in the early 1920s that the

highest principle for all reproduction of music would have to be that what the composer has written is made to sound in such a way that every note is really heard, and that all the sounds, whether successive or simultaneous, are in such relationship to each other that no part at any moment obscures another, but, on the contrary, makes its contribution towards ensuring that they all stand out clearly from one another.[22]

For Gould, too, the clear and precise rendering of notes, phrases, and relationships was a given, and he could be finicky, even obsessive, on this point. A common denominator of many of his performance practices was a desire make musical processes explicit, whether contrapuntal relationships, the component cells of a melodic line, even the relationship of rubato to prevailing tempo. He sometimes spoke of seeking an 'X-ray' view of music in performance, of revealing the 'skeleton' of a piece, of co-ordinating the musical 'flow of information'—remarks that reveal a basic desire to focus on the details of the music's construction rather than its broader rhetorical effects.[23] (In this sense, his playing was more in accord with modern than Romantic aesthetics.) In his copy of Adorno's *Prisms*, he flagged a passage that reflected his own priorities as a performer: 'True interpretation is an x-ray of the work; its task is to illuminate in the sensuous phenomenon the totality of all the characteristics and inter-relations which have been recognized through intensive study of the score.'[24] To illuminate the 'totality' of the work is chimerical, of course, and we have already seen that Gould tended to interpret a piece from a very particular and often highly prejudiced perspective. But within the criteria set by an interpretation, that desire to reveal the work with maximum clarity in all aspects of performance is always palpable. Even exaggerated clarity: the extreme nature of many of Gould's performance practices originated, at least in part, in the desire to make analytical points clear *as* analytical points. In other words, his performances often extend beyond the truism that all performance embodies

21   Nattiez, *Music and Discourse*, 185.
22   Schoenberg, 319.
23   'X-ray': *GGF;* Harris, 52; and Page. 'Skeleton': McClure. 'Flow of information': *GGR* 36.
24   Adorno, *Prisms*, 144; cf. NLC B1, 144.

analysis, by bringing to the fore the analytical process. In this respect, as in so many, Bach was a model. Gould's particular concern for pointing up harmonic, contrapuntal, and motivic events seems to have been tailored most closely to Bach's music, though it was no less a part of his style in Byrd and Gibbons, Mozart and Beethoven, Wagner and Brahms, Scriabin and Schoenberg. It was this special clarity and coherence in his playing that made him such a powerful musical communicator. Like Furtwängler, he was a master at clarifying both the whole and the parts of a musical structure, the large-scale musical argument as well as the fore-ground and middleground connections, with an almost self-conscious explicitness. He could make difficult works of twentieth-century music no less sensible than Bach, even for listeners with no musical training. Listen, for example, to his 1964 recording of Schoenberg's twelve-tone Suite, Op. 25, in which his rendering of themes and motives, contrapuntal lines, relationships between units of phrase, nuances of rhythm, and so on makes the work as clear, accessible, and dramatically coherent to the listener as if it had been a suite of Bach's.

Brahms's Intermezzo in C sharp minor, Op. 117 No. 3, offers a striking example of Gould's fondness for motivic clarity. He stresses dynamically the four-note motives circled in Ex. 3.1 (bars 86–9), bringing them clearly to the listener's attention. His reasoning becomes apparent a few bars later: those left-hand motives anticipate the important four-note motives bracketed in bars 92–4, and first heard in bars 10–12. Gould's reading significantly influences the dramatic structure of the piece: the build-up of dynamic, rhythmic, and textural intensity towards the return of the motive in bar 92 is now enhanced by the incorporation of anticipations that seem to call for that return. Here he uses performance alone to make the sort of observation that an analyst might make on paper, and he clearly sides with those analysts who have recommended articulating hidden motives in performance. The score does not suggest that his interpretation would have met with Brahms's approval, but it offers a good example of a pos-sibility he proposed to Humphrey Burton in 1966, in a discussion of his analysis of Beethoven's Op. 109: that the performer may know more about the work than the composer, in the sense of seeing what is latent within it.[25] With this self-confident (or, less charitably, arrogant) point of view, Gould did not hesitate to amend scores by analytical criteria, where it helped to make an analytical point explicit, a structural relationship more clear. No detail, apparently, was too small to receive attention of this kind: in Ex. 3.2, he makes a small revision to bar 118 of Mozart's score, to make the parallelism with bar 37 more literal, and there are countless such revisions among his recordings.

[25] See Burton, ii.

Ex. 3.1. Brahms, Intermezzo in C sharp minor, Op. 117 No. 3

Gould's ability to convey structural coherence on the largest scale has been noted (though rarely explored in detail) in the critical literature, and many of his readings do create gestures that have analytical significance beyond the foreground level. In the first movement of Beethoven's Sonata in C major, Op. 2 No. 3, he interpreted the passage beginning with the false resolution to A flat major at bar 218, with its tonal digressions and improvisatory texture, as a kind of cadenza; for him the cadenza-like passage that, according to Beethoven's markings, begins with the C major six-four chord at bar 232 really begins fifteen bars earlier. By treating the whole section from bars 218–32 as a cadenza, he made an important analytical point about the movement's harmonic structure. This whole section can be interpreted as a projection of the ornamental progression G–A♭–G, as a decoration of the dominant with the flat-sixth degree to create a kind of parenthesis within the tonal context of C major, one that prolongs the dominant preparation for the final return of the tonic in bar 233. Gould's rhythmic interpretation of this passage makes the analytical observation palpable. By treating bars 218–32 as a cadenza, he separated the whole G–A♭–G progression from the tempo and texture of the surrounding music; as a consequence, it is now clearer to the listener that the tonic cadence at bar 233 takes up where the aborted cadence at bar 217 left off. Gould thus created a rhythmic analogy for a tonal event: he played a tonal parenthesis as a rhythmic parenthesis.[26] It is a characteristic example that recalls Schenker's

---

[26] For a similar example, cf. his treatment of dynamics in the development section of Beethoven's Sonata in D major, Op. 10 No. 3/I.

Ex. 3.2. Mozart, Sonata in A minor, K. 310/I (1969 recording)

concern for the projection of musical levels, including musical parentheses. Gould's reading may not have rested on a formal Schenkerian foundation, but it still suggests an intuitive grasp of structural levels and a willingness to seek means to project them in performance.

His choices of tempo were sometimes determined by the goal of 'architectural clarity'.[27] He claimed that the relative continuity of tempo that he maintained in the first movements of Beethoven's 'Appassionata' Sonata and Brahms's D minor concerto was intended to underscore motivic relationships between theme groups. Speaking of the 'Appassionata' movement, in which he saw a relationship by inversion between the opening theme and the secondary theme (beginning bar 35),

[27] Asbell, 91.

both of which are triadic, he told an interviewer in 1981 that one notices 'in many performances that the beginning is played relatively quickly, but the secondary theme is very drawn-out. My thought, then, was to choose a firmly controlled tempo that would make obvious how the [first] theme and secondary theme take up a single idea.' In the Brahms movement, he again sought a 'tempo structure' that would underscore the 'thematic consistency' of the opening theme and the secondary theme (beginning bar 156), both of which are again triadic and related by inversion.[28] His desire to project these motivic relationships led him in both pieces to reject a tradition in which the broad opening theme is played faster, the lyrical secondary theme growing out of it with what he called 'an artistic ritardando'.[29] In both cases, he took a conventional tempo for the secondary theme, but projected it back onto the principal theme, leading to a notoriously slow opening. Yet he insisted that tempo *per se* was less important than the tempo relationship between the parts.

Many of Gould's rhythmic gestures served the quite commonplace function of commenting on harmonic activity. The first movement of Beethoven's Sonata in F major, Op. 10 No. 2, offers a particularly didactic example of the basic principle, an example Gould himself discussed in print. In performance, he draws attention to the extremely unusual recapitulation in D major (bar 118), articulating this departure from sonata-form convention with a significant shift in tempo not indicated by the composer, and in contrast to the relative continuity of tempo he maintains earlier in the movement. (He plays the opening of the movement at $\downarrow$ = 97, the recapitulation at 76, slowing to 64 before gradually returning to the opening tempo.) In this way, even the listener without perfect pitch is made to feel that the recapitulation is special, a departure from the norm. Gould explained, in an interview with Bruno Monsaingeon:

That *is* a magical moment, and it deserves, in my view, a very special kind of tempo adjustment—something that will allow the main theme to regroup, during the D-major-D-minor sequence, and then gradually come back to life as the F-major tonic returns. Now, nothing of that sort is indicated in the score, but that kind of harmonic drama is something that no one can ignore, surely.[30]

In the first movement of Beethoven's Sonata in A major, Op. 2 No. 2, Gould went even more blatantly against the wishes of the composer to make a rhythmic decision that implied harmonic analysis. In this case, he departed from the score in the matter of placement of emphasis. He ignored Beethoven's rallentando marking at bars 48–53, but inserted his own rallentando in the unmarked passage at bars

---

[28] M. Meyer, 'Interview', 18. See also Page on tempo in the Brahms concerto.

[29] In the case of the 'Appassionata' movement, Philip, 15, offers some quantitative evidence of this tradition, showing examples of the tempo shifts more characteristic of early 20th-cent. performances. Gould's unusual tempo structure in the scherzo-and-trio movement of the Beethoven-Liszt Fifth Symphony offers another similar example; see Kazdin, 17–18, on this performance.

[30] *GGR* 38.

79–83. Both passages are similar harmonically: both imply dominant minor ninth chords heralding a modulation to the dominant key of E. In the first case, the modulation is to E minor, in the second to the more conventional dominant, E major, in which key and mode the exposition closes. (Gould makes comparable rhythmic adjustments at the parallel spots in the recapitulation, bars 267–72 and 298–302.) The second-subject area of this movement, as Carl Dahlhaus points out, is ambiguous, playing on the listener's expectations about 'correct' tonal and thematic behaviour in a sonata-form movement: 'The first melodic idea (bar 59) provides a lyrical contrast to the first subject, begins in the dominant minor (E minor), and returns to it at the end, but is characterized by continuous modulation and sequential process in between. The second idea (bar 84) is tonally closed, and employs the orthodox dominant key, but its motivic material is that of a "display episode".[31] Expected tonal and thematic behaviour is, in short, out of alignment. Beethoven's rallentando marking draws attention to the arrival of E minor, the point at which the misalignment of theme and mode is manifest; Gould, however, preferred to draw attention to the arrival of E major, the point at which the exposition is set on its expected tonal course. His decision shows a characteristic interest in tonal structure at a background level, emphasizing as it does the 'true' dominant modulation rather than the minor-mode diversion.

In his 1981 recording of Bach's Goldberg Variations, Gould's unusual treatment of repeats seems to make class connections between variations, and even to comment upon structure within variations. The treatment of repeats is, of course, crucial in determining the proportions of a work that consists of thirty-two short movements in binary form, and there exists a large body of written and recorded opinion on the subject of repeats in the Goldberg Variations, dating back at least to 1900 and Donald Francis Tovey's ground-breaking analysis. From different performers and writers have come different criteria for deciding which repeats to observe or suppress: position of variation, length of variation, length of bars, clarity, spaciousness, beauty, symmetry, balance, climax, even scholarly obligation and audience attentiveness. In practice, the options range from playing all of the repeats to playing only some to playing none. (The last is Gould's choice in his 1955 recording.) In the 1981 recording, Gould observed a repeat in thirteen variations, the nine canons plus the four variations in strict four-part counterpoint: 4 (a series of stretti), 10 (a fughetta), 22 (a ricercare), and 30 (a quodlibet, with two canons over the ground bass). In this way, he set apart consistently and audibly those variations in which formal counterpoint is of primary importance.[32] Moreover, he

---

[31] Dahlhaus, *Ludwig van Beethoven*, 103–4.

[32] Kirkpatrick, xxvi–xxvii, suggests that the harpsichordist make similar distinctions between classes of variations, through the use of registration. In his table of registrations for the work, 'the same 8' register is employed for all the canons and the same combination for all the two-manual arabesques'. Gould studied Kirkpatrick's edition of the Goldberg Variations in his youth, and may have been influenced by the principle here.

repeated only the first strain—that is, up to the double bar—in the contrapuntal variations, never the second section. (This explains why he did not repeat the fughetta in the second half of Variation 16, even though it features formal counterpoint.) This AAB repeat scheme was once commonplace in performances of Baroque binary-form movements (less so today), and Gould did generally apply it to such pieces, with a few exceptions like Bach's very short Little Preludes. His rationale was primarily harmonic. He treated binary-form movements much like fugues or sonata forms: expandable in the middle, in terms of modulation, but irrevocable at the end, once the tonic key is restored. Indeed, in the Goldberg Variations, he often specially emphasizes the final restoration of the tonic, so that a repeat of the second strain would be anticlimactic. (Note, for example, his tendency to render the bass line with urgency in the drive to the final cadence, in the Aria and Var. 9, among other examples.) He was undoubtedly speaking primarily of harmony when, in a 1963 interview, he likened his tendency to suppress the second repeat to what 'has been said of Bach's cantata about St. Michael': that 'you can't possibly fight the battle twice'.[33] Gould's was generally a 'dynamic' or 'organic' or 'discursive' view of musical form, rather than a 'mechanic' one,[34] and so he was naturally more interested in the goal-oriented nature of Bach's forms than their outward adherence to formal models. For him, the suppression of the repeat in the second strain was necessary to underscoring the music's tonal drama.

But in the 1981 Goldberg Variations, his rationale for repeating seems to have been more specifically dialectical. In the canonic variations, especially, he implies a kind of three-part argument, with the repeat of the first strain serving to set up a thesis-antithesis relationship. In the first strain, he maintains a relatively equable balance of contrapuntal voices, though with some emphasis on the bass line (a tendency throughout this performance). In some cases—for example, Vars. 12 and 18—the emphasis on the bass in the first strain is clearly at the expense of the canon in the upper two voices. But in the repeat of the first strain the priorities are reversed: Gould places less emphasis on the bass, and more on the canon itself. (He makes changes in dynamics and articulation, too.) He generally begins the repeat with an especially strong accentuation of the leading voice of the canon, to draw the listener's attention away from the bass and onto the upper voices. In bars 1r–2r of Var. 3, he adds appoggiaturas that draw even more attention to the canon. Even in the two-voice Var. 27, the canon at the ninth, he lowers the dynamic level and accentuates the downbeats less strongly in the repeat, so that we might say that even here he stresses the canon more and the ground bass less. The second strain, played only once, 'resolves' the contrapuntal disparity between the two readings of the first strain: by the end of the canonic variations, with the return of the tonic

33   Johnson, 2.
34   See the discussion of this distinction in Broyles.

key, Gould restores the relatively equable balance of voices, completing a little dialectical drama that would be upset by a repeat of the second strain.[35] In the four-voice contrapuntal variations, Gould creates similar dramas. In Vars. 4 and 22, he places greater emphasis on the bass in the first strain, on the upper imitative voices in the repeat; again, he 'resolves' the disparity in the closing strain. In Var. 10, in which all four voices participate equally in a fughetta, he still gives special promi-nence to the bass in the first strain; only in the repeat does he highlight each entry of the subject. The quodlibet in Var. 30 is too complicated to conform to the same scheme, though Gould still uses the repeat to readjust his focus—he places more emphasis on the first canon in the first strain (bars 1–2), on the second canon in the repeat (bars 2r–3r)—and he still 'resolves' the disparity in the second strain.

The analytical foundations of a Gould performance could be highly idiosyn-cratic, as his recording of Jacques Hétu's *Variations pour piano* shows. In his liner-notes on the piece, Gould observes—correctly, according to Hétu—that, after an introduction that sets out the tone row, 'each of the four variations becomes occupied with an increasingly dense and/or decreasingly literal utilization of the row'.[36] As Hétu says in his article about this recording, Gould adopts towards the score the same attitude that the composer adopted towards his row. He 'notices that the initial material is treated more and more freely by the composer . . . and this is precisely what he does as performer: he takes more and more liberty, moves farther and farther away from the score, as the work unfolds'.[37] Hétu goes on to record the departures from the score that Gould makes in the variations, partic-ularly in the centre of the work, in Vars. 2 and 3. He notes that 'the *Variations* have an average duration of 8 minutes 45 seconds; Gould's version lasts 11 minutes 19 seconds. Overall, he modifies some tempos considerably, changes legatos to staccato, *pianos* to *forte* and vice versa, he clarifies certain foggy passages, muddies certain others that are normally clear, and so on, a little like the negative of a photo compared with the true image.' In the closing pages of the *Variations*, as in the opening pages, Gould observes the composer's performance directions accurately. As Hétu dryly concludes of the whole performance, 'After having visited the composer's house and moved some of the furniture around, the performer now exits across the threshold as politely and correctly as when he arrived!' In other words, Gould's changing attitude towards the score comments on the composer's approach to his material and the organization of the music. It is a strange premiss for an interpretation, to be sure, yet one that, in its own way, can certainly be called analytical.

---

[35] In Bruno Monsaingeon's 1981 film of this interpretation of the Goldberg Variations, camera angles and splice points often reinforce the dialectical structure of the canonic variations.

[36] *GGR* 207.

[37] This and the following quotations are in Hétu, 24–5.

Performing the Work as *Gestalt*

As the Hétu example suggests, Gould's analytical thinking extended beyond the structural significance of individual musical events to the work as a whole. Like musical modernists and idealists of many stripes, he seems to have viewed musical works as completed objects as much as temporal processes—in Jean-Paul Sartre's words, as 'successive in perception' but 'simultaneous in image'.[38] As Patricia Carpenter puts it, 'Like discourse, a piece of music takes time to disclose its meaning; yet it can be comprehended in a single act of the imagination. Like a melody, a piece can be made to be a single image, which I grasp not only as a successive, but also as a simultaneous, whole.' To objectify a work in this way requires a certain distance from the temporal process of the sound event, which must be rationalized, perceived as a finished product, as an almost spatial entity formed in the imagination after the sound event is complete. Carpenter notes that the distinction between music in time and music as object is an ancient one, and the tendency to 'hear music simultaneously both as it is occurring and as it has occurred' has grown steadily throughout the history of Western music.[39] Schoenberg and his disciples took up the subject with renewed vigour. For Schoenberg a musical 'idea' was not, as most define it, simply a musical motive, theme, melody, or phrase; the real 'idea' of a piece was in fact 'the unified totality of a composition'.[40] Nicholas Cook writes, 'The implication of this highly influential idea is that at the highest formal level an entire composition should be considered to be a single *Gestalt*: that is to say, an integrated structure in which the perception of individual parts is determined by their relationship to the whole.'[41] This was Gould's view of music, too, and it had many practical consequences, first of all in his choices of repertoire. (A tendency to objectify music goes hand in hand with a preference for Baroque fugues and Classical sonatas over Romantic mood pieces.) Even his special comfort with recording technology can be understood in this context. He often spoke in praise of the recording artist's ability to put together an interpretation without being bound by the constraints of real time, but he also noted that for a recording artist to make many takes, retakes, and splices without upsetting the coherence of the performance, he must have a clear and comprehensive image of the work as a whole before he begins to play.[42] An objectified view of music obviously correlates with an analytical mindset, not least because it demands that one know how the parts function within the whole. Arnold Berleant has divided the categories with which we analyse music into the perceptual (pitch,

---

[38] Quoted in Cook, 226 (from Sartre's *The Psychology of the Imagination*).

[39] Carpenter, 63, 59.

[40] Cross, 27. For his own words on this subject, see Schoenberg, 107, 121–3, 220, 269.

[41] Cook, 40.

[42] See Colgrass, 8; McClure; M. Meyer, 'Interview', 19; and Monsaingeon, *Chemins de la musique*, i.

timbre, dynamics) and the conceptual (form, harmonic rhythm, thematic relation-ships).[43] Gould's focus, as both analyst and performer, was always primarily on conceptual categories—those most 'objective' and least dependent on performance. His was goal-oriented playing, in which the details of the work did not merely accumulate but took their places within a precise, preconceived conception of the whole.

One consequence was his fondness for projecting structural events that are significant at a background level. As Rink notes, '[i]mplicit references to "shape" and its importance as a "background" for performance abound' in the literature on analysis and performance, as does the issue of hierarchy, of what events on what structural levels the performer should 'bring out', but precise recommendations to the performer are more rare.[44] Gould offers an unusual example of a performer who attempted to find direct analogies in performance to the kinds of background events to which analysts draw attention. This he accomplished not by literally projecting some kind of abstract *Urlinie*—even Schenker rejected that approach—but by accentuating foreground events (modulations, thematic recapitulations, etc.) that have significance on a background level, often setting in maximum relief what was structurally most important, even if at the expense of some of the musical drama implied by the composer's performance markings. In some of his perfor-mances, the relative structural significance of events is made immediately palpable, and the music acquires a clear overall shape.

The slow movement of Mozart's Sonata in C major, K. 279, offers one such performance (see CD [4]).[45] Here Gould ignores more than a dozen markings in the score calling for contrasts of forte and piano, as he often does in Mozart's sonatas. He plays the exposition and recapitulation at basically a discreet piano dynamic throughout, making some of the expressive inflections suggested by the dynamic markings but within a much narrower spectrum that does not upset the prevailing dynamic terrace. He saves significant changes in volume for certain important structural events. In the exposition, he increases the dynamic level to mezzo-forte only in bars 17–21, where chromatic sequences and a hemiola create a high-point of harmonic and rhythmic tension within the section. In the retransition after the double bar (bars 29–42), he again raises the dynamic level to emphasize the recovery of the tonic, attaining a true forte in bars 33 and 35, tonally the points of furthest remove within the movement (D minor, the relative minor). In the recapitulation, he repeats the basic dynamic plan of the exposition, with two significant exceptions: he raises the dynamic level at the two points at

---

[43] See Berleant, 96–8.
[44] Rink, 324.
[45] For similar examples from Gould's recordings of slow movements by Mozart, see the Sonata in F major, K. 280/II; and the Sonata in C major, K. 309/II.

which a passage from the exposition is extended in the recapitulation, with a resulting increase in harmonic tension. (Compare bars 46–7 with bar 4, and bars 57–63 with bars 17–21.) The extension in bars 62–3, where Gould again permits a forte dynamic, repeats a sequence, and so prolongs its harmonic tension, at just the point at which the final confirmation of the tonic F major is imminent. The two instances of a true forte therefore correspond to important points of tonal departure and return in the centre and near the end of the movement, and the dynamic choices generally seem throughout to manifest Gould's analysis of the play of tonal forces.

Moreover, his suppressing of both repeats in this movement makes his view of its shape—so different from that implied by Mozart's score—all the more direct. His general tendency to suppress repeats in Classical sonata-form works was no less a function of an organic, dynamic view of musical form than his treatment of Baroque binary forms. By suppressing repeats, he was better able to impress a musical structure onto the listener as a single encompassing image, the same reason that analysts do not include repeats in linear reductions, even where they assume the importance of the repeats to the structure of the piece in performance. His 1960 recording of Brahms's Intermezzo in A minor, Op. 118 No. 1, offers a striking example of this principle in just 41 bars (see CD ⑤). Eugene Narmour draws on just this Intermezzo in a study of the relationship between analysis and performance. He demonstrates the importance of the motive C–B♭–A–E, presented in the first two bars, showing how it is intensively developed throughout the piece and is the most important single factor in terms of overall form. But he also points out that because the four-note motive is divided between the hands in bars 1–2, and so somewhat obscured, pianists frequently fail to render it as an integral motive. He makes a point of noting that a 'correct interpretation' of this crucial motive 'is found in Glenn Gould's performance', but adds that Gould then 'ruins the form in other ways', notably by suppressing the repeats, which 'throws the form all out of proportion'.[46] (The timing of the piece in Gould's recording is just 1:03.) In fact, Gould's suppression of the repeats is consistent with his emphasis on the opening motive and its subsequent developments, which he is careful to delineate throughout: hearing the Intermezzo as a continuous 'developing variation' of the opening motive, he plays it, so to speak, in a single gulp. Moreover, the way he conveys the forces of tonal tension and relaxation in the Intermezzo suggests an interpretation as a kind of sonata form in miniature—an interpretation that can certainly be defended. (Exposition: bars 1–10; development: bars 11–20; recapitulation: bars 21–9; coda: bars 30–41.) Gould's decisions about rubato, dynamic levels, dynamic and agogic accents, breaking of vertical textures, and even his

---

[46] See Narmour, 319–21, on this Intermezzo; the quotations are from 321 n.

departures from Brahms's dynamic markings in bars 28–31 all help underscore a sonata-like formal and tonal scheme. And his suppressing of the repeats actually helps him to impress that overall scheme onto the listener as a single controlling image, almost like an analytical graph. Berry writes, 'The details of an interpretation are conditioned by a grasp of broad lines and of whole. This is a most critical point of relation between analysis and performance, between the cognizance of large-scale structural functions and continuities . . . and reasoned decisions of interpretation.'[47] Gould's performance of the Intermezzo might be taken as a demonstration of this principle, with the important exception that for him (unlike Berry) 'reasoned decisions of interpretation' could include the suppression of the composer's instructions.

In many Gould performances, the work appears to the listener as an immediately palpable shape—as a linear progression, arch, double arch, circle. In a number of contrapuntal works by Bach, his conception of overall shape was influenced by his interpretation of a single tonal or contrapuntal event as the dramatic climax. As he noted in a 1964 essay on fugue, 'In Bach's *Well-Tempered Clavier*, a great many of the fugues choose as their moment of highest tension that occasion when, for the first time, the primary subject is heard, or seen, in one of the contrapuntal strands turned upside down.'[48] This climax, usually positioned between halfway and three quarters of the way into the piece, was one that Gould would lead the listener by degrees up to and away from, primarily through dynamics, to create a large-scale arching structure. He seems to have touched on the notion of 'background' crucial to Berry's thesis on music and performance:

it is fundamental to my sense of structure that there is often manifest in the musical structure an underlying dynamic course of events, to and from points—even at times one central, focal point—of primary expressive orientation. Such a 'background,' the content and course of which may constitute a kinetic, all-embracing gesture, is decidedly amenable to explicit awareness and projection in performance. . . . The concept of a dynamic, expressive, gestural whole [is] applicable to many compositions.[49]

Rachmaninov, it is true, always claimed that in his performances he aimed at a single 'culminating point' to which everything else related, but this is still a position with special significance for modernist musicians. Adorno wrote that the Fugue in C sharp minor from *WTC* I,

which begins as though it were a dense network of equally relevant lines, the theme of which seems at first to be nothing more than the unobtrusive glue that holds the voices together, progressively reveals itself, starting with the entrance of the figured second theme

[47] Berry, 65. See also his graphic reduction of the Intermezzo on 40.
[48] *GGR* 240.
[49] Berry, 5.

[bar 35], to be an irresistible crescendo, composed from beginning to end and climaxing with the mighty explosion of the main theme entering in the bass [bar 73], the most extreme concentration of a pseudo-ten-voice *stretto* and the turning point of a heavily accented dissonance, in order then to vanish as though through a dark portal. No appeal to the acoustically static character of harpsichord and organ can cover over the basic dynamism of the compositional structure itself, regardless of whether or not it could be realized as a crescendo on the instruments of the time, or even, as some idly question, whether Bach could have 'thought' of such a crescendo.[50]

Gould's unapologetically anachronistic premisses in terms of analysis and performance are remarkably similar, and indeed his 1962 recording of this fugue realizes just the 'irresistible crescendo' of which Adorno speaks.

Bach's Invention No. 5 in E flat major offers a small-scale but typical example in which Gould took a single climax as the rationale for an overall arch structure; in this case, the climax was the passage in the dominant minor beginning at bar 20. His performance of bars 1–20 features a gradual crescendo that builds tension towards this central point. The forte dynamic then continues through other flat keys in bars 20–5, until the return to the tonic at bar 25, at which point the dynamic level diminishes, especially after the final confirmation of the tonic (coloured by the subdominant) in bars 29–32. The slightly asymmetrical dynamic arch thus creates an audible analogy to the progression into and away from the tonal climax.[51]

Gould did not apply such principles only in early music that includes relatively few performance markings, as his later performances of Berg's Sonata, Op. 1, demonstrate. (There are at least eight preserved Gould performances of this piece, in various media, dating from 1951 to 1974.) The sonata was one of his signature pieces in his concert days, and his preserved concert performances and recordings from the 1950s are relatively true to the performance markings in Berg's score, including the indicated repeat of the exposition, which he observes in his 1951 and 1958 studio recordings. After a long absence from it, Gould took up the sonata again in 1969, for a CBC radio recital; in 1974, for a CBC television programme; and that same year for Monsaingeon's film series *Chemins de la musique*. In these later performances, one observes much slower tempos, a growing tendency to linger over the intense chromatic harmony, an increasing number of liberties with the score, a greater feeling of improvisation, and a tempering of the nervous energy that characterized the earlier performances. Gould conceives of the work more broadly (he staggers many vertical sonorities, for example), undoubtedly because of an increased emphasis on revealing the contrapuntal components of the harmony.

---

[50] Adorno, *Prisms*, 140–1. (*Prisms* appeared in English only in 1967, five years after Gould recorded this fugue.)

[51] For roughly similar examples, see his studio recordings of Bach's Sinfonias No. 2 in C minor and No. 9 in F minor, in both of which the climax is again the modulation to the dominant minor.

(He often used slow tempos to help expose counterpoint.) In the 1969 broadcast, he still observes the repeat (the total timing is 13:33), and observes, for the most part, Berg's dynamic markings. The later television performance is broader still, but now the repeat is suppressed (the total timing is 10:32), and the counterpoint is more obvious.

The 1974 film performance seems the culmination of a process in which the 'Wagnerian' element that Gould observed in the music—the 'molten flow' of melody—moves into the foreground: this is the most extreme expressive statement to be found among the three later performances.[52] He again suppresses the repeat, and again staggers many chords and intervals to clarify counterpoint. The opening tempo is extremely slow ($\quad$ = c.20); the total timing is 12:20, almost as long as the 1958 recording with the repeat (13:07), and certainly far slower than Berg's marking 'Mässig bewegt' suggests. To a greater extent than before, Gould stresses the continuous, gradual unfolding and transformation of the three motivic ideas that form the melody of bars 1–2, and which are the cells that unite the whole sonata, in so doing offering an interpretation of the work as a single arching structure with a single central climax. It is a seamless reading that evokes Schoenbergian 'developing variation', rather than a more articulated reading that reveals the work's roots in Classical sonata form. Gould departs significantly from the score in making this arching structure palpable to the listener. He adjusts dynamics to reduce local-level contrasts somewhat, in order to set the central *ffff* climax in greater relief: for example, he underplays fortissimo interruptions before the climax (bars 8, 23, 44, 67) and after it (bars 154, 157). And he does so not only dynamically: in bars 23–6, for example, he staggers vertical sonorities to undercut the intensity and percussive effect of the fortissimo marking; in bars 41–4, he rolls chords to dilute rhythmic energy, again undercutting the fortissimo marking. (He approaches and renders the central climax as written, however.) The difference in practice between fortissimo and *ffff* on a piano is difficult, if not impossible, to express unequivocally, and this undercutting of some of the indicated fortissimo peaks in the outer sections of the movement is crucial to Gould's emphasizing of the central climax. Moreover, by suppressing the repeat he further emphasizes the arching structure: in Berg's score the *ffff* climax is almost literally in the centre of the work (bar 91, of a total of 179 bars), and without the repeat Gould reaches the climax at 5:46, almost literally in the centre of the performance.

His 1979 film performance of Contrapunctus 1 from *The Art of Fugue* has a dynamic plan that clearly suggests an analysis of the tonal trajectory of the piece. It offers a variation on the arch structure, a double arch that underscores the fugue's twofold movement from the tonic to a half cadence on the dominant and back

52 *GGR* 195.

(see Fig. 3.1). In Gould's performance, the fugue consists largely of two crescendos towards half cadences, the first taking in the whole opening section (bars 1–42), the second leading from bar 48 to the more structurally important dominant pedal beginning at bar 63. One interesting effect of this interpretation is a conspicuous underplaying of the bass entry of the subject at bar 56, which marks a tonal and thematic recapitulation. (Gould had brought it out emphatically in earlier performances of the fugue.) By placing less emphasis on this interim return of the tonic minor, he suggests a return in bar 56 to the subdued character of the opening, making more clear the twofold trajectory of the fugue. He places greatest emphasis on the final achievement of the tonic (now in the major mode) at bar 74 by exceeding the dynamic intensity of the first crescendo in the second: the dominant pedal beginning at bar 63 leads to a fortissimo climax on the diminished seventh chord at bar 70, a high-point of harmonic tension that leads to final tonic resolution. Gould also uses articulation as an analytical tool in this performance. He preserves basically smooth articulation throughout the two arches of the fugue, but prominently introduces staccato articulation just once, in bars 47–52, in the joint between the two dynamic arches; the staccato introduces a 'gap' into the prevailing articulation that makes all the more audible the separation of the first dynamic arch from the second.

The continuous linear progression is another basic *Gestalt* emphasized in some Gould performances; the first movement of Mozart's K. 331 (see CD ③ again) offers perhaps the purest example. In his 1967 recording of Beethoven's 'Moonlight' Sonata, he sought to underscore the accumulation of intensity that he perceived in the sonata as a whole, but in an idiosyncratic way that resulted in one of his most interesting experiments in musical expression. For him, the 'Moonlight' Sonata— by contrast with the *Pathétique*, which 'recedes emotionally' from movement to movement—'escalates from first note to last', from the 'diffident' first movement, through the 'fragile' second to the 'flash flood' of the finale.[53] Thus he considered emotional trajectory to be a primary factor in the organization of the work, and a primary consideration for the performer. This is hardly an unconventional interpretation, of course. The 'Moonlight' Sonata is typically played so as to maximize the contrast between the first and last movements; the performer generally approaches both ends of the expressive spectrum, maximizing the brooding quality of the first movement and the turbulence of the third. (Liszt famously referred to the second movement as a 'flower between two abysses'.) The contrast is conventionally, then, one of kind rather than degree: different expressive qualities, but both as deeply expressed as possible. Gould, however, represents the emotional trajectory of the sonata more in terms of *degree* of expression. In the first movement,

[53]   *GGR* 52.

FIG. 3.1. Gould's dynamics in Bach, *The Art of Fugue*, Contrapunctus 1 (1979 film)

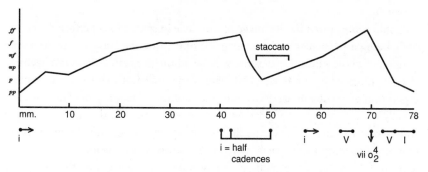

he actually undercuts the brooding quality—an unusual choice for him in an adagio movement. He takes a relatively fast tempo ($\downarrow$ = 72),[54] and maintains it steadily, allowing little rhythmic flexibility even at the end or at the joints between structural units; his tone is dry; he makes the accompanying triplets unusually prominent; and he is sparing with expressive nuances. The effect of the performance is a strange neutrality in terms of expression, precisely the 'diffidence' of which he wrote. He allows considerably more expressive nuance in the second movement: agogic accents articulate an important half cadence at bars 20–4; the movement reaches a definite climax in bars 24–34; and coy use of rubato gives lilt to the syncopations in the Trio. The finale contrasts strongly with the opening movement, not only in character but also in degree of intensity. Gould plays it at an extremely fast tempo ($\downarrow$ = 204), but more important, he gives the impression of veering close to being out of control. The articulation of phrases and larger structural units is rougher than usual for Gould (one phrase seems to spill into the next); note especially his blurred rendering of the quaver chords, marked with staccato wedges, in the opening theme. He ignores important fermatas in bars 14 and 115, maintaining forward momentum with little relief, and his suppression of the exposition repeat seems a by-product of the extreme propulsiveness. He overplays many piano markings, and there is unusual (for him) use of the sustaining pedal to create washes of sound, even during running figuration. The appearance of turbulence threatening control in this movement is uncharacteristic for Gould, and is clearly an exaggeration intended to make his point about the organization—the emotional trajectory—of the sonata: the finale is as unbridled as the first movement is aloof. As in the Hétu *Variations*, the premiss is, in a strange way, analytical: the performer's

---

[54]   In Dubal, 64, David Bar-Ilan, a pianist and friend of Gould's, relates an interesting anecdote about Gould's recording of this movement: 'He once called me when he was in New York and said, "David, I'm recording the *Moonlight Sonata* this afternoon. Should I play it slow or fast?" And since I thought the *Moonlight* is usually played too slowly I said, "Please play it fast." He said "Good," he hung up and then I didn't hear from him for six months.'

varying degree of emotional involvement comments on the character and design of the sonata.

Gould was inspired by the image of the circle in some of his performances, the circle being a particularly direct image of unity, one that inspired some of the composers whose musical structures he most admired, notably Bach and Webern. His 1981 recording of Bach's Goldberg Variations features his most explicit application of circular imagery to a musical structure. The work, of course, returns literally to its point of origin, through the device of the Aria da capo. But Gould underscores the circular effect audibly by applying throughout the principle of proportional tempo relationships from variation to variation, suggesting the continuing presence of the opening Aria, at some level, throughout the work. The 1981 recording, indeed, realizes Edward T. Cone's suggestion that a performer can 'explain an entire composition as one all-embracing rhythmic impulse'.[55] As Gould explained, accurately if verbosely, in the liner notes to his 1955 recording, the Aria 'is not terminal, but radial, the variations circumferential, not rectilinear, while the recurrent passacaille [i.e. ground bass] supplies the concentric focus for the orbit'.[56] Just as in travelling around a circle one remains at the same distance from the centre, he suggests, through the device of rhythmic continuity, that in traversing the variations he remains in constant contact with the Aria, which now assumes a role not just introductory but generative. This 1981 recording (discussed in more detail in Chapter 6) suggests a circular conception as palpably as is possible in an art form that by definition can only move forward through time, and it marked Gould's most extended effort at conveying a musical work as a single all-embracing *Gestalt*.

Criticism and Performance

If it is a commonplace that musical performance implies analysis, it is no less the case that performance can be considered a form of criticism, and many Gould performances imply a discourse on the music that has the character of an essay in music criticism. Sometimes a Gould performance combines with liner notes, published articles, broadcast commentaries, interviews, letters, or other sources to make a critical point, but often a critical discourse is implicit—even foregrounded—within a performance itself. Gould as critic was no less idiosyncratic than Gould as analyst or performer. His music criticism focused at different times on different subjects or combinations of subjects: an individual piece; a body of related works; a composer; a style, genre, or form; a historical period; an issue in performance practice, recording technology, or ethics; even metacriticism—that is, problems in

[55]   Cone, 39.
[56]   *GGR* 28.

music criticism itself. His critical essays, both written and performed, were often polemical, expressing strong value judgements and seeking to make cases for and against different kinds of music. Moreover, one often perceives direct connections between his critical positions and details of individual performances. Many performances discussed in this book embody critical points of view; for the present purpose, his controversial performances of the piano sonatas of Mozart can serve to demonstrate the relationship between criticism and performance practice in his *œuvre*.[57]

Besides embodying analyses of the individual sonatas, Gould's Mozart performances were influenced by his well-defined if often controversial opinions on the nature and development of Mozart's style, on Mozart's historical position, on the moral and intellectual implications of Mozart's music, on Mozart's use of sonata form, and on the proper character, traditional performances, and aesthetic value of the sonatas. His recordings of the complete sonatas, made between 1965 and 1974, were perhaps his most widely and vociferously criticized performances; he was accused of ignorance, insensitivity, even insanity. Otto Friedrich cites one critic who referred to the third volume in the cycle as 'the most loathsome record ever made', and another who expressed the general consensus: 'It is very difficult to see what Gould is out to prove, unless the rumor that he actually hates this music is true.'[58] The brouhaha did prove one of his points: that one criticized conventional wisdom on the perfection of Mozart's art only at one's professional peril. But Gould did not undertake five-volume recording projects just to conduct search-and-destroy missions against great composers. When he referred to the project as 'a joyous task' he was referring both to a body of works most of which he enjoyed, and to a feeling of satisfaction at having successfully realized his ideas about them in performance.[59]

Gould's views on Mozart were expressed with varying degrees of conviction and clarity at different times, and are occasionally inconsistent in some details; moreover, the performances that arose from those views are more interesting than the views themselves, which, like his views on Bach, show a reliance on many conventional ideas about Mozart's musical practices, and on certain simplistic distinctions (contrapuntal-homophonic, German-Italian). He owed much to lingering Romantic clichés about the essential simplicity and unproblematical nature of Mozart's music, and he was not influenced by that strain of modern scholarship (represented

---

[57] The summary of Gould's views on Mozart in the pages that follow is based on the following sources: *GGF*; *GGR* 32–43, 128–30, 458; *GGSL* 108–9; *Le dernier puritan*, 136–64; *Non, je ne suis pas du tout un excentrique*, 192–6; Asbell, 91; Burton, ii; Cott, 54–60; Kent; M. Meyer, 'Interview', 17; 'How Mozart Became a Bad Composer' (both drafts); 'The Art of Glenn Gould: Take 5'; and 'TV Intro No. 7/Abduction from the Seraglio/Draft 2'. See also Jean Le Moyne's 1961 essay 'Meeting Mozart', in *Convergence*, 248–51, an essay whose influence Gould acknowledged.

[58] Friedrich, 149.

[59] *GGSL* 109.

recently by Charles Rosen and Maynard Solomon, among others) that has found more powerful emotional and intellectual implications in it. Rosen notes that in Mozart's G minor symphony, K. 550, 'a work of passion, violence, and grief for those who love Mozart most, Schumann saw nothing but lightness, grace, and charm'; Gould, who saw nothing but 'a half-hour of banality' in that great symphony, was closer to Schumann's position.[60] He considered Mozart's sonatas to be light, unpretentious, unproblematical, largely comic works, the seriousness and intrinsic musical merits of which are generally exaggerated by pianists and scholars. For him they were simple entertainments with undeserved reputations as serious masterpieces, and he challenged not only the conventional evaluations of their character and worth but the conventional—in his word, 'Victorian'—performance practices that grew out of them.[61]

In making this point, he once again showed his allegiance to premises advanced by Schoenberg and his disciples, who, notwithstanding their admiration for Mozart, sometimes criticized his music (and other Classical music) for lacking the particular kind of musical 'logic' they so admired in Bach and Brahms. Mozart's fondness for a relatively large number of independent thematic ideas in his sonata-form works, for example, fitted with difficulty the Schoenbergian aesthetic, with its abhorrence of the musical 'potpourri'. Adorno clearly had such a view in mind when he compared the 'formal types' of Bach and Viennese Classicism, in a passage that Gould flagged in his copy of *Prisms*: 'Despite all its newly won compositional flexibility and effervescence, Mozart's proverbial grace is, as pure musical *peinture*, rather mechanical and crass in comparison with Bach's infinitely involuted, unschematic approach. It is a grace of tone rather than of score.'[62] Adorno's reference to the 'mechanical' is recalled in Gould's comments on Mozart, in which he often points to the relatively high proportion of conventional figuration in the piano music— stock melodic and accompanimental formulas, patterns of scales and arpeggios, routine cadences—which for him seriously compromised its aesthetic value. He sometimes made comparisons between Mozart and Haydn in this respect, predictably preferring the latter's sonatas, which he considered more substantial, more contrapuntal, more fully worked out, more unified, and more strongly differentiated, less predictable in terms of harmony, form, and character. He said in 1962 that Mozart, unlike Haydn, 'doesn't activate all the small details'—that is, doesn't sufficiently develop his material or relate the ornamental to the structural—and he ventured a commonplace criticism of the dearth of true formal development in Mozart's sonata movements, as opposed to those of Haydn or Beethoven.[63] More

---

[60]   Rosen, *The Classical Style*, 324; *GGR* 35.
[61]   Kent, 39.
[62]   Adorno, *Prisms*, 141; cf. NLC B1, 141.
[63]   Asbell, 91.

broadly, he spoke of a worldly, as opposed to philosophical, temperament revealed by Mozart's music; he complained that a Mozart sonata had no aspirations beyond simple pleasure, and did not seek 'something larger than itself'.[64] He spoke in ethical terms of his objections to the sensuousness and theatricality so prominent in Mozart's music, elements that he considered by-products of Mozart's preoccupation with opera, and that he found most prevalent in the later works. In contrast to the conventional view, he believed that 'the early sonatas are under-rated, the late sonatas over-rated',[65] an opinion he applied to Mozart works in other genres, and he admired those early works in which Mozart's Baroque and early-Classical models were most apparent.

Gould made certain connections between structural features of Mozart's music and the sensuous, theatrical quality—in ethical terms, 'hedonism'—that he perceived. Mozart's heavy use of conventional formulas was for him evidence of his reliance upon a 'fantastic facility for improvisation'.[66] Improvisation, as opposed to calculated musical construction, always bothered Gould (as it did Schoenberg), and he considered Mozart's reliance on conventions suggestive of contentment with the immediate solutions that are the province of the virtuoso improviser. And he noted that improvisation is inconsistent with the kind of contrapuntal development that he so admired. Such observations are hardly unique to Gould, even if the intensity of negative value judgement he drew from them is relatively rare.[67]

Typically, he never adjusted his cherished musical values to accommodate Mozart's aesthetic, but instead bent the music to suit his own ends. It was the rigorous application of his personal standards to Mozart's sonatas that produced his provocative performances. One 'Victorian' aspect of Mozart performance that he rejected was the tendency to impose a masculine-feminine dichotomy onto the theme groups in the sonatas, a dichotomy that, in many cases, is justified to some extent by Mozart's dynamics and other performance markings. Gould noted that the actual character and contours of the different themes are often similar, and that the tonic-dominant modulation in the exposition is generally made in a conventional way. These observations, he believed, meant that there was little structural justification for the rhythmic, dynamic, and expressive liberties often taken in performance to distinguish theme groups. His tendency to reduce such conventional contrasts is consistent with the special influence of Baroque music on his aesthetic. He tended to hear long regions of dynamic and rhythmic continuity in the sonatas (in effect, terraces), and it is not surprising that he most admired those earlier sonatas that could be fitted most easily to such standards.

---

[64] 'The Art of Glenn Gould: Take 5', 3.

[65] M. Meyer, 'Interview', 17.

[66] 'How Mozart Became a Bad Composer/(Part II, Draft 5)', 3.

[67] Rosen, The Classical Style, 72, e.g. also notes the 'sometimes astounding' amount of conventional figuration in Mozart's music, though he is more interested in the ways in which Mozart elevates and transcends it.

The opposite of 'Victorian' performance meant *buffa* for Gould: if he thought of the sonatas as light entertainments, he chose to emphasize that character in every aspect of performance. (In many respects, in fact, his Mozart recordings have more in common with recent Mozart performances by early-instrument specialists than with Romantic or conventional modern readings, however far his premisses may have been from those of historical performers.) He was not encouraged to dwell over the music: his tempos tended to be faster, sometimes much faster, than usual, even in the lyrical slow movements. Even in a turbulent work like the Sonata in A minor, K. 310, he was concerned to show that beneath the rhetoric lay an essentially *buffa* conception of rhythm and pace. He also explored the basically homophonic textures of the sonatas for contrapuntal possibilities, however latent— another example of his 'correcting' in performance what he perceived as musical deficiencies, adding 'substance' according to his own aesthetic standards. He played Mozart with a light piano tone and détaché articulation, and applied small-scale rhythmic and dynamic nuances sparingly, in part to suppress lyrical melody and *galant* expressiveness in favour of an atmosphere of *buffa* high spirits. (He considered Mozart's scores too fussy in terms of dynamics and articulation.) Then there were the humorous ornaments—mechanically measured trills, odd arpeggiated chords, sharp acciaccaturas—and the quirks of rhythm and phrasing that had the character of little jokes, puns, pratfalls.

Odd and idiosyncratic Mozart, to be sure—too prejudiced, too uncompromising for most listeners: too much lost and not enough gained. Still, there is an undeniable freshness about these performances; there is infectious rhythmic energy and abandon, wit and sparkle; the very naughtiness is entertaining. The merits of Gould's Mozart sonatas testify as much to his pianistic skills as to his critical judgements, to be sure, but the project as a whole still offers particularly strong evidence that he viewed the performance occasion as a fit opportunity for critical discourse. To embody an idiosyncratic critical position directly, self-consciously, even polemically in performance seems to have been his primary justification for recording this body of works; for him the issues in criticism and performance practice raised by it were important enough to address at length at the keyboard.[68] Mozart being such an important musical figure, yet one so challenging to his aesthetic values, it is understandable that Gould should have devoted a considerable amount of time and effort to addressing what he considered stubborn misconceptions about Mozart's music, and to 'correcting' the music in performance. (The considerable attention he devoted to the no less problematical music of Beethoven was similarly motivated.) It was completely characteristic for him to

---

[68] On the other hand, he never did, in spite of occasional plans, record the complete sonatas of Haydn, which he admired more, but which seemed not to raise any such pressing issues. See the two 1971 letters in *GGSL* 169–72.

undertake a major project for reasons like these rather than use the time to record more congenial repertoire about which he might have a less compelling critical statement to make.

Humour

It is difficult not to hear an element of parody in Gould's whole Mozart project: in the fast movements especially, he not only rejects 'Victorian' performance practices but mocks them. His Mozart cycle was only the most sustained of his many experiments in musical humour, which ranged from small-scale jokes to whole interpretations in which comedy, irony, or parody were fundamental. The humorous streak in Gould's character is often mentioned in the biographical literature, and his extensive and varied uses of humour in performance distinguish him from most classical musicians. The comic spirit that runs throughout his Mozart recordings is especially heightened but is none the less typical of his approach to music of the Classical period. He seems to have agreed with Rosen that the Classical style was, 'in its origins, basically a comic one. I do not mean that sentiments of the deepest and most tragic emotion could not be expressed by it, but the pacing of classical rhythm is the pacing of comic opera, its phrasing is the phrasing of dance music, and its large structures are these phrases dramatized.'[69] (In addition to his Mozart recordings, I would single out his witty recordings of Haydn's late sonatas, but also his frequently tongue-in-cheek readings of those quirky early sonatas, bagatelles, and variations of Beethoven, from Op. 2 to Op. 35, works for which he had a special affection.) The quick tempos, rhythmic continuity, crisp articulation, and leanness of sonority in so many of his performances of Classical music suggest an orientation towards the comic, as do many details of rhythmic nuance, phrasing, and ornamentation that create the musical equivalents of comic turns: acciaccaturas; the suppression of an expected ritardando at a final cadence to create a throw-away ending; intentionally clumsy or halting rhythms; fussy phrasing that seems coy or precious.[70] In a number of Mozart's sonatas, he plays with the comic possibilities of upward and downward arpeggiation of chords: in Ex. 3.3, such interplay has the character of comic crosstalk.[71] In the opening of the Scherzo from Beethoven's Sonata in A major, Op. 2 No. 2, his occasional rolled chords in the left hand have

---

[69] Rosen, *The Classical Style*, 96.

[70] Humorous acciaccaturas: see Mozart, Sonata in C major, K. 279/III, 42–4; Mozart, Sonata in B flat major, K. 281/III, 17–21; and Mozart, Sonata in C major, K. 545/I, 22–3. Throw-away ending: see Mozart, Sonata in E flat major, K. 282/III. Intentionally clumsy or halting rhythm: see the closing bars of Beethoven, Bagatelle in C major, Op. 33 No. 2; and Beethoven, Sonata in G major, Op. 31 No. 1/I. Fussy phrasing: see the left-hand part in the opening of Beethoven, Sonata in E flat major, Op. 27 No. 1/I, where the phrasing is a function of Gould's very slow tempo ($\decrescendo$ = 45).

[71] See also Mozart's Sonatas in F major, K. 280/I, 75–7; D major, K. 284/III, Var. 12, 35–7; and A major, K. 331/I, Var. 6, 5–8.

Ex. 3.3. Mozart, Sonata in C major, K. 309/III (1968 recording)

the effect of cheeky imitations of the arpeggiated chords notated in the right hand (see bars 2r, 5r–6r); they recall, moreover, Beethoven's own use of imitated arpeggios in the Scherzo of his early String Quartet in G major, Op. 18 No. 2, and given Gould's fondness for the Op. 18 quartets, an intended reference is conceivable.[72]

Gould occasionally used suggestions of the mechanical in fast movements to create a comic atmosphere. In many dance movements by Bach and Handel, and most tellingly in some fast movements in sonatas by Classical composers, his rigidly mechanical rhythmic schemes are unmistakably humorous. The device recalls Henri Bergson's comment, in his book *Laughter: An Essay on the Meaning of the Comic*, that 'attitudes, gestures and movements of the human body are laughable in exact proportion as that body reminds us of a mere machine'.[73] As Janet M. Levy shows, in an article on the humorous uses of the mechanical by Classical composers, what Bergson writes of human bodies can apply equally well to musical 'organisms'. She observes that 'when human beings or their musical gestures suspend the animate we may find the effect witty or humorous', and adds that it was this phenomenon—'something mechanical encrusted on the living'—that Bergson considered 'the crux of the comical'.[74] In the finale to Mozart's K. 279 sonata, for example, Gould's tempo ($\downarrow$ = 185) is so fast, and maintained so strictly, that expressive nuance is essentially impossible (see CD [6]), and in the finale to the K. 332 sonata, his precise and blatantly inexpressive semiquaver runs at a very fast tempo ($\downarrow$. = 128) suggest the mechanical churning of a teletype machine. In both cases, the result is a heightened, giddy atmosphere of high comedy, like the ceaseless comic chatter in a finale of a Mozart opera.[75] Gould's frequent suppression

[72] On the Op. 18 quartets, see *GGR* 45, 461.

[73] Bergson, 29.

[74] Levy, 226.

[75] Examples of Gould's comical mechanical rhythms do not always involve breakneck tempos: see Bach's Goldberg Variations/Var. 19, in both the 1955 and 1981 recordings (notwithstanding widely diverging tempos); and the second movement ('adagio grazioso') of Beethoven's Sonata in G major, Op. 31 No. 1.

of the lyrical impulse, especially in Classical music, also had humorous implications. As Levy notes, 'to clip a long-breathed melody . . . is to violate not only its implied life span, but also the essence of its living quality',[76] and as Bergson writes, 'The laughable element . . . consists of a certain *mechanical inelasticity*, just where one would expect to find the wideawake adaptability and the living pliableness of a human being.'[77]

In some whole movements or works there is a clear element of parody in Gould's performance. The parody may lie in the essential character of the performance, in its relationship to the score, or, as with the Mozart sonatas, in its relationship to conventional performance practice. Gould's mock-*pomposo* reading of the famous 'Turkish rondo' finale of Mozart's K. 331 (♩ = 87) can surely be interpreted not only as a parody of martial 'Turkish music', but as a denial, even a send-up, of conventional expectations of this very familiar piece.[78] The clipped phrasing in his performance of the first prelude from *WTC* I is also undoubtedly tongue-in-cheek: he resolutely refuses to play with the 'expressive' pedalling typical in this piece. It was perhaps predictable that in his recording of Schoenberg's Suite, Op. 25, he would stress the wit and parody in the composer's appropriation of Baroque models.[79] (It is instructive to contrast the lightness, charm, even cheekiness in Gould's recording with the sort of modernist Angst that many performers seem to bring to this music.) In the second movement of Prokofiev's Seventh Sonata, Gould's reading of the main theme suggests a parody of a sentimental popular song, or more accurately of a parlour pianist, featuring such Romantic clichés as exaggerated rubato, a fervently 'expressive' rendering of the melody, and 'melodic rubato' (the dislocation between bass and melody parts). The resulting performance is, by Gould's standards, uncharacteristically saccharine—in Pierro Rattalino's view, 'Kitsch'.[80]

Gould's solo-piano transcription of Ravel's *La Valse*, which he played on CBC television in 1975, was certainly intended, at least in part, as a commentary on the parodistic nature of the original work. As Geoffrey Payzant notes, the work is 'already a giddy parody of the sentimental Viennese waltz', and 'Gould's transcription is a parody of those nineteenth-century piano transcriptions of orchestral and operatic masterpieces, and works by Bach for organ, to which he objected in his youth'.[81] The hyper-virtuosity of Gould's performance of the *Vorspiel* from

---

[76] Levy, 251.

[77] Quoted in ibid.

[78] On this movement, see *GGR* 41; and Burton, ii.

[79] On this work, see *GGR* 117, 127; Burton, iii; and Mach, 100.

[80] Rattalino, 375. Gould's parodistic rendering of the theme is more obvious in his 1962 CBC television performance than in his 1967 recording. See *GGR* 166 on this work.

[81] Payzant, *GGMM* 62. See *GGSL* 216 for Gould's comments on how he adapted Ravel's solo-piano transcription to create his own new version. (His annotated score of the Ravel transcription is preserved as NLC Scores 37,9.)

Wagner's *Die Meistersinger*, made possible by four-hand over-dubbing, might also be heard as a commentary in performance on a work with parodistic intentions, in this case a send-up of pedantic academic counterpoint: Gould's 'impossible' transcription underscores the ostentatious complexity of Wagner's polyphony.[82] (Listen to the closing minutes of CD 2.) And in his self-consciously constrained recording of Beethoven's 'Appassionata' Sonata (on which more below), the blustery rhetoric of the work, of which he had such a low opinion, is not only undercut but derided. In all three of these performances, all of unusual Gould repertoire, it is even possible to hear a conscious element of self-parody. (And we might add to this list his performances of the Beethoven-Liszt Fifth Symphony, or Strauss's *Burleske*. Gould admitted that the former performance was 'a bit of a lark'—his jokey liner notes suggest as much—and of the latter work he noted that it was itself a parody of many conventions of the Romantic piano concerto.[83]) Payzant observes in the Ravel performance an uncharacteristic effort 'to dazzle us with the sheer physical improbability' of the virtuoso display,[84] and he is surely right: Gould packs in just those woodwind scales and other orchestral elements that Ravel obviously thought impossible in his own transcription, and it is difficult not to hear this sort of virtuosity—at once punishing and playful—as Gould's send-up of his own musical tastes and priorities. To make sly in-jokes (even album-length in-jokes) for listeners aware of his musical proclivities, to use a virtuoso's technique to poke fun at overt virtuosity—these are motivations highly unusual in a 'serious' classical performer, to say the least. Yet it is admittedly not out of character for Gould to have extended the uses of humour to such lengths in performance. The layers of humour and parody in his playing were not only consistent with certain features of his personality, but with his fondness for broadening or subverting conventional notions about the classical canon, the role of the performer, and the function of performance.

As these examples begin to suggest, there is a more profound element of humour in Gould's whole relationship to his art, not only in his use of explicit comic devices on the piano. Some critics have observed a pronounced streak of irony in his attitude towards received conventions, an irony that is only most explicit in the likes of his Mozart recordings. Nicholas Spice wrote of it in a 1992 review-essay:

the presence of the fool . . . not far below the surface of Gould's playing gives it an exhilarating ambiguity, in which total commitment and peals of laughter, extraordinary beauty and hilarity, seem to alternate. . . . [Gould] understood that humour is not about responding to self-consciously funny things, but about laughing at those aspects of life and art which are deadly serious. Humour arises when the things we most love or fear are tested

---

[82] See 'Transcribing Wagner', 55.

[83] Ibid., 52. On the *Burleske*, see *GGR* 41; and Burton, iv.

[84] Payzant, *GGMM* 62.

to the limit, when we allow ourselves to consider for a moment that what we regard as everything is in fact nothing. In this sense, humour is the capacity to be radical, to pull up settled things and look at their roots. Gould exercised this capacity in a high degree.[85]

José Ortega y Gasset considered irony to be a distinctive characteristic of modern art generally, an observation even more true in Gould's day than when Ortega wrote in 1925, though (as the next section shows), Gould did not, like Ortega's quintessential modern artist, take irony to the point of viewing art itself as a mere game, 'a thing of no consequence'—quite the contrary.[86] But the manifest self-consciousness in his approach to his work, his full awareness of the conventional expectations he was subverting, strongly suggests a fundamentally ironic stance.

But I am becoming too ponderous. Not even the most serious student of Gould's work can ignore the element of simple playfulness in many of his interpretations, and it is certainly not my intention to elevate or rationalize those of his performances—like that famous C major prelude of Bach's—that are really just musical jokes or games. Like Barthes, Gould was at once a serious artist and a nose-thumber, in whose work a tendency *pour épater le bourgeois* is undeniable, and the element of 'play' that Barthes applied in his reading of literary texts is to a degree analogous to Gould's own approach to performance. Some of his interpretations, particularly of over-familiar canonical works, were surely no more profoundly motivated than by a desire to counteract the stifling conformity of classical-music traditions. He combatted with humour and irony the conventions, the predicta-bility, even the boredom inherent in the Classical Hit Parade—in yet another performance of the 'Appassionata' or K. 331. To the extent that such motivations can be inferred from his work, we might say that Gould considered his very task as a performer, no less than the particular pieces he played, to be a proper subject of discourse at the keyboard.

Ethics and Performance

Gould may have been the compleat modern or post-modern ironist when he poked his fingers into Mozart or Beethoven, yet there was at times an almost Medieval seriousness in his attitude towards his art. His thinking about music extended to its ethical, social, and even political and religious implications, and he viewed his performances as reflections not only of his musical tastes but of his philosophical outlook, as arguments for and against certain world-views and ways of life. While the theme of art and philosophy appears frequently in his writings, interviews, broadcasts, and letters, he never wrote a comprehensive treatise on the

---

[85] Spice, 7.
[86] See Ortega y Gasset, 46–52.

subject, and his views were not always clear. Still, one perceives in his scattered musings on non-musical matters some important recurring themes that point to a coherent world-view that influenced all aspects of his work, one that has been explored in some detail in the Gould literature. I will focus here on ethics, the aspect of his world-view that had the greatest impact on his performances. His aesthetic was inextricably bound up with his ethics, and many of his performance practices can be traced back to some ethical standpoint.

Gould believed that aesthetic choices implied ethical correlatives, that music was properly assessed not only in terms of its aesthetic value but in terms of the thoughts and behaviours—the outlook on life—that it encouraged. Music was not ethically neutral, and different musics had different ethical implications. He went as far as to advocate a condition in which aesthetic judgements would be entirely suspended in favour of moral judgements: he described as ideal a situation in which one made aesthetic judgements only about one's own work, as part of the creative process, but judged other musical productions in ethical terms. Perfection 'not purely of a technical order, but also of a spiritual order' was for him a goal that was possible only where one has risen above the need to make aesthetic judgements.[87] Naturally he had ambivalent feelings about music critics, who by profession make, defend, and promote aesthetic judgements: he said that they exercise in society 'a morally disruptive, and aesthetically destructive, influence'.[88] He considered the aesthetic value of a work of art to be irrelevant where the work served a function, or implied a world-view, that he considered immoral. He thus held 'the view of art as an instrument of salvation, of the artist as missionary advocate'.[89] He felt a duty to advocate the kinds of music that, in his view, encouraged moral rectitude, and to challenge those that he perceived to be dangerous, to the extent that, from about the mid-1960s on, he perceived in his own work a 'growing antiart stance'.[90] Because art could be morally dangerous as well as beneficial, he came to believe that art would be unnecessary in a morally ideal world, in which its 'offer of restorative, placative therapy would go begging a patient'.[91] (This was not a position that he ever fully developed, however.)

These views resonate in a number of different contexts. The relating of art to ethics traces back at least to Ptolemy and the ethos of the ancient Greeks, of course, while an anti-art stance has affinities with pre-Enlightenment concerns for the potential dangers of art, even with positions on the future of art taken by such contemporary musicians as John Cage. Gould's outlook does, moreover, ally him with

[87] Colgrass, 10.
[88] *GGR* 258.
[89] Ibid. 297.
[90] Ibid. 446.
[91] Ibid. 353.

some writers (like Jürgen Habermas) who have expressed concern over post-modernism's detachment from real life. His position on music and ethics has often been compared to that of Puritanism, by himself and others, though in spite of some of his terminology his ethics did not have a formal religious foundation, and in reality he did not advocate the degree of restriction associated with Puritans. (In his 1964 lecture 'Music in the Soviet Union' and in a 1974 self-interview, he made it clear that he did not believe that music should be morally 'engaged' in the sense of being forced to conform to political or community standards, and he never advocated a political system in which aesthetic and moral matters were subject to fiat.[92]) There is also something Romantic in Gould's ethics of art, for Romantic theorists of absolute music were much concerned with the higher implications of their aesthetic views. Crucial to Romantic aesthetics was what Lydia Goehr calls the 'separability principle', according to which art is something separated from the ordinary world, something which provides access to 'the higher world of universal, eternal truth'; this is especially true of absolute, instrumental music, the meaning of which is transcendent, derived from within.[93] This principle extends back to the beginning of the era of absolute music, and many Romantic theorists (Herder, Wackenroder, Kant, Schopenhauer, Hanslick) held that music required the listener to withdraw into a state of contemplation, even of 'devotion'. The idea that 'pure music' opened onto the infinite, was a withdrawal into the inward, was a kind of revelation, and so on, implied religious processes for many Romantic writers, who tended to make a religion of art, but for Gould, too, music had ethical implications along these lines. His sympathy with the Romantic view is apparent in his notion of 'ecstasy', which was for him the proper response to music and so the goal of performance. In Payzant's summary, ecstasy was 'a delicate thread binding together music, performance, performer and listener in a web of shared awareness of *innerness*'; it was 'a condition in which the individual has some sense of standing outside himself', growing out of a state of contemplation rather than from the excitation of the senses.[94] The distinction was clearly an ethical one for Gould.

Needless to say, he never attained the state of 'spiritual perfection' that he sought, and he admitted as much. His writings and conversations are rife with aesthetic judgements, about his own work and others', and he was certainly not prepared to live in a world without art. Yet some of his musical choices do suggest that he worked consciously towards his stated ideals. Moral considerations were certainly tied up with repertoire, for Gould no less than his Romantic predecessors. The music to which he was strongly drawn aesthetically, that which satisfied an idealistic penchant for structural integration, was also music which attracted him

---

[92]   See ibid. 166–84, 315–28.

[93]   See Goehr, 121–3, 148–75.

[94]   Payzant, *GGMM* 65, 64; see 63–7, 155–7, on Gould's notion of 'ecstasy'.

ethically, precisely because it encouraged that 'ecstatic' attitude of contemplation rather than excitation. Thus he equated a certain kind of technical order with spiritual well-being. The contrapuntal music of Byrd, Bach, and Schoenberg, for example, was for him music suited to private rather than public audition, to rational rather than sensual apprehension; it was introspective rather than exhibitionistic, and encouraged an attitude of repose rather than one of exhilaration. All of these factors accorded with the way of life that he considered morally healthy: 'The purpose of art', he wrote in 1962, 'is not the release of a momentary ejection of adrenaline but is, rather, the gradual, life-long construction of a state of wonder and serenity.'[95]

By contrast, he deplored music that he considered to be oriented towards theatricality and individual virtuoso display, or designed for mass public consumption—music that, in his view, encouraged a hedonistic outlook. This category included a wide variety of music, from the virtuoso Romantic piano literature (solo and concerted) to Italian opera to large-scale works from Beethoven's 'heroic' period. (Many of the conventional binarisms and categories in Gould's thought— 'Protestant North' versus 'Catholic South', and so on—clearly derived more from the direct application of ethical absolutes than from informed music-historical observation.) He also strongly objected to music, most notoriously Stravinsky's, that in his opinion subscribed to an art-for-art's-sake, or art-as-technique, point of view.[96] He even occasionally applied moral criteria to the assessment of certain musical forms, and to composers' relations with their musical material, with unconvincing results. He insisted, for example, on the moral superiority of such discursive and contemplative musical procedures as the fugue over the more dramatic, 'autocratic', and 'aggressive' procedures of sonata-form works—especially those of Beethoven, and especially when conceived as a conflict and resolution of opposing forces.[97] (He obviously subscribed to the old-fashioned, and now rather discredited, Hegelian interpretation of sonata form, which originated with such early-Romantic theorists as A. B. Marx and was only seriously challenged after the Second World War.) Gould also favoured music that he considered to be served by private audition through recording technology, and denigrated music better suited to concert performance (this issue is explored further in Chapter 10). Indeed, he professed a general ethical objection to all of the live arts—to 'voyeuristically watch[ing] one's fellow human beings' being tested in live situations.[98] The glaring gaps in his musical tastes and knowledge, the apparent contradictions in

---

[95] *GGR* 246. Cook, 183, notes that for Schoenberg, too, a musical work was 'fundamentally a moral entity and not a perceptual one'.

[96] See *GGR* 180–1, 324.

[97] See *GGR* 37–9; and Davis, 282–9.

[98] *GGR* 452.

his musical assessments, his championship of little-known composers like Valen alongside his dismissal of masterpieces by Mozart and Beethoven, Chopin and Liszt, Debussy and Stravinsky—these must be understood in terms of his strong feelings about the ethical implications of different kinds of music, feelings that could influence, outweigh, or even prevent reasoned aesthetic judgement.

At times, and in contradiction to his professed views, Gould attempted to defend ethical opinions by aesthetic standards. His least convincing musical analysis and criticism is generally that which rationalizes a basically ethical objection, for he was rarely able to judge musically masterful a work that he found ethically distasteful. For example, his vigorous dismissal of Bach's early toccatas and Chromatic Fantasy is consistent with his distrust of the element of personal display in improvisatory music; these works also lacked the structural density of the mature fugues he so admired. But his musical objections to such works only demonstrate an inability, or refusal, to appreciate their defining qualities, for to criticize the harmonic promiscuity of the Chromatic Fantasy is simply to miss the whole point of the music.[99] His efforts to find musical rationales to support his views on the rhetoric of Mozart's late piano music and Beethoven's middle-period sonatas and symphonies were weak for the same reason, as were his commonplace critiques of Stravinsky. That his musical analysis was unconvincing in such cases reinforces the ethical origin of the opinions, but also shows how inextricably the aesthetic and ethical were tied in his thought, in spite of his desire to separate them.

Gould's ethics directly influenced his performance practices, perhaps especially in music to which he had ethical objections. His highly controversial 1966–7 recording of Beethoven's 'Appassionata' Sonata, one of his most criticized performances, implies unmistakably a value judgement of the work. The 'Appassionata', like other of Beethoven's 'heroic' works, disturbed him because of the nature of its rhetoric, and this essentially moral reaction is obvious in his failed attempt to rationalize it through musical analysis.[100] His performance, especially of the first movement, amounted to a wilful effort to 'correct' (or, less charitably, sabotage) the original by playing down and even deriding its offensive elements, most notably through the intentional denuding of the work's blustery rhetorical gestures in favour of the kind of dissection that he routinely applied to works like fugues. And where he could not avoid the music's bluster, he undercut it through parody, as in his plodding, ham-fisted rendering of the fortissimo chords at the beginning of the first movement. He adopted an unusually slow tempo ($\quarternote$. = 54) in the first movement, which, along with measured ornaments and clipped phrasing, imposed a tight, cleanly etched profile that undercut much of the rhetorical thrust of the music. The result was a leisurely examination of the music's details, its constituent

---

[99] See his comments in Monsaingeon, *The Question of Instrument*, quoted in Friedrich, 231.
[100] See his liner notes on this sonata, in *GGR* 52–3.

parts, at the expense of the larger drama.[101] It was as though Gould intended to remove the *appassionata* element from the sonata to see what remained. The short answer is: not much. The result is not—cannot be—a good or convincing performance by any conventional criterion, and I do not claim to be more willing than anyone else to sit through this recording. And yet, one is forced to account for it because it was so clearly not made in ignorance of how the piece 'should go'. (The self-consciousness of the interpretation is obvious both in the performance and the liner notes.) The performance makes sense only as a kind of polemical exercise, as a discourse in performance, as a frank experiment in which the work is made to behave as it was never meant to do, in this case to amend a perceived deficiency by standards that were ethical as much as aesthetic.[102] But the performance explained is no less astonishing: Gould was willing to make his ethical and aesthetic point even if it meant leaving a performance that is difficult to listen to, never mind defend.

Some of the non-musical beliefs that directly influenced his preferences among composers and genres, as well as his performances, have already been discussed in the Gould literature: his placing of reason above sensuality; his anti-materialism; his belief that solitude, isolation, and anonymity are important prerequisites for creativity; his insistence that recording technology had important ethical implications. The influence of the Canadian North on his aesthetic has also been much discussed.[103] Images of the Canadian North, as represented in, for example, the paintings of Canada's Group of Seven, influenced Gould from his youth, and he always strongly favoured Nordic attitudes and behaviour. His musical tastes leaned heavily towards the work of Nordic composers, and one might even make some connections between a Nordic outlook and certain characteristics of his style of performance: the importance of silence and repose; an openness and mystery in some of his slow-moving contrapuntal textures; a frequently reticent, brooding quality of emotion. Even his strong, if non-denomenational, religious views, also the subject of some discussion in the biographical literature, influenced his work as a pianist. One can point to his one-sided image of Bach: his idealistic interpretation of Bach's music led him to privilege the abstract element, which he associated with Bach's religious outlook, over the physical element, and this preference affected deeply his manner of playing Bach. His early admiration of Rosalyn Tureck, in fact, was influential in precisely these terms. He told Jonathan Cott in

---

[101] Note e.g. how he breaks up much of Beethoven's sweeping figuration into discrete units, through articulation and dynamic or agogic accents; see bars 17–22, 35–40, 51–6, 79–92, 123–33, 218–26, and 249–61.

[102] Gould's 1974 recording of Beethoven's early Sonata in F minor, Op. 2 No. 1, with its odd rolled chords, clipped and precious articulation, departures from notated dynamics, and other eccentricities seems also to have been intended as a critique of a work renowned for its passionate rhetoric.

[103] See e.g. Payzant, *GGMM* 55–6. As Théberge, 29, notes, the theme of isolation in Gould's thought places him within a distinctly Canadian tradition.

1974 that Tureck's playing of Bach was 'of such uprightness, to put it into the moral sphere. There was a sense of repose that had nothing to do with languor, but rather with moral rectitude in the liturgical sense.'[104] I cannot explore all such ideas and their implications for performance. In the remainder of this chapter, I will focus on the practical implications of perhaps the single most important aspect of Gould's ethics: his disdain for competition.

Competitiveness was, for Gould, the least admirable human characteristic: 'I happen to believe', he said in a 1976 interview, 'that competition rather than money is the root of all evil.'[105] Commentary on competition is woven throughout his writings, interviews, and broadcasts, and Payzant has discussed the subject in detail.[106] Music festivals and competitions were major targets of Gould's criticism, and, excepting childhood events, he avoided the competition circuit.[107] But he also disdained other, indirect manifestations of the competitive impulse in music. He was, as we have seen, a vociferous opponent of music criticism that equated stylistic progressiveness with aesthetic value, and his championing of such reactionary figures as Richard Strauss was in part a defensive reaction against the competitive implications of the idea of progress in music. More significantly, in terms of performance, disdain for competition was at the root of his objection to the concert hall, a subject he discussed in many forums: for him the concert hall called up the image of the arena, and he went so far as to speak of its 'gladiatorial' implications.[108] In the effort of the concert performer to 'conquer' the audience (and the music), in the audience's appetite for feats of skill performed in a live situation with risks of uncertainty and even disaster, Gould sensed manifestations of the competitive spirit at once offensive and injurious to music. 'At live concerts,' he said in a 1964 interview, 'I feel demeaned, like a vaudevillian.'[109] He considered the personal discomforts associated with the competitive aspect of concert performance—adrenaline, stress, stage fright—to be a strong argument against it, because these discomforts interfered with his ability to communicate his musical interpretations. In fact, he even included recordings as a factor in his disdain for concerts: he spoke

---

[104] Cott, 63.

[105] *GGR* 41.

[106] See Payzant, *GGMM* 57–63, 71–2. Payzant, and others, have also discussed some related contradictions, including examples of Gould's own competitive feelings towards other musicians: see ibid. 61–2; Friedrich, 238–41; and Kazdin, 71, 114–15. Certain of Gould's recordings—notably his first two, of Bach's Goldberg Variations and Beethoven's last three sonatas, and the Prokofiev-Scriabin album released in 1969—have been interpreted as tacit confrontations with certain performers (Tureck, Landowska, Schnabel, Horowitz): see e.g. Colgrass, 6; M. Meyer, 'Interview', 16; 'Mostly Music', 3; Friedrich, 240–1; Goldsmith, 55; Ostwald, 222–3; and Roddy, 119.

[107] See Gould's 1966 article on music competitions, 'We Who Are About to Be Disqualified Salute You!', in *GGR* 250–5. On the subject of competition generally, see his 1972 programme for the CBC radio series *The Scene*.

[108] For some of his most notable discussions of this subject, see his 1962 article 'Let's Ban Applause!', in *GGR* 245–50; his 1966 article 'The Prospects of Recording', in ibid. 331–53; ibid. 451–2; Asbell, 90; McClure; Menuhin and Davis; and Monsaingeon, *Chemins de la musique*, i.

[109] Bester, 152.

of the pressure at concerts to compete with his own studio recordings, something he felt unable to do.[110]

Since for Gould 'competition' meant more than actual conflict, but included the whole public spectacle of concert performing, it included many features of that music most indigenous to the concert medium. For example, he found distasteful instrumental virtuosity of an exhibitionistic kind, 'mechanistic' virtuosity that glorified the performer, and that he considered opposed to his cherished standards of musical coherence; as Denis Dutton puts it, he wanted 'to get away from a competitive—one might call it "athletic"—view of excellence in musicianship'.[111] Gould's ethical position here is an old one: musical virtuosity for its own sake was deemed immoral already by the ancient Greeks. But as usual, he pursued the implications of this position with unusual vigour, and the result was some unconventional musical judgements. For example, he deplored the 'empty theatrical gestures' in piano music of the early Romantic period, while admiring the piano music of Sibelius, who 'was disinclined to provide for virtuoso display', and who, in his Sonatines, 'was practically the only composer of his generation to show that one can create piano works without orchestral effects—octave doublings and so on'.[112] Gould did not avoid technically difficult music, and his own technique was universally admired, but he did tend to avoid music like Liszt's in which virtuosity could be considered a positive aesthetic attribute, and the recorded evidence suggests that he was neither technically nor temperamentally suited to such music (it apparently bored him). He was clearly defending his own values when he wrote in praise of the Russian pianist Sviatoslav Richter in a 1978 essay. He divided musical performers

into two categories—those who seek to exploit the instruments they use, and those who do not. In the first category—if we can believe the history books—one could find a place for such legendary characters as Liszt and Paganini, as well as any number of allegedly demonic virtuosi of more recent vintage. That category belongs to musicians who are determined to make us aware of their relationship to their instrument, whatever it happens to be; they allow that relationship to become the focus of attention. The second category, on the other hand, includes musicians who try to bypass the whole question of the performing mechanism, to create the illusion, at any rate, of a direct link between themselves and a particular musical score and who, therefore, help the listener to achieve a sense of involvement, not with the performance per se, but, rather, with the music itself. . . . [Artists like Richter] achieve such a perfect liaison with the instrument that the mechanical process involved becomes all but invisible—totally at the service of the musical structure—and that the performer, and consequently, the listener is then able to ignore all superficial questions of

---

[110] See McClure; Menuhin and Davis, 292; and Gould's spoken commentary in GGC iii.

[111] Dutton, 514. For Gould's comments, see *GGSL* 54, 243; and Mach, 105.

[112] The comment on early-Romantic music is in *GGR* 453. The comments on Sibelius are in ibid. 103; and M. Meyer, 'Interview', 19.

virtuosity or instrumental display and concentrate instead on the spiritual qualities inherent in the music itself.[113]

When it came to musical genres and forms, Gould saw 'a perfect musical analogy of the competitive spirit' in the solo concerto.[114] He revived old-fashioned socio-political analogies to musical forms, viewing the relationship between soloist and orchestra in a concerto—between 'heroic individual and subservient mass'—as fraught with competitive implications.[115] He tended to prefer more 'democratic' concerto types, like the Baroque concerto grosso, or Webern's Op. 24. Among solo concertos, he tended to admire 'parodistic concerto-commentaries' (like Strauss's *Burleske*), or concertos that did not emphasize the element of virtuoso display (like those of Schoenberg and Krenek).[116] The extroversion in solo concertos troubled Gould. In a 1969 CBC radio broadcast, he said:

The great evil of the concerto is that attention is being directed away from the person who is listening. It would seem to me that one ought to make the listener aware of an inward-looking, rather than an outward-looking, process. Surely everything that is mixed up in virtuosity and exhibitionism on the platform is outward-looking, or causes outward-lookingness; and I think that's sinful, to use an old-fashioned word.[117]

Again, he sometimes attempted to use musical analysis to support his basically ethical objections—and again, with mixed results. He argued in 1962 that the musical integrity of some concertos was compromised by the need to satisfy the virtuosic ambitions of the soloist, and by the repeating and embroidering of thematic statements:

Perhaps for this reason, the most popular and successful (though never the best) of concertos have usually come from composers who were somewhat lacking in a grasp of symphonic architecture—Liszt, Grieg, etc.—composers who had in common a confined, periodic concept of symphonic style but who were able to linger without embarrassment upon the glowing melodic moment. Perhaps also for this reason, the great figures of the symphonic repertoire have almost always come off second best in concerto writing, and their relative failures have helped to give credence to the widespread and perfectly defensible notion that concertos are comparatively lightweight stuff.[118]

Characteristically, Gould analysed concertos by the standards of structural 'logic' that he saw in more abstract forms like the fugue; he refused to acknowledge that the dramatic nature of the solo concerto form demanded a different set of standards.

---

[113] 'Sviatoslav Richter', 12. Gould's remark about 'allegedly demonic virtuosi of more recent vintage' is clearly a reference to Vladimir Horowitz.

[114] *GGR* 41. On the concerto, see also Colgrass, 9; and Mach, 104.

[115] *GGR* 270.

[116] Ibid. 41. On the concertos of Schoenberg and Krenek, see *GGSL* 47.

[117] Quoted in Payzant, *GGMM* 72.

[118] *GGR* 129.

And so he found in such formal conventions as 'the orchestral pre-exposition', the 'repetitive thematic structure', and the 'superfluous' cadenza, all of which are essential to the concerto as a drama, mere impediments to great symphonic composers like Beethoven and Brahms.[119]

Most performances of solo concertos only made matters worse, in Gould's view, for performers have traditionally underscored just those features to which he had ethical and musical objections: the exaggeration of the disparity between the solo and orchestral parts; the soloist's indulging in opportunities for personal display, even where the orchestra has more structurally important musical material; and wide fluctuations of tempo and mood between solo and tutti sections.[120] Such practices, he felt, moved the concerto even further from the symphonic unity and continuity that he valued in large-scale works. He told Humphrey Burton in 1966, 'We exaggerate the protagonist's role in concertos. We exaggerate a sense of dualism as between orchestra and soloist, as between individual and mass, as between masculine and feminine statements. . . This is a great mistake.'[121] When he played concertos himself, he sought to minimize virtuoso display and solo-tutti contrast, and to maximize unity and continuity. To use the cliché first applied to Brahms's D minor concerto, he sought to play a concerto as though it were a symphony with obbligato piano.[122] One means was physical disposition of forces. Performing Bach's Clavier Concerto No. 1 in D minor in Lucerne (31 August 1959), he persuaded Herbert von Karajan to conduct 'from the lip of the stage so that the piano could be surrounded by, and integrated with, the strings of the Philharmonia Orchestra', and Edward W. Said has recalled a similar integration of piano with strings in a Boston performance of Bach's Brandenburg Concerto No. 5 (22 October 1961).[123] Both performances were clearly influenced by the model of the Baroque concerto grosso.

The details of performance practice with which Gould brought solo concertos closer to his own ethical position on competition are best exemplified by two interpretations: his controversial 1962 concert performances of Brahms's Concerto No. 1 in D minor, with Leonard Bernstein conducting the New York Philharmonic; and his 1966 recording of Beethoven's 'Emperor' Concerto, with Leopold Stokowski conducting the American Symphony Orchestra.[124] What Gould wrote

[119] Ibid. 70–1.
[120] Gould was caustic in his dismissal of the last-named feature of many concerto performances: see *GGR* 70, 269.
[121] Burton, ii.
[122] Gould uses this description in *GGR* 269; Burton, ii; Colgrass, 10; McClure; and M. Meyer, 'Interview', 18.
[123] *GGR* 269; see Said, 'The Music Itself', 50.
[124] On the Brahms interpretation, see Gould's essay 'N'aimez-Vous Pas Brahms?' from *c.*1962, in *GGR* 70–2. On the Beethoven recording, see the fifth 'scene' in his 1977 essay 'Stokowski in Six Scenes', in *GGR* 269–76. All quotations below not otherwise identified are from these two sources. On the Brahms, see also Page. On the Beethoven, see also Burton, ii; and Mach, 104–5.

of the Brahms interpretation applies to both. The 'peculiarities' of the interpretation 'largely concern themselves with an attempt to subordinate the soloist's role, not to aggrandize it—to integrate rather than to isolate'. For him, typically, there were two ways—two extreme ways—to play such a concerto:

One can stress its drama, its contrasts, its angularities, and can treat the opposition of thematic tonal relations as a coalition of inequalities. This is the fashionable way to interpret romantic music these days. This way reads into it a plot full of surprises, a moral position full of contradictions. It approaches the perfunctory conventions of the classical sonata structure and its inherent and largely stereotyped plan with a naiveté which accepts the masculine-feminine contrast of theme as an end in itself. Alternatively, one can read the future into Brahms. One can see it as Schoenberg would have seen it: a sophisticated interweaving of a fundamental motivic strand; one can read into it the analytical standpoints of our own day.

And this, essentially, is what I have done. I have valued this structure for its similarities; I have chosen to minimize its contrasts.

The most important single element in both interpretations is a continuity of tempo that reduces to some degree the 'competitive' discrepancies between solo and tutti forces and between 'masculine' and 'feminine' theme groups. In both, the tempos are unusually slow (the Brahms runs fifty-two minutes, the Beethoven forty-three), but, as Gould noted, tempo *per se* was less important than the relative stability of that tempo. Of the Brahms, he told an interviewer in 1964 that 'I wanted to play the outer movements . . . [so that] the main themes and second themes were played in exact tempo unless otherwise indicated by Brahms. Unfortunately, a whole virtuoso tradition has been built up otherwise.'[125] One section in which pianists traditionally take rhythmic liberties to heighten the independence of their role is the beginning of the solo exposition from the first movement of the 'Emperor' (bars 107–68). In the second of his televised discussions with Burton, Gould used this section to demonstrate his rhythmic continuity, suggesting that there was no musical need to depart from the basic tempo throughout this section: changes of tone colour, dynamics, and articulation were adequate to underscore the various distinctive moods and textures, while continuity of tempo can offer a locus of unity on a larger level. He maintained relative continuity of tempo to restrain the solo part even in the lengthy cadenza that opens the first movement. He did not take the usual degree of liberty with the notated rhythm, but rather, to a large extent, made a 'measured, metrically unyielding statement' intended to 'link the measured beat of [the] opening orchestra chords to whichever tempo was to govern the movement proper'. Though his performance of that opening cadenza was not literally 'metrically unyielding', he did clearly try to

[125]   Bester, 153.

establish a sense of governing pulse not only at the beginning of the orchestral exposition at bar 11, but already in the introduction.

In both interpretations, Gould seems to have had in mind not so much the variegated drama of the Romantic solo concerto as the relatively greater unity and rhythmic stability of the Classical symphony, but he also made an analogy to the principle of the concerto grosso. He wrote of the 'Emperor' that 'in my view all scales, arpeggios, trills, and other decorative materials, to which so much of the piano's attention is directed in this work, should be treated as supportive elements of the texture—rather like continuo passages in a baroque concerto grosso'. Here the notion of a symphony with obbligato piano is clear, for he played the piano part relatively modestly where the orchestra carried more important musical material. Even within the piano parts themselves, Gould often gave greater emphasis to background harmonic structure than to virtuosic *fioratura*, and used the slow tempos to explore the contrapuntal possibilities latent within accompanimental figuration, making it more 'thematic' and so subordinating it as virtuosic decoration. Moreover, the slow, measured ornaments he played in both works contributed in a small way to the broad time-scale and rhythmic continuity he sought to impose, especially at important joints within the structure, as between orchestral and solo expositions in the first movement of the 'Emperor'. In the first movement of the Brahms, a somewhat terraced conception of dynamics further ironed out the element of solo indulgence, and made the concerto-grosso analogy explicit. In the extended solo statement in F major that makes up the second theme group in the first movement (bars 156–224), Gould maintains a largely piano dynamic throughout, reducing many forte and crescendo markings in the score (see bars 167–70, 187–9, 201, and 204), and setting off the whole section quite audibly as a single structural unit.

Typically, Gould found 'structural' rationales to support what were interpretations founded largely on ethical criteria. As we saw earlier, the levelling of tempo distinctions between theme groups in the Brahms was intended to help clarify 'correspondences of structural material between thematic blocks', as he put it in a 1962 letter.[126] He hoped, in other words, to make developments of the musical material—the element of 'organic unity'—more audible by reducing the dramatic contrasts that clothe those developments. (Moreover, he applied the principle of rhythmic continuity on the largest level, forging tempo relationships between the three movements; see Chapter 6.) In other words, he read into the work the 'analytical standpoints' of Schoenberg's school, and if he sought to 'flatten' the work somewhat in terms of dramatic contrast, it was to permit subtler inner workings of the music—Brahms's 'developing variation' of his material—to be more clearly revealed.

[126] *GGSL* 57.

In both concertos, Gould's decisions about tempo and so on had important consequences in terms of expression. His particular combination of performance practices in each case reduced the excitement of dramatic conflict between forces, creating in its place a sense of the gradual unfolding of a musical argument; an ethic of contemplation replaced an ethic of competition. In each case, Gould's actual ethical position was commonplace, and his ethical-sociological interpretation of the musical form was hardly profound or original. What is interesting, rather—here as in so many of his performances—is his insistence on seeking direct correlatives for his ethical position in his performance practices, revealing the unusually strong unity of purpose between theory and practice that was the major source of his idiosyncratic interpretations.

PART II

PRACTICES

4

Gould and the Piano

GLENN GOULD WAS a pianist. This is, of course, ludicrously to state the obvious, yet it is worth emphasizing the point, for there have been persistent efforts, especially since his death, to exaggerate his achievements in other realms, sometimes at the expense of his piano playing. (It is certainly telling, given the age and size of the posthumous literature, that I am writing the first monograph in English on Gould as a performer.) Gould himself must accept some of the blame: he was always dismissing his instrument of choice as a mere workhorse, denigrating its idiomatic resources, ignoring large parts of its repertoire. But his disingenuous claims to the effect that he was a writer, composer, and broadcaster who played the piano in his spare time can only be taken as tongue-in-cheek polemic—or wishful thinking—for he gave performances that testified in every measure to pianistic gifts of the highest order. He was a pianist who imported a wide variety of ideas, musical and non-musical, into his métier, not a philosopher who happened to express himself through the piano. He may have preferred the latter view of himself, and some in the Gould literature have accepted it uncritically. But thirty years' practice could not make him a better than mediocre writer, while he was, from the beginning of his career, as fluent, accomplished, and natural a pianist as there ever was. We need only watch him play once to recognize an almost effortless mastery of the instrument. And we need only listen to him recall lovingly his boyhood Chickering, or detail endlessly the technical minutiae of his favourite Steinway (he was as fussy as Horowitz or Michelangeli or Kuerti about playing his own, specially adjusted instrument), to realize how much he needed the piano—and not just any piano, the *right* piano—to express his ideas. Even at his most pianistically eccentric, even where he seems almost desperate to convince himself and his listeners that he is doing anything other than playing a piano, there is never a doubt that he is truly at home on the piano, and only there. He may in fact have been the *most* pianistic of pianists, not the least—the pianist with the most intimate, not the most remote, relationship to the piano. As Jacques Drillon, the most vocal opponent of the cliché view of Gould as a kind of 'anti-pianist', put it, there was no happier pianist.

And yet, there remains a grain of truth in Gould's insistence on separating himself from the piano—or, at least, 'the piano' in the sense of conventional pianism. His idealism, his obsession with 'structure', his lack of interest in idiomatic piano

music—all this was not mere rhetoric; he did not make two-volume recordings of
Hindemith brass sonatas or Schoenberg songs just to mask some secret penchant
for nocturnes. And though it is true that only a great pianist could have expressed
so many unconventional pianistic ideas with such conviction at the piano, we
should not trivialize his unconventionality. He often used his pianistic gifts to
challenge basic assumptions about what was proper or appropriate in a piano
performance, and his recordings and pronouncements, throughout his career,
revealed some curious attitudes towards the instrument. Sometimes inspired by
imagined sonorities outside the piano, sometimes by an abstract conception of the
music with no direct instrumental referent, he developed many highly idiosyncratic keyboard techniques in order to communicate his ideas and interpretations.

It may seem self-evident that there is a contradiction between Gould the
professed idealist and Gould the instrumentalist: how could an idealist give
detailed instructions to piano tuners and technicians? In fact, there is no contradiction. As I suggested early on, idealism on its face implies nothing about one's
behaviour as a practising musician. It is simply a way of looking at music and
musical works, and at the relationship of music to sound. An idealist may believe
that music does not need to be played to have meaning, but this belief does not
necessarily imply some particular set of practices when it comes to actually playing.
(Recall Croce: the work of art is internal, mental, *whether or not* we actually play.)
In other words, there is no a priori 'idealist' style of performance, and many
musicians throughout history have reconciled an idealistic view of music with a
perfectly conventional approach to performance. Gould's idealism, I stress again,
was a matter of prioritizing musical values, of making physical realization dependent upon mental conception; it did not mean that he slighted the usual practical
considerations that every performer must address.

But while idealism *can* be reconciled with a conventional attitude towards
performance, Gould did not do so, and herein likes his distinction as a pianist. He
was not an armchair idealist: he sought ways of directly translating that aesthetic
position into practice, and one result was a very distinctive, idiosyncratic attitude
towards the piano. Perhaps most important, he viewed the piano as a 'neutral'
instrument that had little inherent character or colour (unlike orchestral instruments or even other keyboard instruments), a trait he found amenable to his
tendency to think about music in abstract terms. As he told Bruno Monsaingeon,
he sought to exploit the piano's 'predisposition to abstraction', the quality that
makes it suited to playing music for virginals, harpsichord, clavichord, organ, and
even chamber ensemble or orchestra.[1] (He was hardly the only pianist to have

---

[1] *Non, je ne suis pas du tout un excentrique,* 130 ('prédisposition à l'abstraction'); see also Monsaingeon, *Chemins de la
musique,* i. Schnabel, an early influence on Gould, also noted the 'neutrality' of the piano's tone, and its ability to suggest
other instruments: see K. Wolff, *Schnabel's Interpretation of Piano Music,* 154. On this subject, see also Payzant, 'The Glenn
Gould Outtakes', 311–13; and Tovell.

talked about the piano in such terms, incidentally.) The very blandness of the piano's tone, and the evenness of that tone from register to register, served Gould in his efforts to explore pieces in a speculative and analytical way. He professed to have no special affection for the piano as an instrument, and preferred to think of it as a vehicle for the communication of his ideas about music; he claimed to prefer the harpsichord and fortepiano, in terms of instrumental character and sonority.[2] He also viewed the piano as 'most successfully employed as a vehicle for contrapuntal, as opposed to homophonic, music': its neutral character, the evenness of its registers, and its dynamic capabilities made it particularly suited to the communication of polyphonic music.[3] Hence his lack of interest in much 'real' piano music, and his unconventional observation that the early-Romantic composers did not know how to use the piano 'properly', because they wrote for it in 'a melody-oriented, homophonic fashion', and put tonal effect before contrapuntal substance.[4] (Discussing his transcriptions of orchestral music by Wagner, he noted that those pieces that lent themselves most naturally to piano transcription were later works—the *Siegfried Idyll*, the *Vorspiel* from *Die Meistersinger*—that made their 'dramatic points through counterpoint, never through percussive effect', those that 'least depend upon orchestral color'.[5]) As I showed in Chapter 2, Gould used such views to argue for anachronistic performances of early music, especially contrapuntal music: he felt that the piano could reveal the substance of contrapuntal textures better than any more historically appropriate instrument.

Gould's view of the piano as a neutral or abstract instrument does not imply that he considered it inexpressive, or that he was unconcerned about matters of sound and expression when he played. His playing was always vital and expressive even in 'structural' music, like Bach fugues, for which he exploited the piano's neutrality. And of course, his expertise in such matters of pianistic technique as pedalling should never be forgotten. Yet he did seem less interested than most pianists in exploiting the usual tonal resources and idiomatic effects that the piano offers, like the sustaining pedal. Of course, he largely avoided the music that most fully showcases the piano, and he did not, as many pianists did and do, apply the standards and techniques of idiomatic piano music to all music that he played on the piano. He was not, I believe, being disingenuous when he said that he sought his interpretative ideas independent of the piano. He went so far as to describe his goal as 'separat[ing] yourself from the instrument in every possible way'—that is, avoiding an intrinsically pianistic conception of music.[6] Often, it seems, he tried to

---

[2] See Bester, 153; Johnson, 2; Mach, 102–3; and Page.

[3] *GGSL* 220. Schnabel also stressed that the piano was primarily a polyphonic instrument: see K. Wolff, *Schnabel's Interpretation of Piano Music*, 176.

[4] 'Mostly Music', 9; see also *GGR* 453.

[5] 'Transcribing Wagner', 52; *GGSL* 220. See also Cott, 67–70.

[6] Harris, 51.

use the piano to get beyond the piano, or even to get beyond instruments altogether, to present musical ideas as though freed entirely from instrumental trappings.

His motivations were not always so abstract, however. From the beginning of his career, he often sought pianistic analogies for the properties of other instruments, including the voice and even electronic instruments. He felt that the piano, especially in the recording milieu in which he worked, need not 'necessarily sound like a piano'.[7] He spoke at length on this subject in a 1980 interview:

So premise number one is to forget about the specific temptations of the piano, what one might call its 'natural resources.' Now, this obviously doesn't mean that I avoid all use of the pedal or something of the sort. On the contrary, the pedal may on occasion get you closer to an orchestral sonority, or a string quartet sonority, or whatever. But always in the back of my mind, certainly in my post-adolescent period, anyway, there has been a substitute sonority such as orchestra or string quartet to which I have tried to relate whatever I am doing, rather than approaching the music as keyboard music per se. This usually takes the form of superimposing a phrasing system that would be appropriate to the violin, or the 'cello if it's in the left hand, or whatever.[8]

Gould even suggested that 'there are very few composers of quality' who did not tend to imagine instrumental settings when composing for the piano:

when he was writing [the piano sonatas] Op. 2, Beethoven had just finished three piano trios [Op. 1]. He was working with chamber music. To me, the slow movement of [the Sonata in A major,] Op. 2, No. 2, is one of the most beautiful string quartet pieces ever written, and his mental imagery, even his sense of keyboard tactilia, perhaps, seems to have been influenced by chamber music. It really doesn't make sense to think [of] a piece like that as other than music to be shaped, bowed, phrased with some reference to that other performance system.[9]

Much of what was unconventional in Gould's piano style derived from his treating piano pieces as though they were transcriptions of imaginary originals otherwise scored. In this respect, he revived a practice common in nineteenth-century pedagogy, which encouraged pianists to emulate instruments and especially the human voice. But there were important distinctions. The Romantic way was to do so by fully exploiting the 'natural resources' of the piano, even in early music, through pervasive use of the sustaining pedal, legato phrasing, frequent dynamic inflection, and so on. But Gould's way was often to suggest analogies to other instruments by strikingly altering or suppressing those natural resources, straying far beyond the norms of idiomatic piano playing.

Referring to Gould's recordings of Bach's *Art of Fugue* on the organ (1962) and Handel's suites on the harpsichord (1972), Jonathan Cott noted that

    [7] NLC 2/58, 7–8.
    [8] Aikin, 25.
    [9] Ibid. 30. In this respect, he differed from Schnabel: see K. Wolff, *Schnabel's Interpretation of Piano Music*, 155–7. It is interesting to note that Beethoven did in fact transcribe his early Sonata in E major, Op. 14 No. 1, for string quartet, and needed to make relatively few alterations to do so.

you seem to work against the grain of the predominant temperamental characteristics of each instrument. For instance, on the harpsichord, where you can't easily duplicate the arched line and sustained legato of the piano, you seem to aim for just those two qualities. In your piano recordings you aim for the immediacy of attack provided more easily on the harpsichord. And on the organ, you produce a sense of spriteliness more characteristic of both the piano and harpsichord.[10]

Gould agreed that a 'cross-fertilization' of different keyboard influences (organ, harpsichord, clavichord) was a feature of his playing. To Cott's list, we might add the fortepiano. Gould noted that he used a great deal of soft pedal when playing Baroque and Classical music, including early Beethoven, 'in order to thin out the sound'—that is, by striking only two rather than three strings—and he defended the decision as appropriate both musically and historically.[11] The resulting sound, which he emphasized through mechanical adjustments to his instrument and various miking and recording techniques, definitely recalls the distinct registers of the fortepiano, especially the lightness of the high notes and the clarity and precision of the bass notes. Piero Rattalino has compared Gould's piano tone to that of an 1830 Graf fortepiano, the kind of instrument that Albert Schweitzer once recommended for performances of Bach.[12] In the pre-war Steinway grand piano (CD 318) that he used throughout the 1960s and 1970s, Gould admired the 'translucent sound', the 'clarity of every register', the 'very light action', and the incisiveness of articulation—all qualities reminiscent of the fortepiano.[13] He found concert pianos from the 1920s and 1930s generally more congenial than the more powerful post-war instruments.[14] And he often spoke in praise of the 1895 Chickering baby grand piano that he played in his youth, which had a discreet tone and what he called 'tactile grab and immediacy': a light, quick action with immediate damping.[15] His interest in the cross-fertilization of keyboard instruments even extended to short-lived experiments, in the early 1960s, with a so-called 'harpsi-piano', a piano with steel tacks in the hammers, intended to imitate the timbre of the harpsichord while preserving the action and dynamic capabilities of the piano.[16]

[10]   Cott, 48. Gould compared his preferred piano sound, rather unflatteringly, to that of 'an emasculated harpsichord', in a 1959 interview (Braithwaite, 28). On his organ and harpsichord playing, and their effects on his piano playing, see Guillard; Mach, 96; Tovell; and Payzant, *GGMM* 89–108. Incidentally, Michelangeli, another pianist admired for his clear, refined tone, also studied the organ, as well as the violin, and spoke of their influence on his piano playing.

[11]   Cott, 128–9.

[12]   See Rattalino, 368, 373, 376; cf. Schweitzer, i. 354.

[13]   Cott, 47.

[14]   See *GGSL* 191.

[15]   See McClure; and Payzant, *GGMM* 104–5.

[16]   Gould played the 'harpsi-piano' in an 8 April 1962 CBC television programme on Bach, performances from which appear in GGC v and viii. See the discussions of the 'harpsi-piano' in Kind, 56; and Payzant, *GGMM* 104. As he may have been aware, his 'harpsi-piano' was a revival of the tack-pianos or 'harpsichordized' pianos used occasionally by such composers as Mahler and Ravel, early in the twentieth century, to combine a harpsichord-like timbre with the projecting power needed in a concert hall.

The instrumental analogies of which Gould spoke are often apparent in his piano playing. (His notorious vocalizing and flamboyant conducting gestures at the keyboard may have derived in part from his striving after imagined instrumental conceptions.[17]) At times, the instrumental analogy seems to have operated without regard for the inherent qualities and limitations of the piano. For example, he played some works and movements so slowly as to confront the piano's inability to sustain tones infinitely, as though he had transferred directly to the piano, without compromise, interpretative ideas inspired by instruments with greater sustaining powers. When he chose unusually slow tempos for his piano recording of Wagner's *Siegfried Idyll*, he obviously had the orchestral original in mind (and indeed, he used the same tempos in his chamber-orchestra recording); he had to use considerable powers of suggestion to sustain in the listener's mind sounds that he could not physically sustain on the piano to the degree required by his interpretation. Yet, as Joseph Horowitz has rightly observed, it is in the piano performance more than the orchestral that one hears 'a wealth of living, breathing nuance', in which 'all the lines, even the improbably long ones, sing'.[18] The piano recording offers a powerful example at once of Gould's idealism directly influencing an interpretation, and of the remarkable pianistic gifts that allowed him to render that interpretation with conviction, vitality, and beauty.

Many Gould performances suggest that he was 'scoring' a work in his imagination as he played, and not only works in which an instrumental analogy was intended by the composer (for example, early keyboard pieces in the *style brisé* of the lute). His command of simultaneous articulations and tone colours in the rendering of counterpoint was often suggestive in this respect. The Beethoven movement that he singled out above for its quartet-like texture—the second movement of the Sonata in A major, Op. 2 No. 2—provoked such 'scoring' in his recorded performance (see especially bars 68 ff.). Sometimes the instrumental reference was more specific: his *secco* tremolos in the bass in the first movement of Beethoven's *Pathétique* Sonata, and in the Marcia Funebre from Beethoven's Sonata in A flat major, Op. 26, certainly suggest timpani rolls. In several ritornello passages in the second movement of Bach's Clavier Concerto No. 7 in G minor, Gould's use of '16-foot' and '32-foot' doubling of some pedal tones in the bass register suggests the reinforcement of pizzicato contrabass, or even timpani, recalling some of Bach's larger orchestral and choral movements.[19] He occasionally played a repeat of a passage or section of a Bach dance movement an octave higher than written,

---

[17] For Gould's comments on this matter, see Dubal, 183; and McClure.

[18] Horowitz, 136.

[19] See the studio recording as well as the CBC television performance, both from 1967. P. G. D., after observing the recording sessions, wrote of these octave doublings that 'Gould seemed to conjure up the tolling of a great, deep, resonant bell'.

'to give the impression of four-foot registration'.[20] His treatment of register on the piano could also be suggestive. In relatively stable polyphonic textures—for example, in fugues, or in some Classical sonata movements—he sometimes applied to individual lines expressive qualities that evoked distinctions of register in other instruments. Where, say, a tenor voice rose above middle C, he might impart a special urgency or intensity to that line, as though it were a bassoon or cello reaching into its upper register. (On the modern piano, of course, there is no change in tone colour from register to register, and one never strains to sound any note in any register.) The effect is often apparent where he emphasizes some inner-voice activity, as when a tenor voice reaches the top of its register on an accented chord seventh or ninth.

Only in a few cases did Gould specify the instrumental analogy behind an interpretation. Of his performance of the Prelude in E flat minor from *WTC* I, he noted that his rendering of many of the chords—quickly rolled but with a minimum of sustaining—was intended to evoke the strumming of a lute or guitar.[21] Such lute-like strumming was a given in his performances of virginal music, and there are many other Bach performances, mostly sarabandes and other slow movements, in both solo and chamber music, that suggest the lute. Most of Gould's instrumental effects seem to have been inspired by string instruments, not surprising given the string quartet's importance to him as a model of polyphonic texture. (Some of the musicians known to have influenced him at an early age, including Schnabel, Schweitzer, and Kirkpatrick, may have offered encouragement in this respect.[22]) When, in Monsiangeon's 1979 film *The Question of Instrument*, he demonstrates some of the phrasing options that a particular piece (Bach's Little Prelude in D major, BWV 936) offers to a pianist, he does so by explicit analogy with string bowings, including pizzicato. String techniques seem to have influenced many of his decisions about articulation. In the second movement of Bach's Italian Concerto, for example, he rejected the smooth phrasing with which many pianists and harpsichordists render the left-hand part; instead, he emphasized the separateness of the registers implicit within that part, playing the consecutive thirds in the tenor register smoothly, the low pedal tones staccato. A suggestion of string scoring is almost unavoidable—say, paired violas in the tenor register, pizzicato cello or bass below.

---

[20] Johnson, 2. For examples, see the Menuet II from the French Suite No. 1 in D minor, 1r–16r; the Menuet II from the Partita No. 1 in B flat major, 1r–8r; and three movements from the Partita No. 4 in D major (1979 film): Aria, 1r–4r, 8r–16r; Sarabande, 3r–8r; and Menuet, 1r–8r.

[21] See M. Meyer, 'Interview', 16.

[22] For example, Schweitzer, i. 365, writes: 'In general we may lay down the principle that in Bach every theme and every phrase must be delivered as if we were playing it on a bowed instrument. This holds good for the pianoforte not less than for the wood-wind instruments.' And Kirkpatrick, xxii, writes: 'For nearly all the keyboard music of Bach it is extremely illuminating to think in terms of string bowing.'

In the Sarabande from Bach's English Suite No. 5 in E minor (see CD ⑦), Gould's use of sharp staccato in the slow-moving bass part, against smoother articulation in the treble parts, strongly suggests pizzicato, including even staggered 'pizzicato double stops' in bars 13–14; he switches to 'arco' phrasing only near the end, at the high-point of expressive intensity.[23] The effect of 'scoring' is even stronger in his 1979 film performance of the Sarabande from Bach's Partita No. 4 in D major. In this slow, lyrical movement, in a suite that Gould singled out for its warmth, the performance is highly idiosyncratic by conventional standards of pianistic expression, in that he uses a great deal of détaché and staccato, often emphasizes lower voices at the expense of melody, and even plays some left-hand accompaniments an octave higher than written (see bars 3r–8r). But instrumental analogies make sense of the interpretation—analogies to pizzicato and arco strings, to the lute stop of a harpsichord, and to the four-foot registration offered by the harpsichord and organ. (Gould notes in the film that some of the figuration in the Sarabande recalls the lute.) The performance manages to be deeply expressive— even warm—while inverting the pianistic means by which such expression is usually achieved. Gould himself once referred to such use of détaché and staccato as his 'lute stop registration'.[24] That this 'registration' inspired some of his performances of slow music is further suggested by his use of the lute stop in three very slow movements in his harpsichord recording of suites by Handel: the Adagio from the F major suite, the Sarabande from the E minor suite, and the Air from the D major suite. It is probably analogies to pizzicato strings and lute stops that explains the unusual willingness of Gould (like Rosalyn Tureck before him) to use détaché and staccato articulation in pieces that were slow, gentle, intimate, even lyrical, and in which legato would normally be employed to achieve a *cantabile* effect; there are examples throughout his solo and ensemble Bach performances.

Gould even imitated the string player's ability to ease gradually into a note, an effect that is technically impossible on the piano. Often he landed solid chords in such a way that they were slightly broken, though not enough so to be perceived as truly arpeggiated; the result is that they seem to land 'diagonally', rather than truly vertically, counteracting to some degree the percussiveness of the instrument. He even attempted, on occasion, to mimic a true vibrato (as opposed to *Bebung* effect) on the piano.[25] Indeed, he insisted that at least two of his pianos—his 1895 Chickering, and a Steinway concert grand that he discovered in 1955—had slightly

---

[23]   Kirkpatrick, xxvi, suggests the possibility of using the lute stop in the left-hand part in Vars. 13 and 25 of the Goldberg Variations, both of which feature highly ornate, lyrical melodies above slower-moving bass and tenor parts. Gould may well have been influenced by this recommendation, to judge from his performances of these two variations (and many other works).

[24]   P.G.D.

[25]   Horowitz, 136, observes that Gould seems, paradoxically, to have tried to *reduce* vibrato in his one orchestral recording, of Wagner's *Siegfried Idyll.*

more space between keys than is usual, and could actually simulate a vibrato effect
if the keys were wiggled from side to side after being depressed. (To use Joseph
Roddy's terms, he preferred piano keys that were 'vertically tight' but 'laterally
loose'.[26]) In his films and television programmes, he can often be seen vibrating
depressed keys, especially in the lower register, as though executing vibrato on a
cello. As Payzant rightly points out, Gould's attempts at vibrato were technically
absurd: a pianist has no control of a tone once the hammer has struck the strings,
and, of course, he knew much more than this about the mechanism of his instrument.[27] Rather, the anecdote is revealing psychologically; it further suggests that
he sought inspiration from other instruments when he played even where it took
him beyond the physical capabilities of the piano.

Gould always spoke of being much less concerned about his piano's tone than
its action. In fact, he did not view tone colour, any more than articulation or
ornamentation, as a normative consideration, and certainly did not feel bound by
the tonal qualities appropriate to Romantic piano music. Rather, he made tone
colour, too, a function of his conception of a particular musical structure. In fact,
he claimed that 'tone will take care of itself' in a performance in which texture,
rhythm, dynamics, articulation, and other factors have been co-ordinated in the
service of a unified, coherent interpretation of the music.[28] He seems scarcely to
have thought of tone as a separate category at all, though from the Romantic era to
the present day it has often been considered the pianist's single most important
concern. The 'monochromatic' tonal palette, the 'coolness' of expression, that
many critics have observed is valid to a point, but is not applicable to all of his
performances. He intentionally chose to play in (so to speak) 'black and white' in
music that he sought to communicate primarily in terms of structural elements—
for example, works that might be seen as studies in counterpoint, whether from
the Renaissance, Baroque, or modern period. When he performed Sweelinck,
Bach, and Hindemith (among others), it was often in a monochromatic style
because he focused his attention primarily on the technical matters of contrapuntal
and motivic development, rather than on rhetorical effect or topical character or
instrumental flavour. Discussing his performance of selections from Bach's *Art of
Fugue* in Monsaingeon's 1980 film, he recalls Schweitzer's comments on this
music—'a still and serious world, deserted and rigid, without color, without light,
without motion'[29]—by analogy with his own pianistic realization of it as 'an
endless range of gray tints'. When he spoke of sound quality in such music, it was

[26]   See Roddy, 106–8.
[27]   See Payzant, *GGMM* 116; and see Gould's weak reply to Payzant in *GGR* 447. See also Payzant, 'The Glenn Gould
Outtakes', 310–13.
[28]   Page.
[29]   Schweitzer, i. 427. Incidentally, it appears that Gould's eye was no more attracted to vibrant colours than was his ear.

not so much about colour as refinement of sound (as in the reference above to a 'translucent' sound). A 'refined' sound was one that permitted maximum clarity of structure; it meant a sound that was pointed, clean-edged, not flabby or shimmering. In fact, when Gould talked about 'refined' sound he seems to have been talking more about articulation and phrasing than tone colour. Yet, in Strauss's melodrama *Enoch Arden*—and one could cite other of his early performances of nineteenth-century music—his piano playing was the opposite of monochromatic; indeed, he adopted a hyper-Romantic style that recalls earlier generations of pianists more than his own contemporaries. In the matters of tone, pianism, and expression, as in so many others, he characteristically flirted with both extremes of the spectrum. If, statistically, he did favour a monochromatic tonal palette or a 'refined' sound with unusual frequency, it was because of his special interest in the repertoire that he felt most appropriate to that style, and his relative lack of interest in Romantic piano music. In principle, he recognized that different styles of music demanded different approaches to the piano's resources.

It is obvious that Gould was not content to be thought of merely as a great pianist; he dreamed of great accomplishments as a philosopher, a writer, a composer. But in spite of some interesting work in these areas, in the end his real legacy remains his piano performances, and the coherent and highly individual aesthetic they embody. The quality of his piano playing never suffered from his ideas: even as he dismissed concerns like tone colour his playing was beautiful and varied in tone. His unusual piano style, his efforts to counteract the piano's 'natural resources' and conventional conceptions of what is properly 'pianistic', his endless tinkering with the mechanisms of his pianos—these did not, in the end, subvert the piano so much as broaden its range of idiomatic possibilities. For what is 'idiomatic' to the piano includes more than the sounds and techniques of nineteenth-century Romantic piano music; it includes Cage's preparing and Cowell's banging and Crumb's plucking; it includes whatever a piano can be made to do. In this respect, Drillon's comparison of Gould with Liszt is just: far from working against the piano or proving the irrelevance of the piano, Gould, like Liszt, developed a new pianistic language, a new way of playing the piano. (By saying this, however, I do not mean to repeat the common error of playing down his pianistic debts to Guerrero, Tureck, Schnabel, and others.) He was inextricably tied to the piano; it was only the nineteenth-century sense of the piano that he challenged. Gould may have been revealing his idealism in his 'abstract' explorations of counterpoint, or in those resonant silences in his super-slow performances, but he was also exploring new piano sounds and techniques, new kinds of pianistic beauty. And he must certainly have known it: there is no evidence that he ever intentionally wanted the music he played to sound bland or ugly or inexpressive. Even when he spoke of trying to get beyond the piano, or beyond instruments altogether, the result was never bad piano playing, even if it was highly eccentric. When he referred to his piano transcriptions as 'deorchestrations', he implied that he was removing instrumental trappings to make a kind of abstract statement about the music, yet the results of his efforts were in fact beautiful, eminently idiomatic piano arrangements—indeed, arrangements more creative and flattering pianistically than the literal transcriptions of Liszt.[30] But then, as I have noted before, Gould always needed first to rationalize the music he played, to satisfy his 'structural' values, before attending to pianistic matters; to do otherwise was, for him, to give a performance that was sloppy, indulgent, compromised, superficial—in short, 'Romantic', in the pejorative sense of the word. But however late in the creative process, attend to pianistic matters he did, and always with extraordinary results. For all his efforts to transcend the designation, Gould was, in the final analysis, a great pianist, and we would care little about his work and ideas had he not been.

---

[30] For Gould's remarks on Liszt's transcriptions, see 'Transcribing Wagner', 52; and Cott, 68–9.

5

Counterpoint

COUNTERPOINT WAS ONE of the most important factors in Gould's musical thought. It was crucial to his musical judgements, and he was renowned for his ability to clarify contrapuntal textures at the keyboard. He told Humphrey Burton in 1966 that he had 'an inordinate fondness for all music that is in the least contrapuntal',[1] and throughout his career he made comments to the effect that his interest in a piece of music depended greatly on the degree to which it was contrapuntal. For Gould, musical craftsmanship was almost synonymous with the development of musical material in a contrapuntal setting. As Peter Kivy notes, counterpoint has historically been closely allied with such musical values as technical skill, learning, economy, and the development of possibilities—and, moreover, 'since time out of mind, has been associated in the thinking of musicians with the profound and the serious'.[2] Gould's sympathy with this position was emphatic; indeed, he insisted that contrapuntally worked out music was superior not just aesthetically but ethically.

Gould played a wide variety of music, but the composers with whom he had a special affinity were invariably those with a pronounced contrapuntal bent: Byrd, Gibbons, Sweelinck, Bach, Haydn, Mendelssohn, Wagner, Brahms, Scriabin, Strauss, Schoenberg, Berg, Webern, Hindemith, Valen, Krenek. With composers who were more problematic for him (Mozart, Beethoven, the early Romantics), he tended to admire most those works which were explicitly contrapuntal, like Mozart's K. 394 fugue and Beethoven's *Grosse Fuge*. His taste in counterpoint always ran to more strict, formal, abstract works like fugues, and he showed no appreciation for the looser, more 'poetic' counterpoint of composers like Schumann and Chopin—the 'essentially pianistic and colouristic' counterpoint that Charles Rosen has recently analysed so trenchantly in *The Romantic Generation*.[3] Gould's Chopin, to recall a famous jibe of Schnabel's, was a 'right-handed genius'. Ever the idealist, he admired the counterpoint most appreciable on the printed page, the

---

[1] Burton, ii. For similar comments, see Mach, 98; M. Meyer, 'Interview', 17; and Page. The contrapuntal nature of Gould's thinking in even non-musical contexts has been the subject of some discussion in the biographical and critical literature.

[2] Kivy, *Music Alone*, 206. Discussing Mozart in 1978, Gould likewise equated 'a contrapuntal aspect' with 'a life of the spirit' (quoted in Angilette, 143).

[3] Rosen, *The Romantic Generation*, 672.

counterpoint least dependent upon the instrument or the disposition of the hand, but that of Schumann and Chopin is unequivocally *for the piano*, a counterpoint of pedals and thumbs and vibrating strings. (He could admire the *late*-Romantic counterpoint of Wagner and Strauss, however, perhaps because as a pianist there was automatically an element of abstraction in his appreciation of orchestral music.) I do not mean to suggest that there was any lack of vitality, beauty, or dramatic tension in Gould's contrapuntal playing—quite the contrary: he could make counterpoint *sing*. Listen to his early recording of the Praeludium from Bach's Partita No. 1 in B flat major, in CD ⑧: polyphonic lines emerge, evolve, and recede (sometimes unobtrusively, sometimes dramatically) within a continuously transparent texture, yet even as the articulation remains pointed and the tone gentle and clean-edged, the playing is also, in its own discreet way, sonorous, lyrical, deeply expressive. Even in his drier and more closely miked later Bach recordings, with their often nakedly exposed textures, the contrapuntal playing still sings powerfully—if peculiarly. Still, there is no question that Gould's was always an italicized, even didactic approach to counterpoint, not a 'poetic' one; he sought a sun-drenched clarity of texture, not the more mysterious 'shimmer' of inner voices that Rosen observes in so much early-Romantic piano music. It was the clarity of analysis made manifest, and he applied it to all repertoire, including the Romantic. There is a real continuity of purpose in his performances of music from different periods: whether in Bach or Schoenberg, Byrd or Hindemith, Mozart or Wagner, we hear the same leanness and transparency of texture, the same dissection and projection of linear components.

Gould probably did conceive of counterpoint initially as *Augenmusik*, but when it came to playing contrapuntal music he may have had an instrumental model in mind—not the piano, but the string quartet. He greatly admired piano music that suggested such a model. Of Beethoven's Op. 26 and 28 sonatas, and Op. 34 variation set, he observed that 'every texture is as carefully worked out as it would be in a string quartet'.[4] Beethoven's Op. 2 sonatas, he said on another occasion, 'have an incredibly pure, quartetlike concept of voice leading which you never find in the later sonatas, except perhaps for isolated moments like the first movement of Op. 101 or the second movement of [Op.] 109'; he said in a 1981 interview that to reveal this counterpoint was, in fact, one motivation for his recording Op. 2.[5] And of course, his only major published composition was the highly contrapuntal String Quartet, Op. 1. Historically, the quartet texture has long been associated with 'pure music' and with counterpoint. For nineteenth-century theorists, the string quartet was seen as the perfect setting for polyphonic ideas, and so became the epitome of absolute music: it represented the 'cerebral' and 'intellectual' in

[4] *GGR* 459.

music; it realized the 'ideal side of instrumental music', 'the non-material world of the mind'; it was 'a thought-music of pure art'.[6] There is a natural progression, in other words, from Gould's idealism to his fondness for counterpoint to his special admiration for the quartet texture. It should not surprise us that he took the quartet as a model that he applied, as much as possible, to the keyboard music he played—the more so as he got older. Dale Innes, in her study of Gould's preserved performances of the Goldberg Variations, has demonstrated that while he tended to emphasize, even exaggerate, contrapuntal details in the bass and inner voices in the early part of his career, he tended later to make subtler and more discriminating contrapuntal points within a relatively more equalized polyphonic texture. Of the six performances that Innes analyses, she observes the greatest overall transparency, the greatest degree of equality of voices, in the latest, the 1981 studio recording.[7]

In seeking that equable disposition of voices that he so admired in the quartet texture, Gould often played even the most outwardly homophonic music with no less interest in linear action than when he played fugues. His performance style amounts to an extension (or exaggeration) of the commonplace that homophonic textures can be analysed in terms of the voice-leading they imply, and he often brought this voice-leading strongly into the foreground, whether or not the composer wanted it there. All music that conformed to norms of modal or tonal voice-leading offered him the option of contrapuntal performance. As a result, conventional tune-with-accompaniment hierarchies often dissolve in his performances, in favour of a more balanced dialogue between voices. Discussing Oskar Morawetz's *Fantasy in D* with the composer, Gould at one point rejected the conventional tune-with-accompaniment texture that Morawetz wanted. 'All the voices are equally important,' he insisted; 'there are no main voices.'[8] Speaking of his controversial Mozart performances, he told Burton that when playing music not inherently contrapuntal he tried 'to make it contrapuntal; I try to invent happenings for inner voices, even if they don't really exist.'[9] And in a 1968 letter on the same subject, he challenged the whole idea of conceiving of melody apart from 'the component parts of a harmonic environment'.[10] Throughout Mozart's sonatas, he made a point of enlivening inner-voice activity in what are generally two-voice textures with a treble melody and accompaniment. Often he gave special emphasis to the bass line, dwelling less on lyrical melody; often he drew implicit inner voices out of accompanimental figures, or brought out the voice-leading implications of the chord tones that flesh out the harmonies. Ex. 5.1 is typical: Gould enhances

[5]   Ibid. 36–7; M. Meyer, 'Interview', 17. See also Aikin, 25, 30.
[6]   These phrases are quoted in Dahlhaus, *The Idea of Absolute Music*, 16.
[7]   See Innes, 112–21.
[8]   Elliott, 'Glenn Gould and the Canadian Composer', 1. See also Ostwald, 94–5.
[9]   Burton, ii.
[10] *GGSL* 109.

Ex. 5.1. Mozart, Sonata in F major, K. 332/II

the contrapuntal profile of the Alberti bass, sustaining and dynamically accenting certain notes to create integral bass and tenor lines, and so implying a texture of three rather than two real voices.[11] (His increased emphasis on the tenor voice beginning at bar 5 serves to highlight the minor-mode variant of the theme.)

It is revealing to contrast Gould's treatment of Alberti basses with Rosen's description of the technique:

This accompaniment blurs the independence both of the three contrapuntal voices which it theoretically contains and of the chordal or homophonic harmony which it supposedly illustrates. It breaks down the isolation of the voices by integrating them into one line, and of the chords by integrating them into a continuous movement. Linear form is essentially the isolation of the elements of music, and the history of music, until our day, may be seen as a gradual breakdown of all the various isolating forces of the art—contrapuntal independence of voices, homophonic progression, closed and framed forms, and diatonic clarity.[12]

The breakdown of linear thinking in the Alberti bass, as Rosen describes it, is something that Gould, with his musical priorities drawn largely from Renaissance, Baroque, and twelve-tone counterpoint, sought to 'correct' in performance, by isolating the voice-leading components rather than playing arpeggiated block

---

[11] This method of sustaining notes past written length in order to bring out a voice was referred to by Heinrich Schenker as 'Handpedal'; see Rothstein, 18.

[12] Rosen, *The Classical Style*, 29.

harmonies. In short, he resisted the integration of several parts into one that would seem to be the very point of the Alberti bass. John A. Sloboda, in a study of the cognitive psychology of music, observes that in a familiar piece of homophonic music

each chord may be so well known that the listener has the possibility of *constructing* a non-focal line by picking out a given note from each chord and integrating a new line. In such cases all the contrapuntal lines may be *implicit* in what a listener knows, simply awaiting a reorganization of his knowledge to be made explicit. In such a way may a listener suddenly realize that the 'accompaniment' of a well-known passage actually has its own melodic integrity. It is not that there are notes present which he has not noticed before. It is simply that he has not heard them *as* melody before.[13]

Gould's performances often seem dedicated to making explicit for listeners just such implicit contrapuntal possibilities.

There are countless examples among his recordings, not only in Alberti basses but in every kind of accompanimental figuration, even in block chords. Many of his contrapuntal manipulations have significant rhythmic implications, especially where (as in Ex. 5.1) the implicit voices he brings out move more slowly than the part as written. Often, he gave less attention to a busily ornamented melody, to which the ear is naturally drawn anyway, and more attention to slower bass or tenor parts that might otherwise be ignored; or he might use dynamic accents to bring forward an inner voice at a higher rhythmic level that reinforces a basic harmonic progression.[14] By placing special emphasis on the lower voices, Gould treated the melody as the secondary element within the texture—contrary to conventional performance practice, and (usually) to the score. But by bringing forward those slower-moving voices in which the harmonic action is defined, he allowed the listener to perceive the larger processes of modulation and cadence. In this way, he directed the listener's attention to higher rhythmic levels, larger units of structure, longer spans of time, which in part accounts for the perception of many listeners and critics that he was able to convey a sense of musical architecture on a broad scale.

Gould traced his fondness for counterpoint, and his treatment of the piano as a primarily contrapuntal instrument, in part to the influence of his childhood encounters with the organ. As he said in 1962, 'Because I started at the organ very young, I still think of music as being played by three hands—the feet acting as the third hand. So I think of music as more contrapuntally divisible than pianists

---

[13] Sloboda, 171.

[14] For two of many examples of the first technique, from the music of Bach, see Vars. 13 and 25 in the 1981 recording of the Goldberg Variations. For the second technique, see, for example, Bach's Italian Concerto/III, 155–66 (in CD [26]), where he hammers out downbeats with his left thumb, creating a tenor voice at the semibreve level that points up large-scale cycle-of-fifths motion.

generally do.'[15] Organ training thus gave him 'a sense of horizontal line rather than vertical line', and 'an acute sense of bass line and of pedal thinking'—the latter an important characteristic of both his piano playing and his compositions.[16] In his 1974 interview with Jonathan Cott, he agreed that his interest in bass line was one common factor in his perception of music as different as that of Bach, Mozart, Brahms, and Scriabin, and reflected the high priority he gave to tonal structure when analysing a work.[17] Part of his admiration for the music of Strauss was for the 'sure-footedness' and integrity of Strauss's bass lines, compared with those of other post-Wagnerian composers.[18] (Given his interest in bass lines and inner voices, it is worth mentioning that he was left-handed.)

Another important source of Gould's contrapuntal piano style was surely one that he never acknowledged: Romantic piano playing. A propensity for exploring voices and details within a texture was characteristic of many Romantic pianists, at least as early as Chopin, and is apparent in the recordings of such late-nineteenth- and early-twentieth-century pianists as Cortot, Godowsky, Hofmann, Moiseiwitsch, de Pachmann, Aleksander Michalowski and his pupils (among them Landowska), Gould's youthful hero Schnabel, and the Bach specialist Harold Samuel.[19] (The enormous impact of Rosalyn Tureck's Bach style on Gould, in this respect among others, must also be acknowledged, though she sits a little uneasily in the present company.) Like Gould, Hofmann was notably intent on revealing independent inner voices, and on giving unusual and sometimes surprising attention to accompanimental parts; Godowsky went as far as to compose new counterpoints for some of Chopin's works, and he was not alone in this practice. Gould's fondness for emphasizing dissonances and their resolutions, cross-relations, and the like when they occur in inner voices was shared by many Romantic pianists, and was recommended by Schenker and Schnabel, among others.[20] No less Romantic was his lush continuo playing in Bach's concertos and chamber music, in which he often added his own counterpoints or even wove in melodic ideas borrowed from other instrumental parts.[21] Though exploration into musical textures is not nearly so characteristic of post-war piano playing, it was still characteristic of some pianists in the Romantic style who lived into the later twentieth century: Cherkassky (a

---

[15] Asbell, 91.

[16] Bester, 153; Burton, ii. See also *GGR* 383; and Tovell.

[17] See Cott, 51.

[18] See Burton, iv; and *GGR* 87–8, 97, 455.

[19] Though Gould often acknowledged the influences of Schnabel and Tureck, it is tempting to infer the influence of Samuel, too, whose Bach playing often sounds as if it might have served him as a model. But to my knowledge, he never acknowledged Samuel in these terms.

[20] See Rothstein, 14; and K. Wolff, *Schnabel's Interpretation of Piano Music*, 47.

[21] Some of the scores preserved in the NLC show Gould making sketches for his busier continuo parts: see Bach's Brandenburg Concerto No. 5 (NLC Scores 9/4 and 9/5); the cantata *Widerstehe doch der Sünde*, BWV 54 (NLC Scores 1/11); and the Violin Sonata No. 6 in G major/II (NLC Scores 8/3).

pupil of Hofmann's), Horowitz, Michelangeli, Nyiregyházi, Richter. For Gould as for Romantic pianists, texture could be as much a focus of interest, and as open to creative interpretation, as rhythm, dynamics, phrasing, or any other aspect of performance practice. So if his intense interest in counterpoint was unusual among pianists of his generation, it was hardly unprecedented.

Yet his counterpoint also differed significantly from that of the Romantics, and can be considered in part a reaction to it, especially after he stopped giving concerts. That stark, analytical quality of the later Gould's counterpoint certainly had less in common with 'expressive' Romantic polyphony than with the self-conscious anti-Romanticism of the neo-Classicists. Richard Taruskin made just such a distinction in a review of Gould's recording with Leonard Rose of Bach's viola da gamba sonatas. Comparing Gould's priorities with those of Casals, he observed a movement away from 'singing' and towards 'texture'—more specifically, towards a contrapuntal texture realized 'in a crystalline and eerily idealized way', as 'a play of pure sound-pattern'.[22] Furthermore, the degree and extent of Gould's contrapuntal experiments were generally greater than in Romantic performance. But most important, he challenged the Romantic assumption (clear in both the written and recorded evidence) that explorations of inner voices should take place within a context in which the primacy of treble melody is taken for granted. In Romantic playing, unusual textures were usually brief intrusions into a style that was overwhelmingly oriented towards singing melody. Chopin, for example, looked upon piano playing as principally a kind of 'singing' with the fingers, and the influential legacy of Theodor Leschetizky was an emphasis on expressive melody, on tonal beauty and variety, above all. Gould's intention, by contrast, was often precisely to upset the conventional balance of parts, and not only as a momentary variation: often all voices seem more or less equal, for long passages or even whole movements or pieces, and not only in contrapuntal works. The primacy of melody is constantly challenged in his performances. His playing of accompanimental figuration was often unusually loud, and the relationship of parts in his performances tended to be more equable for longer periods of time than in the playing of any Romantic pianist. (Only in Romantic music was he closer to Romantic practice, especially early in his career.) In this respect, his counterpoint differs from that of the Romantics in kind as well as degree.

In arguing against a melody-oriented piano style in the music of Mozart, Gould reasoned that the 'more singable, likeable and memorable the tune one encounters the less likely it is that that particular melodic strain will require any special emphasis', and so the freer one is to explore other parts of the texture.[23] The

---

[22] Taruskin, 304.
[23] *GGSL* 109.

observation has a sound scientific basis in cognitive psychology. Sloboda, for example, writes that, 'all other things being equal, it is the line with the highest pitch range that tends to be focally processed'; moreover, a long tradition of melody-oriented music 'has resulted in a learned disposition to attend to the upper voice when there are no strong counter-signals'.[24] The exaggerating of lower parts in many Gould performances suggests an awareness that 'strong counter-signals' are needed to break conventional listening habits.

Unusual textures abound in Gould's performances, and his reasons for exploring latent counterpoint varied according to the context. As he told Cott, he found that the most structurally interesting or important musical material at a particular moment was often 'something that happens to occur not in the upper voice but rather in some other voice—like the tenor, for example'.[25] (He did have a special fondness for the register controlled by what Brahms called the 'tenor thumb'.) He often made explicit contrapuntal lines implied within a single voice, or clarified lines present but hidden within a busy texture (in this, solo Bach performances by string players might have served him as models). Ex. 5.2 is drawn from the music of Bach, in which Gould brought forward implicit counterpoint as a matter of course. His uncanny command of keyboard texture is evident here: in what is notated as a busy two-part texture, he realizes four distinct voices each at its own dynamic level, emphasizing at the crotchet-level bass and alto voices that move in tandem. His analysis of the components of the texture is by no means controversial, but in performance he exaggerates his point, dynamically and rhythmically, so that the listener unequivocally hears the new alto and bass voices *as* voices. In Sloboda's terms, the exaggeration of these voices is a 'counter-signal' alerting the listener to hear more than two voices within the two notated parts.

In some cases, Gould was more creative in revealing new contrapuntal strands. In most keyboard music, integrity of part-writing is not strictly maintained: the number of real voices fluctuates, and one cannot speak of consistently independent voices, as in a fugue. Gould often 'corrected' fluctuating textures by incorporating notes from several distinct but incomplete voices into a single, coherent counter-melody never intended as such by the composer. In a texture of melody, bass, and fluctuating harmonic filler, he might draw an integral contrapuntal line from that filler, creating the illusion of three real voices. The effect can be heard often in his performances of Mozart's sonatas; it 'adds vitamins to the music', as he told Burton.[26] In Ex. 5.3, the circled notes, which he brings out to form an independent voice in the left-hand part, are all within the same register, but in fact technically

---

[24] Sloboda, 172, 174. L. B. Meyer, *Emotion and Meaning in Music*, 187–8, also emphasizes the role of the 'past experience' of the 'practiced listener' in creating conventional expectations in homophonic contexts.

[25] Cott, 54.

[26] Burton, ii. Gould may have adapted this turn of phrase from Schoenberg, 115.

Ex. 5.2. Bach, Toccata in D major, BWV 912

Ex. 5.3. Mozart, Sonata in D major, K. 284/III, Var. 1 (1968 recording)

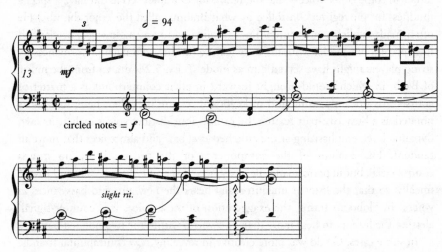

belong to three different voices: first bass, then tenor, then alto. (He adds a note to the score, a g' on the last beat of bar 16, to clarify the transfer of his strand from tenor to alto position.) Many examples of this technique also appear in his performances of virginal music, in which the prominence of imitative counterpoint does not necessarily imply strict adherence to a given number of real voices. In the first strain of Byrd's Sixth Pavan (see CD 9), he links the alto motive of bars 9–12 (which imitates the soprano of bars 8–11) with the tenor voice in bars 13–14, then reconnects this voice with the alto register in bars 14–15; a minor revision to the notes in bar 14 draws more attention to the single polyphonic strand he creates in the middle of the texture. This pavan and galliard offer, moreover, some discreet and beautiful examples of a 'trick' that was no less a trademark of Gould's playing than it was of Horowitz's: the illusion that more than two hands are playing. To be sure, the 'trick' was considerably less self-aggrandizing in Gould's case; his was not the sort of 'look-Ma-three-hands' playing that had audiences buzzing when Horowitz played his transcription of *Stars and Stripes Forever.* But Gould's feat was none the less impressive, technically as well as musically: listen, in the closing strains of the Sixth Galliard, as he easily, casually draws integral voices from harmonic filler and clearly distinguishes them from both bass and treble, pointedly opening up the music for close inspection yet never disturbing the overall atmosphere of tenderness, intimacy, and gentle humour.

One could say that Gould's interest in revealing the linear components of musical textures (like Schenker's) reflected his strong analytical mindset. Certainly his contrapuntal decisions often serve as signposts that make musical relationships unusually clear to the listener. In Ex. 5.4, his drawing out of the tenor voice bracketed in bar 158 reveals its derivation, in terms of rhythm and contour, from the sequential theme bracketed in the treble and bass voices in bars 156–7. In Ex. 5.5, he places great dynamic emphasis on a truncated appearance of the head motive of the fugue subject, which anticipates the full entry of the subject in the same register. The gesture is strikingly unusual on Bach's part, though one that a harpsichordist or organist would have difficulty emphasizing (bass and tenor voices overlap in the low register). Gould, typically, preferred to use the resources of the piano to exaggerate for the sake of analytical clarity, rather than to assume that the natural disposition of voices on a historically appropriate instrument offered the best solution. (His tendency strongly to accent buried augmentations of fugue subjects suggests the same reasoning.) There are times when Gould's contrapuntal playing has almost the character of an analytical graph. In Ex. 5.6a, he uses dynamics to clarify the relationships between different voices and registers. His performance implies an analysis of the new, higher melodic line in bars 44–5 as an outgrowth of the ornamental descending-third figure in bar 43, with the melodic line of bars 41–4 retreating into an inner voice in bars 45–6.[27] (This interpretation points up the implied cross-relation between e♭' and e♮' in bars 44–5, indicated in the example by a dotted line.) It is interesting to compare the diverging performance in his much earlier recording of the same passage (Ex. 5.6b), in which he suggests that a single melodic line in the right hand moves from one register to another in bar 44, while the descending-third figures remain purely ornamental. The later performance in Ex. 5.6a demonstrates not only an alternative analysis, but his increased fondness later in life for maintaining a quartet-like discrimination of registers.

Gould used a variety of performance techniques to clarify real or implied counterpoint. In most of the examples already mentioned, he used dynamic emphasis to give certain lines or notes a privileged position within the texture; this is, of course,

---

[27] See Hagestedt, 26, for a similar example from Mozart's K. 330 sonata.

Ex. 5.4. Brahms, Concerto No. 1 in D minor/I (1962 New York concert)

Ex. 5.5. Bach, *WTC* I, Fugue in B minor

the most natural and common way to make contrapuntal points on the piano. In early music, moreover, the piano permitted him to use subtle dynamic distinctions within larger dynamic terraces—what Schenker called 'layered dynamics'—in the service of contrapuntal clarity.[28] But articulation and rhythm were always at least as important to him when it came to clarifying counterpoint. His ability to impart a distinctive profile and character simultaneously to several voices was frequently praised by critics, and was as much a matter of phrasing as volume. Robert P. Morgan, in a review of Gould's recording on harpsichord of four Handel suites, writes that he 'depended far less than most of his colleagues upon purely dynamic

[28] On Schenker's concept of layered dynamics, see Rothstein, 10, 26–7 (n. 19). Gould discusses this pianistic option in Johnson, 2.

Ex. 5.6. Haydn, Sonata No. 49 in E flat major/II: (*a*) 1981 recording; (*b*) 1958 recording

differentiation—a pianistic device not applicable to the harpsichord—for the definition of complex contrapuntal textures, preferring rather to rely principally upon a careful rendering of the unique shape, character, and inner articulation of the various polyphonic voices. It is an approach eminently suited to the harpsichord.'[29] Through the frequent use of non-legato articulation, and extremely discreet use of the sustaining pedal (where used at all), Gould inserted 'breathing room' into his textures, preventing voices from blurring together and losing their

[29] Morgan, 'Glenn Gould, Extraordinary Harpsichordist', 84.

individual character. (Innes observes how Gould made greater use of non-legato articulation in denser contrapuntal textures.[30]) Rhythmic accents also played a role: a slight holding or clipping of a note often served to draw attention to a particular register, or to draw out components for a new voice from an existing one.

Gould frequently staggered vertical sonorities in order to clarify counterpoint, in a variety of ways and in music of every style. He was generally very casual about breaking intervals and chords, sharing the late-Romantic penchant for (in Robert Hill's words) 'the relaxed alignment of voices on the beat'.[31] In his lute-inspired performances of virginal music he did so as a matter of course, creating a basic texture of arpeggiated accompaniment within which motives and points of imitation could be brought out more effectively than if the accompaniments were realized as solid chords. And he revived the old practice of 'melodic rubato', the expressive dislocation of bass and melody notes that are written as simultaneous (almost always with the bass note anticipating the melodic note). As Robert Philip writes, 'The rhythmic dislocation of melody from accompaniment is one of the most obvious features of much early twentieth-century piano playing.' The practice apparently had its roots in the very beginnings of Romantic piano playing (it was associated with Chopin), was attributed in written records to many pianists (including Brahms), and could still be heard often in concerts and recordings until about the 1920s (most notoriously, those of Paderewski). But, continues Philip, melodic rubato 'has been firmly discouraged in the late twentieth century, and failure to play the left and right hands together is now generally regarded as care-lessness'.[32] (The practice is still used, however, by many modern harpsichordists, as a substitute for dynamic emphasis: I have heard the Aria from the Goldberg Variations played on the harpsichord with a degree of melodic rubato that would have made Paderewski blush.) Once again, Gould can be seen as reviving a Romantic performance practice but with important differences. For one thing, his use of melodic rubato did not imply as much flexibility of tempo as it did among Romantic pianists: he often incorporated the practice within a relatively strict rhythmic framework. Also, he used melodic rubato more often to clarify lines than to accent a melody—the usual Romantic rationale, according to Philip. But Gould was aware of the expressive implications of staggered vertical sonorities, which have an effect analogous to multiple-stopping on a string instrument. There are many examples in his recordings, not all of them in Romantic music, in which he seems

---

[30] See Innes, 116. The idea of '*durchbrochene Arbeit*', which has been applied metaphorically to music by some musicologists, is perhaps relevant to this style of performance. As Mary Whittall writes, the term 'belongs to the vocabulary of a number of crafts such as ceramics and fine metalwork, and refers to decorative pierced work, filigree and the like, all of which have the effect of lightening the texture by literally making holes in it' (translator's note in Dahlhaus, *Ludwig van Beethoven*, 152).

[31] Hill, 39.

[32] Philip, 47; see, more generally, 42–69 on melodic rubato, and 221–3 on the origins of the practice.

to equate degree of dislocation between voices with degree of expressive intensity. In his heady performance of Brahms's Intermezzo in A minor, Op. 118 No. 1 (see CD [5]), or, more subtly, in his recording of the Intermezzo in B flat minor, Op. 117 No. 2, his use of melodic rubato and arpeggiation contribute greatly to the musical tension.

In an interview on the subject of Mozart, Gould acknowledged criticism of his tendency to roll block chords in homophonic textures, but insisted that the mannerism 'originates in a desire to keep the contrapuntal spirit alive, to emphasize every possible connection between linear events'.[33] In a later interview, he said, on the same subject:

I do it in order to try to deliver a certain load of information in such a way that each separate component of the vertical block of the chord carries its own specific weight. This is particularly true in the lower regions of the keyboard. To me, there is a potential ugliness about the sonority of the lower keyboard, especially in Rococo repertoire, the period around Mozart and Haydn when chords began to appear in the texture in lieu of contrapuntal thinking. But more importantly, there is in such chord writing, embryonically anyway, a contrapuntal idea, if the music is good and if the composer knows what he's doing. There is the sense that the chord is the summation of several linear directions, which are not specifically spelled out in the way that a Baroque composer would spell them out, but which are present nevertheless. There is a sense of direction, a sense that a certain note within the chord has a connection with another note that was two bars back, or whatever. And by arpeggiating the chord in some way, one can weight it so as to establish the linear direction in a way that one cannot do if one simply plays a clump of four notes simultaneously.[34]

Gould's arpeggiations sometimes count among the 'counter-signals' he used to draw the listener's ear to an unexpected part of a texture: arpeggiation might help to draw attention to the beginning of a new voice in a new register, to keep voices clear as they cross hands and registers, to emphasize a theme where it enters as an inner voice. Precedent for this sort of arpeggiation can be found not only in Romantic performances but in Romantic scores: Chopin and Liszt, for example, commonly indicated broken intervals and rolled chords (sometimes along with dynamic accents) to draw attention to voices that might otherwise be lost in the texture. Characteristically, Gould took the practice to unusual extremes; he was more finicky and idiosyncratic when it came to clarifying lines, and his rationales for doing so varied widely. In Ex. 5.7, he weights and staggers the final chord to achieve motivic closure, emphasizing the final resolution in the tenor voice of the motive which opens the Intermezzo.[35] The unusual on-the-beat arpeggiations in

[33]   GGR 36.
[34]   Aikin, 26.
[35]   See also his fussy arpeggios in the closing bars of the following works: Byrd, 'Voluntary: for my Lady Nevell'; Byrd, First Pavan; Byrd, 'Hugh Aston's Ground'; Gibbons, Fantasia in C; Gibbons, 'Pavan: Lord Salisbury' (strain 2, 1974 film); Sweelinck, 'Fitzwilliam' Fantasia; Bach, WTC I, Prelude in B minor; and Brahms, Ballade in B minor, Op. 10 No. 3.

Ex. 5.7 Brahms, Intermezzo in A major, Op. 118 No. 2

Ex. 5.8. Brahms, Ballade in D major, Op. 10 No. 2

Ex. 5.8, from the closing section of Brahms's Ballade in D major, Op. 10 No. 2, can only be understood in light of Gould's performance of the whole work. In the outer 'andante' sections of this Ballade, he gives the music a distinctive 'colour' by prominently highlighting the alto register, including fussy and idiosyncratic arpeggiations that emphasize the alto register on downbeats at the expense of the treble (in the closing section, see bars 124–5, 128, 130, and 136). The arpeggios in Ex. 5.8 begin to make sense in this context: as he plays them, the emphasis is on the alto voice, the lowest note of each chord, the upper notes following more casually.

Gould's most unusual arpeggiations suggest that contrapuntal clarity was his highest priority. In the second half (bars 10–18) of the Prelude in B flat major from *WTC* I (see CD 10), he keeps the rhythmic profile of the treble melody largely intact by striking melodic notes alone on the beats, fitting other chord tones

Ex. 5.9. Bach, Chromatic Fantasy in D minor (1979 film)

around the beats in various ways. (In bars 17–18, he also accents rhythmically the new melodic activity in the alto and tenor voices.) The arpeggios allow him clearly to distinguish melodic and harmonic roles, even with the considerable liberties he takes with the tempo. His most distinctive arpeggio type, what I call a 'bordered' arpeggio, is an extension of this principle: he strongly polarizes soprano and bass voices while treating other chord tones as harmonic filler; he plays the outer voices—the most important voices in the texture—in time, on the beat, and slightly louder, allowing the inner voices to fall, less precisely and more quietly, between the beats.[36] As in the Prelude in B flat major, the resulting texture is improvisatory in character, but controlled in terms of counterpoint and rhythm. This 'bordered' arpeggio contributed significantly to many Gould performances, in works both virtuosic and (more often) lyrical.[37] He used it to great effect in his performances of Bach's Chromatic Fantasy. The freedom with which he interpreted the chords that Bach marks for arpeggiation is greater than that sanctioned by modern, published realizations of the chords, but is entirely typical of Romantic performances.[38] (Mendelssohn said of these arpeggios, 'I take the liberty to play

---

[36] Troeger, 139, writing after Gould's death, recommends this arpeggio type as an option for harpsichordists: 'In some contexts, playing the bass and soprano together (or slightly fringed) and following with the remaining chordal members ensures the beat placement and distributes the chord as well.'

[37] See e.g. the Sarabandes from Bach's English Suites Nos. 1, 4, and 6; the Preludes in D major, D minor, and E flat minor from *WTC* I; the passages marked for arpeggiation in the Air from Handel's Suite for Harpsichord in D minor (Var. 5); and the closing bars of the Allegro from the Suite for Harpsichord in E minor.

[38] See e.g. the realizations of the arpeggios suggested in Badura-Skoda, 455–64; Czaczkes, 23–37; David, *Anhang*, 6; Mantel, 149–52; and Schenker, 3–5, 31–7. (See also the comments of von Dadelsen and Kreutz quoted in Badura-Skoda, 453, 455.) Gould's realizations are freer than even the more 'artistic' among these suggestions (Badura-Skoda, Mantel, Schenker). Precedent for a straightforward, up-and-down realization of the arpeggios can, of course, be taken from Bach's own realization of the first arpeggio in bar 27.

Ex. 5.10. Scriabin, 'Désir', Op. 57 No. 1 (1972 recording)

them with all possible *crescendos*, and *pianos*, and *fortissimos*, pedal of course, and to double the notes in the bass,' and he specifically recommended a kind of 'bordered' arpeggio.[39]) Gould varies the speed and direction of arpeggiation, repeats some chord tones, adds passing tones, and treats tempo and dynamics freely. In fact, his performance of these arpeggios—and not for the first time in his career—recalls

[39]   Letter of 14 Nov. 1840 in Mendelssohn, 216–18.

one of the Romantic predecessors whose work he denigrated: Landowska.[40] But in the later 'Recitativ' section, beginning at bar 49, he also asserts his more characteristic priorities: he uses his special 'bordered' arpeggio to clarify the voice leading and rhythmic position of many chords, setting melodic and bass motion in relief and at the same time emphasizing many accented dissonances. (See Ex. 5.9. Some of the earlier writers on this subject recommend playing these chords with no arpeggiation at all.) Moreover, the arpeggios create a texture that (surely not coincidentally) recalls the Baroque recitative, suggesting a treble soloist, a sustaining bass, and rolled continuo chords.

As with other idiosyncrasies among Gould's performance practices, the 'bordered' arpeggio was more common later in his career. (It appeared for perhaps the first time in his 1956 recording of Beethoven's Sonata in E major, Op. 109, third movement, bar 14.) It began to appear often, in a variety of musical contexts, in his recordings from around the mid-1960s, and was not confined to Baroque music: it appears in recordings of works by Mozart, Beethoven, Brahms, Strauss, Sibelius—even Berg and Scriabin (see Ex. 5.10). But regardless of repertoire, this 'bordered' arpeggio served the same function of clarifying rhythm and counterpoint within an improvisatory texture. It was characteristic of Gould to have taken a detail of performance practice normally treated spontaneously and worked out its possibilities for illuminating a musical texture.

[40] See her famous 1935 recording of the work, released on CD on EMI Great Recordings of the Century CDH 7610082 (1987).

6

Rhythm

Tempo

GOULD'S PENCHANT FOR extreme tempos, apparent throughout his career, has received much comment and criticism. Though many of his tempos fell within the limits of common practice, he often exceeded those limits, sometimes strikingly, and he was willing to depart from a composer's tempo directions as well as from documentation on historical performance practice. Tables 6.1 and 6.2 show some of his more extreme tempo choices, at both ends of the spectrum, and Table 6.3 shows that he often chose significantly different tempos in repeat performances of a piece.

In Baroque music, even in movements clearly based on dance types, Gould often ignored both common and historical practice when choosing a tempo, relying instead on criteria like musical character, expression, and even quality. In Bruno Monsaingeon's 1979 film *The Question of Instrument*, in a discussion of the Gigue from Bach's French Overture in B minor, he says that the intensity of expression in this extraordinary movement ('a gigue to surpass all gigues') demands a slower, more probing tempo than usual: it is 'ridiculous to put straitjackets on the music' where it transcends the norms of its genre. (He suggests a tempo of ♩. = 54.) When he played Bach's suites, he generally tried to convey a unified conception of the whole work, and so was concerned as much with the rhythmic relationships between movements as with the tempos of individual movements. He held few, if any, preconceptions as to the 'correct' tempo for, say, a gigue; rather, he adjusted individual tempos for the sake of the consistency of an overall conception, with the result that a 'Gould gigue' might have any of a variety of tempos. As he said in a 1963 interview on Bach's Partitas,

if you play one movement arbitrarily slowly, as a point of experiment, it's going to impose certain demands on the other movements. You could not, in the C Minor Partita, play a very somber and quasi-tragic realization of the Allemande through Sarabande and then do a thoroughly giddy Sinfonia and Capriccio. Obviously, even the movements that are of some dexterity and caprice would still have to maintain that sobriety which you depicted in the other movements.[1]

---

[1] Johnson, 1.

TABLE 6.1 Extreme Gould tempos (slow)

Composer	Work	Tempo
Anhalt	*Fantasia*	♩ = 24
J. S. Bach	*The Art of Fugue*, Contrapunctus 15	𝅗𝅥 = 36
J. S. Bach	Sonata for Viola da Gamba and Harpsichord No. 3 in G minor/III	♩ = 50
J. S Bach	Sonata for Violin and Harpsichord No. 6 in G major/IV	♩ = 20
J. S. Bach	Toccata in C minor, BWV 911, 'adagio'	♩ = 21
J. S. Bach	*WTC* I, Fugue in B flat minor	𝅗𝅥 = 33
Beethoven	Sonata in C major, Op. 2 No. 3/II	♪ = 11
Beethoven	Sonata in D major, Op. 10 No. 3/II	♩. = 13
Beethoven	Sonata in E flat major, Op. 27 No. 1/I (closing)	♩ = c.30
Beethoven	Sonata in B flat major, Op. 106 ('Hammerklavier')/III: opening / closing	♪ = 68 / ♪ = 35
Beethoven-Liszt	Fifth Symphony/II	♪ = 54
Beethoven-Liszt	Sixth Symphony (*Pastoral*)/II	♩. = 30
Berg	Sonata, Op. 1 (1974 film): opening	♩ = c.20
Hindemith	Trumpet Sonata/III	♩ = 27
Mozart	Sonata in A major, K. 331/I, Tema	♩. = 20 (see CD ③)
Schoenberg	Suite, Op. 25 (1964 recording)/Intermezzo	♪ = 18
Valen	Sonata No. 2, Op. 38/I	♪ = 52
Wagner	*Siegfried Idyll* (piano transcription): opening / closing	♩ = 53 / ♩ = 33

Note: In the recorded performance he conducted in 1982 of the first two movements of Beethoven's Concerto No. 2 in B flat major (unreleased as of this writing), Gould apparently wanted the second movement, marked in 3/4 time, so slow that he conducted it in twelve.

Gould felt that flexibility in tempo choice was most appropriate in fugues and other 'abstract' works. In *The Question of Instrument*, he discusses the example of the Fugue in C sharp major from *WTC* II, which he performed twice, on the one occasion twice as quickly as the other (see Table 6.3). Fugues did not so readily imply tempos as dance movements, he tells Monsaingeon, and he compares his variant tempos for the C sharp major fugue to Bach's own use of the devices of augmentation and diminution. That these devices could be applied to the thematic material of a fugue suggested to him that that material was inherently more abstract than, say, the tune of a gigue, and consequently offered a wider range of possible tempos.

TABLE 6.2 Extreme Gould tempos (fast)

Composer	Work	Tempo
J. S. Bach	Goldberg Variations (1955 recording)/Var. 5	♩ = 168
	(1981 recording)/Var. 5	♩. = 152
J. S. Bach	Partita No. 4 in D major (1979 film)/Gigue	♩♪. = 72
J. S. Bach	Partita No. 5 in G major (1957 filmed concert)/Corrente	♩. = 116
J. S. Bach	WTC II, Fugue in G major	♩. = 94
		(see CD 22)
Beethoven	Sonata in C minor, Op. 10 No. 1/I	𝅗𝅥. = 106
	Sonata in C minor, Op. 10 No. 1/III	𝅗𝅥 = 112
Beethoven	Sonata in C sharp minor, Op. 27 No. 2 ('Moonlight')/III	♩ = 204
Beethoven	Sonata in A major, Op. 101 (1952 CBC radio)/II	𝅗𝅥 = 88
	IV	𝅗𝅥 = 80
Beethoven	Sonata in E major, Op. 109 (1956 recording)/III, Var. 4	♩. = 92
Beethoven	Sonata in C minor, Op. 111/I	♩ = 185
Hindemith	Sonata No. 3 in B flat major (1966–7 recording)/II	𝅗𝅥 = 188
Mozart	Sonata in C major, K. 279/III	♩ = 185
		(see CD 6)
Mozart	Sonata in F major, K. 332/III	♩. = 128

Gould adopted a flexible attitude even in those relatively rare Baroque works with tempo markings. In the improvisatory opening section of Bach's Toccata in D minor, for example, he ignores the 'presto' marking in bars 28–32. There is no significant change of musical texture at the point at which 'presto' is marked, and he apparently saw no valid reason for a radical change of affect. As he plays it, the opening section features a continuous, gradual decrescendo and ritardando in its final eighteen bars, a large-scale gesture the integrity of which he chose to preserve: rather than change to presto in bar 28, he continues to play ever slower, quieter, more delicately. He made the same interpretation, doubtless for the same reasons, at the comparable spot at the end of the third section ('adagio') of the toccata, where Bach again indicates 'presto' for the concluding bars. In this case, his disregard for authentic tempo markings reflects his characteristic preference for continuity over contrast.[2] Perhaps the most unusual aspect of his tempo choices is that he applied the same flexibility with tempo markings in much Classical and Romantic music, and even took significant liberties in twentieth-century works for which the composer left metronome markings.

[2] In the Fugue in B minor from WTC I, he disregards Bach's tempo marking ('largo'), and in Mozart's Fantasia in D minor, K. 397, he ignores the 'presto' markings in bars 34 and 44.

TABLE 6.3 Differing Gould tempos

Composer	Work	Performance	Tempo
J. S. Bach	*The Art of Fugue*, Contrapunctus 1	1957 Moscow	♩ = 67
		1959 film	♩ = 59
		1962 recording (organ)	♩ = 124
		1979 film	♩ = 72
J. S. Bach	Clavier Concerto No. 1 in D minor/I	1957 recording	
		1957 CBC television	♩ = 89
		1958 Salzburg	♩ = 103
J. S. Bach	Clavier Concerto No. 5 in F minor/I	1957 CBC radio	♩ = 50
		1958 recording	♩ = 66
J. S. Bach	Goldberg Variations/Var. 19	1955 recording	♪ = 146
		1981 recording	♪ = 90 (see CD 16)
J. S. Bach	*WTC* II, Fugue in C sharp major	1966–7 recording	♩ = 41
		1970 CBC television	♩ = 91
J. S. Bach	*WTC* II, Fugue in E flat major	1963 CBC television	𝅗𝅥 = 50
		1967 recording	𝅗𝅥 = 86
J. S. Bach	*WTC* II, Fugue in E major	1957 recording	𝅗𝅥 = 38
		1969 recording	
		1970 CBC television	𝅗𝅥 = 100
		1980 film	𝅗𝅥 = 35
J. S. Bach	*WTC* II, Fugue in F sharp minor	1957 recording	♩ = 86
		1969 recording	♩ = 102
		1970 CBC television	♩ = 99
Beethoven	*Six Variations on an Original Theme*, Op. 34/Tema	1960–7 recording	♪ = 85
		1970 CBC television	♪ = 43
Beethoven	Sonata in E major, Op. 109/III, Var. 4	1956 recording	♩. = 92
		1964 CBC television	♩. = 50
Gibbons	'Italian Ground'	1968 recording	♩ = 107
		1968 CBC radio	♩ = 88
Haydn	Sonata No. 49 in E flat major/III	1958 recording	♩ = 100
		1981 recording	♩ = 146
Mozart	Sonata in C major, K. 330/I	1958 recording	♩ = 62
		1970 recording	♩ = 96
Mozart	Sonata in B flat major, K. 333/I	1967 CBC television	♩ = 108
		1965–70 recording	
		1969 CBC radio	♩ = 182
Prokofiev	Sonata No. 7 in B flat major, Op. 83/I	1962 CBC television	♩. = 122
		1967 recording	♩. = 161
	III	1962 CBC television	♩ = 152
		1967 recording	♩ = 191

There are several explanations for Gould's extreme tempos. The first is perhaps the most obvious, though not the most important: he experimented with extreme tempos because he could. His digital dexterity and concentration were of an unusually high order, permitting him to play accurately, clearly, and with complete control at both ends of the tempo spectrum. (Listen to breakneck performances like the fifth Goldberg variation as well as super-slow performances like Wagner's *Siegfried Idyll*. The accompanying CD includes a number of performances both very fast ([6], the finale of Mozart's K. 279) and very slow (the opening theme in [3], the first movement of Mozart's K. 331).) Robert Philip writes,

Every modern music student is familiar with the principle that a tempo must be chosen so that the shortest note-values can be played accurately and clearly. The very fast maximum tempos of many pre-war recordings were possible because the modern degree of clarity and precision was not part of the general performance practice of the time. The predominantly slower maximum tempos of modern performances are an inevitable result of the emphasis on rhythmic clarity.[3]

Gould's achievement was often precisely to combine that pre-war fondness for extreme tempos with a post-war clarity of rhythm.

Some of his unusual tempos surely reflected the influence of other performers. His very fast and very slow tempos in works by Bach and Beethoven, to take the most notable examples, were probably inspired to some degree by the examples of Rosalyn Tureck and Artur Schnabel, two pianists whom he admired from his youth, who (he admitted) influenced his playing in many ways, and who also had a penchant for extreme tempos. He may well have been influenced by two Schnabel recordings from 1935, to judge from the following examples from both ends of the tempo spectrum: the third movement ('prestissimo') of Beethoven's Sonata in C minor, Op. 10 No. 1 (Schnabel ♩ = 110, Gould = 112), and the second movement ('largo e mesto') of the Sonata in D major, Op. 10 No. 3 (Schnabel ♩. = 14, Gould = 13). Tureck's 1953 recording of *WTC* II, to take one example, includes a number of unusually slow tempos, and while Gould did not emulate her tempos in those particular preludes and fugues in his own recording, he was undoubtedly influenced generally by her example.[4] Some of his tempo choices were also influenced by such conventional criteria as hall ambiance, piano action, and so on. He noted, for example, that his tempos in the first four of Bach's French Suites (recorded 1972–3) were slower than usual because his recently rebuilt piano had a heavier action and somewhat thicker sound than before.[5]

---

[3] Philip, 234.

[4] The Schnabel performances were both released on Angel Great Recordings of the Century COLH 53, the Tureck performances on Decca Gold Label Series DX-128. K. Wolff, *Schnabel's Interpretation of Piano Music*, 72, notes that in slow movements Schnabel, like Gould, 'tried to play as slowly as possible . . . without ever losing the tension between successive notes or the coherence of harmonic progressions'.

[5] See Cott, 61–2; and *Non, je ne suis pas du tout un excentrique*, 179–80.

Most of Gould's wide departures from given tempo markings suggest a desire to exaggerate the affect implied by the composer—to take it further in the indicated direction. We saw in Chapter 2 that one of his aims was often to present a strongly polarized view of a work, to bring one side of it into high relief, to emphasize some feature present or latent within it—and, frankly, to bring something new to the record catalogues. It was typical of his binaristic thinking that he would consider options in terms of extremes. He would often, for example, treat a movement intended 'andante' as an adagio, exaggerating such qualities as lyricism, languor, introspection, pathos.[6] In multi-movement works, even those with a composer's metronome markings, he often exaggerated prevailing affects in both directions. The extremes in his 1964 recording of Schoenberg's Suite, Op. 25, are typical: he plays the Intermezzo (marked ♩ = 40) at 18, the Gigue (marked ♩ = c.192) at 209. In the two twentieth-century works shown in Table 6.4, he exaggerates all of the tempos:

TABLE 6.4. Exaggerated Gould tempos

Work	Composer's tempo and metronome markings		Gould's tempo
Krenek, Sonata No. 3/I	'allegretto piacevole'	♩. = 90	143
II	'andantino'	♪ = 90	73
III	'vivace ma non troppo'	♪ = 138	186
IV	'adagio'	♪ = 48	33
Morawetz, *Fantasy in D*	'allegro'	♩. = 138	160
	'moderato'	♩. = 120	105, slowing to 58
		♩. = 144	155
		♩ = 108	61
	'più mosso (allegro)'	♩. = c.63	46
	'andante'	♩ = 112	92

Gould would further exaggerate prevailing affect through type and degree of rubato. In many fast movements, he tended to play slightly on the front of the beat (that is, a little early), in slow movements, slightly on the back of the beat, in each case with a subtle but perceptible increase in the prevailing rhythmic effect, whether forward drive or repose. He avoided the very commonplace tendency to move towards middle ground; he generally did not underplay rests, for example, even in the slowest movements, though the practice is very common. In several sonatas in Beethoven's famous 'C minor mood'—the *Pathétique* and Opp. 10 No.1

---

[6]   See the following examples: Haydn, Sonata No. 48 in C major/I; Beethoven, Sonata in E flat major, Op. 27 No. 1/I; Beethoven, Bagatelles, Op. 126 Nos. 1, 3, and 6; Beethoven-Liszt, Fifth Symphony/II; Brahms, Intermezzo in E flat major, Op. 117 No. 1; Sibelius, *Kyllikki*, Op. 41 No. 2; Prokofiev, *Visions fugitives*, Op. 22 No. 2; Anhalt, *Fantasia*; Pentland, *Shadows*; and Hétu, *Variations pour piano* (Var. 3).

and 111—he took extremely fast tempos to achieve a stormy effect, but also allowed little deviation from the basic pulse, even where deviation is marked. In the first movement of Op. 10 No. 1, as he told Humphrey Burton in 1966, he maintained the fast basic tempo ($\downarrow$. = 106) even in the lyrical second theme in A flat major (bars 32 ff.).[7] And in the third movement, as a by-product of his extremely headlong conception ($\downarrow$ = 112), he strikingly refused to obey the 'ritardando', 'calando', and 'adagio' markings in the cadenza, bars 106–14. He maintains the basic tempo through the appearance of the main theme in the Neapolitan in bars 106–10; he obeys only slightly the 'tenuto' marking at bar 112; and he takes bars 113–14, notwithstanding the grace-note arpeggios, almost exactly in time. The effect of slashing through this cadenza, as opposed to lingering over it, is startling, but also consistent with his conception of the movement.[8]

One of the most unconventional aspects of Gould's tempo choices was the place he accorded tempo within the hierarchy of the performer's concerns. For him, tempo was not necessarily the most important interpretative decision, a point of view that runs contrary to common practice. Normally tempo is considered the single most crucial factor in an interpretation, since it is the factor that contributes most to the overall affect or profile of the work in performance.[9] Gould, on the other hand, said in a 1981 interview,

For me the choice of tempo is one of the last considerations in the performance of a work. When I go into the studio, I have made certain preliminary decisions. But basically there are usually several tempi with which the character of the work obviously correlates. . . . It may sound suicidal, but often I only know what tempo I'll take in the studio. And sometimes I even do a second version. Generally it could be said that I subordinate the tempo to the other aspects of a given interpretation. It must then accord with the other forms I choose. Behind everything, naturally, the rule is maximum clarity.[10]

By Gould's standards, tempo was not part of the notation of the work itself, and so was not a factor in analysis and interpretation. In other words, 'the tempo serves the concept' but was not a factor that influenced that concept, since this would assume that it was a necessary feature of the work itself.[11]

---

[7] See Burton, i.

[8] Wilson, 58, writing in 1959, notes that 'Gould's conception of late Beethoven seems to exist in establishing a subtle relationship between passages of continuous, sustained forward movement and others full of the small-scale building up and releasing of tension. Where he sees the first, he minimizes or even ignores Beethoven's continuity-breaking expression marks; where he sees the second, he emphasizes and subdivides them.'

[9] Mozart, for example, considered choice of tempo 'the most essential, the most difficult and the chief requisite in music' (letter of 24 Oct. 1777, quoted in Badura-Skoda, 71 n.). For typical modern expressions of this commonplace position in the literature on performance, see Berry, 220; and K. Wolff, *Schnabel's Interpretation of Piano Music*, 72. As L. B. Meyer, *Explaining Music*, 40, notes, the commonplace approach, in which the performer 'senses the ethos of a composition and then decides upon an appropriate tempo', might seem circular, 'for character is made dependent upon tempo and choice of tempo upon imagined character'.

[10] M. Meyer, 'Interview', 18.

[11] Mach, 105.

Ex. 6.1. Bach, *WTC* I, Fugue in F minor, subject

In his interview on the Bach Partitas, Gould discussed some of the factors influencing his choice of tempo in the Fugue in F minor from *WTC* I, which he was at that time preparing to record.[12] The fugue presented a problem for him in that he found 'two absolutely satisfying ways to play it'—typically, two extreme ways. He recorded one version in which chiselled phrasing—'with pointillistic phrases every two notes in the subject, à la Webern, until you get to the last ones, where I put tenutos and marcatos, apostrophes as it were, over each note'— demanded an 'extremely slow' tempo. (This was the version that he eventually approved for release; Ex. 6.1.) On the other hand, he saw an option of performing it 'in a much more free-flowing, legato fashion, and this would change the character of the fugue entirely'. This connection between tempo and phrasing was a crucial one for Gould: as he wrote in 1966, 'prevailing tempo is almost always the result of phrase delineation'.[13] (Determining tempo on the basis of phrasing is hardly unprecedented—Wagner advocated it in his 1869 essay 'About Conducting'[14]— though I suspect that the reverse is more common among performers.) The analytical implications of the 'pointillistic' version probably influenced his ultimate decision to adopt the slow tempo, but some of the factors he considered with the other version are revealing of his criteria. He cited harmonic reasons to defend the faster, more free-flowing version—notably, the tendency of the fugue to gravitate towards closely related major keys ('it spends a lot of time in A-flat and in D-flat major'). He cited counterpoint, too. The fugue 'proceeds a lot in thirds and sixths', and though not lacking 'independence in voices' it 'doesn't teach one a special lesson in counterpoint or in how to adjust voices; it's a fairly ordinary contrivance in the relation of subsidiary material to main theme', and so did not necessarily have to be presented in the intensely analytical manner that he ultimately chose.

Counterpoint was, in fact, a major factor in Gould's tempo choices generally: he often slowed tempos significantly to allow himself more time to explore real or latent counterpoint.[15] (Most of the slow tempos in Table 6.1 were clearly inspired,

---

[12]   See Johnson, 1, for those quotations not otherwise identified in the paragraph that follows.

[13]   *GGR* 338.

[14]   See Wagner, 314.

[15]   In 'Sviatoslav Richter', 12, he recalls hearing Richter's notoriously slow interpretation of the first movement of Schubert's Sonata in B flat major, and praises the 'analytical calculation', the revealing of the structural significance of details, permitted by the slow tempo. He heard this performance at a Richter recital in Moscow in 1957, and it is tempting to assume (as his essay suggests) that he was both impressed and influenced by it.

at least in part, by contrapuntal considerations.) In his 1968 CBC radio performance of the Beethoven-Liszt *Pastoral* Symphony, his interest in revealing contrapuntal possibilities within the largely homophonic textures of this work is obvious throughout, and as a consequence his tempos (except in the storm movement), shown in Table 6.5, are significantly slower by as much as 40 per cent than the metronome markings published by Beethoven in 1817.

TABLE 6.5. Gould's tempos in the Beethoven-Liszt *Pastoral* Symphony

Movement	Composer's tempo and metronome markings		Gould's tempo
I	'allegro ma non troppo'	♩ = 66	40
II	'andante molto moto'	♪. = 50	30
III	'allegro'	♩. = 108	68
IV	'allegro'	♩ = 80	92
V	'allegretto'	♪. = 60	48

In his recording of Scriabin's Sonata No. 3 in F sharp minor, Gould reconceived the basic character of the work, playing down drama in favour of introspection. His obvious desire to explore the work's counterpoint was a crucial factor in this conception, and his tempo choices followed accordingly. In the first movement, which Scriabin marks 'drammatico' (♩ = 69), he plays much more slowly (40).[16] And his tempos merge consistently with other changes to Scriabin's performance markings: for example, he backs away from the forte dynamics in the opening bars (except in the initial octaves), and allows a great deal of rhythmic freedom where he plays quietly; both decisions help in clarifying counterpoint. Late in his career, Gould noted his growing penchant for slower tempos, seeing it as a corollary of his growing interest in exploring counterpoint, and in many of his later recordings, broadcasts, and films, the connection between tempo and counterpoint is unmistakable.[17] (See his performances from the 1970s and 1980s of Bach's Goldberg Variations, Haydn's last sonatas, Beethoven's early sonatas, Brahms's Ballades and Rhapsodies, Wagner's *Siegfried Idyll*, and Berg's Sonata.)

Rhythm: Premisses and Criteria

For Gould, tempo was clearly less important than rhythmic order, and the expression of musical form in performance was above all a matter of shaping the rhythmic profile.[18] He was admired throughout his career for his exceptional

[16] See his comments on the movement in *GGR* 165.

[17] See Page. Innes, 67–72, confirms and quantifies Gould's observation, in the context of his six preserved performances of the Goldberg Variations.

[18] Cf. Cone, 25, 31, for whom 'musical form . . . is basically rhythmic', and for whom a 'valid and effective performance' is achieved primarily 'by discovering and making clear the rhythmic life of a composition'.

rhythmic control, and indeed he seems to have had a highly developed sense of musical time, even on the largest scale. Even in those patently 'wrong' Mozart performances that are difficult to accept because of fast tempos, there is invariably a buoyant energy in Gould's playing, a control of rhythmic tension and relaxation, that at least superficially commends the playing, and this is no less true of his slowest performances. And where his sensitivity to rhythm met his insight into counterpoint, there was a marriage of horizontal and vertical tension in his playing that was powerful, dramatic, yet always immaculately controlled. (Some of his 'wrong' performances are, in fact, among his most entertaining precisely because of his ability to invigorate his playing rhythmically and contrapuntally.) Gould used rhythm, more than any other single factor, to communicate his interpretation of formal divisions, harmonic action, and other important structural features. With rhythm, as with so many other factors, he valued unity and continuity above variety and contrast; indeed, rhythmic unity and continuity formed a principal locus of over-arching order in most, if not all, of his performances. In this respect, he was in accord with a basic priority of twentieth-century, and especially post-war, performance. As Philip and others have shown, the kind of controlled organization that Gould sought is typical of modern rhythm, in contrast to the rhetorical flexibility and spontaneity of Romantic performance. Indeed, it is in the matter of rhythm—of musical time—that one finds perhaps the most important distinction between Romantic and modern performance. Philip writes,

In general, written sources suggest that the changing of tempo within movements was practised and accepted by the majority of performers and composers in the early twentieth century. Some writers urge caution, others do not. A number of musicians stand out against the general acceptance of tempo fluctuations, notably Weingartner, Toscanini and Stravinsky, and from the viewpoint of the late twentieth century we can see these as pioneers of a stricter attitude to tempo which was to influence a later generation of musicians.[19]

Among the features of modern rhythm, Philip notes 'a trend towards stricter control of tempo . . . more emphatic clarity of rhythmic detail, more literal interpretation of note values, and the avoidance of rhythmic irregularity and dislocation'. He summarizes these elements 'as a trend towards greater power, firmness, clarity, control, literalness, and evenness of expression, and away from informality, looseness, and unpredictability'. Thus modern performances, compared to Romantic ones, tend to be 'accurate, orderly, restrained, deliberate, and even in emphasis'.[20]

These values are evident throughout Gould's performances—more evident, indeed, than in the work of many pianists considered 'modern' or 'classical' in temperament. Of course, degree of rhythmic strictness varied according to repertoire,

[19]   Philip, 15. See also Hill.
[20]   Philip, 229, 234.

with Gould as with everyone else: stricter in Bach, looser in Brahms. But generally, his rhythm places him among the 'geometrical' performers, to use the term with which Richard Taruskin characterizes modern performance, be it neo-Classical or historical. Gould noted late in his career that he was always 'very *aware* of constant pulse', preferring 'very firm, very tight rhythmic features'.[21] But this is not to say that he advocated only metronomically rigid tempos. Certainly by comparison with early twentieth-century tastes, he preferred consistency to contrast in terms of tempo. But the Gould criticism has tended to exaggerate the degree of rhythmic strictness in his performances; even some of his own remarks, usually made in polemics against Romanticism, seem to advocate a degree of strictness that he did not always practise. He suggested to Burton that relative continuity of tempo could provide a 'spine' for an interpretation,[22] and one does indeed sense the unifying rhythmic order in his performances, yet his use of rhythmic nuance was subtle, considered, and often generous, and he *suggested* strict time more often than he literally observed it. He was in fact highly critical of some of the performers whose rhythm was considered a paragon of the modern, most notably Toscanini and Stravinsky.[23]

Perhaps the most important difference between Gould's rhythm and that of his Romantic predecessors—and that of many of his contemporaries, too, including harpsichordists—was in the degree of inflectional detail that he permitted, and the scale on which he made departures from a prevailing tempo. He tended to infuse music with rhythmic energy while permitting relatively little rhythmic inflection within a phrase or paragraph, tending to use significant inflections on a larger scale, to articulate major cadences or formal divisions. In Romantic practice, as Philip and others have documented, real shifts of tempo—that is, interruptions or changes that are not compensated for, that cannot be interpreted simply as rubato—were common. Wagner, for example, throughout his essay on conducting, advocated a principle of tempo 'modification' that applied to whole movements and works, and he believed that different thematic ideas had their own proper tempos. The practice has roots at least as far back as Beethoven and Czerny, but is still audible in many early recordings, in which one sometimes hears shifts of tempo on an almost phrase-by-phrase basis; in fact, I have heard old recordings by pianists like de Pachmann and Paderewski of passages in which literally no two consecutive quavers are in the same tempo. Gould vehemently rejected this style. But because he sought to avoid such shifts of tempo while still not entirely forsaking rhythmic inflection, the scale of his inflections tended to be correspondingly smaller, more

---

[21]   Cott, 60, 61. Here he also compares his rhythmic preferences with those of Schnabel. (Asked once if he played 'with feeling' or 'in time', Schnabel famously replied, 'Can't one feel in time?')

[22]   See Burton, ii.

[23]   See e.g. *GGR* 264, 344.

SUITE I

G. F. Händel.

Prélude
(Original.)

Arpeggio

Edition Peters.

7903

*) In der Ausgabe der Deutschen Händel-gesellschaft steht hier:

In the edition of the German Handel Society we find here:

L'édition de la Société Händel allemande indique ici:

1. Handel, Suite for Harpsichord in A major/Prelude, in Gould's Peters edition of the score (NLC Scores 28/5, 6; photo reproduction supplied by the Music Division of National Library of Canada, and reproduced with the permission of the C. F. Peters Corporation and the Estate of Glenn Gould)

2. Handel, Suite for Harpsichord in A major/Prelude, 1–7, from Gould's autograph manuscript of his arrangement, final draft (NLC 27/6/1, 1; photo reproduction supplied by the Music Division of the National Library of Canada, and reproduced with the permission of the Estate of Glenn Gould)

3. Gould in the recording studio, March 1963 (photograph by Don Hunstein, supplied by and reproduced with the permission of Sony Classical)

4–5. Scriabin, *Two Pieces* ('Désir' and 'Caresse dansée'), Op. 57 (photo reproduction supplied by Photographic Services, University of Victoria, and reproduced with the permission of Dover Publications)

2. Caresse dansée

6. Sibelius, Sonatine in F sharp minor, Op. 67 No. 1/I, 47–72; Gould's copy of the score, marked with his instructions for 'acoustic choreography' (NLC Scores 44/2, 4; photo reproduction supplied by the Music Division of the National Library of Canada, and reproduced with the permission of the Estate of Glenn Gould)

7. Sibelius, *Kyllikki*, Op. 41/II, 1–29; Gould's copy of the score, marked with his instructions for 'acoustic choreography' (NLC Scores 43/5, 8; photo reproduction supplied by the Music Division of the National Library of Canada, and reproduced with the permission of the Estate of Glenn Gould)

8. Sibelius, Sonatine in F sharp minor, Op. 67 No. 1/III, 38–54; Gould's copy of the score, marked with his instructions for 'acoustic choreography' (NLC Scores 44/2, 10; photo reproduction supplied by the Music Division of the National Library of Canada, and reproduced with the permission of the estate of Glenn Gould)

discreet. Often, when making small-scale expressive or analytical points, he abandoned rhythmic inflection almost entirely, preferring to rely on subtleties of dynamics or phrasing. A Romantic performer (or a harpsichordist) who uses continuous and significant rhythmic inflection for immediate expressive purposes must use even larger inflections in order to mark an event of greater structural significance; Gould, on the other hand, tended to maintain a more modest level of rhythmic inflection so that he could articulate even the most important events without upsetting the prevailing tempo. As Philip writes, 'Old-fashioned playing uses rubato to create a sort of relief, in which significant details are made to stand out. By comparison, a modern performance is much smoother and more regular. Any points of emphasis are carefully incorporated into the whole, nothing is allowed to sound out of place; the relief has been, so to speak, flattened out.'[24] Gould's performances often suggest a rhythmic analogy to terraced dynamics: he would maintain a relatively 'flat' rhythmic profile through a large structural unit, where he saw no compelling reason to do otherwise, saving significant rhythmic articulation for events whose structural importance is at a middleground or background level. There was also a connection between rhythmic inflection and phrasing. As George Barth has shown in a study of Beethoven's playing, the need for rhythmic stress becomes greater where legato articulation becomes the assumed norm, as throughout the Romantic era.[25] Given Gould's generally more articulated non-legato style, it is not surprising that he could get by with more discreet rhythmic nuances.

His recording of the Fugue in C minor from *WTC* II offers a concise case study of his rhythmic priorities in action (see CD |11|). The exposition of this fugue (bars 1–8) leads seamlessly into a series of subject entries and sequences in which harmonic resolution is constantly deferred until bar 14, with the cadence to the dominant (G minor), by which point the fugue is already half over. Gould strictly maintains his opening tempo ($\downarrow$ = 83) through bars 1–14, creating a rhythmic analogy to the deferral of thematic and harmonic resolution. The passage from bar 14 to the tonic cadence in bar 23, a series of entries including stretti and augmentations, has the same effect of continuous spinning out, and Gould plays it too as a strictly controlled rhythmic unit. Within these two major paragraphs, he uses phrasing and dynamics to clarify counterpoint and motivic development, using rhythmic continuity for the larger purpose of conveying these paragraphs as discrete units within the overall structure. He strongly punctuates only the cadences in bars 14 and 23, yet even here he does not upset the prevailing tempo. Rather than articulate the cadences with a ritardando or fermata or even slight

---

[24] Philip, 69.
[25] See Barth, 131.

tenuto, he does the opposite, playing the cadential chords in bars 14 and 23 with a sharp staccato that abruptly breaks off the preceding spinning out of material; in bar 14, the two paragraphs seem to bump up against each other. This abruptness of articulation allows him to set off clearly the end of one paragraph, and insert a moment's breath, but still proceed immediately into the next paragraph without breaking the prevailing pulse. (Changes in texture and dynamics at these joints also help to set off the paragraphs one from the other.) Only in the final five bars of the fugue does Gould relax rhythmically, through the stretti over a tonic pedal in bars 23–6 and in the cadenza-like penultimate bar. His manipulation of rhythm in this performance conveys, in an immediately palpable way, his interpretation of the form of the fugue as two large paragraphs punctuated by perfect cadences, followed by a coda in which the preceding tension unwinds as the tonic key is restored and confirmed. This recording dates from 1966–7, after Gould's retirement from the concert stage, and is typical of the importance he gave to rhythm in communicating form in his mature recordings. As Dale Innes shows in her study of his performances of the Goldberg Variations, 'his tempi became more uniform later in his career, after he left the concert stage', a fact that reveals his growing interest in conveying unity and order on the largest structural level, and his correspondingly greater discrimination in the application of local rhythmic inflection.[26] This fugue demonstrates on a very small scale a feature typical of all of his performances, regardless of time scale, tempo, or degree of rhythmic flexibility: his ability to combine the analytical clarity and 'geometrical' orderliness characteristic of modern rhythm with the sense of large-scale rhythmic structure and drama that we associate with performers like Furtwängler.

What Gould considered rhythmic waywardness and indulgence in much conventional (and especially Romantic) piano playing was precisely deviation from the prevailing tempo that was not 'essentially structural and analytical in motivation', not 'clearly part of the structural plan', and so 'expressive' only in a superficial or exaggerated sense;[27] it disturbed him most in pre-Romantic music. Here again we come up against the conflict between emotion and reason in Gould's psychology. He did not reject rhythmic inflection, but demanded that it be rationalized by the criterion of 'structure', and where that criterion was satisfied he could be as rhythmically flexible as any Romantic. His own rhythmic models were not pianists, in fact, but conductors. As he said in a discussion of Mozart, he felt that pianists should not indulge in a degree of rhythmic licence that a conductor would not

---

[26] Innes, 72; see also the tables on 73 and 74.

[27] GGR 39; Aikin, 26. As so often, his rejection of Romantic rhythm implies a false dichotomy between 'Romantic' and 'structural', which are hardly incompatible concepts. Even Wagner rejected tempo modifications that were merely random or whimsical, and the rhythmic nuances of Furtwängler, a true Romantic among twentieth-century performers, have been admired precisely because they help project the music's structure, a criterion he explicitly cites in his writings.

attempt with an orchestra, especially in early music, and he denied that most of the liberties taken by Romantic pianists could be justified as rubato. Indeed, his interest in using rhythmic nuances that did not upset the prevailing tempo actually brought him closer than many Romantic and modern performers to the true rubato effect advocated by C. P. E. Bach, Mozart, Türk, Chopin, and others, according to which the right hand 'bends' the rhythm for expressive purposes while the left keeps good time. Modern 'rubato', as Philip notes, is more derived from the Romantic practice of frequently speeding up and slowing down, shifting the prevailing tempo entirely.[28] In an interview for a 3 December 1968 CBC radio recital, Gould referred to the relatively strict rhythm in his Mozart performances as a feature 'which conductors always bring to this music but which instrumentalists very often do not, out of a curious deference to a Victorian prejudice as to what Mozart was supposed to be like'.[29] He noted the harpsichordist's tendency to take many rhythmic liberties to substitute for dynamic inflections, for which

there is no comparable excuse . . . on the piano. I'm not even convinced that one should exploit the instrument that way in late romantic music. I'm not saying that one shouldn't be free to employ subtle tempo gradations . . . but this other thing, which to my ear is a combination of structural negligence and a certain lack of control instrumentally, is something else altogether. I find it disturbing even in Scriabin, say; but in Mozart it's simply grotesque.[30]

Gould was as good as his word, not only in Mozart but in Scriabin: it is revealing to compare the relative sobriety and continuity of rhythm in his performances of Scriabin's Fifth Sonata with the more extreme, almost schizophrenic contrasts of tempo and mood brought to this music by most other pianists.

Gould explicitly cited Baroque music (meaning Bach) as a general rhythmic model. As he told an interviewer in 1964, the flexible Romantic approach to rhythm 'offends my Baroquish notion of what tempo is all about. I'm much influenced by the Baroque incessant rhythmic pulse.'[31] The trait that Gould interprets as 'Baroque' is, of course, more accurately described as Baroque interpreted in light of the neo-Classical values of mid-twentieth-century music, for, as Taruskin observes, the assumption of a 'classical' or 'geometrical' rhythmic style in Baroque music is a reflection of twentieth-century taste 'uncorroborated by

---

[28] On rubato, see Philip, 37–69, 221–2. (Epstein, 371, uses the term 'romantic' for Philip's 'modern' rubato, and the term 'classical' for the 'real' rubato of C. P. E. Bach, Mozart, and others.) Philip's comment on 'modern' rubato calls to mind Virgil Thomson's analysis of Arthur Rubinstein's rubato, in a 1940 concert review. Rubinstein's rubato, he writes, 'is of the Paderewski tradition', and does not accord with 'Chopin's prescription for rubato playing, which is almost word for word Mozart's prescription for playing an accompanied melody', namely 'that the right hand should take liberties with the time values, while the left hand remains rhythmically unaltered'. The 'Paderewski tradition', however, 'is more like the Viennese waltz style, in which the liberties in the melody line are followed exactly in the accompaniment', resulting in 'a flexible distortion of strict rhythm' (Thomson, 194).

[29] Kent, 39.

[30] *GGR* 40.

[31] Bester, 153.

any contemporary [i.e. seventeenth- or eighteenth-century] witness'.[32] (The rhythmic features that Gould admired in Bach's music were the same ones that Stravinsky admired, though Gould would have balked at the comparison.) According to Taruskin, Edward T. Cone was only reflecting modern prejudices when he wrote that the style of Bach and Handel

is most memorably characterized by an important rhythmic feature: the uniformity of its metrical pulse. This is in turn but one facet of a regularity that pervades the texture of the music. As a result the typical movement of this period is indeed a *movement*, i.e. a piece composed in a single unvarying tempo. . . . Even when a movement juxtaposes two or more such units in clearly contrasted tempos, there is often an underlying arithmetical relation that, if observed in performance, unifies them. In this music, events of the same kind tend to happen either at the same rate of speed, or at precisely geared changes of rate. . . . In the best of this music, the contrapuntal texture, either actual or implied, sets up a hierarchy of events, each proceeding at its own rate, yet all under a strict metric control that extends from the entire phrase down to the smallest subdivision of the beat. . . . The beats seem to form a pre-existing framework that is independent of the musical events that it controls. One feels that before a note of the music was written, the beats were in place, regularly divided into appropriate sub-units, and regularly combined into measures; and that only after this abstract framework was in place, so to speak, was the music composed on it. . . . In performance, the result should be a relative equalization of the beats.[33]

If Cone's analysis of Baroque rhythm is questionable historically, it still provides a valuable summary of the modern interpretation to which Gould's playing largely conformed. An 'abstract framework' of beats performed at a 'single unvarying tempo' was precisely the effect that he seems to have sought, especially in Bach. His admiration for post-war German performances of Bach, like those of Karl Richter and Karl Münchinger, was based on a perception of rhythmic solidity that he felt appropriate as an antidote to the excesses of more Romantic Bach players like Casals, even though his own sense of rhythm was considerably more subtle than that of performers in the so-called 'sewing-machine' style.[34] (This is a case in which he may have exaggerated his admiration for polemical purposes.) Gould was also influenced by Ralph Kirkpatrick's 1938 edition of the Goldberg Variations, which he studied in his youth; he seems to have followed many of the prescriptions in the edition itself and in the preface. On the subject of rhythm, Kirkpatrick, like

---

[32] Taruskin, 115. Taruskin may be correct as to contemporary accounts of actual Baroque practice, but there was in fact some advocacy of relative uniformity of tempo among Baroque theorists and composers, including Schütz, Muffat, and Quantz. The famous obituary of Bach that C. P. E. Bach and Johann Friedrich Agricola published in 1754 alludes to the composer's preference for a steady tempo (see David and Mendel, 222).

[33] Cone, 59, 62, 70.

[34] On Richter's and Münchinger's Bach, see Cott, 64; and Johnson, 2. In addition to the relative strictness of rhythm in these performances, Gould surely also heard the detached articulation, cleanliness of phrasing, and terraced dynamics as bracing alternatives to Romantic practice, even if, again, his own playing in these respects was more subtle.

Cone, warns that 'in most Bach movements, all harmonic and melodic detail is arranged in such a symmetrical relation to the whole phrase or movement that the musical structure can often be distorted by rhythmical fluctuations'.[35] These rhythmic priorities influenced Gould's performances of later repertoire, in varying degrees. Philip notes that pre-war performances tended to treat Baroque and Classical music 'with much greater volatility of tempo than is now considered appropriate'.[36] Gould put an eminently modern spin on this relationship: he applied to music of all periods the standards of rhythmic order that he considered most appropriate for early music.

Where he did make significant rhythmic inflections, he was influenced above all by harmony. Tonal structure was for him the most important factor in determining the profile of a piece, and rhythmic inflection was his most important means of communicating that profile. The basic principle here is conventional: tonal considerations were crucial for many Romantic players, for writers on the subject of analysis and performance, and for performers (notably Tureck) who served Gould as models. But once more, he took this conventional principle to unconventional ends, in some cases through the degree of exaggeration with which he made his point, but most notably in the degree to which he allowed harmonic criteria to dictate rhythmic responses even where a composer's markings to the contrary existed in the score. Here again, he applied a principle developed to suit particularly the music of Bach—and harmony is the most important criterion for making interpretative decisions for most Bach players—even to music in which rhythmic matters are more explicitly dictated by the composer. His use of harmonic criteria (like Tureck's) was unusually intense and consistent, and because of the framework of relative rhythmic continuity within which he worked, his rhythmic articulations of harmonic events were often unusually pointed.

Gould felt that rhythmic inflection was justified to the extent that tonal predictability was upset, that rhythmic inflections could act as a kind of analytical marker to the significance of tonal events. He said in a 1980 interview that 'the further away you are from the conventional modulatory expectation . . . the more reason there is at that point to consider that there should be a radical departure from the rhythmic, motoric norm that you have established'.[37] Discussing his performances of Mozart's sonata-allegro movements, he invoked a 'theory of modulatory distance' as justification for relatively unyielding tempos: since he considered that the modulation from tonic to dominant, in the piano sonatas, was generally routine and unsurprising, he saw no need for rhythmic underscoring. On the other hand, 'if some genuine, untoward event intervenes to keep the sonata-

[35] Kirkpatrick, xxiii.
[36] Philip, 20.
[37] Aikin, 26–7.

allegro from its appointed rounds, then I'm all for the creation of a tempo shift appropriate to the magnitude of that event'.[38] (By way of example, he cites here the D major recapitulation in the first movement of Beethoven's Sonata in F major, Op. 10 No. 2, which he articulates by slowing down dramatically; see Chapter 3.) In an interview for a 1969 CBC radio programme, he applied his harmonic yard-stick even to Baroque dance movements, insisting that significant harmonic events justified considerable departures from the norms of dance rhythm.[39]

Gould's rhythmic inflections were often responses to changes in tonal tension or relaxation. This criterion has been important since at least the early Romantic era, though in modern playing responses to harmonic events tend to be less extreme. Gould's use of the practice was somewhat more strict than usual, more concerned with middleground- and background-level tonal activity, and again less concerned with performance markings to the contrary. The importance of tonal tension and relaxation in his performances is clear in his differing treatment of rhythm in the development sections in two first movements from late Beethoven sonatas: Op. 109 in E major, and Op. 110 in A flat major. In the case of Op. 109, he strongly pushes the tempo through the development section, first through bars 16–21, up to the cadence (and momentary pause) on G sharp major, then through bars 21–48, building to the dominant pedal in the upper register that ushers in the recapitu-lation. His pushing of the tempo responds to the conspicuously sharpward harmonic motion that characterizes the development, which moves as far from the tonic key as D sharp major and its dominant. His performance of this section responds directly to its tonal function as one of continuous and mounting tension. In fact, the movement as a whole manifests sharpward tension until the sudden appearance of C major at bar 62, just after the recapitulation, and it is only at this point, and in the plagally coloured coda that follows, that Gould relaxes rhyth-mically. His rhythmic scheme amounts to an analysis of the tonal trajectory of the movement: he pushes through the opening 'vivace ma non troppo' and 'adagio espressivo' sections, pulling back slightly only with the achievement of the long-delayed dominant modulation in bar 15;[40] he pushes through the development section, pulling back only to articulate the temporary goals G sharp and B; and he pulls back significantly only with the extreme plunge to the flat side after the recapitulation, with the final achievement of the tonic in the coda, and with the tonic pedal in the closing bars. (His rhythmic inflections are complemented by his dynamic plan, for the most part, often in contradiction to the score.) Similar

[38] GGR 38.

[39] See 'Take 16', 2–3.

[40] According to K. Wolff, *Schnabel's Interpretation of Piano Music*, 19, Schnabel also heard 'one long line that goes from the first note to the end of the exposition, without stop and without a break of any kind. The initial E major chord opens a phrase which is continued until finally the E major key is replaced, in bar 15, by a B major chord implied in the *sforzato* bass on B.'

reasoning produced opposing results in the development section of the first movement of Op. 110 (bars 40–55). Here, the section is continuously flatward in harmonic orientation, moving in sequence from the relative minor (F minor), through the subdominant (D flat major) and its relative minor (B flat minor), returning to the tonic with only a hint of dominant preparation in bar 55. As a result, Gould's performance is now marked by a continuous slowing of the basic tempo throughout the section. The return to the tonic at bar 56 amounts to a harmonic move sharpward, and it is here that he returns to the basic tempo established in the exposition.

Gould used the momentary relaxation of a strict prevailing tempo to articulate harmonic events of many kinds, some of them conventional: for example, trios in a contrasting key or mode in Baroque dance pairs; deceptive cadences; modulations to distant keys; false recapitulations; and thickets of chromaticism within a largely diatonic context. And he gave conventional attention to the articulation of cadences, though at times was unusually careful about revealing their relative structural weight. (See the last sixteen bars of the Gigue from Bach's Partita No. 6 in E minor (1974 film), in which he uses rhythmic articulations of growing intensity to place the various half and full cadences with which the Gigue gradually draws to a halt into an audible hierarchy.) Harmonic criteria are obvious in some more unconventional examples in which he applied cadenza-like rhythmic licence in passages not so designated in the score. In the same interview in which he discussed Beethoven's Op. 10 No. 2, he discussed the cadenza near the end of the third movement of Mozart's Sonata in B flat major, K. 333. It has all of the expected features of a cadenza: it begins with a tonic six-four chord, includes modulations to distant keys, varies some thematic material, and concludes with flourishes over a dominant seventh chord. Yet Mozart marks the passage 'cadenza in tempo' (at least until the closing flourishes, which are marked 'ad libitum'). Gould plays this passage with all of the rhythmic licence of a typical cadenza. As he told Monsaingeon, he felt that the tonal meandering demands rhythmic adjustment: 'It *is* a cadenza, no matter what Mozart says, and I simply can't imagine how he could possibly expect anyone to charge through the tonic minor [B flat minor] and its submediant [G flat major] without going into low gear.'[41] Gould goes into 'low gear'—that is, slows down—precisely during the move through B flat minor to G flat major (bars 175–8); he speeds up during the following sequence, which builds tension towards a dominant pedal.[42]

[41] *GGR* 38.

[42] For a similar example, see his performance of the 'cadenza' in Beethoven's Sonata in G major, Op. 31 No. 1/III, 206–48. In Strauss's Sonata in B minor/IV, 92–113, he ignores the composer's 'allegretto molto vivo' marking and plays this D major section slowly, gently, with considerable rhythmic freedom, returning to the quicker tempo only with the 'animato' passage in F sharp minor beginning at bar 114. He seems to have interpreted bars 92–113 as a kind of cadenza separating the end of the exposition from the 'real' beginning of the development proper in bar 114.

If tonality was the most important, it was not the only criterion that influenced Gould's rhythm. He made telling use of agogic accents (that is, the lengthening of notes or chords to provide articulation or accentuation) to make musical points on various structural levels, mostly in his recordings, broadcasts, and films after 1964 (his control of rhythmic nuance was considerably greater away from the concert hall). Of course, one finds numerous conventional cases in which he, like any pianist, used agogic accents, without disrupting the basic tempo, to draw attention to foreground details—prominent dissonant notes and chords, points of arrival, fugal entries, and so on, sometimes details of some importance. In his 1979 film performance of Bach's Partita No. 4 in D major, he plays the quick fugal Gigue with almost metronomic strictness until bar 85, where he makes a strong agogic accent to announce the thematic and tonal recapitulation and the drive to the final cadence. His accent makes explicit a thematic recapitulation that might otherwise have passed unnoticed. It occurs at the c''' in bar 85, the flat-seventh degree and the highest note of the movement. This note, approached by an octave leap, proves in retrospect to be part of the principal fugue subject in the tonic, which enters here in truncated form, without its head motive; as it turns out, this is the last entry of the subject in the movement. The agogic accent reinforces the octave leap, and sets the theme in relief against the less important thematic material that precedes it.[43] Gould sometimes used rhythmic gestures of this sort to make what might be called 'middleground' connections. In the central 'allegro' section of the first movement of Beethoven's Sonata in E flat major, Op. 27 No. 1, he used agogic accents to point up a long-range modal shift. In bar 49, he holds slightly the initial e'' on the downbeat, stressing the expected C major harmony; at the parallel spot in bar 57, he puts a stronger agogic accent on the e♭'' on the downbeat, which now initiates a surprising shift to C minor (and through it, a return to the original key of E flat major). His pointing up of the expected e'' in bar 49 makes more striking the unexpected shift to e♭'' eight bars later, projecting a cross-relation audibly across a lengthy span.

Metrical Counterpoint

Gould's interest in underscoring the play of harmonic and thematic forces led him frequently to rhythmic interpretations that contradict the prevailing nominal metre. He was always eager to seek out cross-rhythms and syncopations that contradicted the notated metre—what have often been called 'metrical dissonances' or, more recently, 'shadow metres'.[44] These could involve the temporary shifting of

---

[43] In the same performance, he makes a comparable rhythmic gesture to mark the point of recapitulation (bar 104) in the fugato that closes the Ouverture movement.

[44] The latter term was coined in Samarotto.

metre in all voices simultaneously, but in many cases, his metrical counterpoint was more overtly a function of his interest in linear counterpoint: emphasizing the integrity of individual contrapuntal lines often led him naturally to the super-imposition of contradictory metres. He enhanced the rhythmic independence of lines as a matter of course, and he always sought opportunities to impose it, whether briefly or broadly, and not only in music by the most inherently contra-puntal composers (Byrd, Bach, Brahms, Schoenberg). He often treated barlines and time signatures as mere typographical conveniences, where the 'inner time' of the music—the organization of motives, themes, phrases, patterns of figuration—seemed to contradict them.[45] Ex. 6.2 is typical. In bars 25–6, his hemiolas (com-mon time imposed on a larger triple metre) preserve the rhythmic profile of the imitated motive in the soprano and alto voices, and conform to the syncopation Byrd has written in the bass. In bars 27–8, the same motivic rationale justifies the hemiolas in the right-hand part, but now this metre is superimposed on a left-hand part that Byrd clearly wanted to conform to the notated metre. Shifts of metre like this imparted a real sense of action and variety in Gould's rhythm even where the tempo remained relatively strict; the metrical action to some degree made up for the relative discretion about nuances of tempo. Indeed, Johanne Rivest has sug-gested that Gould's fondness for metrical counterpoint in part explains his fondness for relatively stable tempos, for the impact of cross-rhythms is heightened where the basic rhythmic profile is strict.[46]

In stressing a syncopation or cross-rhythm, the performer has the basic options of maintaining or upsetting the nominal metre. He can, for example, make a syncopation by accenting a weak beat (agogically, dynamically, or through phrasing alone) but still preserving the prevailing metre by properly acknowledging the strong beats as notated. In such a case, the expressive effect of the syncopation comes from the contradiction between the accent and the metrical position of the accented note. Gould tended to favour the other option: injecting a stronger sense of rhythmic interruption by suggesting a sudden and complete shift to a new metre (and then back), a maximizing of rhythmic tension that is analogous to his exaggeration of contrapuntal tension within vertical textures. Exx. 6.2–6.5 are all typical in that I have had to rewrite the metrical notation of the original scores in order to convey the effect of Gould's cross-rhythms. Ex. 6.5 in fact demonstrates the distinction between the two syncopation effects: his rendering of Brahms's accents in the left hand creates a conventional syncopation, a dynamic accent that contradicts (but does not completely upset) the prevailing metre; his rendering of the accents in the right hand, however, creates a clear impression of a 3/4 metre

---

[45] The phrase 'inner time' is taken from K. Wolff, *Schnabel's Interpretation of Piano Music*, 98.

[46] See Rivest, 113, and her examples on xxxii–xxxiv.

Ex. 6.2. Byrd, 'Hugh Aston's Ground' (arrows indicate barlines in the score)

Ex. 6.3. Bach, Goldberg Variations (1981 recording)/Var. 8

both hands *sempre détaché*

being imposed on the notated 6/8. Moreover, his syncopations provide a firm metrical footing for the sense of broadening one perceives in the opening fourteen-bar period of this piece; the clear sense of movement from 6/8 to 3/4 to 3/2 slows the pace of the music by degrees.[47]

In this respect, too, some of his youthful influences undoubtedly played a part—Tureck's Bach recordings, for example, but also Schnabel, one of whose 'most emphatic goals' was to break the 'rule' that stated that a downbeat must receive a metrical accent, and who, 'wherever possible . . . adopted a reading which permitted him to have more than one rhythm going on at the same time'.[48] Gould's tendency to seek out and project rhythmic 'dissonance' and counterpoint

---

[47] In the minuet movement from Bach's Partita No. 5 in G major, which features hemiolas throughout, Gould created an unexpected additional rhythmic twist—indeed, a rhythmic 'climax'—in bars 41–2, by adding a hint of 3/2 to the already conflicting 3/4 and 6/8.

[48] K. Wolff, *Schnabel's Interpretation of Piano Music*, 56, 109.

Ex. 6.4. Beethoven, Sonata in D major, Op. 28 ('Pastoral')/I (arrows indicate barlines in the score)

is especially pronounced in his performances of Bach's fugues, in which his articulation of phrase units and dynamic points of emphasis within individual lines create complex rhythms not easily reconciled with the prevailing time signature. In Bach especially his approach to rhythm allies him with a long tradition of scholarship and performance practice that privileges the 'inner time' implied by the various lines over the notated barlines. Some of the older literature advocates a degree of syncopation at least as extreme as Gould's; indeed, he was probably influenced by such concepts as Schweitzer's 'syncopated accentuation', though it is unlikely that he was familiar with the considerable literature in German on the subject.[49] In any event, though his rhythmic premises were largely commonplace, his special gifts as a contrapuntal performer allowed him to project them with an unusual degree of clarity and emphasis.

The principal subject of the Fugue in D sharp minor from *WTC* I has appeared often in the literature on Bach performance as an archetypal example of a Bach theme that contradicts the notated metre on its first appearance. Exx. 6.6*a–d* show

[49]   The term 'syncopated accentuation' is introduced in Schweitzer, i. 379.

Ex. 6.5. Brahms, Ballade in B minor, Op. 10 No. 3 (arrows indicate barlines in the score)

the subject as written and in the metrical interpretations suggested by Schweitzer, Hellmuth Christian Wolff, and Paul Badura-Skoda over a period of eighty-two years.[50] Gould's interpretation, in Ex. 6.6e (see also CD 18), is not exactly the same as any of them, but certainly reflects similar principles. He heard this subject as consisting of two phrases, one in 3/2, the other in common time. He plays the two phrases smoothly, ignoring the barline; he introduces a significant comma, before the ninth note, to separate the two phrases, and places slight dynamic stress on that note to confirm the effect of a downbeat. He obviously made a motivic connection between the rising fifth and rising fourth intervals, both of which are followed by dotted notes and melodic descents, and he reinforced this connection by creating a similar rhythmic profile for each of the two phrases. Moreover, his performance emphasizes the connection between the note a♯' at the beginning of bar 1 and the note g♯' at the end of bar 2, implying that he interpreted as the melodic backbone of the subject the descending fifth from a♯' to d♯'. His perfor-

---

[50]   See ibid.; H. C. Wolff, 91; and Badura-Skoda, 29–30. (In Wolff's article, the example is transcribed into E flat minor.)

Ex. 6.6. Bach, *WTC* I, Fugue in D sharp minor: (*a*) subject; interpretations of the subject proposed in (*b*) Schweitzer (*c*) H. C. Wolff (*d*) Badura-Skoda; (*e*) subject in Gould's recording

mance is unconventional by pianistic standards (though characteristic) in that he used phrasing and rhythm almost exclusively to make his point; he used almost no dynamic inflection in shaping the theme. He gives a modernist, analytical reading of the subject in terms of its component parts, as opposed to a Romantic reading of the subject as a single *Gestalt* conveyed largely through dynamic profile. The fugue subjects in Ex. 6.7, both also discussed in the literature on Bach's rhythm, show the same principles in action. In each, Gould again shows little concern for barlines or even regular metre; shapes the subject more with articulation, phrasing, and rhythm than dynamics; and places metrical accents to emphasize a melodic backbone, implying an interpretation of the subject as the ornamentation of a basic falling or arching line.

In works like these fugues, the rhythmic profile of the subject inspires some significant rhythmic counterpoint as the fugue proceeds—for example, when the subject is accompanied by secondary material that conforms more closely to the

Ex. 6.7. Bach, *WTC*: (*a*) I, Fugue in F sharp minor, subject (*b*) II, Fugue in F sharp minor (1969 recording), subject

nominal metre. (Extreme rhythmic counterpoint of this sort is sometimes recommended in the literature as a by-product of the interpretation of the subject; Wolff's article offers many examples.) One common result of such rhythmic counterpoint is elided cadences; another is that sometimes no one metre is demonstrably in control of the texture, and only the regular pulsation of the lowest common denominator rhythmically—say, running semiquavers—is common to all voices. The Fugue in A flat major from *WTC* I offers a striking case in which Gould's metrical interpretation of the subject inspires later 'dissonance' and counterpoint that ultimately defines the work's form (see CD 12). His reading of the subject conforms to the nominal time signature (common time), but is displaced relative to the barline: the four beats of the subject, written as 2–3–4–1, are heard as 1–2–3–4; the fugue begins with a full bar in common time that seems 'consonant' to the ear but is in fact 'dissonant' in relation to the notated metre.[51] (Gould's slight dynamic emphasis of the first note, written on a weak beat, creates a palpable downbeat.[52]) As he applies this reading of the subject later in the fugue, the 'inner time' of the performance often contradicts the barlines. At times, the metre of the music is ambiguous, and only the persistent crotchet pulses and running semiquavers convey rhythmic unity and continuity. The whole fugue, as Gould plays it, divides up into cycles of displacement and restoration of metre:

[51] Krebs, 106, refers to this effect as 'subliminal metrical dissonance', adding that it is 'analogous to non-tonic scale steps in harmonic theory, which are consonant in their immediate context but dissonant against the background tonic'.

[52] In his reading, the crotchet rest with which the fugue begins becomes an upbeat, not a downbeat—an upbeat with a special significance. He creates a proportional tempo relationship between the prelude and the fugue by playing both at ♩ = 96 (the prelude is in 3/4 time). And so he does not 'lose' the crotchet rest, but makes it serve as a joint between related tempos.

passages featuring the subject proper are metrically displaced (including those featuring the head motive only, as in bars 21–2), while the sequences and other transitional passages between subject entries serve to restore the metrical 'correctness' of the music. Moreover, cadences that mark important modulations within the fugue are almost invariably those which also mark joints between these cycles of displaced and 'corrected' metre (see, for example, the cadences that fall on the downbeats of bars 8, 10, 16, 21, and 23).

Gould's metrical displacement of the subject is generally clear throughout this performance; in fact, it is metre that most characterizes the subject, rather than one consistent dynamic level, articulation, or phrasing. But his creation of metrical dissonance is especially obvious at certain spots. In bar 3, for example, the nominal downbeat of the bar, corresponding to the end of the subject in the bass, has the conspicuous feel of an upbeat, as does the following beat, and one hears no strong beat until the third beat of the bar, where the suspension dissonance is obvious. Likewise, in the tenor voice in bar 11, and in the soprano voice in bar 22, the juxtaposition of two upbeats—the collision of two different metres—sounds especially obvious. In bars 6–7, Gould displaces the subject metrically in the alto voice, but preserves as written the metrical profile of the soprano voice, which is descending to a cadence on the downbeat of bar 8; the alto and soprano voices on the downbeat of bar 7 thus belong, in effect, to different but superimposed metres. Likewise, in bars 14, 19, and 25, the first beat is both an upbeat, in terms of the subject, and a downbeat, in terms of the sequence that follows. In bar 5 (soprano) and 17 (tenor), Gould imposes a definite sense of downbeat on beats that are metrically weak but harmonically strong, and he does so in bar 27 (bass) to mark a thematic and tonal recapitulation.

In the eight bars that follow this recapitulation and conclude the fugue, he begins to restore metrical order, as though making an analogy between tonal and rhythmic resolution. One hears metrical ambiguities being ironed out within the stretto in bars 27–30: the bass entry in bar 27 is clearly displaced, but by the time of the soprano entry in bar 30 the subject conforms to the notated metre, as does the subsequent sequence. Finally, Gould makes no special effort to emphasize the last entry of the subject (soprano, bars 33–4), whether through rhythm, dynamics, or phrasing: it is now fully integrated into the prevailing metre and texture. In short, his treatment of rhythm and metre in this fugue defines its form: metrical displacement characterizes the subject in the exposition (bars 1–8); cycles of displaced and restored metre reveal developments of the subject and articulate major cadences and modulations (bars 8–27); and metrical order is gradually restored after the recapitulation in bar 27. As in the performance of the C minor fugue from *WTC* II, rhythm is here the primary carrier of the interpretation, the most important single element in the communication of form.

Gould's interest in counterpoint influenced him in matters like overdotting and synchronization. As a rule, he shared the modern preference for the accurate rendering of note values, as opposed to the Romantic tendency, in Philip's words, 'to lengthen the long notes and hurry and lighten the short notes', and to 'overdot dotted rhythms', creating 'a rather casual, "throwaway" style of rhythm' with an air of informality and improvisation.[53] He sometimes regularized rhythms in passage-work that is notated as rhythmically free, integrating it into the prevailing metre, as in Ex. 6.8. (Here his professed fondness for 'very firm, very tight rhythmic features' on the local level is apparent.) In Baroque music, he generally avoided synchronizing the rhythms of different contrapuntal voices. Though the issues of overdotting and synchronization in Baroque music are controversial, due in large part to the writings of Frederick Neumann, common practice, among both conventional and historical performers, overwhelmingly favours the aligning of musical lines that are dotted at different rhythmic levels, and the synchronizing of them where duple and triple rhythms coincide. Yet Gould generally preferred to preserve such rhythmic clashes.[54] In movements in the style of the French overture, in which dotted-crotchet-plus-quaver figures coincide with dotted-quaver-plus-semiquaver figures, he did not sharpen the quavers of the slower-moving lines to align them with the semiquavers of the faster-moving ones; he also tended not to rush *tirades* in order to align voices. Examples from his performances include not only overtures proper but movements that recall the style only fleetingly.[55] His contrapuntal rationale was especially persuasive in two pieces from Bach's *Art of Fugue*. Contrapunctus 7 is marked 'per Augment[ationem] et Diminut[ionem]', and Contrapunctus 6 also features diminution; often, in both fugues, the same subject is accompanied by itself at a different rhythmic level. By avoiding synchronization in these fugues, Gould seems to argue that there is no more important goal in performing a fugue that features augmentation or diminution than to preserve the rhythmic identity and integrity of the individual entries of the subject, at whatever rhythmic level they occur.[56] In the opening movement of Bach's French Overture in B minor, there are no clashes of rhythm between lines, but it is common for performers to overdot the quaver upbeats in bars 1, 11–13, 144, and 147–8—that is, to synchro-nize them with the prevailing semiquaver dotted rhythm of the movement. But

---

[53] Philip, 70.

[54] There is recorded evidence that he was not simply ignorant of the principle of synchronization in Baroque music. He was aware of it at least as early as 1954: see the Allemande from Bach's Partita No. 5 in G major, in his 1954 CBC radio performance (and in his 1956–7 studio recording), in which he aligns dotted figures with prevailing triplets.

[55] See Bach, Goldberg Variations (1955 and 1981 recordings)/Var. 16, 3–5; Bach, Partita No. 2 in C minor/Sinfonia, 1–6; Bach, Partita No. 4 in D major (1962–3 recording and 1979 film)/Ouverture, 5–6, 11; Bach, Partita No. 6 in E minor/Sarabande, 33; and C. P. E. Bach, 'Württemberg' Sonata No. 1 in A minor/I, 4–5 and elsewhere.

[56] Once again, he may have been directly influenced in his youth by Kirkpatrick, who, in his edition of the Goldberg Variations, xviii, makes just this point about the examples from *The Art of Fugue;* moreover, in Var. 16 (marked 'Ouverture') Kirkpatrick recommends avoiding synchronization in bars 3–5, advice Gould followed in both of his recordings.

Ex. 6.8. Beethoven, Bagatelle in E flat major, Op. 33 No. 1

Gould played these upbeats as written, and moreover seems to have taken them as a cue to lengthen some of the other, shorter upbeats, as well as some of the demisemiquaver *tirades*. By changing the rhythmic notation in the unconventional direction of *under*dotting, he imposed more rhythmic independence of contrapuntal lines than is indicated in the score.[57]

Contrapuntal considerations also led Gould to maintain—even exaggerate—clashes of, say, duplets against triplets; for some well-known examples, in all of which both conventional and historical performers generally 'dot' the duplets to align them with the triplets, see the Prelude in D major from *WTC* II, the third movement of Bach's Brandenburg Concerto No. 5, and the third movement of Bach's C minor violin sonata. More interesting was his decision not to synchronize the demisemiquaver arpeggios in Bach's Sinfonia No. 15 in B minor, which is notated in 9/16. The result is triplet motion at both the semiquaver and demisemiquaver levels, with the arpeggios now cutting across the basic metre of the Sinfonia, creating hemiola clashes of two against three in bars 13, 16, and 19. (Rendered clearly in a busy texture at top speed, these hemiolas reveal Gould's mental and digital agility, too.) In the Fugue in D major from *WTC* I, written in the French-overture style (and the subject of some debate in this respect), Gould's

---

[57] In his 1971–3 recording of this movement, Gould underdots upbeats and *tirades* in bars 1–2, 5–7, 10, 14, 1r–2r, 5r–7r, 10r, 14r, 16r, and 154; in the repeat of the opening section, and in the closing section, he does sharpen some notes (bars 4r–5r, 11r–12r, and 144), mostly to maintain the rhythmic independence of lines while accommodating changes in ornamentation. His 1969 CBC radio performance of the French Overture seems more perfunctory and less idiosyncratic, like a 'rough draft' for the later recording. In the opening movement, his tempo is considerably faster (CBC radio ♩ = 56, recording = 46), and he maintains to a greater extent the sharper rhythmic profile as written. He underdots upbeats only in bars 4–5, 7, and 10, and sharpens upbeats in bars 11–12 and 16; he does not lengthen any *tirades*. (He does not observe the repeat in this performance.) Hagestedt, 20–1, discusses Gould's recording of the French Overture, and suggests that his reading of the opening movement might be interpreted as a blending of rhythmic elements from the two surviving versions of the movement: the original C minor version, preserved in two manuscript sources, in which the rhythmic profile is softer throughout; and the later B minor version, published in 1735 in the second part of Bach's *Clavier-Übung*, in which the rhythmic profile is consistently sharper, more dotted. (The significance and implications of Bach's change of rhythmic notation in the published version are matters of considerable controversy, and this case arises often in discussions of overdotting and synchronization: see e.g. Hefling, 98–101; and Neumann, *Essays in Performance Practice*, 99–110.)

Ex. 6.9. Bach, *WTC* I, Fugue in D major, subject

inconsistent rendering of the dotted figures can be criticized as needlessly perverse, as an unwillingness to choose between playing as written and overdotting: he overdots the first dotted figure of the theme but plays the second as written, as in Ex. 6.9. Konrad Wolff offers a plausible rationalization for this practice: 'The first of the dotted eighths is repeated after the dot, while the second opens a descending diatonic progression in which the 16th following the dot—G—forms an essential step.'[58] The performance thus acknowledges a difference in melodic importance between the two semiquavers: the second B becomes an ornamental grace note, the G a true melodic tone.

Tempo, Rhythm, and Large-Scale Form

Gould's interest in manipulating tempo and rhythm to help communicate musical structure on a large scale extended to his creating rhythmic relationships between whole sections or movements. For example, in the Prelude and Fugue in E flat major from *WTC* I, his scheme of tempo relationships creates a cumulative dramatic structure. Bach gave no tempo markings for the prelude, but it comprises three sections, all distinct in terms of texture. The opening section (bars 1–10) is a series of toccata-like scale figures that modulates from the tonic to a half cadence on the dominant. An imitative section follows (bars 10–25), moving at a slower pace and again leading to a half cadence on the dominant. The final section (bars 25–70) brings together passage-work from the first section as a counter-subject to the imitated theme of the second, and develops this premiss at some length. Bach's notation suggests one tempo throughout, in which case the two themes would combine in the third section at the tempo in which they were earlier exposed. Gould, however, seems to have been inspired by such Bach movements as the opening Sinfonia of the Partita No. 2 in C minor, which comprises several sections in ever-faster tempos, marked as such by the composer. (In the Sinfonia, the first two sections are marked 'grave-adagio' and 'andante'; the third section, a fugato in 3/4 time, is unmarked but is clearly an allegro.) In the E flat-major prelude, Gould

---

[58] K. Wolff, *Masters of the Keyboard*, 3 n. Gould sometimes overdotted purely for expressive effect: see the principal themes of the Prelude in G minor from *WTC* I and of the 'largo' from Bach's Violin Sonata No. 6 in G major.

plays the opening section in an improvisatory manner, at about ♩ = 36; the imitative section at about 60; and the long final section at 87. He plays the fugue, which is written in the same metre as the prelude, at ♩ = 98, suggesting that he thought of the prelude and fugue together as forming a single dramatic structure, with the growing rhythmic intensity of the prelude reaching a culmination in the fugue. (Dynamics underscore this dramatic interpretation throughout.[59])

On a larger scale, in a number of works in variation form, Gould used tempo relationships to impose a clear dramatic profile onto the set as a whole. We saw in Chapter 3 how he often sought to convey a work as single shape or *Gestalt*, and as his career progressed he conceived of works like variation sets increasingly as unified wholes rather than as collections of discrete units. In his 1970 CBC television performance of Beethoven's *Six Variations on an Original Theme*, Op. 34, more so than in his 1960–7 recording, he seems to have been intent on using rhythm to fashion the highly disparate variations into a single cycle. In the later performance, the variations build in rhythmic intensity towards a central high-point (Var. 4), while the tempo and character of the opening return at the end. The later performance thus suggests an overall arching rhythmic structure; in the earlier recording, the variations are treated more as isolated units. As Fig. 6.1 shows, three major reinterpretations of tempo in the later performance contribute to this arching structure. Gould takes a much slower tempo in Var. 3, and so moves the high-point of rhythmic activity (now the beginning of Var. 4) almost exactly to the temporal centre of the performance. Further, in the later performance, there is no longer an extreme disparity of tempo in Vars. 3–5. Most important is Gould's decision to play the opening theme at the same tempo as the da capo. In the studio recording the theme is considerably faster, in accordance with Beethoven's tempo markings ('adagio' for the theme, 'adagio molto' for the da capo). Gould's decision in 1970 to bring the two into line by slowing the theme makes explicit his intention to treat the work as a cycle that returns to its point of departure after a series of wanderings. His recording is truer to the score as written, the broadcast (like many of his later performances) truer to his interest in long-range unity and continuity.[60]

In some works, Gould conveys a sense of order on the largest structural level, by suggesting rhythmic continuity between independent movements according to the principle of proportional tempos. He did not apply this principle in all, or even

---

[59] For a similar example, see the final two movements from Handel's Suite for Harpsichord in D minor. In the Air and variations, Gould conveys a sense of cumulative drama by gradually increasing the tempo and volume (i.e. the number of harpsichord registers). The concluding 'presto' becomes the culmination of this process, featuring the fastest tempo and the most registers.

[60] A propensity for cyclical formal order of this kind can occasionally be perceived in even his earliest performances—for example, the variation-form finales of Beethoven's sonatas in E major, Op. 109, and C minor, Op. 111, in his 1956 recording—though the cyclical possibilities are not pursued as rigorously as in some later recordings.

Fig. 6.1. Gould's tempos in Beethoven's *Six Variations on an Original Theme* in F major, Op. 34 (1960–7 recording and 1970 CBC television)

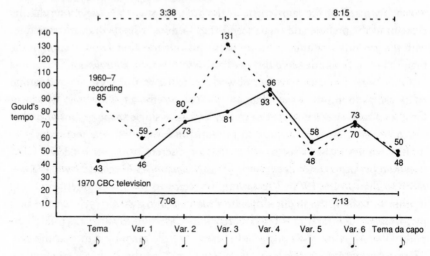

most, of his performances, but he did do so in a significant number of major works. According to this principle, two adjacent movements share, at some level, a common pulse, which creates an audible relationship between the two tempos. A movement in 3/4 time might share a crotchet pulse with an adjacent movement in 4/4 time, or the dotted-crotchet pulse of a 6/8 movement might become the minim pulse in a subsequent alla breve. The tempo relationship between movements might be even (say, ♩ in 2/4 = ♩ in 3/4), in which case it would be immediately audible because the shared pulse corresponds to a principal beat within each metre; or the relationship might be uneven (say, ♪ in 2/4 = ♪ in 9/8), in which case it would be more subtle because the movements share a common rhythmic referent only at a lower, more subliminal level that does not correspond to a principal beat. But the point in both cases is the same: to suggest that the pulse of one movement continues, at some rhythmic level, in the next.

The word 'suggest' is carefully chosen: Gould intended the method just described to work in performance, not on paper. The rhythmic relationships were meant to be heard and felt as such, but did not necessarily have to be demonstrably exact or quantifiable. (Indeed, there are some Gould performances in which it is difficult to determine, whether by calculation or intuition, whether he intended to convey a rhythmic relationship.) Rarely did he create mathematically exact relationships between adjacent movements, especially between opening tempos; rather, he took care at the joints between movements to suggest such relationships. Thus, he would derive the opening pulse of Movement Y from the closing pulse of Movement X, even if Movement X, because of a ritardando, closed considerably more slowly than it opened. In works featuring such a scheme of tempo relationships, there may actually be no mathematical correspondences between the opening or average pulses of adjacent movements, yet they may still be perceived subjectively as exchanging a common pulse because of Gould's interpretation of the transition between them. In a recorded interview with Tim Page about his 1981 recording of the Goldberg Variations, he made clear his intention to suggest rhythmic continuity subliminally, not literally exactly, and he was aware that rhythmic order carried to extremes would sound 'relentlessly clinical . . . ruthlessly sterile and antimusical'. His working methods are revealing. In outtakes from Monsaingeon's 1981 film of this performance, Gould never consults a written plan or metronome as he moves from variation to variation.[61] But he can be seen ensuring that each variation begins with an audible connection to the previous one. Before beginning a new variation, he would first hear a playback of the end (though never the beginning) of the previous one, and at times, in both the outtakes and the finished film, he actually conducts through a transition between variations, making the exchange of common pulse even more explicit.

The sources for Gould's interest in proportional tempos are not immediately clear; it is difficult to assess to what degree he was influenced by specific writings or performers. He was familiar from his teens with the work of Arnold Dolmetsch, who was an advocate of proportional tempos (as his surviving recordings show).[62] Erwin Bodky's book *The Interpretation of Bach's Keyboard Works*, which Gould reviewed in 1960, contains recommendations for some proportional tempos in multi-movement works. But Bodky, like many writers but unlike Gould, supports mathematically precise relationships between *opening* tempos of adjacent movements, and supports the application of generic tempos between adjacent dance movements (for example, $\quarternote$ = 80 for many allemandes, $\halfnote$ = 80 for many courantes). The specific tempo scheme in Gould's 1981 recording recalls the premises and recommendations in Walter Schenkman's 1975 article 'The Establishment of Tempo in Bach's *Goldberg Variations*'; both even choose the same initial pulse in the Aria: 60—that is, one beat per second, a kind of rhythmic middle C. But Gould diverges widely from Schenkman's table of suggested tempos, and the table is precisely what Gould's performance is not: mathematically exact. The article is not listed among Gould's effects in the NLC, and anyway his interest in rhythmic organization of this kind dates back more than a decade before the article was written. One can speak more broadly of Gould's interest in tempo relationships as a reflection of his very modern tastes in rhythmic order. (Recall Cone's reference

---

[61] See NLC videotapes nos. 42A–50A. On these outtakes, see Forfia.

[62] Beckwith, 'Glenn Gould, The Early Years', 59, notes that Alberto Guerrero had his piano students study Dolmetsch's book *The Interpretation of the Music of the XVII and XVIII Centuries, Revealed by Contemporary Evidence*, first published in 1915 and reissued in 1946, when Gould was 14.

above to the 'underlying arithmetical relation[s]' that can produce rhythmic unity in Baroque music.) And, of course, the whole principle of proportional tempo relationships in multi-movement (or multi-section) works in Renaissance and, to a lesser extent, Baroque music is surely relevant. Gould's interest in Renaissance music is documented, and though the extent of his scholarship on the subject (especially performance) cannot be determined, it is possible that this repertoire might have influenced him, even if no more than to plant the idea of an overarching *tactus* as a locus of structural organization. Modern musicology has tended to stress the decline of the proportions through the Baroque period, and the essential demise of the idea in later music, though David Epstein has recently collated an impressive amount of historical documentation and modern scholarship to show the relevance of the principle, in varying degrees, throughout Western music history, including a (largely unwritten) Viennese tradition that persisted through the Classical and Romantic periods and into the twentieth century.[63]

Though it is tempting to cite such sources, it is difficult, for lack of evidence, to place Gould's practices solidly in any tradition: he never specified sources for his proportional tempos, whether in ancient principles, living tradition, or modern scholarship. Take one example: there is a good deal of theoretical literature advocating the use of proportional tempos to underscore motivic relationships within a piece, and we saw in Chapter 3 how, in Beethoven's 'Appassionata' Sonata and Brahms's D minor concerto, Gould definitely made connections between motive and tempo in performance; yet, there is no evidence that he knew any such literature. It is not inconceivable that he simply reinvented the wheel when it came to proportional tempos, for the practice was, after all, entirely consistent with his interest in unifying musical devices, an interest that can be discerned early in his career and that grew stronger with age. Epstein is undoubtedly correct when he says of Gould's 1981 Goldberg Variations that it 'reflects no particular historical awareness of the principle of proportional tempo and the role it played in earlier eras', and that it 'seems that he came upon these relationships intuitively, and developed his temporal consciousness along these lines largely from practical experience'.[64] Given his background and learning, it is doubtful that Gould was looking to scholarship on Renaissance performance or some Viennese tradition when, for example, he applied proportional tempos in an unlikely place: the second movement of Beethoven's 'Hammerklavier' Sonata. Twice in this movement, he relates adjacent sections of triple and duple metre by making them share a common crotchet pulse, eliminating indicated contrasts of 'assai vivace' and 'presto'.

---

[63] Much of Epstein's book *Shaping Time*—97–363—is devoted to the subject of proportional tempo, and he offers a wide range of bases, criteria, and examples for the practice. Most relevant here is his collation of 'historical aspects', 109–34.

[64] Ibid. 124.

Where the composer marks 'presto' at bars 81 and 168 (2/4 and cut time, respectively), Gould simply maintains the crotchet pulse of the previous 'assai vivace' (3/4) section. With the change of metre from triple to duple, one still senses subjectively some quickening of tempo, though nowhere near the indicated 'presto'. But if the principle here can be shown to have deep roots and a large literature, it is probably more relevant to hold it up as a typical example of Gould's preference for unity and continuity over dramatic contrast.[65]

The 1981 recording of the Goldberg Variations, in which he sought to convey the shape of the work in circular terms, offers the most rigorous example of his proportional tempos. In his 1955 recording, one senses at times that he recognized relationships of pulse between some adjacent variations—especially in such obvious cases as Vars. 28 and 29. But he never explored the larger possibilities of rhythmic unity, instead treating the variations as self-sufficient entities, separated by significant pauses. But in 1981, as he said in Monsaingeon's film, he no longer thought of the variations as 'thirty very interesting but somewhat independent-minded pieces going their own way', but sought to make 'some sort of almost arithmetical correspondence between the theme and the subsequent variations'. Gould wanted each variation to relate intimately to its neighbours, and so to convey the impression that the pulse established in the opening Aria is present at some level throughout the variations. But that 'almost' is crucial. While one can find some truly 'arithmetical correspondences' in the final performance, those which can be considered meaningful are relatively few. For example, while Vars. 10, 14, 18–19, 22, and 28–9 all share the same timing of 1:03 (give or take a second), only in the two adjacent pairs is the continuity audible and meaningful; the other correspondences are probably coincidental, as Gould's working methods would suggest. (Exaggerating the mathematical nature of his tempo relationships, especially in this performance, is quite common in the Gould literature.)

There are varying degrees of subtlety to the rhythmic relationships between adjacent variations. In some cases, they are related by such even ratios as 1:1, 2:1, and 4:1: Vars. 1–2 and 28–9, for example, share the same crotchet pulse; the crotchet of Var. 9 becomes the minim of Var. 10; and the minim of Var. 18 becomes the quaver of Var. 19.[66] In such cases, Gould simply proceeds from the end of one variation directly into the beginning of the next, with no break in the

---

[65] Similarly, he ignored the 'presto' marking and simply maintained the previous tempo in the closing section of the Beethoven-Liszt *Pastoral* Symphony/III. (In such cases, did a precedent like the proportional switch from 3/4 to alla breve and back in the Scherzo of Beethoven's *Eroica* Symphony (bars 381–4) perhaps influence him?)

[66] Here and elsewhere, I follow Epstein in considering as proportional not only tempos that are in extact integral ratio, but also those that deviate by less than 5 per cent, 'the Just Noticeable Difference of the Weber Fraction'; see his discussion of Weber's Law and the Weber Fraction on 166–7. He writes, 'The practical import of this information with respect to performance is that within this range [i.e. between metronome marks 30 and 150] a tempo would have to change by more than 5 percent for the change to be noticed.' But he also acknowledges (and I concur) that this 'rule' must be applied somewhat flexibly under real-life, as opposed to laboratory, circumstances.

Ex. 6.10. Bach, Goldberg Variations (1981 recording)/Aria-Var. 1

continuity of the pulse, or with a short break evenly divisible in terms of the pulse. (Between Vars. 18 and 19 he interpolates a pause of four pulse beats, notwithstanding a slight ritardando that is not statistically meaningful; see CD 15–16.) Var. 16, a French overture with fugato (see CD 13), offers the one case in which there is a change of metre *within* a variation, and here Gould takes the dotted-crotchet pulse of the fugato directly from the crotchet at the end of the opening strain. (The new metre and tempo of the fugato are anticipated in the ornamental turn he appends to the trill at the very end of bar 15—a good example of the ornamental made 'structural'.) It is worth noting that his opening tempo in Var. 16 ($\textrm{J}$ = 60) takes up anew the pulse of the opening Aria ($\textrm{J}$ = 60). This tempo relationship significantly underscores the sense that Var. 16 marks a new beginning, since it opens the second half—'Act Two'—of the work (and hence the appropriateness of the overture topic).

More interesting are those examples in which Gould made special gestures to effect more subtle transitions between variations. Several times, as he noted, a ritardando at the end of one variation assumed a larger role than that of immediate expressive nuance, by cueing in the pulse of the next variation. This is the case with the Aria and Var. 1, which open at much different tempos ($\textrm{J}$ = 60 and $\textrm{J}$ = 83, respectively). At the end of the Aria, Gould slows the tempo to the point that the closing appoggiatura and its resolution each last the length of a whole bar of the variation to come (see Ex. 6.10); the ritardando thus leads the listener from one rhythmic plane to the next. This example shows, moreover, how Gould's method of creating tempo relationships is more direct and plausible than a strictly mathematical interpretation. Given the opening tempos of the Aria and Variation 1, one might tempted to posit a mathematical ratio of 3:4 between these movements, but while this is literally true it is essentially meaningless, especially given the ritardando at the end of the Aria. What the listener *hears* is not the abstract 3:4 relationship of opening tempos separated by more than three minutes, but the more immediate 1:1 ratio that Gould creates between the final beats of the Aria and the first variation.

There are, however, examples in which Gould does create very clear uneven ratios (3:1, 3:2) between adjacent variations. Vars. 5 and 6 have almost the same timing, though they are respectively in 3/4 and 3/8 time. The closing tempo of Var. 5 ($\dotted{\text{♩}}$ = 52) and the opening tempo of Var. 6 ($\dotted{\text{♩}}$ = 75) relate by a 3:2 ratio: three bars of Var. 5 equal two bars of Var. 6. What aids the listener in making intuitive sense of this ratio is the silence, equivalent to one full bar of Var. 5, that Gould interpolates between these variations. It makes the relationship palpable though less shocking than it might have been had the two variations literally bumped up against each other; it allows him, and the listener, a moment to change gears from old to new metre—from one pattern of accents to another relative to a common pulse. The joint between Vars. 16 and 17 offers a particularly complicated example in which Gould passes on a common pulse in spite of both an expressively appropriate ritardando and an uneven tempo ratio (see CD 13 – 14). He plays the closing fugato of Var. 16 (up to bar 45) at ♩. = 70, the opening of Var. 17 at ♩ = 108, creating an uneven relationship in which there is a common pulse only at the eighth-note level (♪ = 210 and 216, respectively). But he also plays the expected ritardando in bar 46 of Var. 16, observes the change to cut time in bar 47, and interpolates a moment's pause before continuing with Var. 17. It might seem on the surface that these gestures would undercut and confuse any tempo relationship between the two variations; yet, if one takes together the three beats of bar 46, the four beats of bar 47, and that moment's pause, one finds eight beats with an average pulse of 108—precisely the pulse of Var. 17. This observation might sound valid only 'on paper', but the sense the listener gets from this transition is precisely one of connection operating through apparent divergence. It is a remarkable (though not unique) example of Gould's extraordinary sensitivity to musical time, and his ability to control time in performance in ways that the listener, even if only intuitively, can appreciate.

Perhaps most impressive in Gould's 1981 recording is that he is able to *suggest* continuity of tempo where it is demonstrably lacking, at least mathematically. With Vars. 2 and 3, for example, there is a strong sense that they share a common quaver pulse, even though the metre changes from 2/4 to 12/8 and so the natural grouping of quavers changes from pairs to triplets. But in fact, the closing tempo of Var. 2 (♩ = 78) is in no sense proportionally related to the opening tempo of Var. 3 (♩. = 62), the less so given the ritardando in the final bar of Var. 2. Gould, however, plays the variations without a break between them, and phrases the first six quavers of Var. 3 in pairs—there is a small but obvious dynamic accent on the first D in the bass—before continuing with the usual 12/8 triplets (see Ex. 6.11). By emphasizing crotchet motion in the first few beats of Var. 3, he strongly suggests the carrying over of the crotchet pulse of Var. 2, even though this is not literally the case.

Ex. 6.11. Bach, Goldberg Variations (1981 recording)/Vars. 2–3

As in most cases where Gould made a didactic point about a piece, here some parts fit less naturally into the scheme than others, and certain compromises were required for the sake of the whole, including compromises with historical dance tempos. His reading of Var. 7, for example, which Bach marked 'al tempo di Giga' in his *Handexemplar* of the original published edition, has the more leisurely pace of a loure or siciliano ($\downarrow$. = 52), and he plays Var. 19, a passepied, almost as slowly as a sarabande ($\downarrow$ = 90; see CD $\boxed{16}$).[67] It cannot be said that Gould distorts these variations, but clearly the tempos that these dance movements would imply if played separately, and at which he himself played them in his 1955 recording, were tempered for the sake of their rhythmic relationships with neighbouring variations. Sometimes, the end of one variation actually collapses into the beginning of the next. In Vars. 19, 21, and 27, rhythmic motion stops only on the last semiquaver of the last bar, and in each case Gould allows no break in the pulse before moving on to the next variation (see CD $\boxed{16}$–$\boxed{17}$ for Vars. 19–20). The resulting tension between the natural urge to slacken the pace at the end and the insistence on immediately beginning anew can perhaps be said to underscore the feeling of driving, inexorable rhythmic continuity. While this is expressively appropriate, in all three cases Gould also uses the device to 'trick' the listener into perceiving a sense of tempo continuity where, mathematically, there in fact is none: the collapsing of variations disguises (or inspires?) an actual increase in basic pulse, while still maintaining a sense of continuity. It is doubtful that Gould or anyone else would end any of these three variations as he does in the 1981 recording if it were being performed as a separate piece; the expressive effect only makes sense within a context that assumes the present type of rhythmic continuity. Moreover, as Innes points out, there is in this recording a greater degree of stability of tempo

---

[67] Gould's tempo in Var. 7 was not, incidentally, chosen in ignorance of Bach's marking. In outtakes in NLC videotape no. 47A (though not in the final film or recording), he plays ornaments in Var. 26 that appear only in the *Handexemplar*, and in videotape no. 50A he can be seen with the 1979 Henle edition of the score, in which the 1975 discovery of the *Handexemplar* is noted and incorporated. In videotape no. 45A, he says that his very slow reading of Var. 19 was intended to create 'an intermezzo' between the faster Vars. 18 and 20, and shows how he used the silence between Vars. 18 and 19 to 'explain by way of a pause' the tempo of the latter.

(and dynamics) within variations than in any of Gould's previous performances of the Goldberg Variations, a feature consistent with his insistence on overall rhythmic continuity. By allowing little rhythmic (or dynamic) nuance *within* variations, he sets in higher relief the distinctions in character *between* adjacent variations, and draws the listener's attention to the macro, rather than micro, level of musical structure. He emphasizes in this way that the individual variations should be heard as units within a larger structure, not (or at least, not only) as complete, closed dramatic entities within themselves.[68]

There is no question that Gould's rhythmic scheme in his 1981 recording greatly enhances the audible sense of unity in the work. Of course, any set of variations by definition implies total order on at least one level; in this case, the recurring ground bass, which led Ralph Kirkpatrick to liken the work to 'an enormous passacaglia', is the primary organizing principle.[69] The Aria da capo, the dramatic organization of the variations, the presence of a canon every third variation, the progress of the canons through intervals ever-widening from the unison—all impose large-scale order. Ingrid Kaussler and Helmut Kaussler have proposed intervallic and motivic relationships between adjacent variations, as well as parallels between variations throughout the set; Owen Jander has proposed a hidden rhythmic symmetry based on the time signatures of the nine canons; and the Canadian pianist Reginald Godden (among others) has observed that the 'Aria has thirty-two bars and the thirty variations plus the two presentations of the Aria number thirty-two items'.[70] Gould's rhythmic scheme adds a further layer of unity, one that is, moreover, immediately audible—a performer's rather than a theorist's unity.

As he told Tim Page, he applied long-range rhythmic schemes of this kind with increasing frequency as he grew older, and came to feel later in his career that every work should have one basic rhythmic reference point. There are isolated cases in early performances of definite continuity of pulse between sections or movements— for example, the final movement (or, more accurately, complex of sections) in Beethoven's Sonata in A flat major, Op. 110, which he recorded in 1956. Here he applied a principle similar to that in Bach's E flat major prelude and fugue, only more precisely: he took the accumulating urgency built into the music and set it on a precise rhythmic foundation. He exactly doubled the basic pulse from section to section: 'adagio ma non troppo', ♩ = 20; 'Klagender Gesang, Arioso dolente', ♪. = 40; and Fuga ('allegro ma non troppo'), ♩. = 80. This doubling of speed provides a neat rhythmic analogy for the organic connection from one section to the next. Moreover, one effect of the scheme is a telling rhythmic identity between

---

[68]   See Innes, 72–7, 94–9. Kirkpatrick, xxvii, recommends not changing registers within a variation.
[69]   Kirkpatrick, vii.
[70]   See Jander; Kaussler and Kaussler, 182–230; and Godden and Clarkson, 251.

the quaver triplets in bars 110–13 and the semiquaver triplets in bars 114–15, at the return of the 'Arioso'. Gould may, indeed, have taken this transition as evidence that Beethoven intended a rhythmic relationship between the 'Arioso' and fugue tempos, and then projected this observation back onto the beginning of the movement.

Gould claimed that his first important use of the principle of long-range continuity of pulse was in 1962, in his performances of Brahms's D minor concerto. He did not offer details, but continuity is apparent in the performance that has been commercially released: the pulse at the end of the first movement ($\dotted\ = 52$) continues in the following 'adagio' ($\ = 51$); and the closing pulse of the 'adagio' ($\ = 42$), which incidentally corresponds to the opening pulse of the first movement, is taken up in the closing rondo ($\ = 84/\ = 42$).[71] Gould applied such rhythmic schemes more often after his retirement from concert life in 1964, and his recordings offer some revealing comparisons. In his recordings of Bach's Partitas, made between 1956 and 1963, he treated the individual movements of these works, at least in rhythmic terms, as isolated and independent (with a few exceptions), and used relatively long pauses to separate them. As his 1963 interview on the Partitas shows, he was not, at the time, generally concerned with continuity of pulse, in spite of his professed interest in other unifying aspects of performance in multi-movement works.[72] However, continuity of pulse is an important, almost pervasive, feature of his later recordings of Bach's English Suites (1971–6), French Overture in B minor (1971–3), and, especially, French Suites (1971–3). In all of these dozen suites, the pauses between movements are much shorter, and the movements are not conspicuously set apart in terms of rhythm. In some of the suites—for example, the French Suite No. 1 in D minor—the continuity of pulse from movement to movement seems clear and precise. In others, where the correspondences are less precise, Gould still suggests long-range rhythmic order by regulating the joints between movements so as to minimize the degree of separation.[73]

Various performances from the 1960s forward show Gould experimenting with continuity of pulse in different contexts. His 1967–71 recording of music by Byrd and Gibbons features proportional tempos between pavans and galliards, perhaps by analogy with the structural relationships between them as described by Thomas Morley in *A Plaine and Easie Introduction to Practicall Musicke* (1597).[74] In the

---

[71]   Leonard Bernstein's recollections in 1983 (see Bernstein, 17–19) about the tempos in this performance are misleading, and do not accord with Gould's comments on the subject or with the evidence of the concert recording. He claims, for example, that the first two movements had the same tempo; that 'the first movement alone took about as much time as it should take to play the whole concerto' (in fact, twenty-five minutes); and that the concerto 'took well over an hour to play' (in fact, fifty-two minutes).

[72]   See Johnson, 1.

[73]   Outtakes from his recording sessions for the Sarabande and Bourrées from the English Suite No. 1 in A major can be seen in Monsaingeon, *Chemins de la musique*, ii, and reveal a working method similar to that seen in the outtakes for the Goldberg Variations.

[74]   See Morley cited in Strunk, 87.

Ex. 6.12. Bach, Violin Sonatas: (*a*) No. 5 in F minor/I–II; (*b*) No. 4 in C minor (1975 recording)/ III–IV

First Pavan and Galliard of Byrd, for example, Gould took the closing pulse of the pavan (♩ = 32) for the tempo of the following galliard (♩ = 64); likewise, the tempo of the Sixth Galliard (♩ = 100) was drawn from the basic pulse of the final strain of the pavan (♩ = 52; see CD 9). He created similar tempo relationships in a number of paired works by Bach, for which there is some precedent in the scholarly literature, as he may have known. In his 1963–4 recording of the two-part Inventions and three-part Sinfonias, he played each Sinfonia directly after the Invention in the same key, and tended to minimize the degree of separation between them. In each case there is a suggestion of rhythmic continuity from Invention to Sinfonia, though sometimes the rhythmic relationship between the two is more obvious and exact (see especially Nos. 4–7, 9–10, 12, and 14–15). There are further examples in his recordings of preludes and fugues from *WTC* I and II.[75] In the Prelude and Fugue in E minor from *WTC* I, he maintains continuity of pulse both within and between movements: within the prelude itself, the crotchet pulse of the opening (unmarked, but suggesting 'andante'; ♩ = 47)

---

[75] For straightforward examples, see the following, in each of which the tempo relationship between prelude and fugue is ♩ = ♩: *WTC* I, C major; *WTC* I, D minor; *WTC* I, A flat major; and *WTC* II, F minor.

Ex. 6.13. Chart of Gould's scheme of rhythmic relationships in Bach's Partita No. 4 in D major (1979 film)

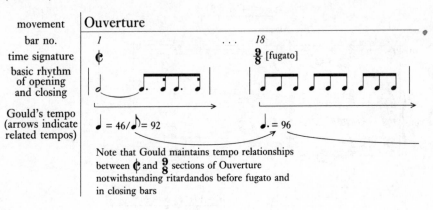

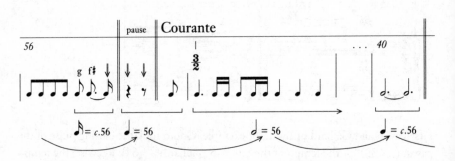

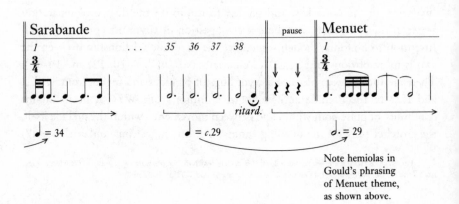

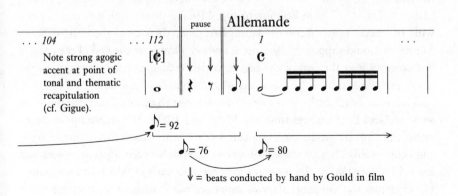

... 104   ... 112   pause   **Allemande**

Note strong agogic
accent at point of
tonal and thematic
recapitulation
(cf. Gigue).

♪ = beats conducted by hand by Gould in film

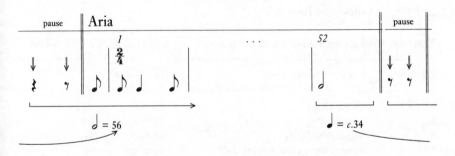

pause   **Aria**

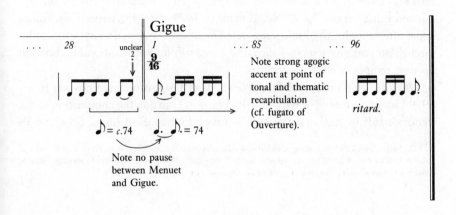

... 28   unclear   **Gigue**   ... 85   ... 96

Note strong agogic
accent at point of
tonal and thematic
recapitulation
(cf. fugato of
Ouverture).

ritard.

Note no pause
between Menuet
and Gigue.

becomes the minim pulse of the 'presto' that begins in bar 23; the same pulse is then passed on to the dotted minim of the fugue (unmarked, but suggesting 'allegro'). The effect, as in Beethoven's Op. 110, is a precise quickening of tempo, with the same pulse accommodating first one, then two, then three beats. Moreover, Gould suppresses the written *tierce de Picardie* at the end of the prelude but observes it at the end of the fugue, further evidence that he considered the whole prelude-and-fugue pair as a single formal and dramatic unit.[76]

The most noteworthy examples of long-range rhythmic order are found in some of Gould's recordings from the 1970s and 1980s. His recordings of Bach's violin and viola da gamba sonatas, made 1973–6 with (respectively) Jaime Laredo and Leonard Rose, feature many proportional tempos between adjacent movements; Ex. 6.12 shows two of the more obvious cases, in each of which ornamentation (appoggiatura and mordent) plays an important role in making the closing pulse of one movement clear enough for the listener to hear its relationship to the tempo that follows. There are isolated cases of proportional tempos in his later recordings of Beethoven's early sonatas, too, including the so-called 'Pastoral' Sonata, recorded in 1979, and shown in Table 6.6.

TABLE 6.6. Gould's proportional tempos in Beethoven's Sonata in D major, Op. 28 ('Pastoral')

Movement	Composer's tempo marking	Gould's tempo	
I	'allegro' (3/4)	(closing)	♩. = 60/♩ = 180
II	'andante' (2/4)	(opening)	♪ = 180
III	'allegro vivace' (3/4)	(closing)	♩. = 90
IV	'Rondo, allegro ma non troppo' (6/8)	(opening)	♩. = 94

(The second movement ends too slowly, with too great a ritardando, for any connection to the third to be audible. Between the third and fourth movements, he interpolates a pause of six pulse beats that makes the rhythmic connection obvious.) Even in his recordings of the fantasy-like Sonatas in A flat major, Op. 26, and E flat major, Op. 27 No. 1, made in 1979 and 1981 respectively, Gould apparently sought rhythmic cross-references and large-scale rhythmic order through proportional tempos—including (unusually for him) relationships between opening tempos of some movements.

One of Gould's most careful applications of proportional tempos was in his 1979 film performance of Bach's Partita No. 4 in D major, the culmination of the trend towards increasing integration in his performances of suites. (I believe, in

---

[76] In Monsaingeon's 1980 film on fugue, Gould deplores the disparity, the lack of integration, between the Prelude and Fugue in E major from *WTC* II, but once again his standards were anachronistic: for a composer of Bach's day, formal or dramatic 'integration' was not the point of a prelude and fugue—quite the opposite.

fact, that it is one of his greatest performances in any medium, in terms of conception as well as pianism.) More than in his 1962–3 studio recording, in his film performance he seeks an audibly unified conception of the work. Various aspects of performance practice contribute to a consistent profile of the music from movement to movement: approaches to counterpoint and texture; choices of repeats; octave displacements used as a special 'registration'; choices of dynamics and agogic accents; even ornamentation. But continuity of pulse, above all, welds the constituent movements into a whole. This continuity is already apparent within the Ouverture, in which the quaver pulse of the slow, dotted opening strain becomes the dotted-crotchet pulse of the fugal conclusion. As the chart in Ex. 6.13 shows, there are no mathematical relationships between the opening or average pulses of the various movements, but a palpable effect of continuity is still achieved through the careful rendering of the joints between them. The short pauses that Gould places between movements are evenly divisible in terms of the pulse that is being passed on, and in several cases (indicated in the chart) he conducts through the pauses with a free hand, making his rhythmic intentions explicit. Of this extraordinary performance—as of the C minor and A flat major fugues, or the 1981 Goldberg Variations—one might say that rhythm *is* form.

7

Dynamics

GOULD'S CONTROL OF dynamics was no less extraordinary than his control of rhythm; indeed, the two generally operated in tandem. Listen to his piano recording of Wagner's *Siegfried Idyll:* on the immediate level the dynamic level rises and falls as the mood of the music demands, yet on the largest level one hears him realizing the whole work—all twenty-four minutes' worth—as a single, great dynamic hairpin that reaches a climax in bars 295–307, the passage in which the trumpet makes its only appearance in the original; in the final pages, from that climax to the end, his control over the gradual slackening of tempo and reduction in dynamic level must count as one of his most astonishing (if least showy) pianistic feats. It is a remarkable example, on a very large time scale, of a performance structured around a 'single culminating point' (to recall Rachmaninov's phrase). But it is only one example among many; Gould's control over small- and large-scale dynamic nuance was admired from the beginning of his career.[1]

Moreover, in his treatment of dynamics the freedom with which he interpreted musical scores is readily apparent, and not only in early music for which the composer provides no dynamic markings. At first glance, he seems to treat dynamics almost casually, much as Romantic pianists once did, with little regard for what is written in the score; he seems to have had no more regard for a composer's dynamics than most modern actors have for a playwright's directions. As Carl Morey has shown, Gould's compositions often reached completion with no dynamic markings at all, and his written transcriptions of orchestral music did not, as a rule, incorporate the composer's dynamics, or expression markings, as integral aspects of the piece. In the final draft for the *Siegfried Idyll* (NLC 28/3), for example, he entered dynamic markings, along with recording and editing markings, in different (and obviously later) ink than the notes, probably at the time of his recording of the work. This is one of many pieces of evidence suggesting that he thought of dynamics as a function of a specific performance, of a particular interpretation of a musical structure, not as part of the notation that (in Nelson Goodman's terms) defines a musical work. Each interpretation implied its own dynamic plan,

---

[1] Schafer, 59, writing in 1958 of the Toccata in Gould's recording of Bach's Partita No. 6 in E minor, observes 'a beautiful pacing of dynamics here, from high to low to high to low again. The long four-and-a-half-page *Durchführung* of the middle part of the movement [bars 27–88] which Mr. Gould plays as a careful almost unbroken crescendo is a miracle.'

whether or not compatible with the composer's dynamics. This is not to suggest that he was indifferent or careless about dynamics. When he told an interviewer in 1962 that he had 'never been fond of exploiting the dynamic potentials of the piano', he meant only that he favoured less dynamic fluctuation than did Romantic pianists, and sought rationales for dynamic nuance in the music's structure.[2] He tended to avoid pervasive use of what Ralph Kirkpatrick has called 'pianistic chiaroscuro';[3] indeed, his performances frequently suggest a throwback to that pre-Romantic era when keyboard players discriminated more through articulation and phrasing than dynamics.[4] Yet, his performances are far from static dynamically, and he did exploit dynamics in a variety of ways to serve his interpretations.

Many Gould performances feature departures from written dynamic markings that indicate nothing but a disagreement with the composer as to the degree of expressive intensity appropriate to a particular passage.[5] He often smoothed over dynamic markings that he found too fussy—for example, chains of alternating piano and forte markings in slow movements by Mozart—and often replaced dynamic accents with more subtle agogic accents. He would often draw attention to a particular event by pulling back dynamically, even at the top of a melodic phrase, where many pianists would make a definite dynamic climax, thus using the denial of an expected accent as a kind of 'negative accent'. He generally avoided or minimized sforzandos and other dynamic accents, even in music by composers (like Beethoven) who made them a distinctive part of their personal style. He cited a Puritan's abhorrence of 'theatricality' as one reason,[6] but another was surely that dynamic accents can disturb the relatively equable disposition of contrapuntal voices that he often sought in performance. There is a notable sobriety in terms of dynamics (as well as tempo) in many performances in which he focused with special intensity on counterpoint, from Sweelinck's 'Fitzwilliam' Fantasia to Bach's *Art of Fugue* to twentieth-century works like Valen's Sonata No. 2. In such works, Gould seems at times to flirt intentionally with being 'inexpressive', with creating a relatively neutral expressive framework in which dynamic and rhythmic fluctuations are not permitted to disturb the deliberate surveying of musical materials and relationships, except where such fluctuations can serve to make a contrapuntal point, articulate a motive or cadence, or in some other way clarify the music's

---

[2] Asbell, 91.

[3] Kirkpatrick, xxvii.

[4] As Barth, 159, notes, it was Czerny, following Beethoven, who 'helped to popularize the practice of substituting changes in dynamics for articulation'.

[5] He discusses one such example, from the Intermezzo of Schoenberg's Suite, Op. 25, in Monsaingeon, *Chemins de la musique*, ii.

[6] See *GGR* 36. He always associated 'theatricality' in performance more with concert than studio performance, and Innes, 80–4, observes that, predictably, he made considerably more use of dynamic accents during his concert years than later.

structure. In some of his performances of contrapuntal music, dynamic fluctuations are almost exclusively by-products of the pointing up of contrapuntal events as they occur, rather than the result of real changes in basic dynamic level. Even with a less overtly contrapuntal work like Mozart's K. 330 sonata, he spoke of conveying an 'X-ray' view of the music, an approach that demanded restraint in terms of dynamics and tempo.[7]

Gould sometimes eliminated dynamic accents where he preferred to keep the listener's attention focused on a larger structural level, as in the second movement of Beethoven's Sonata in F major, Op. 10 No. 2. Here the composer marks dynamic accents to create syncopations (bars 9–15), to emphasize dissonant notes and chords (bars 23–4, 27–8, and 49), and to mark the top note of a phrase (bar 33), but in each case Gould reduces the intended dynamic effect, applying a much more subtle crescendo or a slight agogic accent, never disturbing the quiet, *misterioso* quality of the opening. Only in the dissonant passage that leads to the final cadence in the Trio (bars 79–86, repeated bars 103–10) does he permit the significant increase in volume marked in the score. He creates a single, central climax for the movement, at the crux preceding the return of the opening at bar 125, reducing earlier dynamic accents to set this climax more strongly in relief.[8]

Gould's departures from written dynamics sometimes suggest a disagreement with the composer as to the nature of expression, as well as the degree of intensity. An extreme example comes at the end of the Trio section (bars 78–86) of the third movement of Beethoven's Sonata in D major, Op. 10 No. 3—that is, the transition from the end of the Trio back into the Minuet. While he retains the notes and rhythms exactly as written, he inverts every indicated aspect of expression, creating (to recall Jacques Hétu's phrase) a negative image of the score. What Beethoven indicates as in time, loud, clipped, dry, and broken off, Gould plays as slowing down, soft, smooth, pedalled, and fading away. It is as though a line in a play meant to be shouted were whispered instead (common enough in the theatre, in fact). Beethoven asks for a sudden return to the gentle texture of the Minuet; Gould prefers that the Trio fade gradually into it. Nothing in the notation of the music is changed, but the movement as a drama is completely rethought.

Gould's rationales for departing from written dynamics ranged widely. Some were conventional, as when he used dynamics to help convey the relative structural weight of cadences, or responded to a thinning of texture. Sometimes tempo alone seems to have inspired new dynamics. Hétu, in his response to Gould's recording of his *Variations pour piano*, notes that his tempo in the third variation ($\textrm{\musEighthNote} = 60$,

---

[7] See *GG* (He refers here only to the first movement in his 1958 recording.)

[8] For comparable examples, see the second movements of Beethoven's Sonatas in A major, Op. 2 No. 2, and C major, Op. 2 No. 3. In each movement, Gould emphasizes a single fortissimo climax, at the entrance of the main theme in a distant key, by underplaying written fortissimo dynamics elsewhere in the movement.

exactly twice as slow as the metronome marking) rendered impractical certain dynamic nuances, most notably the triple-forte climax.[9] In several slow movements by Haydn, Gould's reductions of indicated dynamics seem tied to his unusually slow tempos, and throughout Grieg's E minor sonata his emphasis on the work's gloom and melancholy led him to unusually moderate tempos, and many reductions of indicated dynamic contrasts.[10] In the second movement of the Clavier Concerto No. 1 in D minor, Bach clearly intended the opening tutti (like the closing tutti) to be played forte, since the orchestra is instructed to play piano when the soloist first enters. But Gould, in his 1957 recording of the movement, opted for a *misterioso* reading with a very slow tempo ($\downarrow$ = 38), and with it a new dynamic plan. The opening tutti now begins piano; with the hemiolas in bars 6–8 there is a crescendo that builds to the dissonant climax on the Neapolitan note A♭ in bar 11, then a return to piano in the closing tonic cadence.

Such examples suggest that Gould's dynamic plans, like his decisions about rhythm, were often motivated by tonal events—one of the most important criteria for his performance practices, as we have already seen, and a crucial factor in his performances of Bach, who left few dynamic markings. He was not immune to making simple, conventional dynamic analogies to rhythmic events, including the Romantic cliché that Stravinsky so deplored: the pairing of a crescendo with an accelerando (and the inverse effect).[11] An accelerando in a passage of harmonic tension (some sequences, dominant pedals) might be accompanied by a crescendo, a ritardando in a passage of harmonic relaxation (tonic pedals, flatward modulations) by a decrescendo. But harmonic criteria are often apparent in Gould's dynamics where the tempo remains constant; Bach fugues, in particular, provide many examples. Linking dynamics to harmonic action is by no means radical: the principle is centuries old, is well documented among Romantic performers and editors (notably in the music of Bach), and continues to be recommended for Baroque music. Gould's relative reticence about detailed dynamic nuances does set him apart from most Romantic performers (and from many of his contemporaries), but his use of harmonic criteria also led to some revealing similarities to Romantic performances.

Less conventional, especially by post-war standards, was his willingness to allow harmonic criteria to suggest major revisions to written dynamic markings in later repertoire. (Recall the *Meistersinger* Prelude, discussed in Chapter 2.) In the first movement of Beethoven's *Pathétique* Sonata, he moved the sudden piano marking at bar 163 to bar 167—arguably a more logical choice. He retained the forte

[9] See Hétu, 25.

[10] See Haydn's Sonata No. 42 in D major/I, Sonata No. 48 in C major/I, and Sonata No. 50 in C major/II. In the first movement of No. 48, Gould ignores the forte markings in the opening presentation of the principal theme, saving a true forte for bar 27, where the theme appears in the tonic minor. For his comments on Grieg's sonata, see *GGR* 80.

[11] See Stravinsky, 129.

dynamic until the dominant pedal is reached, then reduced the dynamic level to begin building tension towards the recapitulation. (Beethoven's change to piano at bar 163 comes, in terms of harmony and texture, in the middle of a phrase.) And he maintained that dominant tension into the recapitulation (bar 195) by ignoring Beethoven's *fp* marking at bar 187, retaining forte through the flourish in bars 187–94. In the second movement of Beethoven's Sonata in D major, Op. 10 No. 3, in the ornamented repeat of the main theme beginning at bar 65, Gould replaced the quick crescendo that Beethoven marks, which calls for a move from pianissimo to forte in two bars, with a more gradual crescendo extending through this whole passage, to a climax on the tonic six-four chord in bar 72. The crescendo mimics the growing harmonic tension, and the slow chromatic ascent of the bass line towards its goal, the dominant note A, in bar 72; it ties the whole passage together as an integral unit. In the second movement of Beethoven's Sonata in C minor, Op. 10 No. 1, in the final presentation of the theme (bars 91–102), he changed dynamic markings to place the peak of volume at the final achievement of the tonic at bar 102, then diminished the volume gradually in the confirmations of the tonic in the eleven bars that follow.

All of these examples have in common a correlation of dynamics with harmonic tension and relaxation, and all reveal Gould's analytical mindset even as they contradict the score. So, too, do those cases in which he 'corrects' written dynamics to create or underscore similarities between otherwise parallel spots in the music— say, making a recapitulation of a theme more obvious by presenting it at its original dynamic level.[12] In Scriabin's Prelude, Op. 33 No. 3, a piece of just twelve bars, he ignored *sff* and *ff* markings in bars 8–9 to preserve the quiet dynamic level of the phrase in bars 7–9. (The previous three-bar phrases, bars 1–3 and 4–6, had both been presented at consistent dynamic levels—fortissimo and forte, respectively.) By ignoring Scriabin's interjections in bars 8–9, Gould established a pattern of ever-quietening phrase units, and so set in greater relief the dramatic surprise of the closing phrase, bars 10–12, in which a pianissimo dynamic is shattered by cadential chords marked *sfff*. In this case, his dynamic plan, though it upsets one of the twists in Scriabin's 'plot', has a dramatic logic of its own, but some of his dynamic changes, no less 'structural' in motivation, can only be considered impoverishments of the music. In his recording of the Echo movement that closes Bach's French Overture in B minor, for example, he dropped the echo effects—the forte-piano contrasts—that are the point of the movement. His decision may not have been entirely perverse. The passages marked piano by Bach are those which already

---

[12]   For dynamic parallelisms of this kind, see the following examples: C. P. E. Bach, 'Württemberg' Sonata No. 1 in A minor/II: cf. bars 1 and 21; Mozart, Sonata in B flat major, K. 281/I: cf. bars 1 and 70; Beethoven, Sonata in F major, Op. 10 No. 2/II: cf. bars 36–7 and 168–9; Beethoven, Sonata in G major, Op. 31 No. 1/I: cf. bars 3–7 and 48–52; Beethoven, 'Appassionata' Sonata/III; cf. 20 and 64; and Grieg, Sonata in E minor, Op. 7/II: cf. bars 7–8 and 47–8.

have the thinnest textures (sometimes only a single line); those marked forte are the thicker, busier chordal passages. (Compare, for example, bars 22 and 23.) In other words, if the movement were played at a continuous dynamic level subtle distinctions of volume would still appear as the number of voices in the texture changes. Gould may have felt that the music did not demand the dynamic underscoring of its contrasts that Bach indicates. Typically, his dynamic plan speaks less to foreground variety of expression than background tonal design: he drops those of Bach's dynamic markings that create echo effects (as at bars 5–7), but observes those that correspond to important points of articulation in terms of the tonal plan (as at bars 13 and 45). Once again, these are 'structural', 'logical' dynamics by Gould's standards, but I doubt there is a listener anywhere who would find the rather conventional tonal plan of this movement more interesting than the dramatic contrasts of texture and volume that Gould stubbornly refuses to highlight.

It should be noted that he was generous with dynamic nuances at the harpsichord—more so than most contemporary harpsichordists, in fact. This is an interesting paradox: he was cautious at the piano, which is inherently rich in dynamic potential, but liberal at the harpsichord, which traditionally is not. Once again the rationality of the Gould aesthetic is apparent: the piano demands more careful control precisely because it can be more readily indulged. In his recording of Handel's suites, and in his CBC television performances of preludes and fugues by Bach, he used a large Wittmayer harpsichord whose many registers, controlled by pedals, permitted a wide range of tone colours and volume levels which he exploited freely. Notwithstanding his insistence that Landowska did not influence his playing, his harpsichord playing in fact recalls her more than any more recent historical performer, and the Wittmayer resembles Landowska's notorious Pleyels more than any Baroque instrument.[13] As much as Landowska, he wanted at the harpsichord the same dynamic possibilities offered by the piano. He played the Allegro from Handel's F major suite as a continuous crescendo by gradually adding registers throughout, and in his performances of Bach fugues he used registers generously to clarify counterpoint and set off tonal regions.

In at least one instance, Gould's thinking about dynamics seems to have been influenced by analogies to other works. In the second movement of Beethoven's Cello Sonata in A major, Op. 69, he and Leonard Rose change the whole character of the music in the third appearance (after the second Trio) of the opening Scherzo material. In the score, Beethoven indicates that the Scherzo here is to be played as in its two earlier appearances, with frequent forte interjections and crescendos. But in a performance for CBC television in 1961, Gould and Rose play this whole section conspicuously pianissimo throughout. They seem to have been influenced by another middle-period Beethoven work in A major, the Seventh Symphony, which sets a precedent for such dynamic variants in a five-part Scherzo-and-Trio movement. Their performance recalls even more closely the Scherzo movement of the String Quartet in C sharp minor, Op. 131, in which Beethoven, in the third presentation of the opening material, calls for just the kind of quiet, rarefied variation that Gould and Rose offer in the cello sonata.

In Chapter 3, we saw how Gould sometimes used dynamics to convey a whole work as a large arch or some other controlling shape or *Gestalt*. This practice was not incompatible with the conventional use of dynamics to underscore musical events on a more immediate level. In a 1963 interview, he noted how the piano could serve Bach's music by allowing the performer to suggest dynamic continuity (a plateau, or a long crescendo or decrescendo) while still making small dynamic adjustments for the sake of clarifying counterpoint—that is, to convey minor local variations within a basic *Gestalt*, a practice Schenker called 'layered dynamics'.[14] The piano allowed him often to mimic the stable registers of the harpsichord without requiring him to employ the degree of rhythmic fluctuation typical of harpsichordists in order to make detailed expressive, contrapuntal, analytical points. His recording of the Fugue in D sharp minor from *WTC* I shows this simultaneous control of both the 'architectonic dynamic' and 'the dynamic of detail' (to borrow Albert Schweitzer's terms), in response to the harmonic and contrapuntal criteria that always directed his Bach performances (see CD [18]).[15] The first half of the fugue (bars 1–44) features a continuous crescendo from piano to fortissimo, creating a central dynamic climax at the point at which a half cadence on the dominant introduces an unusually early return of the tonic key, along with the first appearance of the subject in inverted stretto. (This, for Gould, was the turning-point of the piece.) Throughout the fugue, he uses small-scale dynamic plateaus, crescendos, and descrescendos to underscore local harmonic events and entries and developments of the subject, and his dynamic peaks correspond to the most important joints in the structure: the central tonal recapitulation (bar 44); the thematic recapitulation of the original subject in the tonic (bar 52); the high-point of fugal artifice (bar 77); and the final achievement of the tonic with *tierce de Picardie* (bar 87). Yet he manages to articulate these events dynamically without compromising the larger dynamic action, the gradual move towards and away from the central climax that determines the basic shape of the fugue as a whole.[16]

[14]   See Johnson, 2; and Rothstein, 10, 26–7 (n. 19).

[15]   Schweitzer, i. 363. He adds that 'nothing is gained by besprinkling his compositions with *pianissimo, piano, mezzoforte, forte, fortissimo, crescendo* and *decrescendo*, as if they were written for the accordion', and speaks of 'a broad dynamic plan . . . richly shaded in detail'—that is, layered dynamics—as most appropriate to Bach.

[16]   In 1964, two years after recording the D sharp minor fugue, Gould wrote that many of the fugues in the *WTC* reach a point of highest tension where the principal subject appears in inversion; see *GGR* 240. In the present case, the high-point is the first stretto of the inverted subject, which coincides with the tonal recapitulation and is set in high relief (it begins in the bass after a bar's rest). The simple inversion of the subject appears earlier, at bars 30, 36, and 39, and is less strongly articulated.

We can begin to see certain recurring features in Gould's treatment of dynamics: the reduction of detailed dynamic inflection; the pointing up of important structural (usually tonal) events at a background level; the use of dynamic continuity to set off major units of structure. Taken together, they make it plain that he was influenced by the old convention of terraced dynamics, modelled on the registrations of the harpsichord and organ and on the principle of the concerto grosso. Terracing was already common in the 1950s, at the beginning of Gould's professional career (and his musicology never extended much beyond the standards of that day); yet the term 'terraced dynamics' is no more than a century old, and today the practice is somewhat discredited. At least as early as the 1930s, considerable historical evidence had been discovered revealing detailed dynamic indications and graded dynamics in seventeenth- and eighteenth-century music, even in places where stark dynamic contrasts might seem to be indicated.[17] But terracing of dynamics was advocated in the early post-war historical performances of Bach that Gould admired, in the 1938 Kirkpatrick edition of the Goldberg Variations that he studied in his youth, and in much of the early Bach scholarship with which he was familiar. Schweitzer, for example, whose views on Bach and Bach performance seem to have had a significant influence on him, advocated dynamic terracing at the turn of the century, and many of his recommendations, both general and specific, are apparent in Gould's performances: to play some whole works or movements (for example, some preludes and dance movements) at one continuous dynamic level throughout, where no justification for dynamic nuances exists; not to use crescendos and decrescendos to make transitions between dynamic terraces; and not to accent the subject throughout a fugue at the expense of other voices. Schweitzer further recommended avoiding dynamic swells in presenting a fugue subject, advice Gould followed. The implied confrontation with Romantic practice in many of Schweitzer's comments on dynamics, and his invoking of harpsichord registration and Bach's organ and concerted works as models for imitation by the modern pianist, however dated, clearly influenced Gould. Indeed, he pointed to the influence of his own early organ playing when he noted, in a 1959 interview, his tendency to articulate fugue subjects through rhythm and phrasing more than dynamic nuance, precisely along the lines suggested by Schweitzer.[18] (This tendency can be seen as a microcosm of his very modern tendency to view fugues primarily in terms of structure and only secondarily in terms of rhetoric and drama.) Finally, the concept of terraced dynamics undoubtedly also reached Gould through the influential example of Rosalyn

---

[17]   See e.g. the historical and modern sources cited in Boyden (which dates from 1957).

[18]   See Schweitzer, i. 355–64. Cf. also Schweitzer's recommendation for the opening bars of the Prelude in D major from *WTC* II, in i. 359–60, with Gould's recording. Gould's comment on his early organ playing is quoted in Payzant, *GGMM* 97.

Tureck, who was an early and eager proponent of the view that 'the pianist's habit of continual rise and fall [of dynamics] does not suit Bach'.[19]

But Gould's dynamic terracing also differed in some ways from the conventional principle and from some of his specific influences. For one thing, he was considerably less strict and literal in his application of terraces, by comparison with early historical performers and especially Tureck, whose dynamic plateaus are generally much more strongly etched. And he was less rigorous than Tureck when it came to making dynamic analogies to musical events. (Tureck, for example, in her recording of the *WTC*, almost invariably applies a crescendo to an ascending sequence, a decrescendo to a descending sequence, while Gould's performances suggest no such regulations.) Moreover, with Gould the concept of terracing must be understood more broadly than usual. It applies in the usual sense of dynamic continuity used to create plateaus, but it also applies to the use of crescendos and decrescendos over a long span, as in the first half of the D sharp minor fugue, which suggests a kind of 'diagonal' terrace. 'Terracing' for Gould meant not only stark concerto grosso-like contrasts, but large-scale dynamic responses to accumulating tension or relaxation. (Such 'diagonal' terraces are most obvious in his recordings of Bach fugues from the 1950s and 1960s.) It is not the flatness of dynamic level that defines a terrace in this sense, but the continuity of the dynamic event.

Terraced dynamics meant Bach, first and foremost. In a 1963 letter, Gould wrote:

I feel that if one is going to use the piano for Bach's music at all, one has to attempt to some degree to simulate the terraced registration of the harpsichord. While I am far from puritanical in this matter and do not believe in any case in carrying such theories to excess, I feel that the main progress in Bach interpretation which has occurred in the last generation or so, has been that so many people have been willing to attain the necessary clarity and delineation by sacrificing to some degree colouristic qualities of the piano.[20]

But he applied the concept of terraced dynamics, to varying degrees, in many performances of later repertoire, too, often with provocative results. (An example from Brahms's D minor concerto was mentioned in Chapter 3.) In Classical sonata-allegro movements, he often used dynamics to articulate large units of structure, especially tonal units, while smoothing over some smaller-scale expressive nuances and contrasts. In C. P. E. Bach's 'Württemberg' Sonata No. 1 in A minor, he departed from the score on several occasions to set off musical paragraphs one from the other, and to tie together dynamically material that is alike in texture and

---

[19]   Tureck, *An Introduction to the Performance of Bach*, i. 6. Her major criteria for dynamic decisions, like Gould's, are harmony and counterpoint.

[20]   *GGSL* 69. He goes on in this letter to defend 'layered dynamics' on the piano. As Innes, 87–99, 149–53, shows, his performances of Bach relied less on 'inflectional' dynamics (i.e. crescendo and decrescendo) and more on 'sectional' (i.e. terraced) dynamics as his career progressed; see especially her Table 7 (87–92).

function. In the exposition of the first movement, for example, he plays forte the two statements of the opening theme (in the tonic and dominant, respectively); plays the sequences that follow each statement piano; and plays the cadence into the double bar forte. These dynamics suggest the solo-tutti contrasts of a Baroque concerto grosso—the two forte statements of the main theme have the character of tutti ritornellos—and he changed markings in bars 5 and 12 to create the effect.

He noted on several occasions that his performances of Mozart's sonatas were informed by standards he usually applied to Baroque music, in terms of tempo, rhythm, counterpoint, and dynamics.[21] Most of his performances of the sonatas tend towards terraced dynamics, with many local dynamic effects and contrasts eliminated or minimized. This is particularly true of slow movements, in which he made expressive nuances within a narrower range than that implied by the many forte-piano contrasts in the score, and in which he generally saved strong dynamic effects for moments of climax on the largest structural level. As with the Bach Echo movement, he often let variations of texture alone provide dynamic contrast, without further emphasis. An example from a Mozart slow movement was discussed in Chapter 3 (see CD [4]), but his performances of Mozart's larger sonata-allegro movements also reveal dynamics used to articulate large-scale rather than local-level events. In the first movement of his 1969 recording of the Sonata in A minor, K. 310 (see CD [19]), his dynamic terraces, especially the extended sections of continuous crescendo, seem functions of his very propulsive tempo ($\downarrow$ = 175). In this performance, large areas of either static dynamic level or of crescendo or decrescendo correspond to major tonal activity.[22] In the exposition, he maintains a continuous forte dynamic throughout the first key area (bars 1–22)— that is, until the first modulation, articulated by the half cadence in the relative major. He does not change the expressive quality of the movement until this point; he ignores the piano markings in bars 5–6, 15, and 18. (Dynamics go hand-in-hand with rhythm here: he also maintains constant forward momentum through the first key area, ignoring the calando marking in bar 14.) He plays the subsequent scampering section in the relative major at the indicated piano dynamic through to the major cadence at bar 35. The next section, bars 35–45, offers a series of cadential confirmations of the relative major, which he renders with a continuous crescendo to forte. He reduces the volume slightly in the last five bars of the exposition, as the relative major is reiterated. He makes further significant dynamic changes in the development section. He begins moderately, but in the long sequential passage leading back into the tonic (bars 58–79), he creates a dynamic analogy to the continuous build-up of tonal and rhythmic tension, at the

---

[21] See Burton, ii; and *GGR* 35–6.

[22] In the rondo finale of K. 310, which he also plays very quickly ($\downarrow$ = 123), he applied the principle of dynamic terracing for similar reasons and to similar effect.

expense of the strong pianissimo-fortissimo contrasts with which Mozart articulates the reiterated units of the sequence. In the recapitulation, he largely repeats
the dynamic plan of the exposition, though plays somewhat louder in the second
key area, where material exposed in the relative major returns in the tonic minor.

Such dynamics seem even more provocative in Gould's performances of sonatas
by Beethoven. In his 1968 recording of the second movement of Beethoven's
Sonata in F sharp major, Op. 78 (see CD 20), terraced dynamics are again
consistent with a headlong approach to rhythm, though here they seem definitely
at odds with the capriciousness, the quirkiness of the movement. Again, Gould
creates much larger units of dynamic continuity than the score calls for, and again
his rationale seems to have been tonal. Passages in which he suppresses or minimizes
dynamic variation tend to be tonally stable: see, for example, the parallel passages
of cadential confirmation in bars 12–22, 43–51, and 100–10; and the parallel
cadential passages in bars 65–74 and 124–33. (He also smooths over dynamic
contrasts in the tonally stable, though modally mixed, passages in bars 57–65 and
116–23.) He reserves crescendos and decrescendos for modulating or unstable
passages, and he also reduces the dynamic contrasts built into the main theme.

In his dynamic plans for K. 310 and Op. 78, Gould characteristically revised
the musical text according to his own musical standards. He allowed the play of
tonal forces (and, to a lesser extent, rhythm, texture, and register) to determine
dynamic response no less than if the music had been Bach's, and he was more
concerned to clarify structural events of background significance than to highlight
every foreground detail (or to obey the score). Both performances are exciting, and
as always expertly played, but they also reveal typically prejudiced, intentionally
one-sided views of the music. As so often with Gould, the interpretations impov-
erish the music in one sense, highlight it in others; expressive detail is lost, dramatic
sweep and a certain kind of analytical precision gained. I do not necessarily defend
this trade-off when I point to such performances as evidence of Gould's remarkable, if highly personal, control of dynamics.

8

Articulation and Phrasing

A S A GENERAL rule, Gould preferred articulation that can best be
described as non-legato or détaché (I consider these terms interchangeable).
His desire for clarity, so basic to his musical personality, extended to his rendering
of phrases and even individual notes. Landowska once remarked that even her
staccato was legato; Gould had the opposite priority: even his legato was détaché.
Rarely, even in his smoothest phrases, did he blur the boundaries of individual
notes. As he told an interviewer in 1981, he wanted 'each individual note to be
heard precisely'; he felt 'that music did not have to be tied together with pedal and
legato'.[1] Thus 'the non-legato state . . . between two consecutive notes is the norm,
not the exception';[2] it was legato that had to justify itself as a special effect, as a
departure from the norm. He attempted, he said in another late interview,

to make the isolated legato moment a very intense occasion. I happen to adore the
cleanliness, the clarity of texture that one gets when the prevailing touch is of a détaché [*sic*]
nature. But in addition, when into that prevailingly detaché sonority, in which virtually
every note comes equipped with its own space separating it from the note that follows it,
there is injected a legato element, then there's something quite moving that happens, a kind
of emotional sweep that the music does not have if the prevailing assumption is that the
piano is a legato instrument, and the slicker the sound the better.[3]

Many writers on harpsichord performance have advocated *cantabile* playing to
counteract the innate 'dryness' of the instrument; Gould, by contrast, advocated
more detached playing to counteract the innate 'wetness' of the piano. He described
his usual articulation in different terms at different times; in the same interview, he
once used all of the following: 'secco, pointillistic, détaché', 'deliberate and dry',
'clean'.[4] Like some of his critics, he used the term 'staccato', too, but it is misleading. His basic touch was not a true staccato, and his references above to non-
legato and détaché are more accurate.[5] He avoided the blurring of adjacent tones
with fingers or pedal and largely preserved note values as written, not holding them

---

[1] M. Meyer, 'Interview', 16.
[2] Page.
[3] Aikin, 26.
[4] Cott, 49, 62.
[5] Kazdin, 116, quotes Gould's reference to the 'very staccato articulation' in his Bach performances. The 'extreme
staccatissimo' that Siepmann, 27, refers to is clearly an exaggeration, though exaggeration and even parody of Gould's
articulation is common enough in the critical literature.

beyond their written value (as in the legato effect that harpsichordists call 'over-legato'), but not shortening them as significantly as a true staccato implies. His use of a very short, sharp staccato was, like his use of legato, a special effect. Moreover, détaché was the norm for Gould regardless of tempo, and many of his performances contradict (sometimes spectacularly) Schenker's assumption that détaché 'automatically results in a more moderate tempo' and is 'incompatible with a rapid tempo, especially with a very rapid tempo'.[6]

Of course, Gould made use of considerable variation in articulation, even within a specific category like 'non-legato' or 'staccato'. In Bach's music, for example, he often distinguished between what Paul Badura-Skoda calls 'soft, "evanescent" staccato' and 'vigorous staccato', the former being more appropriate to light, flute-style pieces with arpeggiated figuration, the latter to many gigues in both French and Italian styles. (See his performances of two of the pieces Badura-Skoda cites: the Fugue in G major from *WTC* II, (CD $\boxed{22}$), and the Gigue from the French Suite No. 2 in C minor.[7]) Gould generally observed the conventional rule that stepwise passages should be played more smoothly than intervals or leaps (though he tended to play 'walking' bass lines relatively détaché). And his articulation tended to be lighter in fast movements and smoother in slow movements— a centuries-old convention.[8] But even where he did apply smoother articulation, he almost always preserved the integrity of the individual note. Frequently his legato was what Richard Troeger calls 'structured legato', defined as 'the near connection of notes'; even at its most intense, his legato rarely extended beyond what Troeger calls 'simple legato', defined as 'the bare linking of notes'.[9] Even in an intensely expressive, fluid, idiomatic piano piece like Scriabin's miniature 'Désir', which features a significant amount of exposed, unaccompanied melody, his legato did not extend to the blurring of adjacent tones, which remain clearly independent. In short, while he made use of a variety of articulations, and often applied them in conventional ways, his whole range of articulations was shifted towards the détaché end of the spectrum, to a degree unusual for a pianist.

His discreet use of the sustaining pedal was an important factor. For him the pedal was not the 'soul' of the piano, as it was for most pianists from the beginning of the Romantic era. As he told an interviewer in 1959, he had 'a very strong aversion' to Romantic indulgence in the pedal, and preferred to use it very selectively, 'as a factor of punctuation'—that is, to articulate, or to mark beats—rather than as a ubiquitous feature in the service of a singing tone.[10] In most repertoire, he created

---

[6] Schenker, 63.

[7] See Badura-Skoda, 112–17.

[8] For historical references to both rules just mentioned, see e.g. Bach, 149, 154–5.

[9] See Troeger, 65–7.

[10] Tovell. In his copy of Erwin Bodky's book *The Interpretation of Bach's Keyboard Works*, Gould flagged and approved of Bodky's plea for 'utter discretion' with the sustaining pedal, which should never be used to create 'veils of harmony', at least in Bach's music; see NLC B12, 93.

relationships between notes, even in legato passages, as much as possible with the fingers alone, using the pedal only where physically necessary or advantageous to make a connection, or as a special tonal effect—a kind of 'stop'—that he felt had some structural rationale. (In this he may have been following Tureck's example.[11]) Gould had exceptional control of the pedal, to be sure, and when he did use it to create a kind of 'sheen' it was not at the expense of clarity of articulation; he never allowed the pedal to make the music muddy or ambiguous. While it is not literally true that (as he sometimes said) he 'never' used the pedal in early music, he did avoid it far more often than most pianists. In many of his performances, passages normally played with the sustaining pedal—for example, broken chords—are played *secco*.

Gould's approach to articulation challenged that which prevailed among pianists active in his youth. The 'objective' school of nineteenth-century Bach playing that Glen Carruthers identified did advocate a dry, staccato touch, and Schenker was one early twentieth-century advocate of a 'non-legato' touch 'in most early works'.[12] But as a general rule, and regardless of repertoire, most Romantic pianists, well into the recording era, sought a 'singing' style that emulated the human voice, and assumed legato phrasing as a norm except in special circum-stances. (Like the sustaining pedal and a wide dynamic palette—both also assumed in Romantic playing—legato phrasing reflected the Romantic pianist's interest in exploiting the 'natural resources' of the piano, even in early music.) Gould's challenge to Romantic articulation, which he developed primarily to serve the contrapuntal music of Bach, has sometimes been interpreted as a response to the growing post-war presence of historical performance, and in the early part of his career he was considered something of a historical performer himself. There is, in fact, considerable evidence, from theorists like C. P. E. Bach, Marpurg, and Türk, and from the evidence of early fingerings, that some kind of non-legato touch was the assumed norm in Baroque keyboard music, at least among German musicians; many early theorists also distinguished non-legato from true staccato. Moreover, Forkel's biography suggests that J. S. Bach, as a general rule, favoured clean, even, and brilliant articulation, 'as if each tone were a pearl'.[13] Even in the Classical era, bright and clearly articulated playing—'choppy' playing, to its critics—was associated with important players like Mozart and Hummel. The practice of pedalling for special effect rather than pervasively was in fact the norm before

---

[11]   Tureck, too, preferred to use the fingers alone wherever possible, and advocated using the sustaining pedal in Bach's music only to articulate structure (as a harpsichordist might change registers), not as a pervasive tonal effect; she rejected the transplanting of Romantic pedalling practices to early music. See *An Introduction to the Performance of Bach*, i. 7.

[12]   See Carruthers, 35–6; and Schenker, 63. Schenker believed more generally that non-legato was more natural to keyboard instruments than was legato.

[13]   See Ch. 3 ('Bach the Clavier Player') in Forkel's 1802 biography, in David and Mendel, 306–12; the quoted passage is on 308.

about 1830 (Beethoven and Czerny were decisive figures in the transition to a more legato, pedalled style of piano playing).[14]

Yet, one must wonder how extensive was Gould's scholarship about early performance, his occasional appeals to historical criteria notwithstanding; it probably did not extend much beyond what he learned from the sources to which he was steered in his youth by Alberto Guerrero. But even if one can identify some coincidences between Gould and historical performance, it is surely more pertinent to see his non-legato articulation as a function of that analytical approach to music that owed so much to the structural values of Schoenberg and other modern musicians, even the neo-Classical Stravinsky of whom he disapproved so strongly. Gould admitted as much on several occasions, when he expressed a fondness for the kind of cell-like phrasing that he considered 'Webernesque'. His very precise reading of a fugue subject like that in F minor from *WTC* I recalls nothing so much as Webern's phrasing in his orchestral transcription of the six-voice Ricercare from Bach's *A Musical Offering*, a transcription Gould was familiar with. In a passage that he flagged in his copy of *Prisms*, Adorno writes of Webern's transcription that 'the surface interweaving of lines is dissolved into the most minute motivic interrelations and then reunited through the overall constructive disposition of the orchestra'.[15] Gould's articulation and phrasing often served to clarify just those 'minute motivic interrelations' of which Adorno speaks. Moreover, as Nicholas Cook notes, the 'clean, rather dry textures' in the music of Schoenberg and many of his contemporaries in the 1920s reflected broader aesthetic positions like idealism, formalism, and objectivity.[16] Gould's seeking 'cleanliness' in articulation can likewise be traced to his idealistic orientation, which made elucidating musical structures—clarifying the parts that made up the whole—perhaps his highest priority in performance.

Gould once referred to his finger-oriented technique as resembling that of a harpsichordist.[17] But Geoffrey Payzant has rightly emphasized that his early organ training was a major influence on his piano style; it taught him, especially in the music of Bach, 'the organist's accentuation by spacing rather than by weight of touch'.[18] In 1959, he told an interviewer,

The organ was a great influence, not only on my later taste in repertoire, but I think also on the physical manner in which I tried to play the piano. . . . [By my teens] certain aspects of

---

[14]   The more articulated Classical style of playing, at least before Beethoven, is documented throughout Chapter 3 ('Inflection: The "Speaking Style" Transformed') of Barth, 38–131.

[15]   Adorno, *Prisms*, 146; cf. NLC B1, 146.

[16]   Cook, 227.

[17]   See Bester, 153.

[18]   Payzant, *GGMM* 95. Liszt encouraged students to think like an organist, so as not to overlap sounds, when playing fugues (see Carruthers, 20), and Schenker, 63, draws an analogy to 'organ sound, which excludes true legato in the strictest sense', in explaining non-legato touch for the piano. (He also draws an analogy to détaché on the violin.)

organ playing—the physical aspects—had made a great impression on me. I learned that when you played Bach, the only way to establish a phrase, a subject, a motive of any kind, was *not* to do as one would with Chopin—you know, try to make a crescendo in the middle of the thing—but to establish it by rhythmic gasps and breaths. One had to have an entirely different approach, something that was based, really, on the tips of the fingers being responsible for the whole action, something that could almost produce the wonderful whistling gasp of the old organs. So that expression, consequently, was accomplished with practically none of the slurrings and over-fadings, not to speak of pedalings, with which Bach is so often played on the piano. And I really feel that this is entirely due to the fact that, at an early age, I was playing the organ.[19]

(Gould's own organ playing, it should be noted, was highly articulated—and much criticized for it.) The influence of the organ in his youth was complemented at the same time by his absorption of the work of Tureck, whose highly articulated Bach style was decisively influential: she was the one pianist in whose work he heard reflected his own confrontation with the Romantic, *cantabile* style of playing Bach, as he acknowledged.[20] (I am also tempted to cite Landowska's articulated and rhythmically vigorous style as an influence, despite Gould's claims to the contrary.) These influences were augmented in his youth by the training he received from Guerrero. As he occasionally acknowledged, and as other former pupils have recalled, Guerrero helped lay the groundwork for his non-legato, finger-oriented style, including exercises designed to reduce dependence on muscular weight, enhance the isolation of the fingers from the rest of the hand and arm, and so enhance the clear articulation of individual notes, even at fast tempos.[21] Guerrero also encouraged the notoriously low seating posture that Gould (like both Tureck and Schnabel) came to prefer. Gould told an interviewer in 1980 that he always sat on a chair whose seat was fourteen inches from the ground (about twenty inches is normal), in addition to which he would raise the piano on blocks about one and a quarter inches high. He felt that 'control increases in direct relationship to one's proximity to the keyboard', and that his sitting posture was well suited to the articulation of early music, especially contrapuntal music, which demands a technique oriented to 'the tips of the fingers'.[22] He noted in a 1974 interview that his finger technique and posture was most relevant to repertoire that did not

---

[19] Quoted in Payzant, *GGMM* 97.

[20] See Cott, 62–5; Mach, 103–4; and M. Meyer, 'Interview', 16. Like Gould, Tureck often applied détaché articulation at very slow and very fast tempos. It is important to note, however, that she also advocated much greater use of legato and *cantabile* effects in Bach's music than Gould ever did.

[21] For comments by other Guerrero pupils, see Aide; Beckwith, 'Glenn Gould, The Early Years', 60–1; Beckwith, 'Shattering a Few Myths', 68–70; and Friedrich, 31. Guerrero had studied the comparison made in Otto Ortmann's 1929 book *The Physiological Mechanics of Piano Technique* between 'weight technique' and 'pure finger technique', and passed on to Gould his preference for the latter. On Guerrero's influence, see also Ostwald, 70–4, 104.

[22] Mach, 111.

demand a widening of the hands—say, Bach or Mozart or pre-Bach. But you cannot, you simply cannot play Scriabin in that position, for the simple reason that the leverage required to support a widening of the hands is such that you have to be further away from the keyboard, you couldn't be that close. But you *can* play Bach that way, and should, because by so doing you refine the sound, you minimize the pianistic aspects of it, and you increase your control . . . by a considerable measurement.[23]

This way of playing the piano did undermine his ability to play the virtuoso effects of nineteenth-century piano music, as he admitted, but he sacrificed them willingly in exchange for the control and contrapuntal clarity that his style afforded him in his preferred repertoire. And though he was incapable of the volcanic fortissimos of a Horowitz, he had, by way of compensation, unusual control over dynamic gradations at the lower end of the spectrum, from pianissimo to mezzo-forte, the part of the spectrum most important to his repertoire. Like such predecessors as de Pachmann and Gieseking (who also sat unusually low), and such contemporaries as Michelangeli and Kuerti, Gould was one of the great pianissimo pianists, more comfortable with clarity, intimacy, tenderness than demonic fury.

Because he valued clarity in articulation, Gould sought 'tactile grab and immediacy' from his pianos, rather than rich tone colour; he was more concerned with 'the rites of passage *between* notes' than with the sound quality of individual notes themselves.[24] As Payzant and others have noted, Gould was unusually sensitive to both the beginnings and endings of his tones, and so to the amount of silence between notes, and to the evenness of tones in passage-work. In his filmed performances, especially of Bach and especially in slow and moderate contrapuntal music at moderate and low volumes, he can often be seen lifting his free fingers high off the keys; he would drop a finger onto a key from a high position to assure a precise attack, then lift the finger quickly and high off the key to assure a precise termination to the sound. (For a good view of this sort of fingerwork, see the photograph from 1963 reproduced as Plate 3.) Payzant, commenting on the incisiveness that Gould sought both with the attack and the damping of a tone, invokes a linguistic analogy: 'He wants to give shape to each individual sound envelope, including not merely the timbre of the vibrating strings, but the distinctive patterns of onset and termination, the *consonants* of individual musical notes.'[25] In Payzant's view, Gould's interest in the articulating power of musical 'consonants' led him actually to increase the amount of 'chink'—that is, percussive

---

[23] Cott, 46.

[24] McClure; *GGR* 447. In addition to the sources cited here and below, there are many letters from Gould's concert days that recount his travails with various pianos, and they suggest that a piano's action was always more important to him than its tone.

[25] Payzant, *GGMM* 117. Guillard, 150, also invokes the analogy of vowels and consonants in a discussion of Gould's articulation and the influence of his organ playing.

noise—at the beginning of each tone.[26] (Recall Gould's reference above to articulation that suggests the 'whistling gasp of the old organs'.) On the other hand, it was precisely works and performances that stressed the percussive aspect of the piano that Gould despised. On many occasions he seems clearly to undermine the percussiveness of the instrument, creating an almost disembodied sound by *reducing* the 'chink' accompanying each note, mimicking a string or woodwind instrument's ability to ease into a note, with a minimum of audible attack. Samuel Lipman rightly observed that Gould could play 'as if the piano keys were being played on an upward rather than a downward stroke'.[27] This effect, cherished as suggestive of the human voice, was sought by many Romantic pianists (Debussy once said that in his music the piano should sound as though it had no hammers), and it remains a goal of many pianists. In Gould's case, there is a certain consistency between his fondness for a sort of disembodied sound and the tendency towards abstraction in his thinking about music, and the quality of tonal neutrality that he praised in the modern piano would certainly have been undermined by excessive 'chink'. It is perhaps more accurate to say that Gould did not so much seek to maximize 'chink' as willingly put up with it where it was an unavoidable by-product of increased incisiveness of articulation.

This point is strikingly substantiated by at least one anecdote. Gould used one particular Steinway concert grand piano (CD 318) for most of his recordings throughout the 1960s and 1970s, and admired it for its tight action rather than its tone. In 1963, shortly after he acquired it, the piano was adjusted mechanically to maximize control of articulation and minimize the amount of muscular weight required. In the process, however, it acquired a pronounced anomaly that he called a 'hiccup': in the middle register (from about g to g'), in quiet passages at a slow or moderate tempo, a hammer would sometimes unintentionally restrike a tone lightly, creating tonal 'shadows'. The hiccup intrudes in the first recording Gould made on this instrument in 1963–4, Bach's Inventions and Sinfonias, so much so that an explanatory note was printed on the album cover.[28] Over the years, his piano technicians were able to work out the anomaly without loosening the piano's action; by the early 1970s it was rarely noticeable.[29] What is telling in this anecdote

[26] See Payzant, *GGMM* 113. Said, *Musical Elaborations*, 24, also notes Gould's 'unidiomatic heightening of the piano's percussive traits'.

[27] Lipman, 81. For a clear example of this effect, see the demisemiquaver *tirades* in the seventh Goldberg variation (1955 recording).

[28] This note, which explains the mechanical adjustments to the piano, is reprinted in full in Payzant, *GGMM* 106; and in part in Kazdin, 3. See also Payzant, *GGMM* 104–8 on the general subject of Gould and his pianos.

[29] The 'hiccup' is apparent throughout the album of Inventions and Sinfonias (see e.g. the opening of the first Invention), and frequently in the Byrd-Gibbons album (1967–70). For other prominent examples, see Bach, *WTC* II, Fugue in E flat major (1963 CBC television); Scarlatti, Sonata in D minor, L. 413; Beethoven, Sonata in G major, Op. 14 No. 2/II, 85; Beethoven, Sonata in F sharp major, Op. 78/I, 1; Beethoven-Liszt, *Pastoral* Symphony (1968 CBC radio)/I, opening bars; and Scriabin, Sonata No. 3 in F sharp minor/I, 107–8.

is that Gould should choose to accept a significant tonal anomaly in his piano rather than sacrifice any degree of precision in the action—in his power to control articulation.

From at least the mid-1950s, Gould and his technicians fussed inordinately with the mechanisms of his pianos in order to get a lighter and tighter action, and a cleaner, more refined sound, always in the service of articulation, and usually with early keyboard instruments like the harpsichord and fortepiano serving as models. (In outtakes from his 1981 film of the Goldberg Variations, he can be heard instructing his piano technician, between takes, to 'think harpsichord' when voicing and regulating the instrument.[30]) The inherently light action in his preferred Steinway piano was enhanced by reducing the draft of the keys (that is, the distance the key is allowed to fall when depressed). As he explained in a letter from c.1972, he deplored the tendency in modern pianos to increase the draft of the key, and hence the sheer projecting power of the instrument: 'I prefer an instrument which is regulated with a touch-block of a slightly shallower than average measurement partly because, assuming all the correlative factors such as after-touch etc. are accounted for, it does, generally speaking, increase one's control over the instrument and provides a more precise and usually more even tonal quality.' This adjustment, he said in a later letter, allowed him 'a rather exceptional clarity for contrapuntal styles'.[31] He also had his piano's hammers moved closer to the strings, to achieve a quicker and more controllable attack, an adjustment that also contributed to his discrimination at lower dynamic levels at the expense of fortissimos.[32] But it should be noted that the instrumental qualities just described, while certainly the norm in Gould's performances, and suited especially to early music, were adjusted to some degree depending on the repertoire. As he noted in a 1968 interview, the same Steinway that was made to evoke the virginals in his performances of Byrd was regulated to produce a 'fat, fluffy' sound when he took up the Beethoven-Liszt Fifth Symphony, though of course digital technique, too, plays a large part in such distinctions.[33] Gould wanted total control of such factors as action and tone, through both digital and mechanical means, and did not assume that the instrument and technique appropriate to nineteenth-century piano music offered necessary models for imitation.

Characteristically, his decisions about articulation, phrasing, and even note values frequently departed from the score. And as Hermann Danuser has pointed out, he was not particularly concerned with historical relationships between rhetoric and music as they relate to articulation and phrasing—with the conventional (and

---

[30] NLC videotape no. 49A.
[31] GGSL 192, 220.
[32] See Aikin, 27.
[33] McClure.

now somewhat discredited) doctrines of the affections and musical figures, the so-called *Affektenlehre* and *Figurenlehre*. Danuser cites the Prelude in F minor from *WTC* I, in which Gould's short-long phrasing of the two-note 'sighing motives' directly contravenes historical practice.[34] In some notable cases, he actually replaced sound with silence, as in Ex. 8.1, where he uses silence as a kind of 'negative accent' for a note that Bach highlights by sustaining.[35] Most of his changes to written articulation were, predictably, in the same direction: from legato to détaché, even in passages of broken chords or unaccompanied melody. ('Away with the phrasing slur!' might have been his motto, to borrow an article title from Schenker.) He tended to shorten rather than lengthen phrase units. Except in particularly intense passages, he was rarely interested in the Romantic 'long line' of melody; rather, he would set off the component parts into which a melody divided, as when he revealed counterpoint implied within single voices in Bach, or gave highly punctuated readings of melodies. Here is Gould's analytical bent once again: he was as interested in dissecting horizontal lines as he was in clarifying vertical textures. His sometimes microscopic examination of the music applied even to some secondary or accompanimental material. In the second movement of Beethoven's Sonata in C major, Op. 2 No. 3, he subdivided the demisemiquaver figuration throughout (beginning at bar 11), though the composer has slurred these figures as smooth units (see Ex. 8.2). His extremely slow tempo ($\lrcorner$ = 11) permits this rather bizarre dissection of the music.

Gould often adjusted articulation by analogy with rhythm and dynamics. In many cadences, where the musical energy diminishes in terms of dynamics and tempo, he also 'diminishes' the articulation, by reducing the amount of sound relative to silence—that is, gradually shortening the note values by playing progressively more détaché.[36] As the music grows more restrained and intimate in other ways, silence increasingly replaces sound; the effect might be described as an application of brakes. Some of Gould's departures from score involved the pedal. He seems to have been unusually fond of the possibilities for contrapuntal clarity offered by the middle pedal, with which the pianist can 'catch' and sustain certain notes while allowing subsequent notes to remain detached. In the first movement of Beethoven's Sonata in A flat major, Op. 26, he emphasizes the notes marked sforzando by holding them through the bar using the middle pedal, ignoring the

---

[34] See Danuser, 22. In this respect, Gould did *not* follow the precepts of Schweitzer, who was an enthusiastic proponent of the *Figurenlehre* in Bach's music; Gould's view of Bach's music was more abstract, not pictorial. And Schweitzer discusses the *Figurenlehre* in his volume on Bach's vocal music, while Gould derived his image of Bach largely from the instrumental works.

[35] See also his 1979 film performance of the Allemande from Bach's Partita No. 4 in D major. In one series of outtakes from the 1981 film of the Goldberg Variations (NLC videotape no. 44A), Gould replaces ties with rests in the syncopated melody of Var. 13, 9–10, though he did not adopt this reading in the final film, or in the 1981 recording.

[36] See e.g the closing bars of Byrd, 'Sellinger's Round'; Bach, *WTC* II, Prelude in E major (1969 recording); Bach, *WTC* II, Fugue in G major; and Bach, Sinfonia No. 6 in E major (1963–4 recording).

Ex. 8.1. Bach, *WTC* I, Prelude in C sharp minor

Ex. 8.2. Beethoven, Sonata in C major, Op. 2 No. 3/II

staccato wedges with which the composer articulates these notes (see Var. 3, bars
9–14 and 27–32). And in Beethoven's Bagatelle in A flat major, Op. 33 No. 7,
where the composer asks that the sustaining pedal be held throughout arpeggiated
passages in which tonic and dominant harmonies blur (bars 21–35 and 77–91),
Gould sustains the fortissimo bass notes with the middle pedal, but plays staccato
the pianissimo, arpeggiated triads above them. Harmonies do not blur, though the
pedal tone sounds strongly throughout. The effect is reminiscent of the fortepiano,
on which the upper register tends to sound relatively dry even when the sustaining
pedal is deployed, though Gould used it strikingly in modern music, too (see
Hétu's *Variations pour piano*/Var. 2).

   Dale Innes, writing of Gould's performances of the Goldberg Variations, shows
that articulation is generally 'much more distinct and uniform' in his later
performances, and adds that the later Gould was more likely to apply non-legato
articulation to short notes and notes in the lower register.[37] Johanne Rivest has
found examples in which he arranged units of consistent articulation in 'blocks'—
a kind of 'terraced' approach to articulation.[38] Sometimes, he could be precise about
phrasing in order to make a specific point: in Ex. 8.3, his phrasing, along with
dynamics, serves to clarify cycles of fifths and stepwise sequences within a walking

---

[37]   See Innes, 104–7, 155.
[38]   See Rivest, 111–12, xxxii.

Ex. 8.3. Bach, Violin Sonata No. 4 in C minor (1975 recording)/IV (piano only)

bass line. He applied the same principle on a larger scale in the Prelude to Bach's English Suite No. 6 in D minor. He maintains legato articulation throughout the opening period (bars 1–15), which features a modulation from the tonic to the dominant. In the four-bar, single-voice transition that follows, he switches to a more detached articulation, then returns to legato at the return of the opening theme and texture (now in the dominant) at bar 19. The change in articulation reflects the function of bars 15–18 as an interpolation or transition between similar thematic statements.

The degree of strictness and consistency in Gould's articulation could vary considerably, however. At times, he pursued a particular pattern of phrasing rigorously to make a point; at other times, he was more casual, improvisational. (He frequently used the conventional device of varying articulation in repeats in Baroque binary-form pieces.) In the second movement of the Beethoven C major sonata, he did not maintain consistently the initial phrasing shown in Ex. 8.2, though in his score for this movement he marked the phrasing consistently throughout.[39]

---

[39] See NLC Scores 16/2, 53–5.

Perhaps he considered small variations within a basic pattern of phrasing in performance to be essentially equivalent to literally strict phrasing on paper. Even in the music of Bach, his articulation was generally less strict and consistent, and featured more subtle variations, than that of many other Bach pianists—notably Tureck, whose articulation is more obviously 'terraced', but also the many earlier pianists who adopted an unvaryingly *secco* approach to Bach. (He was not fanatical about maintaining consistent phrasing for a fugue subject, for example.) When it came to phrasing, Gould commonly allowed himself a certain amount of improvisational freedom within limits that established the general character for a movement, section, or passage. The thirteenth Goldberg variation (see CD $\boxed{21}$) offers a typical example: he maintains a consistent relationship of détaché melody against more sustained lower parts, yet allows considerable variety in the melody in terms of degree of détaché, placement of small slurs, and so on. These small variations inject considerable vitality into the playing, without sacrificing overall unity of mood and dramatic profile. 'Layered articulation', by analogy with Schenker's 'layered dynamics', is perhaps an appropriate term for this style.

Clearly, Gould's articulation, while based on a given norm of détaché, was not static; it ranged widely according to the musical context. There was a certain development in his non-legato sound over the course of his career. There is often a sweetness, even a delicate sheen, to the non-legato sound in his earlier recordings, including the Bach Partitas and the first Goldberg Variations. The dry, 'disembodied', even 'dehumanized' sound noted by many critics is much more apparent in his later performances, especially in his Bach recordings from the 1970s and early 1980s—the toccatas, the short preludes, fugues, and fantasies, the violin and viola da gamba sonatas, the second Goldberg Variations. (Compare the Praeludium from Bach's B flat major Partita in CD $\boxed{8}$, recorded in 1959, with the Goldberg variation in CD $\boxed{21}$, recorded in 1981.) At times in the later recordings, each individual note seems to occupy its own acoustical space, as though played on a synthesizer. It was a matter not only of digital technique, interpretation, and piano mechanism, but also recording quality. Gould miked his piano increasingly closely and in an increasingly dry acoustic as his career progressed; even his chamber-orchestra recording of the *Siegfried Idyll* is recorded tightly. Not surprisingly, many listeners and critics find these recordings chilly, clinical, and not only in Bach. Yet, his later non-legato playing is often strikingly expressive, even warm, evidence once more of his considerable pianistic gifts: to invest the leanest textures with power and beauty, to maintain immaculate technical control under acoustical circumstances that are almost cruelly exposed, is quite a trick. There is a peculiar tension in Gould's non-legato playing that is compelling—that literally compels listening; often, indeed, that tension is more powerful and pregnant than the most sweeping legato, legato on the piano being more 'sonorous' but also more banal. Silence plays a crucial role in this perception. The background of silence, of stillness, is palpable 'between the cracks' in Gould's non-legato playing, especially in his super-slow performances; one 'hears' the open space surrounding the sounds. (Needless to say, I am not referring here to reverberation or hall ambiance.) Gould was not concerned that 'clarity could be an enemy of mystery';[40] in his non-legato playing, at least, clarity was in fact the *source* of mystery. Gould's was certainly a distinctive sort of piano poetry: no shimmering kaleidoscope of pedalled sonorities, but instead the bracing clarity of tones cleanly etched against a background of vast open spaces. (A poetry of the North, one is tempted to say.) 'Dehumanized' is not really an appropriate term for piano playing so personal, so deeply (albeit strangely) expressive. The 'Gould sound' may have subverted many conventional notions about expression at the piano, but it was ultimately in the service of a new and heightened brand of pianistic expressiveness.

[40] *GGR* 337.

9

Ornamentation

I N THE MATTER of ornamentation, Gould differed from most performers in the degree to which he avoided generic solutions to individual problems. Adapting ornamentation to articulate a musical event, or to suit the general character of a work, he often permitted himself to depart significantly from conventional and historical practices. While his ornamentation could only occasionally be described as analytical in motivation, it did often contribute to the unity of an interpretation. His attitude towards ornaments was, again, consistent with the intellectual premises of Schoenberg and his followers: Schoenberg, for example, wrote in 1922 that 'in true works of art nothing is an ornament in the sense that one could leave it out'.[1] As we will see, Gould's ornamentation, in repertoire from all periods, reflects this aesthetic premiss in the ways it serves the music.

As early as the 1940s, Gould was introduced to matters of historical practice in ornamentation, largely through Alberto Guerrero,[2] though his insight into the historical sources did not keep pace with the explosion of post-war scholarship on the subject. Still, it is apparent throughout his discography that he had a respectable working knowledge of ornamentation, and his early recordings especially are relatively uncontroversial in this regard. (With ornamentation, too, his experiments grew more idiosyncratic after his retirement from concert life in 1964.) He often rendered trills, turns, mordents, appoggiaturas, slides, and other commonplace ornaments in conventional ways, in terms of melodic and rhythmic profile, auxiliary notes, phrasing, and character. In Baroque and Classical music, he played brief ornamental cadenzas at appropriate spots marked with a fermata. And many of the less common ornaments that appear in his recordings are accounted for in historical sources: the appoggiatura used to replace an indicated or expected trill; the grace-note (i.e. pre-beat) appoggiatura; the long mordent; the *Schneller*, a sort of inverted mordent; the sharp (often humorous) acciaccatura; the anticipation; the leaping *Vorschlag* (i.e. an accented grace that leaps to the main note); the unaccented *Nachschlag* (i.e. a grace that connects two main notes); the five-note

---

[1] Schoenberg, 299.

[2] Beckwith, 'Glenn Gould, the Early Years', 59, says that Guerrero, in the 1940s, steered his students towards Dolmetsch, and to some of the original treatises cited by Dolmetsch (C. P. E. Bach, Couperin, Quantz, Leopold Mozart), then just beginning to appear in modern editions.

turn beginning on the main note; the addition of passing tones; the downward rolling of a chord; the repeating of individual notes within an arpeggiated chord; and the positioning of a trill between two notes, rather than (as marked) on one of the two notes, as in the French Baroque *tremblement lié* or *tremblement feint*.[3] In some sarabandes and other slow movements in solo and chamber music by Bach, Gould's application of ornamentation could be lavish—occasionally garish[4]—though rarely unusually so by the standards of some recent historical performers, and many of his more heavily ornamented passages are consistent with the Baroque practice of improvising *agréments* and diminutions. His recordings offer enough evidence to suggest that his ornamentation, in music from the Elizabethan to modern periods, was often acceptable by conventional and historical standards, and that he broke conventional rules of ornamentation intentionally.

Gould's deviations from the norm were, of course, more noteworthy. They included invention of new ornaments, unusual placement or suppression of ornaments, unusual rendering of standard formulas, and unusual interpretation of expressive character. Jens Hagestedt names three ornaments as Gould's own inventions: the staccato double grace note ('der punktierte Doppelvorschlag'); the trill beginning with a mordent ('der mit einem Mordent beginnende Triller'); and the trill that accelerates in measured increments ('das gestufte Triller-Accelerando'), a variant of the French Baroque *tremblement à progression*.[5] One could add to Hagestedt's list, especially drawing from Gould's later recordings. On a few

---

[3] Examples of some of the more noteworthy of these ornaments follow. Appoggiatura replacing trill: Bach, Goldberg Variations (1955 and 1981 recordings)/Aria, 12. Grace-note appoggiatura: Bach, Goldberg Variations (1955 and 1981 recordings)/Vars. 24 and 25, *passim*. Long mordents: Bach, WTC II, Prelude in E major (1969 recording and 1970 CBC television), 54; Bach, French Overture in B minor/I (1971–3 recording), 18–19, 18r–19r, 161–2; and Handel, Suite for Harpsichord in A major/Gigue, 22, 22r, 45. Sharp, humorous acciaccaturas: Mozart, Sonata in C major, K. 279/III, 42–4, 128–30 (see CD ⑥). Leaping *Vorschläge*: Bach, Goldberg Variations (1981 recording)/Var. 3, 1r–2r; and Handel, Suite for Harpsichord in A major/Courante, *passim*. Unaccented *Nachschlag*: Bach, Goldberg Variations (1955 and 1981 recordings)/Var. 30, 4. Downward rolling of chords: Bach, WTC I, Prelude in E flat minor, 22–4; Bach, Partita No. 2 in C minor/Courante, 7; and Bach, Goldberg Variations (1955 and 1981 recordings)/Aria, 11. Five-note turn: Bach, Goldberg Variations (1955 recording)/Aria, 6. Trills between notes: Bach, Clavier Concerto No. 3 in D major/I, 14; Bach, Partita No. 1 in B flat major/Praeludium, 3, 14 (see CD ⑧), and Allemande, *passim*; and Bach, Goldberg Variations (1981 recording)/Var. 3, 9–10, Var. 5, 20, and Var. 13, 9 (see CD ㉑). Examples of passing tones are given in the text below. Gould's repeating of individual notes within arpeggiated chords appears frequently in his recordings of Baroque music, but also in later repertoire, including Bizet's *Variations chromatiques* and the final chords in Scriabin's 'Désir'. He may have been influenced by Romantic practice in this respect: the effect is quite common in scores by Chopin and other Romantic composers (see the last bar of Chopin's Nocturne in G minor, Op. 37 No. 1).

[4] In the Violin Sonata No. 3 in E major/I and II, and the Violin Sonata No. 6 in G major/III, his excessive ornamentation and arpeggiation actually detracts from the violin part; he comes across like a supporting stage actor mugging in the background. Taruskin, 304, writing of Gould's recordings with Leonard Rose of Bach's viola da gamba sonatas, notes that he 'improvises melismata to the point where they become virtual graffiti'.

[5] Hagestedt, 156; his examples of each follow. Staccato double grace notes: Beethoven, Cello Sonata in A major, Op. 69/III, 9–15. Trills beginning with a mordent: Mozart, Sonata in C major, K. 330 (1958 recording)/III, 39–45, 138–44. Trills that accelerate in measured increments: Bach, WTC I, Prelude in G minor, 1, 3, 7, 11; Bach, Clavier Concerto No. 3 in D major/II, 7–8; Bach, Clavier Concerto No. 7 in G minor/II, 17, 31, 33; Bach, Viola da Gamba Sonata No. 1 in G major/I: 1–2, 16–17, 25; and Beethoven, 'Emperor' Concerto/II, 39–44. For the latter ornament, see also Bach, Violin Sonata No. 1 in B minor/I, 33; and Mozart, Sonata in A minor, K. 310/II, 17–18, 70–1.

occasions in music by Byrd, he plays rapid trills that dissolve into repetitions of the main note alone, suggesting the early Baroque Italian *trillo*, or even *Bebung*,[6] in Bach's English Suite No. 6 in D minor/Gavotte I, he uses simultaneous appoggiaturas in thirds in two passages (bars 2 and 10); in Bach's Little Prelude in E minor, BWV 938, he uses a rising appoggiatura (or *port de voix*) along with a repetition of the main note (bar 12r); in the Adagio from Bach's Violin Sonata No. 5 in F minor, he uses a variety of odd combinations of ornaments, like a leaping *Vorschlag* combined with an unaccented mordent. He took unusual liberties in post-Baroque music, too, and not only where the composer has only sketchily notated the music (as in several spots in Mozart's C minor concerto). In Classical music, he occasionally added trills, appoggiaturas, and grace notes, though by the standards of some recent performances by fortepianists his intrusions were relatively discreet. He did so as late as the last sonatas of Beethoven, however.[7]

Where Gould did observe written ornamentation, his realization was often idiosyncratic in terms of expression. Smooth and elegant performance is typical of Baroque ornamentation, including that of Bach, which is modelled largely on the French style. But Gould was liberal in his use of détaché, even sharply staccato, ornaments. His staccato appoggiatura at the end of the Fugue in G major from *WTC* II is striking but typical (see CD 22). There are a few precedents for such ornaments that may have influenced him: he may, for example, have heard the staccato appoggiaturas in Landowska's 1936 recording of the Bourrée from Bach's French Suite No. 6 in E major,[8] to judge from his own recording of that piece. But generally speaking, Baroque and Classical treatises, not to mention common practice, are unanimous that such ornaments as the appoggiatura are to be played smoothly, in a vocal manner, with dynamic or agogic emphasis on downbeat dissonance. (Daniel Gottlob Türk, in his *Klavierschule* of 1789, made a point of including a musical example resembling Gould's staccato appoggiatura, and labelling it 'incorrect'.[9]) Gould's priority in both the fugue and the bourrée was to render the ornaments consistent with the general character of the piece as he interpreted it. The fugue he plays in a notably light and jaunty manner, at a rapid tempo (♩. = 94), with détaché phrasing throughout; in this context, especially given his beautifully calibrated relaxation of the tempo at the end, the witty throw-away ending provided by the closing staccato appoggiatura does not obtrude. Gould often applied staccato ornaments for the sake of consistency where the prevailing articulation of thematic material was détaché—more frequently with age, in fact.

---

    [6] See Byrd, First Galliard, 17–18, 28.

    [7] For examples from Beethoven's music, see the following: Bagatelle in F major, Op. 33 No. 3, 41, 43, 47, 55, 61; Sonata in E major, Op. 109/III, 6; and Sonata in A flat major, Op. 110/I, 56.

    [8] This recording was released on CD in *Landowska plays Bach*, Pearl GEMM CD 9489 (1991).

    [9] Türk, 218. See also Bach, 97.

Ex. 9.1. Bach, French Suite No. 5 in G major/Allemande

(His recordings of solo and chamber music by Bach from the 1970s and 1980s provide many examples.) Such consistency could even apply from movement to movement. The lightness and wit that characterize his interpretation of Bach's French Suite No. 5 in G major are reflected in his basically détaché articulation throughout, but also in his ornamentation, most notably the staccato appoggiaturas in the opening Allemande (bars 1, 4–5, and 13) and the staccato ornaments in the Sarabande. Indeed, his light measured trill and staccato appoggiatura in the first bar of the Allemande (see Ex. 9.1) seem like announcements of the mood he will maintain throughout the suite. His staccato ornaments have always horrified purists, yet they usually make sense in context, and in fact they often have great beauty—once you get used to them. In a later recording like the first movement of Bach's B minor violin sonata, the staccato ornaments are delicate, not sharp or abrasive, played with a softness of tone that gives them a 'bouncing' quality; the notes are very short yet speak fully and clearly, and the precision and focus of the rendering gives the ornaments real intensity. Many of the ornaments are also strictly measured rhythmically, but their beauty of tone counteracts their stiffness.

Other of Gould's unusual ornaments were adaptations to prevailing affect or character, and some clearly recall the recordings of Rosalyn Tureck, whose ornamentation (like other aspects of her Bach performances) must be counted a major influence on him, both generally and specifically. The unusual ornament transcribed in Ex. 9.2 is characteristic of both pianists, and shows unequivocally that Tureck served at times as a direct model for Gould;[10] there are countless 'Tureck ornaments' in his recordings. His frequent use of measured ornamentation also recalls Tureck, who in fact wrote that trills in early music 'are almost always measured'.[11] (The historical basis for this claim is questionable, incidentally, probably based on a misinterpretation of theoretical writings and historical tables of ornamentation. The French practice, and by extension that of Bach, always favoured elegance and flexibility in ornamentation.) In his performances of Mozart's sonatas,

[10] The Tureck ornaments in both Exx. 9.2 and 9.3 appear in her 1953 piano recording of *WTC* II, Decca Gold Label Series DX-128. Tureck herself notes her influence on Gould's ornamentation in Lelie, 31.

[11] Tureck, *An Introduction to the Performance of Bach*, i. 8. The influence of Ralph Kirkpatrick's 1938 edition of the *Goldberg Variations* should again be noted. As Innes, 123, writes, 'Generally in all his recordings of the *Goldberg Variations* Gould followed the realization of ornamentation given by Kirkpatrick.' (There were some notable exceptions, too, however.)

Gould's crisply articulated measured trills seem to be by-products of the strict rhythmic profile he imposed on the music, and his conspicuously unsentimental rendering of ornaments contributes to the atmosphere of *buffa* humour that he sought to convey. As this suggests, he made conscious decisions about ornaments that were based on factors like tempo and character. He did not (as some early sources did and as many performers do) assume that all trills must be rapid fluctuations. The slow measured trills in Wagner's *Siegfried Idyll*, in the slow movement of the Beethoven-Liszt *Pastoral* Symphony, in the 'Emperor' and Brahms D minor concertos, have an effect of gentle undulation that suits the extremely slow tempos and broad time scales of these interpretations. (The hideous measured trills in the first movement of the 'Appassionata' Sonata, however, are more subversive and parodistic, I would say.) Gould may again have been directly influenced by Tureck, who wrote in 1960:

> On the whole, ornaments should be thought, felt, and played slower than one usually hears them today. This rule holds good for most music preceding Mozart. Trills are never played with the nervous speed typical of virtuoso performers of recent years. . . . Ornaments in a slow movement are apt to be slower than in a fast movement. The surest guide to the tempo of an ornament is to fit the speed to the time value, rhythm, and character of the motive, not forgetting the tempo and character of the piece as a whole.[12]

Dale Innes has noted that the ornaments in Gould's 1981 recording of the Goldberg Variations 'are generally slower and more clearly articulated' than in his earlier performances of the work, and it is no coincidence that the 1981 performance is the slowest and most clearly articulated generally.[13]

Gould's decisions as to the exact configuration of notes making up an ornament, including starting note and auxiliary notes, did not always conform to historical prescriptions, and even when they did he seems to have been inspired less by documentary evidence than such musical needs of the moment as clarity of line or harmony. In virginal music, for example, he declined to make a firm decision about the meaning of the single- and double-stroke ornaments, which litter this music but which are still subject to scholarly dispute. Rather, he tended to follow the standard Baroque practice and use ornaments that follow the direction of the musical line in which they appear—usually, short trills with the upper auxiliary in descending lines, mordents in ascending lines. As a rule, where prolonging a dissonant note was the main point of a trill, Gould did not begin in the conventional manner with the upper auxiliary. He seems to have agreed with Frederick Neumann and others that the trill with accented upper auxiliary was relevant only in stepwise melodic contexts in which rhythmic and harmonic circumstances

[12]   Tureck, *An Introduction to the Performance of Bach*, i. 8.
[13]   Innes, 124.

Ex. 9.2. Bach, *WTC* II, Fugue in C sharp major (Gould: 1966–7 recording)

Tureck

Gould

would permit an appoggiatura to stand in its place.[14] Where the main trilled note itself contained the accented dissonance or was more important melodically or rhythmically, he tended to use a trill that began with that note. He would, for example, use a main-note trill to maintain the integrity of a repeated-note motive.[15] In chains of ascending or descending stepwise trilled notes, he used main-note trills to accent the basic melodic progression.[16] When he leaped to a trilled note, it was generally to a main-note trill, to keep the basic melodic contour clear,[17] and where a series of trilled notes formed an arpeggio, he used main-note trills to clarify the chord.[18] (His use of five-note turns beginning on the main note in stepwise melodies, in Baroque and Classical music, was probably also motivated by melodic and rhythmic clarity.) In the well-known case of the subject of the Fugue in F sharp major from *WTC* II, which begins with a leading-tone trill, Gould predictably played a main-note trill, there being no harmonic context on the first note to justify an accented upper auxiliary; his rendering of this trill also suggests once again the influence of Tureck (see Ex. 9.3). In the opening bars of Mozart's Sonata in C major, K. 330, in both his 1958 and 1970 recordings, he played a main-note

[14]   This principle is clear in Neumann's discussions of the Baroque trill in 'Couperin and the Downbeat Doctrine for Appoggiaturas', *Essays in Performance Practice*, and *Ornamentation in Baroque and Post-Baroque Music*. The importance of harmony in determining the shape of Gould's trills is apparent in his annotations on the subject in his copy of Erwin Bodky's *The Interpretation of Bach's Keyboard Works* (see NLC B12, 165–6, 182–3), and in his 1960 review of Bodky (see *GGR* 28–31, esp. 30). This is one respect in which he departed from Kirkpatrick, who writes, xiii, that it 'cannot be too emphatically stated that the Bach trill *always begins with the upper note*, in accordance with the nearly unanimous directions of eighteenth-century instruction books'.

[15]   See Bach, English Suite No. 6 in D minor/Gavotte I, 1; Bach, Clavier Concerto No. 4 in A major/III, 82–3, 86–7; Bach, Little Prelude in D minor, BWV 935, 3–4; Mozart, Sonata in C major, K. 330 (1958 and 1970 recordings)/II, 15; Mozart, Fantasia in C minor, K. 475, 31–2, 37–8; Beethoven, Concerto No. 1 in C major/II, 106–7; and Beethoven, Concerto No. 3 in C minor/III, 72, 74.

[16]   See Beethoven, Sonata in C minor, Op. 111/II, Var. 4, 34–6; Beethoven, Concerto No. 1 in C major/II, 66, 107–8; Beethoven, Concerto No. 2 in B flat major/III, 154–5; Beethoven, Concerto No. 3 in C minor/I, 219–25, 336–9, and cadenza; Beethoven, 'Emperor' Concerto/II, 39–44; and Bizet, *Variations chromatiques*/Var. 11, 13–14.

[17]   See Bach, Clavier Concerto No. 4 in A major/III, 94; Bach, Clavier Concerto No. 5 in F minor/III, 120; Mozart, Concerto No. 24 in C minor, K. 491/I, 199; Beethoven, Concerto No. 4 in G major/I, 129; and the fugue subject from Beethoven's 'Hammerklavier' Sonata/IV.

[18]   See Beethoven, Concerto No. 1 in C major/II, 20, 80–3; and Beethoven, Concerto No. 4 in G major/II, 55.

Ex. 9.3. Bach, *WTC* II, Fugue in F sharp major, subject

Ex. 9.4. Mozart, Sonata in C major, K. 330 (1958 and 1970 recordings)/I

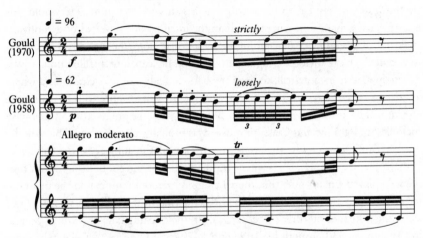

trill to create a satsifying mordent-like effect (c"–b'–c") between bars 1 and 2 (see
Ex. 9.4). As in most comparable circumstances, he avoided the less elegant melodic
shape that would have resulted from reaching from b' past the main note c" to the
upper auxiliary d' on the downbeat. Still, the two ornaments reflect two very
different interpretations of the music. In the faster, wittier 1970 performance, the
trill is rhythmically strict, and exactly rhymes with the demisemiquaver passage
that precedes it, forming a two-bar phrase with the neatness of an epigram.

Of Gould's rationales in ornamentation, harmony—consonance and dissonance—was perhaps the most important. This is immediately apparent in the
third movement of Bach's Clavier Concerto No. 5 in F minor, where his renderings
of adjacent, identically notated trills differ according to the harmonic circumstances (see bars 73–5, 81–3, 165–7, and 173–5). In Ex. 9.5, he plays an upper-
note trill in bar 74, creating an accented dissonance against the bass, but a main-

Ex. 9.5. Bach, Clavier Concerto No. 5 in F minor (1958 recording)/III

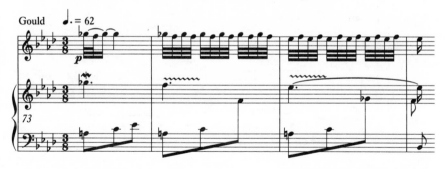

note trill in bar 75, where an upper-note trill would replace an existing tritone dissonance with a consonant sixth. (He also loved to add the spice of cross-relations in his ornaments, wherever possible.) At the end of the Gigue from Bach's French Suite No. 4 in E flat major, Gould's ornamentation serves along with rhythm and dynamics to underscore a harmonic arrival. The final seven bars of the Gigue remain solidly in the tonic, and his response to this tonal relaxation is a gradual ritardando and decrescendo. But his ornamentation, too, might be said to relax: his unmeasured trills in the final bars contrast noticeably with his strictly measured trills elsewhere in the movement.

In such ornamentation, we begin to confront again Gould's analytical mindset, his tendency to underscore structural points or increase the load of musical information in some way; his obsession with 'structure' thus asserted itself even in this most detailed and (usually) spontaneous aspect of performance. He sometimes used ornaments to create or enhance parallelisms, to smooth out minor inconsistencies, and so on.[19] But he also tried to increase the significance of ornamental detail—to make the ornamental 'structural' or 'thematic', in Schoenberg's sense. Apparently no ornamental detail was too small in this respect, as Ex. 9.6 shows. By adding an appoggiatura on the downbeat of bar 66, he suggests that the later, notated two-note figures grow organically out of the cadence, and so increases the motivic significance of the passage in a small way. (He also plays the two-note figures bracketed in bars 67–8 as though the first note were an ornament, by bringing in the second note slightly early.) In many of his performances, a recurring ornament, especially if it is an idiosyncratic one, makes enough of a contribution to the profile or character of the piece to qualify as a minor locus of unity. In his studio recording of Bach's English Suite No. 1 in A major, for example, his

---

[19]   When he added or adapted ornaments in music composed after about 1800 it was generally for such reasons. For example, in Beethoven's *Thirty-two Variations on an Original Theme*, WoO 80/Var. 9, on the notes marked '*tr*' in bars 7–8, he plays measured main-note trills, continuing the pattern of the measured main-note trills that Beethoven writes throughout the variation.

Ex. 9.6. Mozart, Sonata in C major, K. 330 (1958 recording)/I

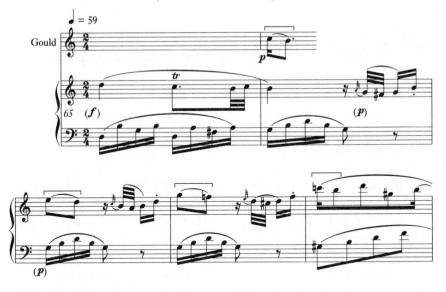

rendering of written thirds as broken intervals with an added passing tone recurs in several movements: Prelude, Courante I and Double I, and Sarabande—all of the movements, in fact, in which such thirds appear. The effect is minor but still palpable, a recurring splash of colour unique to that performance of that work. In Bach's Partita No. 6 in E minor, his distinctive arpeggiated rendering of chords in the Sarabande definitely implies a connection with the written-out arpeggios in the opening Toccata.[20] More striking on a larger scale are his idiosyncratic trills in the first movement of the 'Emperor' Concerto. In this movement, the opening of the solo exposition proper is preceded in the piano part by a chromatic scale that leads to a trill (bars 107–10); the soloist's entrance in the development section is also preceded by the same chromatic scale and trill (bars 264–7). In both cases, Gould plays a slow, delicate, measured trill, a reading that conforms to Beethoven's *dolce* marking at bar 111, and to the slow tempo, rhythmic continuity, and broad time scale of his interpretation of this concerto. But its real significance becomes apparent in the coda, where a chromatic scale, in the same harmonic context (dominant seventh), appears again, leading into a chain of elaborate measured trills written out by the composer (bars 559–68).[21] Gould's measured trills at the earlier parallel spots look ahead to Beethoven's own in the coda, suggesting that he intended to

---

[20] In Haydn's Sonata No. 50 in C major, his arpeggiation at the start of the second movement sounds like a slow-motion reference to his unusual arpeggiation of chords in the first movement (bar 7 and elsewhere).

[21] Beethoven's trills here begin with the upper auxiliary, Gould's earlier trills with the main note. The discrepancy is explained by the slightly different approach to the trilled note in bar 560, as compared with bars 108 and 265.

underscore in an immediately audible way the similar structural functions of these three passages. Of course, the music as written—the dominant preparation, the chromatic scale—already makes the connection between these three passages clear, but it was typical of Gould to seek any opportunity, however minor, to increase it still further. Sometimes, he even used the conspicuous *absence* of expected ornamentation to clarify structure. In his studio recording of Bach's Sinfonia No. 8 in F major (see CD $\boxed{23}$), he leaves undecorated some standard cadential figures that, in most cases, he or any other player would ornament, as a natural part of the style (see bars 3, 7, 11, 15, and 23). This is an especially dense piece, with twenty-one complete entries of the principal subject in just twenty-three bars, in addition to a number of other entries of the subject's head motive alone. To set in relief the entries of the full subject, Gould, following Bach's suggestion in bars 1–3, plays a short trill on the fifth note of each entry. And by not ornamenting the head motive when it appears alone (as in the bass in bars 13–14), and by leaving out expected cadential ornaments, he increases the degree to which the trill identifies and sets off the complete subject.[22]

These examples may appear subtle, minor, even trivial, but then ornamentation is inherently a matter of details. What is revealing is how much thought Gould invested in his ornaments, and how much they reveal about his musical priorities. Occasionally they had implications on the largest time scale. In Chapter 6, I mentioned several examples of ornaments that contributed to the rhythmic scheme in his 1981 recording of the Goldberg Variations. In the final bar of the opening Aria, he observes the written appoggiatura and makes it serve in the crucial first joint of his scheme. At the end of the Aria da capo, however, he suppresses the ornament. In doing so, he underscores the effect of closure: the absence of the ornament implies that the rhythmic continuity it originally helped set in motion is now at an end; it punctuates the end of an otherwise circular conception of the work. He builds structural significance into two details separated by fifty minutes of music, using ornamentation as something more than simple decoration.

---

[22]   There is one exception to this pattern: he does observe the 'extra' short trill that Bach adds in the soprano in bar 10.

10

Recording Technology

THE SUBJECT OF Gould's relationship to recording technology is a large and complex one, and has been discussed at length by Gould himself and others.[1] Among classical performers, he was widely known by the 1960s as the greatest proponent of the electronic media—of studio recording, radio and television broadcasting, and film. He was, in Denis Dutton's words, 'the closest thing we have to a philosopher of music recording'.[2] He was also a leading opponent of live performance, and of the music most appropriate to the concert hall. He felt that concert performance should no longer be the standard of musical behaviour in the late twentieth century. His views on the advantages of recording and the disadvantages of concert performance are well documented, and need not be rehearsed in detail. Relevant here are those aspects of recording technology that directly influenced his performance practices, for he used technology as a way of extending the range of interpretations available to him as a performer, to transcend the limitations of conventional piano performance.

Gould's interest in recording began in his youth, with private recordings on the relatively crude home equipment of the 1940s and 1950s, and grew with his early broadcasting for the CBC.[3] In an internal CBC questionnaire from 1952, the 19-year-old Gould already made a strong statement in favour of recording and broadcasting and against live performance: 'the concentration on purely musical detail', which 'is of utmost importance for any performance', is 'much easier to achieve when there is no need to feel responsibility for the visual pleasure of the listener'.[4] Despite his early interest in technology, his interpretations did not immediately show the influence of it, but there was a noticeable development in his appropriation of technology in those recordings made after his retirement from concert life in 1964. As he noted in a 1980 CBC radio broadcast, his early record-

---

[1] See the following, *passim*: *GGF*; *GGSL*; 'What the Recording Process Means to Me'; Burton, i; Davis; Eisenberg; Forfia; Kazdin; McClure; Monsaingeon, *Chemins de la musique*, i–ii; Théberge; and most of Gould's published periodical interviews. See also *GGR* 315–95; Cott, 81–103; Menuhin and Davis, 290–5; Payzant, *GGMM* 21–50, 119–39; and Rivest, 4–44.

[2] Dutton, 513.

[3] Gould discusses his earliest radio work in *GGR* 353–4; and Mach, 90–1.

[4] 'Glenn Gould's CBC Questionnaire from 1952', 5. In a 1974 self-interview, he spoke of the concert performer 'savor[ing] the ego gratification' of 'communicating with an audience from a power-base' (*GGR* 318).

ings were 'contaminated by the concert experience'—that is, they merely preserved conventional performances and were not founded on a real aesthetic of recording, a distinction he considered crucial. By contrast, he added, 'the first records that really reflect a total concentration, a total respect for the [recording] medium, were done about two years later [than 1964] . . . and it just happens that that was the period in which I began to do all my own editing and, through that experience, became aware of exactly what could be done and should be done with the medium'.[5] Throughout his career, he was quick to explore new technological options as they appeared. (At the time of his death, digital recording was in its infancy, and CDs of his recordings had not yet appeared.) In notes for a 1966 CBC radio programme, he claimed that 'most of the ideas that occur to me as a performer relate in some measure to the microphone'.[6] His mature style of performance, in short, was geared entirely to recording.

Jean-Jacques Nattiez has shown that there was a unity of purpose between Gould's most basic premises about music and his attraction to recording technology, and Gould himself noted in 1974 that his 'total immersion in media represented a logical development' in his thinking.[7] The recording medium promoted just that atemporal vision of music so essential to his aesthetic. The studio, he wrote near the end of his life, is 'an environment where the magnetic compulsion of time is suspended—well, warped, at the very least. It's a vacuum, in a sense, a place where one can properly feel that the most horrendously constricting force of nature—the inexorable linearity of time—has been, to a remarkable extent, circumvented.'[8] In the studio, as opposed to the concert hall, the work is assembled outside real time, a process that, according to Gould, encourages a view of the work as an independent structure standing apart from the historical circumstances of its creation. This position on recorded versus concert performance was echoed by Walter Benjamin, who observed, in his famous 1936 essay 'The Work of Art in the Age of Mechanical Reproduction', that 'mechanical reproduction emancipates the work of art from its parasitical dependence on ritual', and frees it from the 'aura' of occasion.[9]

Technology permitted Gould to exercise maximum control over a performance, to present his conception of a work as fully, clearly, and definitively as possible. One of his main objections to live performance was that the inevitable element of chance can undermine even the most carefully prepared interpretation. The importance of control in Gould's psychology has been discussed by several writers,[10] and

[5] 'Mostly Music', 17. For a list of Gould recordings released around this time, see Canning, 180 ff.
[6] 'The Art of Glenn Gould—Programme No. 13/Draft II (Final)', 1.
[7] *GGR* 317. See Nattiez, 'Gould singulier', 68–79.
[8] 'What the Recording Process Means to Me', 36. See also *GGR* 342–3.
[9] Benjamin, 226, 231.
[10] See e.g. Friedrich, 294–7; Kazdin, 84–91; and Ostwald, *passim.*

is certainly obvious in many of his performance practices. (He was uncomfortable generally with chance elements in art, including aleatoric composition, jazz improvisation, and live theatre; in fact, he abhorred attending live events as much as performing in them.) There is no doubt that his objections to the concert hall were in large part motivated by personal discomfort, and that his intellectual arguments rationalized a basically instinctual response.[11] His descriptions of the studio recording environment as 'womb-like', 'cloistered', 'monastic', and so on, reveal the importance of control—and privacy, solitude, security, concentration—to the communication of his ideas about music.[12] Moreover, these working conditions were for him conducive to truly creative interpretation; he was a conspicuous exception to the view—pervasive among musicians—that recording encourages timidity and sterility in interpretation. He considered the studio a kind of laboratory that encouraged and rewarded experimentation: the performer had the opportunity to approach a work afresh, without preconceptions, and the listener had the leisure to adjust to an unconventional interpretation through close and repeated listening. By contrast, he felt that the concert milieu encouraged the satisfaction of conventional expectations, the repetition of that which is tried and true. (The Beatles abandoned the concert hall for the recording studio for much the same reasons.)

Gould also made the case that the recording studio was a more appropriate medium than the concert hall for much of the music he played.[13] He insisted that the public concert hall, a relatively recent phenomenon in historical terms, was most appropriate to the nineteenth-century solo and concerto repertoire he disdained, and that the kinds of music he preferred—works for virginals, Baroque fugues and suites, Classical sonatas—were better served by private audition in the home.[14] (This argument was by no means original, and in fact has recently been revived in some discussions of historical performers, who often play early music in anachronistic concert settings.) Such works as Byrd's pavans and Bach's fugues were conceived more for private study and contemplation than for public performance; in Gould's view, they required solitude in order to be best appreciated, and were distorted by projection in the concert hall. Recording technology, more than the concert hall, offered him a twentieth-century equivalent to the intimate venues for which much of the keyboard music written before about 1800 was conceived. He also applied the same reasoning, by extension, to some twentieth-century reper-

---

[11] He admits as much in Monsaingeon, *Chemins de la musique*, i.

[12] The quoted phrases appear in Bester, 156; Mach, 107; McClure; and 'What the Recording Process Means to Me', 36.

[13] In his 1966 essay 'The Prospects of Recording' (see *GGR* 335–6), he also noted that recording encourages performers to explore repertoire with limited concert appeal, and he is certainly not the only writer to have suggested that the widespread dissemination in the twentieth century of many types of music outside the traditional concert-hall and opera-house repertoires is due in large part to the availability of such music on recordings.

[14] See *GGSL* 15; Bester, 156; Burton, i; and Monsaingeon, *Chemins de la musique*, i.

toire, especially twelve-tone music. In his 1966 essay 'The Prospects of Recording', he wrote, 'Schoenberg's theories, to simplify outrageously, have to do with attributing significance to minute musical connections, and they deal with relationships that are on the whole subsurface and can be projected with an appropriate definition only through the intercession of electronic media.' Hindemith's highly contrapuntal music was, likewise, 'a "natural" for the microphone'.[15] Schoenberg himself noted in 1933 how the relatively thin scoring of most modern music, including his own, made it 'very suitable for broadcasting', and Gould cited a 1928 dialogue between Schoenberg and Erwin Stein to underscore the same point in his 1966 essay.[16] As usual, his reasoning was more aesthetic than historical: most of the music he considered historically inappropriate to the concert hall was also structurally complex music in which specific sonorities were less important than in Romantic or impressionistic piano music. For Gould, music whose impact was primarily through its counterpoint or motivic developments, rather than its rhetorical effects or tone colours, was best served by the electronic media, which permit private, concentrated, and repeated listening.

Regardless of the repertoire at hand, the 'contemplative climate' of the recording studio suited his style of playing, which aimed for a detailed inspection of the music.[17] As Geoffrey Payzant writes, he used recording in search of 'greater intimacy between performer and listener, and deeper awareness of the inner workings of the music than are achievable in public performance'.[18] He discovered that recording technology could help him to make a musical structure transparent. The characteristics of recorded performances that he valued most—'analytic clarity, immediacy, and indeed almost tactile proximity'—are the same characteristics that he sought through his performance practices; recording allowed him to heighten his basic pianistic style.[19] Given his often-stated desire to reveal the 'backbone' or 'skeleton' of a work, it is no surprise that he preferred the microphone, which he praised for its 'capacity for dissection, for analysis'; indeed, he once spoke of cultivating 'a very intimate, perhaps even clinical sound, which gives you all the details, all the data—in effect, an almost computer-like read-out of the music'.[20] His usual preference for close-up miking and a relatively dry acoustic further enhanced the clarity of his recordings, and further distanced them from concert-hall sound.

[15]   *GGR* 346, 344.

[16]   Schoenberg, 151. The 1928 dialogue is cited in *GGR* 346.

[17]   *GGR* 452.

[18]   Payzant, *GGMM* 44.

[19]   *GGR* 333. He contrasted these characteristics with the 'acoustic splendor', the 'cavernously reverberant' and 'cathedrallike' sound, preferred by many concert-goers (and even by some record listeners), and he rejected the importation of concert acoustics into recordings.

[20]   Ibid. 355; 'CBC Radio Script from 1978', 15. Gould used the image of 'dissection' often: see e.g. *GGR* 337; Burton, i; McClure; Menuhin and Davis, 291; and Payzant, *GGMM* 45–7.

Though he sought analytical clarity in his playing even as a concert artist, Gould insisted that his style was betrayed in the concert hall. He spoke of the futility of trying to communicate subtle contrapuntal points to audiences in large halls, in situations fraught with nervous perils.[21] He even held that the continuity—the 'long line'—often praised by proponents of concert performance was largely illusory, a merely superficial feeling of 'sweep', and that a unified performance could in fact be better achieved through efficient recording and editing.[22] He did not assume that the real-time circumstances of the concert guaranteed the authenticity or integrity of a performance. The comparison he made in 1981 between concert and recording artists reflected his belief that recording fostered greater insight, for both performer and listener, into musical structures:

I think a concert artist is somebody for whom the individual moment is more important than the totality. . . . and having given a lot of concerts I know that what one really does in concert is concentrate on an individual collection of moments and string them together to create a superficial impression of a coherent result. . . .

The true recording artist, who really understands the values and implications of recording, is someone who is looking at the totality—see[ing] it so clearly that it doesn't matter if you start with the middle note in the middle movement and work in either direction like a crab going back and forth. The mark of a true recording artist is an ability to be able to cut in at any moment in any work and say, 'This works in a way that's only appropriate for this recording.'[23]

Robert Philip, in his study of early recordings, notes that the recording medium has greatly influenced a general shift in emphasis among twentieth-century performers. Early recordings show that performers were then concerned above all to 'put across' the overall drama of the music, as in a live concert, whereas recent recordings show performers more concerned with '[d]etailed clarity and control' in the presentation of the musical text.[24] In Gould's playing this general trend became a polemical point. The kind of playing that James Methuen-Campbell describes as 'the romantic school at its most romantic'—that is, playing 'for overall effect rather than detailed point-making'—was precisely that which Gould associated with the concert medium, and it was in the service of 'detailed point-making' that he turned so definitively to recording.[25]

In a 1962 interview, he defined Romantic playing as that in which the imagination of the performer was employed at the expense of, rather than in the service of,

---

[21]   He wrote in his 1974 article 'Music and Technology' that recording could exercise a morally beneficial effect by enabling a person 'to operate at increasing distances from . . . his animal response to confrontation' (*GGR* 355).

[22]   See ibid. 355–7; and Payzant, *GGMM* 119–27. In his 1975 article 'The Grass is Always Greener in the Outtakes: An Experiment in Listening', he reported the results of a controlled experiment that provided some statistical evidence for his claims about the potential 'unity' of recorded and spliced performances (*GGR* 357–68).

[23]   Colgrass, 8.

[24]   Philip, 230–1. Gould made this same point in a 1965 article, quoted in Payzant, *GGMM* 44.

[25]   Methuen-Campbell, 51.

the 'architectural framework' of the music, and such playing he always associated with the concert hall.[26] The projection of pieces to a dispersed crowd in a large space was, for him, the source of unnecessary nuances that had no justification in a structural event—or at least, were out of proportion to the importance of the event. He spoke often of the detrimental effects of concerts on his own performances, of the temptation to make exaggerated expressive gestures in live performance without sound musical reasons: because of nervousness, to make up for digital errors, to adjust for hall resonance, to keep the audience's attention.[27] (His own preserved concert performances bear him out, and I reject the quite common tendency in the Gould literature to find his live performances superior to his recordings.) He applied this criticism even to studio recordings that he made during his concert years, which he felt were detrimentally affected by concert performances.[28] In a number of interviews and broadcasts, he used his 1956–7 studio recording of Bach's Partita No. 5 in G major as an example of an inter-pretation whose musical integrity had been compromised by repeated concert performances; in 1968 he called it the worst recording he had ever made.[29] The interpretation was 'compromised' in the sense of featuring rhythmic and dynamic inflections that did not correspond to structural joints, and so marred intended rhythmic and dynamic plateaus; exaggeration of legato melody at the expense of more articulated phrases and a more contrapuntal texture; and use of the sustain-ing pedal for purely colouristic effect. Such features created a performance that was more 'rhetorical' than 'analytical'—'piano playing', in a pejorative sense.[30] For Gould, a concert performance of this kind was inappropriate to the recording medium because it ignored the options that the medium offered.[31]

He repeatedly made an analogy between studio recording and film-making, and often adopted the terminology of film-making when describing the recording

[26] Asbell, 92.

[27] Gould was scathing about such gestures, which he referred to as 'party tricks' (Mach, 95–6), 'bad scene-stealing habits' ('The Art of Glenn Gould: Take 1', 2–3), and 'interpretive "niceties" ' intended to woo the upper balcony' (*GGR* 336).

[28] In 'Mostly Music', 17, he notes how his early recordings were relatively 'performance-oriented' and 'pianistic' by his later standards.

[29] McClure. For a published discussion of this recording, see Mach, 95–6.

[30] Mach, 95; Burton, i. There is extant film footage of Gould playing the Allemande, Sarabande, and Corrente (in that order) from this Partita, as an encore in a 1957 concert in Toronto (released in GGC iii). Compared with his usual style of performing Bach in the studio, the footage shows precisely the rhythmic and dynamic exaggerations about which he complained. And as he pointed out, it is instructive to compare his 1956–7 studio recording with his 1954 recording of the Partita for Radio Canada International: the 1954 version, made before he had become an international concert pianist, is, as he noted, 'less exhibitionistic . . . unspoiled by concert wear and tear' ('The Art of Glenn Gould: Take 1', 2–3); it is stylistically closer to his later studio recordings of Bach. (The same is true, to a lesser degree, of the 1951 performance of the Partita preserved in NLC acetates nos. 142–4 and 158–9.)

[31] Several studies have validated and even quantified Gould's observation of the more 'rhetorical' and 'pianistic' style of his early performances. The point is made throughout Dale Innes's study of his performances of the Goldberg Variations. And Guertin, 19, uses a semiological analysis of the results of a listening experiment to validate Gould's perception of his 1955 recording of the Goldberg Variations as more conventionally pianistic than his more 'analytical' 1981 recording.

process.[32] He believed that recording and concert performance were distinct art forms, each with its own premisses, priorities, ethics, and possibilities, and he used a comparison between cinema and theatre by way of analogy; indeed, he considered the basic principles and processes of film-making and recording to be identical. He denied, for example, that splicing tape to create a recording was any less ethical than shooting a film out of sequence and assembling it in an editing studio: the recording musician need no more be bound by the conditions of live performance than the film director or actor is by those of the theatre. And he demonstrated that recorded music could be assembled to create as coherent a result as a film—that it could convey a sense of continuity and coherence without being bound by limitations of real time.[33]

Gould's cinematic analogy is a telling one: it is precisely the inherent differences between film and theatre that separate recording from live performance. Benjamin wrote that a film audience identifies with the camera, a theatre audience with the actor, and his comments on the inherently analytical nature of the film experience recall Gould's own on recording:

behavior items shown in a movie can be analyzed much more precisely and from more points of view than those presented on paintings or on the stage. As compared with painting, filmed behavior lends itself more readily to analysis because of its incomparably more precise statements of the situation. In comparison with the stage scene, the filmed behavior item lends itself more readily to analysis because it can be isolated more easily.[34]

Gould wanted to lead the listener's ear the way a film director leads the viewer's eye. The distinction often made between stage acting and screen acting might, by analogy, be applied to his performance style. Like a film actor, he was aware of the magnifying potential of the electronic media: small inflections are more telling in a recording, as in a film.[35] The reticence about expression in many of his performances, and the often narrow spectrum within which he made nuances of rhythm, dynamics, articulation, and so on, seem tailored to the intimate scale of studio recording and home playback, and were compromised in a concert setting.

Though Gould was a leading proselytizer on behalf of recording technology, and understood the mechanics of it better than most performers, his applications of technology in practice were often conservative.[36] Most Gould recordings were

[32]   For general comments on this subject, see *GGF*, Aikin, 31; Colgrass, 8, 10; Harris, 51; McClure; and Menuhin and Davis, 193. Dutton, 513, writes: 'The analogy has sure validity: record manufacturers still very often boast that their discs provide "concert hall realism." How many film makers would brag that their production of a dramatic work presents the play "exactly as one would see it in a theatre"?'

[33]   Gould used the same argument to defend the assembly of performances at a synthesizer (see Davis, 293).

[34]   Benjamin, 237–8. Marshall McLuhan, likewise, wrote that the camera 'records and analyses the daylight world with more than human intensity' (quoted in Théberge, 19), and Lyotard, 74, notes the ability of photography and cinema to 'stabilize the referent' to permit analysis of it; both observations could be extended to the microphone.

[35]   In the field of popular music, the influence the microphone had in encouraging the more intimate style of singers like Frank Sinatra has often been noted.

[36]   Some of his record producers have made this point: see Kazdin, 19–20, 63; and Scott *et al.*, 80. His usual working methods in the studio are discussed in these two sources, and in Aikin, 32; Burton, i; Colgrass, 8; McClure; Monsaingeon, *Chemins de la musique*, ii; and Payzant, *GGMM* 33–50, 119–27.

made in the conventional way (basic takes supplemented with inserts and edited into a polished product), and some in fact consist of continuous, unedited single takes. According to Gould himself and to the colleagues, technicians, and producers with whom he worked, he used tape splicing no more often than the average recording pianist, and used it, moreover, less to correct finger slips than as a creative tool.[37] He was interested in the possibility of intercutting between takes in order to arrive at an interpretation that was superior to that offered by any single complete take. One example that he discussed on several occasions was the Fugue in A minor from *WTC* I, the finished recording of which combines two takes alike in tempo but distinct in character, one in the outer sections of the fugue, one in the centre.[38] The splice, and change of character, comes at a structurally significant point in the music: the moment at which the subject first appears in inversion, in bar 14. The significance of this example for him was that the post-production process, here as in film-making, allowed him more interpretative options than the actual performances of the takes themselves. The editorial function offered by technology became part of the creative process, altering the impact of performance practice on the interpretation. As he put it, 'By taking advantage of the post-taping afterthought . . . one can very often transcend the limitations that performance imposes upon the imagination.'[39]

The basic recording methods that he used in the A minor fugue—recording sections out of sequence, repeated takes, splicing—did not create a performance that was necessarily impossible to attain in a concert setting, but other of the techniques that he exploited did do so, and can properly be considered aspects of performance practice. Some were commonplace: the regeneration of segments of tape in order to create an exact repeat; the admission or suppression of reverberation (natural or electronic) according to prevailing affect, tempo, and articulation.[40] Over-dubbing permitted Gould to play, in a four-hand duet with himself, the complex counterpoint in the closing minutes of Wagner's *Meistersinger* Prelude, in his 1973 piano transcription (see CD 2).[41] In the last years of his life, he investigated the possibility of recording concertos by taping orchestral and solo tracks separately, with himself both playing and conducting, and assembling a finished performance in the studio. A private recording made in April 1982, in which he

[37]   Gould often used such terms as 'creative cheating', 'creative lying', and 'creative dishonesty' to refer to his use of splicing.

[38]   See *GGR* 386; Burton, i; McClure; and Payzant, *GGMM* 38–9.

[39]   *GGR* 339.

[40]   On Gould's use of regeneration and reverberation, see *GGR* 366; and Kazdin, 64–7, 116–17, 131. For a clear example of regeneration, cf. Bourrée I with the da capo repeat of it, in his 1973 recording of Bach's English Suite No. 1 in A major.

[41]   Over-dubbing is common—indeed, ubiquitous—in the recording of popular music, as he was aware. Rumours of pervasive over-dubbing in his recordings still circulate occasionally, but are unfounded: Kazdin, 18–19, notes that only in the *Meistersinger* Prelude and in a brief passage in the fourth movement of the Beethoven-Liszt Fifth Symphony did he ever use over-dubbing. But there was certainly one other instance. In the 'Siegfried's Rhine Journey' section of his transcription of music from Wagner's *Götterdämmerung,* he used over-dubbing to create a three-hand texture in some complex passages. This is obvious in the recording itself, but is also confirmed by the final draft of his score for the transcription (NLC 27/11).

conducted the Hamilton Philharmonic and pianist Jon Klibonoff in the first two movements of Beethoven's Concerto No. 2 in B flat major, was apparently a trial run for such a project.[42] In his performances for television from the 1950s to the 1970s, and especially in his later films, he experimented with using visual ambiance, background projection, camera placement and movement, and editing to underscore affects, and even articulate structural joints, in the music. His most accomplished such work is in his CBC television programmes from the 1970s, and, especially, in his films with Bruno Monsaingeon, but he admitted that his success was generally limited, and he never worked out a fully satisfying, comprehensive theory or set of practices for presenting music visually.[43] He also made tentative experiments with a technique that he could not control sufficiently to produce a polished recording, but whose benefits he extolled in theory: recording the individual voices of a fugue on separate tracks, and mixing them for quadrophonic playback, to enhance the independence of those voices more than conventional performance and recording permit. In a 1970 letter, he wrote:

I had occasion last year to record several of Bach's fugues experimentally—wearing earphones, performing one voice at a time only. The experiment which, in view of the deficiencies of ensemble that inevitably resulted, will not, of course, be made public, was intended purely as an in-house demonstration at Columbia Records of the possibilities for a quadrophonic sound-system—i.e. each voice was recorded on a separate tape track and emanated from a different speaker (one at each corner of the room). For me, however, the real benefit of this never-to-be-released recording was that it offered conclusive proof of the appropriateness of the one-voice-at-a-time approach to Bach. I have rarely been able to enjoy so clear a perspective on the fugues in question and I do believe that some modification of that principle remains the most rewarding approach to the keyboard music of Bach.[44]

This recording technique extends Gould's interest in clarifying contrapuntal textures well beyond the limits permitted to the concert performer.

Perhaps the most conspicuous use to which he put recording technology in the service of performance practice was a process that he applied in the 1970s, and that he called 'acoustic choreography'.[45] This technique involved treating microphones the way a film director treats a camera. Gould would record a piece using several

---

[42] See Black; Friedrich, 278–83; and Bruno Monsaingeon's liner notes to GGC vi.

[43] For his comments on his television work, see GGR 368–73; GGSL 153–8; and McClure.

[44] GGSL 123–4. In the 1970 CBC television programme The Well-Tempered Listener, the text of which is transcribed in Davis, Gould discussed the same principle, and used split-screen technology to show a one-hand-per-part performance of an excerpt from the Fugue in C sharp major from WTC II.

[45] He also used the terms 'sonic choreography' and 'acoustic orchestration'. For discussion of this technique, see GGR 381–2; 'CBC Radio Script from 1978'; Aikin, 36; Cott, 87–95; Davis, 292; Kazdin, 137–40; Mach, 97–8; Menuhin and Davis, 295; and Monsaingeon, Chemins de la musique, ii. He even applied this technique for dramatic effect in his music for the 1972 film Slaughterhouse-Five (see Goddard, 28). Théberge, 27–8, not only considers acoustic choreography to be 'completely in keeping with Gould's predilection for the analytical capabilities of the recording medium', but relates it to the 'labyrinth' (or 'mosaic' or 'cubist') structure that McLuhan defined as 'the acceptance of multiple facets and planes in a single experience', and that he considered a model of human cognition.

ranks of microphones in different locations, ranging from adjacent to the piano strings to facing the back wall of the hall, and conveying the sonic equiavalents of close-ups, medium shots, and long shots. After recording a work, he could then mix it, as a director edits a film, by moving back and forth between different microphone perspectives, or combinations thereof. The technique permitted a variety of means of transition between microphone perspectives—cuts, dissolves, pans, and so on. The ambiance of the recording could be varied to underscore aspects of the music, just as, in a film, camera angles and movements, and the mixing of perspectives, underscore relationships and emotional connotations within the images shot.[46]

Even when recording in the studio using a conventional, stationary microphone pick-up, Gould adjusted overall ambiance in accordance with the repertoire and style of performance at hand: a tight, analytical microphone perspective for contrapuntal music by Bach, a somewhat more distant, reverberant sound for music by Wagner and Brahms. Acoustic choreography likewise applied to different degrees depending on the composer and the music. Predictably, Gould discussed conventional miking and acoustic choreography by analogy with, respectively, black-and-white and colour film, with each having its place according to the kind of expression desired and the subject-matter at hand. One composer who, he thought, 'cries out' for the possibilities of acoustic choreography was Scriabin, especially given Scriabin's interest in using the piano to express ideas that transcend the piano.[47] He first used the technique of acoustic choreography in his 1970 recording of Scriabin's Fifth Sonata, which was recorded on eight tracks. As he told Jonathan Cott, the microphones were arranged in four ranks: one inside the piano, as in a jazz recording ('ultra-percussive'); one about five feet from the piano (his usual perspective, which is closer than usual); one about nine feet away (a more conventional perspective); and one pointing at the back wall of the hall, picking up only indirect hall ambiance. His intention was to 'choreograph' or 'orchestrate' the music in the editing studio, 'to look at the score and decide what it might offer in terms of a cinematic projection'.[48] But the mix was never done: though he had intended to record other Scriabin sonatas the same way, even a complete cycle, he did not pursue the project further.[49] The Fifth Sonata was never released in his lifetime, and when it was released posthumously in 1986, Andrew Kazdin, who directed the digital remixing process, used the conventional perspective only; he did not create his own Gouldian 'choreography' out of the various perspectives preserved.

[46] Gould also used the technique of 'pan-potting'—moving a sound source from one place to another within a stereo spectrum—in his CBC radio documentaries in the 1960s and 1970s: see Cott, 90–2.

[47] Gould also used video technology in the 1970s to enhance his television performances of Scriabin, which are available in GGC vii, xi, and xvi. See also GGSL 204, 210.

[48] Gould's comments in this and the following paragraph are in Cott, 92–4.

[49] On his aborted Scriabin cycle, see GGSL 171; 'CBC Radio Script from 1978', 10–11; and Kazdin, 138.

From Gould's interview with Cott, however, it is possible to imagine one important gesture in the sonata that the acoustic choreography was to have created. The sonata 'starts with a trill in the lowest octave of the piano, supported by a tritonic passage playing as a tremolando, and in the course of about ten seconds this trill plus the accompanying tritone moves up the keyboard, octave by octave, until it gets to the very top, at which point the score unrealistically asks for fortissimo, and, of course, you can't play fortissimo at the top of the piano'. Gould's plan in mixing this opening passage was to begin 'with the hindmost mikes, those that faced the wall, and which picked up a sort of a distant rumble, which was really quite an unearthly sound. . . . with each octave, as it moved up the piano, we'd kick in another rank of mikes, but never so many that the sound lost its basic clarity'. At the end of the passage, with the fortissimo at the top of the keyboard, the closest microphone perspective alone was to be used. The increasing 'close-up' of the microphone perspective thus mimicked, and enhanced, the crescendo marked in the score. (In bar 12, following this introduction, there is a long pause, and then the first theme proper of the sonata begins, at which point Gould planned to pull back to Rank 2 for a more conventional perspective.) He compared the audio effect in the introduction to a zoom in a film.

He applied similar acoustic choreography to Scriabin's two pieces 'Désir' and 'Caresse dansée', Op. 57. His 1972 studio recording of them featured a conventional microphone perspective only, but when he recorded them again in 1974, for the second film in Monsaingeon's series *Chemins de la musique,* he used four ranks of microphones as in the Scriabin sonata. An extended sequence in the film shows him at work in the editing studio, 'conducting' his engineer during a playback of the pieces, to cue the entrance, exit, and combination of the four ranks as the tape is mixed. He refers to this as a 'very rough' test only, though like most 'impromptu' sequences in his films it was surely planned in advance. Fig. 10.1 shows his mixing of microphone perspectives—in cinematic terms, his 'storyboard'—for this recording, according to his spoken directions in the film; 'Rank 1' refers to the closest set of microphones, 'Rank 4' to the most distant. (The 1974 film, as of this writing, has been released only by a French company on a European-format video-tape, and is not yet part of Sony Classical's Glenn Gould Collection. Readers without access to the film can compare my Fig. 10.1 with the score of Op. 57, which is reproduced in Plates 4 and 5, and with the 1972 studio recording, which is available on CD.)

In Gould's view, the 1974 film version, unlike the earlier recording, 'made a real statement about Scriabin which was very vivid and absolutely in keeping with the nature of the music'.[50] It is certainly clear that he used acoustic choreography, as

---

[50] 'CBC Radio Script from 1978', 11.

FIG. 10.1. Gould's 'acoustic choreography' in Scriabin's *Two Pieces* ('Désir' and 'Caresse dansée'), Op. 57 (1974 film)

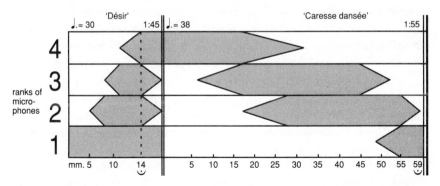

much as rhythm or dynamics, to give the pieces a distinctive shape in performance. He conveys the two pieces as a continuous, arching structure: 'Désir' opens, and 'Caresse dansée' closes, with the closest perspective alone; the first piece offers motion from an intimate to a distant perspective, the second piece motion back to the point of departure. Moreover, Gould adds and subtracts microphone perspectives at important points in the musical structure. In 'Désir', he adds Rank 2 to the original Rank 1 through the modulating section in bars 3–4, having Rank 2 fully present at bar 6, where the opening theme returns in the dominant. Rank 3 is introduced in a similar way. And Rank 4 is introduced to enhance the final cadence. As conceived by Scriabin, 'Désir' describes a gradual progression outward in terms of register and dynamics, and Gould mimics this progression by gradually moving outward in terms of microphone perspective, like a camera gradually pulling back and taking in ever more space. While mixing 'Caresse dansée', he instructs the engineer to leave the perspective stable in the sequential passage in bars 33–48: the sequence implies a static texture, and no need for a change in sonic perspective. On the other hand, as the energy of the work gradually dissipates in the closing bars, he gradually subtracts microphone perspectives until, in the final bar, only the closest perspective remains—that with which 'Désir' had begun.

Acoustic choreography was applied most extensively in Gould's 1976–7 recording of pieces by Sibelius, the only studio recording using this technique to be released in his lifetime. The Sibelius pieces were recorded using a disposition of microphones similar to that in the Scriabin projects, and in the editing process the different perspectives were likewise mixed to enhance features of the music.[51]

---

[51] The NLC holds two copies of each Sibelius score, one containing Gould's splicing notes, the other his notes for the mixing of microphone perspectives: NLC Scores 43/4–5 and 44/1–6. (The mixing notes do not always seem to correspond to the finished recording, however.) The analyses that follow are based on consultation of both the mixing notes and the recording. All quotations in the text below are taken from 'CBC Radio Script from 1978'.

Gould discusses this recording, and the whole technique of acoustic choreography, in an interview with Andrew Marshall (actually scripted by Gould alone) used as programme notes for a 1978 CBC radio broadcast featuring some of the pieces. He again draws a cinematic analogy in making a distinction between his approaches to recording Scriabin and Sibelius, the latter 'a much more reserved musical figure who doesn't really need that much sonic assistance', as Marshall puts it.[52] He replies:

Yes, that's quite true—the point about his being reserved, anyway—but I would like to think that we 'shot' it, accordingly. For example, in the ORTF Scriabin filming [of 'Désir' and 'Caresse dansée' in 1974], there were no hard cuts whatsoever; every change of perspective was approached by a very slow dissolve. But, in the Sibelius, on the other hand—precisely because, as you say, it is very restrained music—I attempted to draw up a 'shot list' that would reflect that restraint in various ways. For example, many of the perspective-swaps occur during pauses—of which there are many, pregnant ones, in these pieces, so they're obviously hard cuts. The dissolves, when they occur, and with a couple of notable exceptions, are negotiated gently and rather quickly; that sounds like a contradiction in terms but it isn't, because they're almost always between perspectives, or combinations of perspective, which are rather similar.

As with the Scriabin pieces, Gould's 'only yardstick' when making decisions about microphone perspectives was 'the structure of the music itself'. A particularly clear example occurs in the last of the three lyric pieces *Kyllikki*, Op. 41 (see CD $\boxed{24}$), in which the outer 'commodo' sections and the central 'tranquillo' section are distinct in character. Moreover, he notes,

there's a considerable harmonic spread between them—the outer segments are in B flat major and minor, which is the tonic key for all three movements of Kyllikki, while the center episode is in G flat major and there's absolutely no modulatory preparation between the two harmonic areas. So, it seemed to me that the way to characterize that transition—or lack of transition—was through a 'zoom shot'. The outer segments, which are virtually identical, are also 'shot' identically—hard cuts only, very bright colours, very tight perspectives—but the moment we hit the G flat major segment, we go to a sort of crow's nest pick-up . . .

Here the distance between aural perspectives mimics the tonal distance between sections.

The first movement of Sibelius's Sonatine No. 1 features 'an extraordinary happening, harmonically', which Gould underscored through miking and mixing. Though the piece is in F sharp minor, the tonic is not solidly confirmed until near the end. Gould notes that there are

earlier moments in which [Sibelius] hints at what the tonic might be—the second theme, if one can call it that, is first presented in the dominant, C sharp minor—but, all in all, it's

---

a very elusive piece and I wanted to find an audio metaphor for that rather slippery modulatory quality. So I chose, as a basic registration, a combination of the closest and the most distant of our perspectives. . . To switch from the lingo of film editing to that of organ playing, it was the fundamental stop of the movement; and it was modified to the following extent: whenever Sibelius gave some hint of where the tonic really was—whether through the dominant episode I spoke of earlier, or through a series of chords immediately prior to the recapitulation—each of which shows an increase of F sharp minor-ness, so to speak—I replaced the ethereal quality of the basic sound by something a little more earthbound, a little closer to conventional pick-up ranks. So that, in this movement, the choice of registration—the choice of 'shot'—whichever terminology you want to use—was absolutely determined by that rather curious structural drama which Sibelius plays out in it—the search for a home-key.

Plate 6, from Gould's mixing notes for this movement, shows him moving the microphone perspective increasingly close in the approach to the recapitulation (at the end of the first system), then retreating to a distant perspective at the point of recapitulation (the start of the second system), where the sense of tonic return—of 'F sharp minor-ness'—is immediately undercut by a pivot to D major. (In Plates 6–8, '1' again refers to the closest microphone perspective, '4' to the most distant.)

In the second of the *Kyllikki* pieces, Gould cuts sharply from a modest, conventional microphone perspective to a distant one to set off the mysterious trills that interrupt the chordal texture at bar 17 and elsewhere: now they interrupt not only texturally, but acoustically, too (see Plate 7). In the same piece, he accentuates the distinctions of affect between the outer chorale-like sections in D flat major and the more turbulent and virtuosic central episode in B flat major (beginning at bar 25), by reserving the closest, most robust microphone perspective for that central episode alone. He thus employed three acoustic perspectives—'long shot', 'medium shot', and 'close-up'—to articulate major units of the piece. Similarly, in the first movement of the Sonatine No. 3 (see CD 25), he used microphone perspectives to set off the sections of a slow-movement sonata form: a close-up, 'dry' acoustic perspective for the first theme in both exposition and recapitulation; a more distant, 'wet' perspective for the lyrical second theme in both sections; and a conventional 'medium shot' for the six bars of 'andante' introduction.

Gould sometimes even applied acoustic choreography on a much smaller level, that of the phrase. In the third movement of the Sonatine No. 1, bars 13–20, he alternated between two microphone perspectives to distinguish the two-bar units that make up a phrase, colouring the triplet flourishes in the right hand by introducing the most distant rank of microphones (see Plate 8). In these flourishes, his addition of distant hall ambiance (Rank 4) seems to have served as a more subtle substitute for the sustaining pedal, and elsewhere in the Sibelius Sonatines he added Rank 4 to achieve some sustaining power without the sacrifice of tonal and melodic clarity that the sustaining pedal would bring. (See, for example, the spare opening bars of Sonatine No. 2, and the busy figuration in the 'allegretto' finale of Sonatine No. 3.)

Pianists normally modify instrumental tone colour to suit a particular piece and to distinguish structural units, and they adjust tone, articulation, pedalling, and the like to accommodate a given concert hall or recording studio. For Gould, acoustic choreography was simply a recording artist's extension of such performance practices. It was an option granted only by twentieth-century technology, of course, and so could not have been intended by the composers to whose music he applied it; as such, it can be both criticized and defended by the standards one would apply to the debate about playing early music on 'incorrect' modern instruments. Characteristically, Gould was no more reluctant to enhance his performances through the anachronistic application of technology than he was to play Bach on the modern piano, and, as we saw in Chapter 2, he repeatedly rejected the aesthetic and ethical arguments against recording. By accepting the premisses of recording so completely, and building his aesthetic of performance around them, he made a radical and conspicuously modern contribution to performance practice.

Conclusion

THIS STUDY HAS revealed both consistencies and contradictions in Glenn Gould's work and thought, and it was, of course, the sum of these consistencies and contradictions that formed the Gould aesthetic. Many conclusions about his achievement are possible, but he cannot be assigned to any one intellectual stream or school of performance: he was too eclectic. One source of his eclecticism was surely the relative insularity of his upbringing: his provincialism, amply documented in the biographical literature, certainly helps explain both the strengths and weaknesses, the originality and the banality, in his thinking. From the beginning of his musical life, he obviously felt less pressure to conform to mainstream conventions than do more cosmopolitan musicians moulded by peer pressure, the conservatory system, and the competition circuit. Throughout his career, he proved to be unusually open to ideas and practices from a wide range of sources, some of them seemingly conflicting, and he was always willing to let non-musical ideas directly influence his playing. His work reveals an idiosyncratic union of many aesthetic ideas and styles; Romanticism, early modernism, neo-Classicism, postmodernism, even aspects of pre-Enlightenment thought, have all been cited, in different contexts, in this book. But no one 'ism' suffices to characterize him, and he never felt the need to conform consistently to any one aesthetic school. (The Romantics' insistence on creative interpretation but not their devotion to instrumental sonority; the modernists' structuralism but not their teleological view of history; the neo-Classicists' orderliness but not their claims to objectivity.) Yet the final result of Gould's eclecticism was not chaos, but rather a peculiar and coherent synthesis that defined his aesthetic.

We have seen that he was decisively influenced by many precepts of such modernist traditions as structuralism and formalism, especially as applied to music by Schoenberg and his disciples. The idealist, analytical, and contrapuntal orientations of his thinking about music; his privileging of structure over sonority, of unity over variety, of the 'thematic' over the 'ornamental'; his fondness for 'logical' procedures like fugue and developing variation; his acceptance of (indeed, snobbishness about) the Austro-German canon of absolute music; his desire to convey a work in performance as an integral 'idea' or *Gestalt*—all were clearly influenced by the Schoenberg aesthetic. Yet in many ways the distinctive piano style that he developed had as much in common with the neo-Classicism of Stravinsky as with Schoenberg, Berg, and Webern, who as composers and performers never rejected their Romantic roots as insistently as Gould (and Stravinsky) did. The mostly 'classical' or 'geometrical' profile; the fondness for lean, highly articulated, contrapuntally transparent textures; the tendency towards rhythmic and dynamic terracing; the nourishing of such values as clarity, control, consistency, precision, discretion, balance, economy, sobriety, even irony—these are hallmarks of Gould's playing, the roots of which can be traced in large part to the neo-Classical aesthetic. (As we saw, the revealing if superficial similarities between Gould's playing and that of post-war historical performers can be traced to shared roots in neo-Classicism.) His appreciation of Bach's compositional art may have owed much to the structural values of dodecaphony, but when he advocated imitating harpsichord registrations when playing Bach's keyboard music on the piano, he revealed a musical and historical perspective more in line with Stravinsky than Schoenberg.

So Gould was certainly justified in considering himself a 'modern' performer *par excellence*, and to speak of his playing as a confrontation with Romanticism: in terms of repertoire, approach to the piano, attitude towards concert performance, and many specific stylistic traits and practices, he did directly challenge assumptions held by pianists since the nineteenth century. Yet some of his performance practices did have precedents in Romanticism, as he was surely aware (recall his fondness for exploring inner voices, or his using the piano to suggest other instruments). And there were times when his playing *was* Romantic, pure and simple, and not only in Romantic repertoire (recall his staggering of vertical sonorities, or his florid continuo playing). Moreover, and notwithstanding his dislike of early-Romantic piano music, he admitted to a strong Romantic streak: witness his admiration for the late-Romantic styles of Wagner, Bruckner, Brahms, Reger, Mahler, Strauss, Scriabin, Sibelius, and the early Schoenberg and Berg. It is true that he often drew on his cherished structural values to justify this admiration, as we have seen, but it is no less obvious that there were simply Romantic 'blips' in his tastes, and in his discography, that cannot (and should not) be dismissed or explained away. Nothing is served by seeking evidence of latent idealism or analytical thinking in his *echt*-Romantic recording of Strauss's salon piece *Enoch Arden;* rather, it must be simply accepted as one of those peculiar pockets in his musical taste that cannot be reconciled with the prevailing values that supported his work on most other occasions. (Such exceptional products in his *œuvre*, even if they do not undermine the validity of his basic value system, should certainly serve as cautions—as reminders that that value system cannot be accepted completely uncritically, because it does not account for every facet of his artistic personality.) But more important, the influence of Romanticism on Gould extended beyond a few exceptional practices and predilections, for some of his most basic aesthetic premises—his idealism, his allegiance to the concept of absolute music, his one-sided image of Bach, his notion of 'ecstasy'—can be situated within the Romantic aesthetic tradition that includes such figures as Hanslick and Schoenberg. And of course, when he insisted that a performer should offer a highly personal gloss on the music he played, he could not have been a more compleat Romantic.

But I have also explored aspects of his work and thought that suggest a close temperamental allegiance with contemporary post-modernism. His treatment of the musical work as a 'text', in Roland Barthes's sense of the word; his view of the interpreter's role as necessarily creative and critical; his very personal sense of 'authenticity'; his ahistorical vision of music, rejection of 'progress' as a value, and advocacy of the mixing of musical styles; his position on the roles of the composer, performer, and listener—such ideas often ally Gould more closely with post-modern theory and practice in literature than with most contemporary thought in musicology, music criticism, and classical-music performance. The self-consciousness in Gould's œuvre is also typical of post-modernism—self-consciousness towards his work in its cultural context, towards his role as a performer, towards the classical canon, and towards conventions of performance practice; self-consciousness in the way his performances and writings address aesthetic issues, argue for new criteria and standards, even take at times a metacritical stance. The streak of irony—even parody and self-parody—in Gould's work, and his playful, tweaking performances of some of the staples of the repertoire, have parallels in post-modern critical practice. (Such performances were the musical manifestations of an artist and thinker who was serious about his work but was also not above appearing on television singing Mahler to elephants, or playing awful ethnic characters *in maschera*.) In many respects, Gould's work was tuned in to the post-modern culture of the 1950s and 1960s, whether or not he thought of it in those terms; I have explored a number of alliances between Gould and contemporary thought in music composition, literature, theatre, semiology, media studies, and other disciplines. Indeed, the very eclecticism characteristic of his aesthetic was itself utterly symptomatic of his times, as he was keenly aware.

Yet, if his views often resonate with his cultural contemporaries, they also at times hearken back to a pre-Enlightenment, even pre-Renaissance, view of art. And he was conscious of it: he sometimes advocated ideas that he considered 'Medieval' (temperamentally, if not necessarily historically). I have cited: his position on the ethical implications of music; his advocacy of a principled suspension of aesthetic judgement; his belief that anonymity was a proper condition for an artist; his hope for the reunion of the roles of composer, performer, and listener; and his rejection of the teleological view of history implicit in such concepts as originality, individuality, fashion, and progress, values that he rejected ethically because of the competitive implications he perceived in them. Even the creative licence he demanded as a performer sometimes suggests an approach to music more relevant to an era before concepts of a stable musical work and 'fidelity' to the work existed.

But even as I have revealed the extent of Gould's eclecticism, I have tried to document the sometimes remarkable stability and internal consistency of his aesthetic, and the many respects in which there was a unity of purpose between his premisses and his practices. Recording technology offers one convenient example treated in detail in the book and discussed often by Gould himself. As I showed in various chapters, his intense interest in recording was consistent with his idealism; with his atemporal vision of musical works; with his analytical bent; with the repertoire he favoured; with the contemplative or 'ecstatic' mode of listening he encouraged; with his belief in the creative function of the interpreter; with his views on the proper relationship of composer, performer, and listener; with such basic musical values of his as clarity and the primacy of structure; with his fondness for revealing counterpoint; and with some of his specific choices in terms of articulation, tone colour, piano action, and expressive nuance. I even showed how he applied specific recording techniques *as* elements of performance practice in themselves. In other words, a whole complex of diverse but related ideas and practices converged on his interest in recording.

Many other consistencies in Gould's aesthetic should now be apparent. We have seen some recurring themes in his thought—idealism, atemporality, structure, counterpoint, the ethic of non-competition—that had far-reaching implications. We have seen a persistent tendency towards polarization in his thinking, a tendency to view issues in terms of often simplistic binarisms, and with it a tendency to see performance options in terms of opposed extremes. We have seen certain recurring musical criteria in his performance choices, like the importance of harmonic criteria in determining rhythmic and dynamic inflection, articulation and phrasing, even ornamentation and miking. We have seen how he consistently applied musical values derived from his special interest in Bach to music from all historical periods—values relating to the performer's attitude towards the score, but also to such practical matters as counterpoint, rhythm, dynamics, articulation, and instrumental tone and action.

We have also seen how countless aspects of Gould's playing and thinking, from his disregard for the composer's intentions to his interest in large-scale rhythmic control, developed significantly after his retirement from concert life in 1964. Countless times we have seen him make his most provocative practical experiments, or consolidate the most characteristic aspects of his style, only after 1964, in the solitude of the recording studio. We have also seen a growing strictness and control of all aspects of performance as his career progressed, and a growing tendency to forgo conventional pianistic solutions to musical problems. And, of course, it is no coincidence that the implications of the recording medium itself were increasingly influential on his performances. Critical opinion will undoubtedly always be divided as to the proper evaluation of Gould's development. Some critics admire him as a great pianist while rejecting his most characteristic quirks, and as a result consider his best work to be his least idiosyncratic, namely that from the 1950s and early 1960s, especially his early recordings of Bach, Beethoven, and Brahms. But whether we see his work as becoming increasingly interesting and significant as his career progressed, or increasingly self-indulgent and bizarre, it cannot be denied that the intellectual and stylistic features that most characterize him came into focus and matured after his retirement from public performance.

It is undoubtedly this consistency and coherence in Gould's aesthetic, translated directly into performance terms, that accounts for the peculiar conviction of his playing, and that make his performances—even at their most controversial, most obviously 'wrong'—worthy of serious attention and discussion. This is not to suggest that his playing is convincing in the sense that it is always, or even often, likely to win converts to the specific premises, ideas, and values at the heart of the performances. The quality of conviction that I refer to is difficult to define, though one gets a sense of it from the Gould literature: reviewers and critics often acknowledge and praise the integrity, consistency, clarity, and strength with which he realized his vision at the keyboard, even where they have no sympathy for that vision and do not recommend the resulting performances as models for imitation. In his best performances, even where highly idiosyncratic, there is a real sense of unity between idea and practice, between thought and sound. The extreme tempos, the upside-down textures, the absurd ornaments—Gould could make such eccentricities sound convincing in performance because *he* was convinced by them, because they were such honest reflections of his aesthetic ideas, and also, of course, because he had the keyboard technique to render them in an engaging manner. (Not surprisingly, as his orchestral and chamber-music recordings show, those quirks that sounded so natural under his fingers sounded awkward and contrived when he induced colleagues to try them.) In other words, there is a sense of conviction in Gould's successful bridging of his theories and his practices, a bridging capable of stimulating productive discussion on a wide range of music-related issues. Substantiating and developing this point has been one of the principal goals of this book.

Moreover, I have sought to emphasize, in the face of persistent claims to the contrary, that Gould's primary achievement remains that of a performer, not a writer or critic or philosopher. It is true that he sought to use the piano to communicate a comprehensive vision of music and life, more directly than most performers, and it is true, as we have seen repeatedly, that the aesthetic and philosophical positions he advocated were not merely empty claims. In this sense, we cannot fully account for his work if we limit him to someone who simply played the piano. Yet, he never undermined the vitality of his piano performances in the process of communicating his aesthetic and intellectual positions. We can call him (as Jerrold Levinson did) a 'theory-driven' performer, and can identify the theoretical discourses embedded in his performances, but we cannot say that his performances have the quality of dry essays, for he never abandoned the basic musical values that any performer must hold in order to create performances that were (for want of a better word) *alive*. Reason may have modulated beauty in his playing, but never undermined it; as Nicholas Spice once put it, his aesthetic was cold, not his performances. I have held back one musical example until now, and it should quash any doubt about this point: the finale of Bach's Italian Concerto, in Gould's original 1959 recording (see CD $\boxed{26}$). This is a performance that could certainly be used to exemplify many aspects of the rational Gould—his idealist's image of Bach; his clear, controlled, analytical playing style; his obsession with counterpoint and structure; his ability to clarify for the listener both the musical details and the architecture of the whole; his special affinity, both aesthetically and ethically, with the medium of recording. Yet this is also a performance of boundless energy and joy, a remarkable display of mental and digital facility, a powerful rendering of the music's inherent tension and drama. It is a thoughtful performance that repays analysis, yet it never seems calculated; it seems all spontaneity and abandon. We can, to be sure, admire the musical thinker behind this interpretation, but we also do well to notice that this is some of the most accomplished, compelling, and entertaining piano playing on record.

There was generally a potent synthesis of calculation and spontaneity in Gould's playing, and indeed a greater level of intuition than he was willing to admit (hence his rationalizations after the fact). Contrasting himself with Alberto Guerrero, he said in 1960 that Guerrero was a 'heart' man, whereas he wanted to be a 'head' kid. But he always protested too much in this respect: like Charlie Chaplin or Bertolt Brecht or Orson Welles, he was a highly intuitive artist who fancied himself an intellectual. To say so does not invalidate the study of Gould in a variety of intel-lectual contexts—I hope this book has made that point—but it should caution us about accepting his rationalizations of his practices at face value. There is often in his performances a pregnant tension between the imperatives of theory and practice, which coexisted in fluctuating degrees depending on the circumstances at hand, even within the same performance. The necessary compromises between theory and practice in his performances did not amount to flaws; rather, an effective synthesis of these two forces was his principal point, and remains the source of much of what is interesting and characteristic about his work.

Gould's refusal to abandon basic standards of performance in communicating his ideas is obvious in the frequent contradictions between the polemical strength of his convictions and the compromises he made in putting them into practice. We have seen, for example, that though he held extreme notions about the degree of interpretative licence proper to a performer, he did not feel bound radically to rethink every aspect of every piece he performed. And he did not—could not—entertain such basic values as idealism, anti-Romanticism, analytical calculation, and the like as strictly in practice as in theory. Compromises are apparent in many of his performance choices. His rhythmic premises may have fallen into the 'geometrical' camp, but he allowed countless compromises to make particular musical points. His application of rhythmic continuity in works like the Goldberg Variations was typical: the operative principle might seem clinically calculated, yet the result in performance was achieved (and was intended to be perceived) intuitively, directly, and in fact is better understood through the study of outtakes from recording sessions than through quantitative analysis. Likewise, though he theoretically defended the principle of dynamic terracing in Bach's music, his terraces were not absolutely strict, certainly never as strict as those of a harpsichordist, or of a pianist like Tureck who applies the analogy of harpsichord registrations more literally; his more 'layered' dynamics gave him both the terracing he sought in theory and the inflections that vitalized the performance. Gould's arrangement of Handel's Prelude in A major showed another typical compromise: inspired by Schoenbergian premises, but not taken to Schoenbergian extremes; recomposed to satisfy certain structural values, yet put over in performance with an improvisatory spirit that all but disguised its calculated motivic developments. Even his love of the recording medium reflected the twin forces of calculation and spontaneity in his playing. As he observed, recording offers, on the one hand, a forum in which one initially can improvise, experiment, literally 'play' with the music at hand without being bound by the real-time limitations (what he called the 'non-take-two-ness') of the concert medium; yet, on the other hand, it encourages greater reflection on the work than the concert medium, and offers complete control over the finished product, by postponing final interpretative decisions to the post-production process. In other words, for Gould the studio offered greater freedom than the concert hall, the editing booth greater control.

This synthesis of control and freedom, of calculation and spontaneity, has been the source of the necessarily *ad hoc* nature of much of my foregoing analysis of Gould's performance practices. Since his interest in theoretical issues was generally not far removed from performance-related concerns (whether he acknowledged this or not), one's analysis of his playing often bumps up against his compromises between theory and practice. His analytical bent offers a good example. I explored many ways in which his thinking about music could legitimately be considered analytical; I proposed, in fact, a basically 'analytical' mindset, and showed how many of his specific practices reveal analytical motivations and yield analytical insights. But there is no comprehensive body of theoretical work in which Gould addresses the issue of analysis and performance; there are no signs of advanced, professional training in analysis, not even many surviving analyses that he actually wrote down. For the most part, his interest in analysis extended only to its relevance to performance, and a great deal of the analysis manifested in his performance was clearly more intuitive than formal. I have not suggested that every note in Gould's performances had a demonstrable analytical function, that he sought to make only analytical points at the expense of conventional expression, that he somehow 'played analyses' (if such a thing is even possible), that his performance choices were exclusively logical rather than intuitive, thought about rather than felt. Even in those performances in which he sought to impose an almost graph-like image of the work as an overall *Gestalt*, he did not realize his analytical goal at the expense of the work's expressiveness, dynamism, or drama, though he may have significantly altered the score for his own purposes. And yet, for all his concessions to the imperatives of performance, that analytical mindset remains evident and relevant, and too many aspects of his playing make little sense unless one acknowledges it.

Were his *œuvre* to consist of everything but his performances, Gould would almost certainly be a relatively insignificant musical figure: to find in his performances reflections of a coherent aesthetic does not necessarily imply that that aesthetic makes a major contribution on its own merits. Compared with true polymaths like Furtwängler and Bernstein, or even with pianist colleagues like Rosen and Kuerti, Gould appears to be the less complete musician—the greater figure at the piano, perhaps, but the more amateurish away from it. Furtwängler, Bernstein, and Kuerti all married performance at the highest level with a true calling as a composer, while Gould was always a dabbler as a composer, and Rosen's writings on music history and style make Gould look like an undergraduate. His efforts to build a productive musical and intellectual career away from the piano were often frustrating and rarely wholly successful; the posthumous attention accorded his work as a conductor, writer, broadcaster, and composer is certainly out of proportion to its merit. But his ability to develop and communicate ideas directly at the keyboard never faltered. (This was immediately obvious in broadcast recitals in which he gave unconvincing or cliché-ridden spoken introductions that were followed by deeply personal performances of great conviction.) His diatribes against the piano might be seen as reflecting his frustration that much of his best thinking was more closely tied to the keyboard than he would have liked.

Still, the debate over Gould's importance has been coloured by perceptions of him as a writer and thinker. His writings and ideas have had some passionate champions (Payzant, Nattiez, Said), and recently his work has begun to be cited by scholars in a variety of musical and non-musical contexts. His writings constitute a quite coherent body of thought, but they can also be surprisingly uneven in terms of originality, intellectual rigour, clarity, and style. He certainly did not encourage serious attention by publishing his writings in popular magazines, with titles like 'The Future and "Flat-Foot Floogie"' or '"Oh, for heaven's sake, Cynthia, there must be something else on!" ', not to mention the (mercifully?) unpublished 'How Mozart Became a Bad Composer'. Gould had no advanced formal training in musicology, criticism, philosophy, aesthetics, logic, and his private reading in such subjects was highly selective. His writings betray the quirks that might be predicted in a brilliant but idiosyncratic mind operating outside of its métier: flashes of insight stand next to loftily expressed banalities, fluent argument next to obscure, laboured, and pretentious prose. The hilariously bad high-school writing that Otto Friedrich quotes in his biography contains stylistic flaws that Gould never wholly outgrew. (A degree of pretentiousness in his work away from the keyboard cannot be denied: he was the sort of person who liked to use fancy words but often misspelled or mispronounced them.) His insecurity as a writer was obvious from the beginning. He was always more sensitive to criticism of his writing than of his playing, and, once he had the authority to do so, he did not permit his writings to be edited before publication.

But we should not exaggerate either side of this issue. Some of Gould's published and broadcast writings can certainly stand alone as original, insightful, well-developed, even influential work. His prescient theorizing on the subjects of recording and broadcasting; his polemics against the 'progressive' view of music history; his writings on the roles of composer, performer, and listener; his early championship of modern music, and his early reassessment of the work of Richard Strauss; his continuing critique of conventional expectations about the role and repertoire proper to a professional pianist—with such work, Gould did make worthy contributions, away from the piano, to subjects of interest in post-war music. My point is only that it is not too harsh to assume that most of his work away from the piano would have attracted little attention were it not for the performances that grew out of it. Many times in this book, I have cited Gould writings that do not offer new insights based on searching critical analysis or historical investigation, so much as simple portraits of his temperamental prejudices. But these writings, even where of indifferent quality, shed much light on his thinking, and so are essential for the serious student who seeks a comprehensive understanding of his work.

Often I have cited idiosyncratic and provocative Gould performances and performance practices that turned out to be based on commonplace, even banal, premises. Some of his ideas (*The Art of Fugue* as 'paper music', terraced dynamics in Baroque music, ethical analyses of musical forms, and so on) were certainly conventional, simplistic, even widely discredited. His achievement was not in merely propounding such ideas, but in synthesizing them in unusual ways, importing them into unexpected contexts, pursuing them to striking extremes, and, of course, finding direct performance corollaries for them—doing so, moreover, in ways that frequently yielded original, provocative, and distinctly personal perspectives on the music. Guerrero once said that the secret to teaching Gould was to let him discover things for himself; it was predictable that he would 'discover' commonplace ideas as though they were his own, yet for precisely this reason he could re-energize such ideas, too. He loved what he called 'aesthetic cross-breeding', the synthesizing of apparently conflicting ideas in performance, whether it was importing the principles of Baroque counterpoint into Mozart's sonatas, the principles of developing variation into Bach's fugues, or the principles of the concerto grosso into Brahms's D minor concerto. Such behaviour cannot be defended by standards like historical performance or the composer's intentions, and Gould generally did not defend his work in such terms; certainly it was more successful in some cases than others. But 'aesthetic cross-breeding' was at the heart of many of his important performances, because he so insistently imposed his cherished personal priorities into almost every musical context.

This aspect of Gould's work is likely to remain controversial. Many of his performances will undoubtedly always be seen as travesty, subversion, parody, deconstruction; some will always see in his steadfast vision the mark of an arrogant, ignorant, or immature artist; some have already found the consistency of his style in all musical contexts—the relentless linearizing of textures, the dissecting of melodic lines, the extremes of tempo, the very predictability of his unpredictability—as too restricting, simply boring. One could say that Gould did not grow much as an artist. His development consisted of the constant refining of a set of ideas and practices that was basically established by the start of his professional career. He was unusually stubborn in his tastes, and had gaps in his knowledge surprising for a professional pianist: colleagues have testified that he could play whole Strauss operas from memory in improvised transcriptions, but could not recognize a warhorse like Chopin's 'Military' Polonaise. (It is no wonder that by the age of 50 he was claiming to have exhausted the keyboard music that interested him.) Gould was like the enthusiastic adolescent who settles definitively on his heroes and villains and then defends his choices against all comers. This is the uncharitable way of putting it, of course, for it is the same stubborn integrity of vision, the highly personal take on the repertoire, that attracts so many listeners to Gould's work. Some listeners of this persuasion have seen in his provocative performances something like the 'bisociation'—the multi-level thinking, the juxtaposing of seemingly alien concepts in resonant new syntheses—that Arthur Koestler once defined as vital to creativity and discovery, not to mention the sense of wonder that Koestler considered an essential quality of genius.

The stubbornness with which Gould imposed his own vision onto the music he played is worth considering for a moment, for it offers a revealing insight into his particular creative ego. It is safe to say that most professional performers, in acquiring a varied repertoire, aim to appreciate different musical styles and aesthetic positions on their own terms, to get 'under the skin' of different composers and try to convey their particular works in informed and responsible ways. It is not surprising that the performer who seeks to act as a discreet conduit or advocate for the composer is often complimented, while the performer who imposes his own vision onto the music in contradiction to that of the composer is often criticized. In this context, Gould presents a challenge—even a provocation—to music criticism. He had (to steal a line from Kenneth Tynan) the courage of his restrictions. Perhaps more than any other performer, he insisted that his proper function was to present not Mozart but *his* Mozart, and his admirers seem to be precisely those whose primary interest is *his* take on the repertoire. (No one puts on a Gould recording to find out how Mozart 'should go'.) His attitude may explain why he played relatively little music by Sweelinck or Krenek, though he often praised it, while playing a great deal of music by Beethoven and Mozart, though he often criticized it: it was with the better-known, canonical works that there were more traditions and expectations to be challenged.

Gould had a creative ego that might properly be called 'composerly'. I do not seek merely to excuse his more unusual and 'delinquent' positions when I suggest that his thinking reveals a narrowness, and an attendant strength, of purpose that seems more consistent with a composer—that is, with a *creator*—than with a typical performer, as some in the Gould literature (including composers) have already suggested. Many composers require a highly selective, idiosyncratic, even blinkered view of music and music history in order to protect and validate their own peculiar creative vision. This is apparent throughout music history in many composers' comments about each other's work—in Beethoven's contempt for Rossini; in the Wagner-Brahms rivalry; in the need of Debussy and Stravinsky (among others) to reject, at least nominally, the legacy of Wagner; in Ives's snide remarks about Mozart, Chopin, Wagner, Tchaikovsky, and other 'ladies' who had 'emasculated' music; in the young Boulez's need to reject Schoenberg in favour of Webern; in Schoenberg's own barbed dismissal of Stravinsky's aesthetic (and vice versa); in the disdain of modernists of many stripes for the stubborn, lingering Romanticism of Strauss. Such disputes generally do not reveal the subtle and open-minded positions that we expect from responsible performers, musicologists, and critics; rather, they reveal the transparent partisanship that is frequently symptomatic of the creative ego—particularly the more original, and hence more protective, creative egos. ('For me to be right, *he* has to be wrong.') Gould's positions were often of just this sort. His superficial broadsides against Chopin and Liszt, his defence of indefensible positions like the banality of late Mozart and middle-period Beethoven, can be seen as the exaggerated polemics of an essentially creative mind. Yehudi Menuhin remarked to Gould, in their 1966 CBC television recital, that someone who likes something generally knows more about it than someone who does not, and in this motto might be a clue to how to receive some of Gould's polemics. It is usually more profitable to follow his enthusiasms—for Byrd, for Bach, for Strauss, for Schoenberg—than his *bêtes noires*: when he enthused, he was thoughtful and informed; when he dismissed, he merely rationalized. His arguments *for* recording were always more convincing than his arguments *against* the concert hall; the former were intellectually considered, the latter simply necessary intellectual scaffolding.

This 'composerly' mindset, though perhaps unusual in a professional performer, was in fact what made Gould's work so provocative, for his principal achievement was surely in the creative approach to performing the works of others. His creative ego, compared with that of most performers, was stronger in that it enforced a given set of values and priorities even in unsympathetic contexts, but was also more fragile in that it needed to be protected from hostile influences. Single-mindedness of creative vision partly explains his tendency towards binaristic thinking: in protecting and validating his vision, he tended to paint conflicting views in the strongest, and so least flattering, terms; the greater his commitment to a particular point, the greater his tendency to exaggerate the position of his 'opponents'. Predictably, there is some evidence of double standards: he would defend his own heroes but deplore artistic partisanship in others; he neglected to notice that the rhythmic licence of many Romantic players was based on the same harmonic criteria as his own; he deplored virtuoso Romantic music that glorified the performer, yet overtly displayed his own virtuosity in countless breakneck Bach performances, and drew no end of attention to himself through his eccentric interpretations. He seemed prone to simplifying issues for his own polemical purposes even where it is apparent that he had considerable insight into the more subtle stylistic and historical realities of the situation. Hence the sometimes studied naïveté in his defending of his positions, his tendency to play down evidence contradicting his views ('monster-barring'), and, as the biographical literature suggests, his tendency to seek the company of peers who would not seriously challenge his positions. (Acquaintances have testified to his inability to synthesize or even appreciate opposing views.) Again, whether one interprets such evidence as proof of strength or fragility of vision, or both, it does suggest that Gould viewed his work as the output of a creator rather than of an executant or scholar or critic.

This suggestion of a highly focused, 'composerly' ego in his psychology helps explain some of his attitudes towards his contemporaries and influences, especially his tendency to exaggerate the degree to which he was self-taught. (Much of the Gould literature has also exaggerated his iconoclasm.) That he was aware of the extent of his theoretical and practical debts to the various schools of thought and practice discussed here is not always evident. He did, as we have seen, have an informed grasp of his position in terms of cultural currents of his day, though there is little evidence that he was conscious of, say, his debts to Romantic aesthetics, or his affinities with post-modernism. Like many creative artists, he was sometimes reluctant to acknowledge influences, especially when it served some purpose to deny them. While he was forthcoming about some early influences on his work, like Schnabel and Tureck, he was disparaging, at times with revealing excess, about others (Romantic pianists, Landowska, the neo-Classical aesthetic) where they did not fit easily with his later theoretical positions. His hatred of the idea of competition notwithstanding, there was an element of competitiveness in his relationships with predecessors and colleagues, as some in the posthumous literature have noted. He often praised older musicians (Furtwängler, Stokowski, Rubinstein) who differed greatly from him in terms of style and aesthetic values, who exercised no direct influence on his playing and so were not direct 'competitors', while saying little or nothing about contemporaries whose playing had more in common with his own. His attitude towards Guerrero was certainly revealing: he did tentatively acknowledge debts on some occasions, but more often stressed their adversarial relationship, going as far as asserting that he had really learned nothing from him. Yet the surviving evidence, especially that of other former pupils, shows that Guerrero was clearly instrumental in nourishing many important aspects of Gould's work: his interests in Bach and Schoenberg, his analytical mindset, his fondness for détaché and contrapuntal playing, even his trademark low, hunched seating position. There is no denying that in many respects, especially in extra-musical matters, Gould *was* largely self-taught; he made especially great efforts on his own to broaden his intellectual horizons after his retirement from concert life. But there is also no denying his tendency to underplay his roots and influences. Indeed, the claim to being self-taught seems to have been necessary to him, as though the integrity and individuality of his particular aesthetic ideas and pianistic style would be compromised if his debts were too easily acknowledged.

In finally assessing Glenn Gould's achievement, it seems appropriate to consider his performances and statements as he seems to have considered them: as suggestions, propositions, arguments, experiments, rather than as attempts at ideal performances or permanently valid statements. As Johanne Rivest puts it, to 'interrogate' seems to have been one of his principal goals as both thinker and performer. Gould was never the considerate interpreter, the careful scholar, the open-minded critic: he was too restless intellectually, and too caught up in his own peculiar vision. Rather, he seems to have seen himself as a kind of musical explorer or provocateur, and in his work one can find both the flaws and the virtues inherent in such an enterprise. The flaws include, of course, the inevitable miscalculations, the unconvincing productions that can result from the rush to put a focused, idiosyncratic set of ideas directly into practice. But the virtues include the striking freshness of much of his playing, the refusal to conform to conventional expectations, the sense of challenge, dialectic, defamiliarization. He calls to mind such figures as Barthes and McLuhan, or any number of post-modern critics, who aim to throw out new ideas for consideration, perhaps rashly but with conviction, risking errors (even howlers) yet often yielding precisely the sorts of insights and products that more careful, reasoned, and responsible behaviour might not entertain. (McLuhan once said he found questions more interesting than answers.) Such figures are interested principally in posing provocative theses that encourage new avenues of thought and interpretation, and shed new light on works and issues. However we interpret Gould's approach to performance—naïve or open-minded, arrogant or courageous—it is fair to say that the label of explorer or provocateur is to some extent justified, given his constant testing of basic assumptions about the purposes and priorities of performance.

As the scope and tone of this book suggest, I obviously believe that the aspects of Gould's work that I have been summarizing here make him a valuable and important artist, rather than a mere aberration (as many believe), and one of my aims has been, obviously, to validate my position. I believe, moreover, that his *œuvre* as a performer has an importance that extends beyond the accumulated quality of his various performances, for his work as a whole implies discourses and challenges that can be assessed quite apart from one's critical response to the individual performances themselves and the intellectual positions they embody. Given a project like his integral recording of Mozart's sonatas, one can, of course, examine the individual performances and the pianist's implied vision of the composer, and come to critical conclusions about them. But it is also possible and fruitful, regardless of how one evaluates each sonata, to interpret the Mozart project *in toto* as an extended critical discourse in performance—indeed, as a model for how such a discourse can be conducted in practical terms. In my view, Gould's work, both in its parts and as a whole, offers many similar examples of layers of discourse on aesthetic issues.

I would suggest, in fact, that his *œuvre* merits consideration by standards very like those of the so-called *auteur* theory of cinema, as propounded by French (and later American) film critics in the 1950s and 1960s. According to the *auteur* theory, the personality of the director was a criterion of value, particularly where there was a manifest tension between that personality and the material of the work. Moreover, with a canonical director who had a particularly distinctive personal vision, the *auteur* critic was interested not only (or even especially) in evaluating the individual films but in appreciating the *œuvre* as a whole, and so in situating the individual films within an overall conception of the director. Put bluntly, the *auteur* critic was as interested in a director's artistic failures as in his successes, where that director's work as a whole was deemed important; failure illuminates the *œuvre* no less than does success. The *auteur* theory was not intended to sanitize the

canonical directors, to find reasons to excuse or forgive their weak and unconvincing productions, but rather to acknowledge that those productions existed
within an *œuvre* that had a value greater than the sum of its constituent works.
Indeed, *auteur* critics were often more interested in the bad works of great directors
than the exceptional successes of mediocre ones.

I hold a similar view of Gould. Moreover, I consider the performances that even
I find ultimately weak and unconvincing to merit study precisely because they are
no less a part of the discourses embedded in his *œuvre*. This explains why I have
not thought it worthwhile to identify and deplore, or else dismiss and ignore, what
I consider to be his artistic miscalculations and failures—or, for that matter, to
document his artistic successes; this is mere book-keeping. The more interesting
critical work is in situating his various productions within the *œuvre*. This implies,
rightly, that I consider his strange performances of K. 331 and the 'Appassionata'
Sonata more worthy of attention within the context of his *œuvre* than they might
be if they were simply isolated aberrations of a more conventional artist. So I do
not mean to advocate on behalf of his K. 331 or 'Appassionata' Sonata when I
suggest that it is more productive to explore than to dismiss them. (Still, I can
forgive the critic who wrote that Gould's Mozart recordings brought to mind 'a
tremendously precocious but very nasty little boy trying to put one over on his
piano teacher'.) Listening to his more eccentric productions is like reading Brecht's
Lehrstücke, or watching Chaplin's sound films: you would never claim that they
were the artist's important work, but you would not want to be without them,
because of the light they shed on the *œuvre*, and you would probably ignore them
if they were the work of a lesser artist. This may appear to be a controversial
position—to be over-generous, even credulous, too sympathetic to Gould, even an
attempt to shield him from conventional critical scrutiny. Yet I believe it to be a
necessary position if one wishes to understand his work as fully as possible in the
most conducive terms. Conventional critical scrutiny and evaluation are always
relevant to Gould's (or any) performances; this goes without saying. But the
broader implications of his work demand, frequently, that one at least supplement
conventional critical criteria in order fully to elucidate and situate (and by implication, evaluate) a performance. To document and deplore how he disregards a
composer's intentions is merely to state one of his premises.

Gould, in short, requires of us some readjustment of the critical standards we
often take for granted; this, indeed, was one of the achievements of his playing, a
by-product of the conviction with which he conveyed his idiosyncratic vision. As
Wordsworth once said, the original poet 'must himself create the taste by which he
is to be relished'. One of the goals of this book has been to elucidate the taste by
which Gould's work demands to be relished, by clarifying and contextualizing his
premisses and practices. I have not necessarily sought to make him a less contro-

versial figure. I have not attempted to resolve all of the issues and answer all of the questions raised by his work, but I have sought to bring those issues and questions more clearly into focus. Some long-standing Gould clichés I have tried to revise, and I have not accepted uncritically his own views on his work. (Always take an artist's self-promotion with a grain of salt: the ageing Chaplin once claimed that *A Countess From Hong Kong* was his best work.) But some received ideas about Gould I have only confirmed: I have not, for example, tried to explode as a myth the commonplace view of him as a pianist of 'classical' temperament at his best in the contrapuntal music of Bach and Schoenberg. But I have tried to flesh out the picture of Gould enough to shed new light on the clichés, while accounting for other aspects of his work. It remains for every reader and listener to evaluate Gould for himself, and it should prove interesting to track his growing posthumous renown and his growing impact on our culture. My intention in this book is not necessarily to prod future Gould reception and Gould studies in any particular direction, but to lay a scholarly and critical foundation to help readers and listeners towards more informed, if no less personal, responses to his work.

LIST OF GOULD PERFORMANCES CITED

THE FOLLOWING IS a list of all of the performances by Glenn Gould—concerts, studio recordings, radio and television broadcasts, films—that are referred to in this book and that have been made available to the public; it includes commercial releases on LP, CD, videotape, and laserdisc, as well as performances preserved on acetate discs in the NLC. (Not all of the commercial releases are necessarily in print at the present time, however.) The list also includes three posthumous commercial recordings of works composed by Gould.

Only performances of complete works or movements are listed, not the shorter excerpts that Gould occasionally played in his broadcasts, films, and recorded interviews.

All Gould performances are on the piano unless otherwise specified.

For performances released on CD in Sony Classical's Glenn Gould Edition (GGE, 1992–7), and/or on videotape and laserdisc in Sony Classical's Glenn Gould Collection (GGC, 1992–4), I simply note the relevant series and volume numbers. These comprehensive series—the official Gould *opera omnia*—are readily available internationally and are likely to remain in print indefinitely; for these reasons, I do not provide cataloguing numbers, details about original LP releases, or other discographic information for performances contained therein. I do, however, provide cataloguing numbers and release dates for those performances available only on labels other than Sony Classical or on acetate discs in the NLC, though in these cases I cite only the particular release I consulted, not whatever alternatives may exist. (Some of Gould's concert and broadcast performances appeared posthumously on CD from as many as half a dozen different labels.) This list, in other words, is intended to reveal the sources I used and to point readers interested in finding a particular recorded performance in the right direction; it is not intended to duplicate detailed information already available in published Gould discographies.

If I refer at various points in the book to all or most of the works in a series or set—Bach's *WTC*, Mozart's sonatas, Brahms's Intermezzi—I give a single citation for the whole set in order to simplify the list, especially where the whole set appears on a single CD or boxed set in the GGE. To locate discussions of specific performances in the text, see the references to individual composers and works in the index.

As of this writing, the GGE comprises eight untitled volumes (totalling more than seventy CDs), and I cite them here simply as 'i' to 'viii'. The GGC comprises sixteen titled volumes, each a little less than an hour in length; I cite them here simply as 'i' to 'xvi'. A list of titles for each volume follows:

GGC i: *Prologue*
GGC ii: *Sonatas and Dialogues*
GGC iii: *End of Concerts*
GGC iv: *So You Want to Write a Fugue?*
GGC v: *The Conductor*

GGC vi: *The Earliest Decade*
GGC vii: *A Russian Interlude*
GGC viii: *Interweaving Voices*
GGC ix: *Mostly Strauss*
GGC x: *Rhapsodic Interludes*
GGC xi: *Ecstasy and Wit*
GGC xii: *Epilogue*
GGC xiii: *The Goldberg Variations* (*Glenn Gould Plays Bach*, 3)
GGC xiv: *The Question of Instrument* (*Glenn Gould Plays Bach*, 1)
GGC xv: *An Art of the Fugue* (*Glenn Gould Plays Bach*, 2)
GGC xvi: *On the Twentieth Century*

ANHALT, *Fantasia* (1967 recording): GGE i.
BACH, C. P. E., 'Württemburg' Sonata No. 1 in A minor (1968 recording): GGE viii.
—— 'Württemburg' Sonata No. 1 in A minor (1968 CBC radio): Music and Arts CD-663 (1991).
BACH, J. S., *The Art of Fugue*, Contrapunctus 1–9 (organ) (1962 recording): GGE viii.
—— *The Art of Fugue*, Contrapunctus 1, 2, and 4 (1957 Moscow concert): Harmonia Mundi France/Le Chant du Monde LDC 278 799 (1983).
—— *The Art of Fugue*, Contrapunctus 1 (1959 film): NFB, *Glenn Gould: Off the Record*.
—— *The Art of Fugue*, Contrapunctus 1 (1979 film): GGC xiv; GGE viii.
—— *The Art of Fugue*, Contrapunctus 2, 4, and 15 (unfinished) (1980 film): GGC xv; GGE viii.
—— *The Art of Fugue*, Contrapunctus 4 ('harpsi-piano') (1962 CBC television): GGC viii.
—— Brandenburg Concerto No. 5 in D major, with Peter H. Adler conducting the Baltimore Chamber Orchestra (1962 Baltimore concert): Music and Arts CD-298 (1989).
—— Brandenburg Concerto No. 5 in D major ('harpsi-piano', and conducting an unidentified string orchestra), with Julius Baker, flute, and Oscar Shumsky, violin (1962 CBC television): GGC v.
—— Cantata: *Widerstehe doch der Sünde*, BWV 54 ('harpsi-piano', and conducting an unidentified string orchestra), with Russell Oberlin, countertenor (1962 CBC television): GGC v.
—— Chromatic Fantasy in D minor (1979 film): GGC xiv.
—— Chromatic Fantasy in D minor (1979 recording): GGE viii.
—— Clavier Concertos Nos. 1–5 and 7, with Leonard Bernstein conducting the Columbia Symphony Orchestra (No. 1 in D minor), and Vladimir Golschmann conducting the Columbia Symphony Orchestra (Nos. 2 in E major, 3 in D major, 4 in A major, 5 in F minor, and 7 in G minor) (1957–69 recordings): GGE i.
—— Clavier Concerto No. 1 in D minor, with Thomas Mayer conducting the Ottawa Symphony Orchestra (1957 CBC television): GGC vi.

—— Clavier Concerto No. 1 in D minor, with Dmitri Mitropoulos conducting the Concertgebouw Orchestra (1958 Salzburg concert): Nuova Era 013.6306 (1986).

—— Clavier Concerto No. 5 in F minor, with Nicholas Goldschmidt conducting the CBC Symphony Orchestra (1957 CBC radio): Music and Arts CD-654 (1990).

—— Clavier Concerto No. 7 in G minor, with Vladimir Golschmann conducting the Toronto Symphony Orchestra (1967 CBC television): GGC iv.

—— English Suites (Nos. 1 in A major, 2 in A minor, 3 in G minor, 4 in F major, 5 in E minor, and 6 in D minor) (1971–6 recordings): GGE vi.

—— French Overture in B minor (1969 CBC radio): Music and Arts CD-654 (1990).

—— French Overture in B minor (1971–3 recording): GGE vi.

—— French Suites (Nos. 1 in D minor, 2 in C minor, 3 in B minor, 4 in E flat major, 5 in G major, and 6 in E major) (1971–3 recordings): GGE vi.

—— Goldberg Variations (1955 recording): GGE i.

—— Goldberg Variations (1981 recording): GGE ii.

—— Goldberg Variations (1981 film): GGC xiii.

—— Fifteen Two-Part Inventions (1963–4 recording): GGE ii.

—— Italian Concerto (1952 CBC radio): CBC Records PSCD 2005 (1993).

—— Italian Concerto (1959 recording): GGE viii.

—— Little Prelude in D minor, BWV 935 (1979 recording): GGE iv.

—— Little Prelude in D major, BWV 936 (1979 film): GGC xiv.

—— Little Prelude in E minor, BWV 938 (1979 recording): GGE iv.

—— Partitas (Nos. 1 in B flat major, 2 in C minor, 3 in A minor, 4 in D major, 5 in G major, and 6 in E minor) (1956–63 recordings): GGE iv.

—— Partita No. 4 in D major (1979 film): GGC xiv.

—— Partita No. 5 in G major (1951 CBC radio): NLC acetates nos. 142–4, 158–9.

—— Partita No. 5 in G major (1954 CBC radio): CBC Records PSCD 2005 (1993).

—— Partita No. 5 in G major/Allemande, Sarabande, Corrente (1957 filmed Toronto concert): GGC iii.

—— Partita No. 6 in E minor (1974 film): Monsaingeon, *Chemins de la musique*, iv.

—— Preludes, Fugues, Fughettas, and Fantasies (various) (1979–80 recordings): GGE iv, viii.

—— Fifteen Three-Part Sinfonias (1955 CBC radio): CBC Records PSCD 2005 (1993).

—— Fifteen Three-Part Sinfonias (1957 Moscow concert): GGE iv.

—— Fifteen Three-Part Sinfonias (1963–4 recording): GGE ii.

—— Sonatas for Viola da Gamba and Harpsichord (Nos. 1 in G major, 2 in D major, and 3 in G minor), with Leonard Rose (1973–4 recordings): GGE vi.

—— Sonatas for Violin and Harpsichord (Nos. 1 in B minor, 2 in A major, 3 in E major, 4 in C minor, 5 in F minor, and 6 in G major), with Jaime Laredo (1975–6 recordings): GGE vi.

—— Toccatas in F sharp minor, BWV 910; C minor, BWV 911; D major, BWV 912; D minor, BWV 913; E minor, BWV 914; G minor, BWV 915; and G major, BWV 916 (1963–79 recordings): GGE v.

—— *WTC* I (complete) (1962–5 recordings): GGE iv.

—— *WTC* II (complete) (1966–71 recordings): GGE iv.

—— *WTC* II, Fugues in C major, C minor, D minor, and E flat major (1966 CBC radio): Music and Arts CD-679 (1991).

—— *WTC* II, Prelude and Fugue in C sharp major (1970 CBC television): GGC xii.

—— *WTC* II, Fugue in E flat major (1954 CBC radio): CBC Records PSCD 2007 (1995).

—— *WTC* II, Fugue in E flat major (1963 CBC television): GGC iv.

—— *WTC* II, Fugue in E major (1952 CBC radio): CBC Records PSCD 2007 (1995).

—— *WTC* II, Fugue in E major (1957 recording): GGE i.

—— *WTC* II, Prelude and Fugue in E major (harpsichord) (1970 CBC television): GGC iv; GGE iii.

—— *WTC* II, Fugue in F sharp minor (1954 CBC radio): CBC Records PSCD 2007 (1995).

—— *WTC* II, Fugue in F sharp minor (1957 recording): GGE i.

—— *WTC* II, Prelude and Fugue in F sharp minor (harpsichord) (1970 CBC television): GGC i; GGE iii.

—— *WTC* II, Prelude and Fugue in B flat minor (1954 CBC radio): CBC Records PSCD 2007 (1995).

—— *WTC* II, Prelude and Fugue in B flat minor (1963 CBC television): GGC iii.

—— *WTC* II, Prelude and Fugue in B flat minor (1970 CBC television): GGC xii.

—— *WTC* II, Fugue in B flat minor (1980 film): GGC xv.

BEETHOVEN, Bagatelles, Op. 33 (complete) (1974 recording): GGE i.

—— Bagatelles, Op. 126 (complete) (1952 CBC radio): CBC Records PSCD 2013 (1997).

—— Bagatelles, Op. 126 (complete) (1974 recording): GGE i.

—— Bagatelles, Op. 126 Nos. 1 in G major, 2 in G minor, and 5 in G major (1967 CBC radio): Music and Arts CD-680 (1991).

—— Bagatelle in E flat major, Op. 126 No. 3 (1970 CBC television): GGC iii.

—— Concertos Nos. 1–5, with Vladimir Golschmann conducting the Columbia Symphony Orchestra (No. 1 in C major, Op. 15, with cadenzas by Gould), Leonard Bernstein conducting the Columbia Symphony Orchestra (Nos. 2 in B flat major, Op. 19, and 3 in C minor, Op. 37), Leonard Bernstein conducting the New York Philharmonic (No. 4 in G major, Op. 58), and Leopold Stokowski conducting the American Symphony Orchestra (No. 5 in E flat major, Op. 73, 'Emperor') (1957–66 recordings): GGE i.

—— Concerto No. 2 in B flat major, Op. 19, with Sir Ernest MacMillan conducting the Toronto Symphony Orchestra (1951 Toronto concert): Music and Arts CD-284 (1988).

—— Concerto No. 2 in B flat major, Op. 19, with Ladislav Slovák conducting the Academic Symphony Orchestra of the Leningrad Conservatory (1957 Leningrad concert): GGE iv.

—— Concerto No. 2 in B flat major, Op. 19, with Georg Ludwig Jochum conducting the Swedish Radio Symphony Orchestra (1958 Stockholm concert): BIS CD-323 (1986).

—— *Six Variations on an Original Theme* in F major, Op. 34 (1952 CBC radio): CBC Records PSCD 2004 (1993).

—— *Six Variations on an Original Theme* in F major, Op. 34 (1960–7 recording): GGE i.

—— *Six Variations on an Original Theme* in F major, Op. 34 (1970 CBC television): GGC viii.

—— Sonatas in F minor, Op. 2 No. 1; A major, Op. 2 No. 2; C major, Op. 2 No. 3; C minor, Op. 10 No. 1; F major, Op. 10 No. 2; D major, Op. 10 No. 3; C minor, Op. 13 (*Pathétique*); E major, Op. 14 No. 1; G major, Op. 14 No. 2; A flat major, Op. 26; E flat major, *quasi una fantasia*, Op. 27 No. 1; C sharp minor, *quasi una fantasia*, Op. 27 No. 2 ('Moonlight'); D major, Op. 28 ('Pastoral'); G major, Op. 31 No. 1; D minor, Op. 31 No. 2 ('Tempest'); E flat major, Op. 31 No. 3; F minor, Op. 57 ('Appassionata'); E major, Op. 109; A flat major, Op. 110; and C minor, Op. 111 (1956–81 recordings): GGE v.

—— Sonata in D minor, Op. 31 No. 2 ('Tempest') (1960 CBC television): GGC iii.

—— Sonata in D minor, Op. 31 No. 2 ('Tempest') (1967 CBC television): GGC xi.

—— Sonata in E flat major, Op. 31 No. 3 (1967 CBC radio): Music and Arts CD-680 (1991).

—— Sonata in F sharp major, Op. 78 (1968 recording): GGE iii.

—— Sonata in F sharp major, Op. 78 (1968 CBC radio): Music and Arts CD-663 (1991).

—— Sonata in A major, Op. 101 (1952 CBC radio): NLC acetates nos. 131, 139–40.

—— Sonata in B flat major, Op. 106 ('Hammerklavier') (1970 CBC radio): GGE iii.

—— Sonata in E major, Op. 109 (1964 CBC television): GGC iv.

—— Sonata in A flat major, Op. 110 (1962 CBC television)/III–IV: GGC i.

—— Sonata for Cello and Piano in A major, Op. 69, with Leonard Rose (1961 CBC television): GGC viii.

—— *Thirty-two Variations on an Original Theme* in C minor, WoO 80 (1966 recording): GGE i.

—— *Thirty-two Variations on an Original Theme* in C minor, WoO 80 (1967 CBC television): GGC vi.

BEETHOVEN-LISZT, Fifth Symphony (1967–8 recording): GGE i.

—— Sixth Symphony (*Pastoral*) (1968 CBC radio): GGE ii.

BERG, Sonata, Op. 1 (1951 recording): Turnabout TV 34792X (1982).

—— Sonata, Op. 1 (1952 CBC radio): CBC Records PSCD 2008 (1995).

—— Sonata, Op. 1 (1957 Moscow concert): Harmonia Mundi France/Le Chant du Monde LDC 278 799 (1983).

—— Sonata, Op. 1 (1958 recording): GGE vii.

—— Sonata, Op. 1 (1958 Stockholm concert): BIS CD-324 (1986).

—— Sonata, Op. 1 (1969 CBC radio): Music and Arts CD-679 (1991).

—— Sonata, Op. 1 (1974 CBC television): GGC iv.

—— Sonata, Op. 1 (1974 film): Monsaingeon, *Chemins de la musique*, iii.

BIZET, *Variations chromatiques* in C minor (1971 recording): GGE i.

BRAHMS, Ballades, Op. 10 (Nos. 1 in D minor, 2 in D major, 3 in B minor, and 4 in B major) (1982 recordings): GGE ii.

—— Concerto No. 1 in D minor, Op. 15, with Leonard Bernstein conducting the New York Philharmonic (1962 New York concert): Music and Arts CD-682 (1985).

——Intermezzi in A major, Op. 76 No. 6; A minor, Op. 76 No. 7; E major, Op. 116 No. 4; E flat major, Op. 117 No. 1; B flat minor, Op. 117 No. 2; C sharp minor, Op. 117 No. 3; A minor, Op. 118 No. 1; A major, Op. 118 No. 2; E flat minor, Op. 118 No. 6; and B minor, Op. 119 No. 1 (1959–60 recordings): GGE ii.

——Rhapsodies, Op. 79 (Nos. 1 in B minor and 2 in G minor) (1982 recordings): GGE ii.

BYRD, First Pavan and Galliard (1967 recording): GGE iii.

—— 'Hugh Aston's Ground' (1971 recording): GGE iii.

—— 'Sellinger's Round' (1971 recording): GGE iii.

—— Sixth Pavan and Galliard (1967 recording): GGE iii.

—— 'Voluntary: for my Lady Nevell' (1967 recording): GGE iii.

CHOPIN, Sonata No. 3 in B minor, Op. 58 (1970 CBC radio): GGE vii.

GIBBONS, Fantasia in C (1968 recording): GGE iii.

—— 'Italian Ground' (1968 recording): GGE iii.

—— 'Italian Ground' (1968 CBC radio): Music and Arts CD-659 (1991).

—— 'Pavan and Galliard: Lord Salisbury' (1951 CBC radio): NLC acetates nos. 142–4, 158–9.

—— 'Pavan and Galliard: Lord Salisbury' (1956 CBC radio): Music and Arts CD-272 (1987).

—— 'Pavan and Galliard: Lord Salisbury' (1968 recording): GGE iii.

—— 'Pavan and Galliard: Lord Salisbury' (1968 CBC radio): Music and Arts CD-659 (1991).

—— 'Pavan: Lord Salisbury' (1974 film): Monsaingeon, *Chemins de la musique*, i.

GOULD, 'Solitude Trilogy' (three 'contrapuntal radio documentaries'): *The Idea of North* (1967), *The Latecomers* (1969), and *The Quiet in the Land* (1977): CBC Records PSCD 2003–3 (1992).

—— 'Lieberson Madrigal'; String Quartet, Op. 1; Two Pieces for Piano; Sonata for Bassoon and Piano; Piano Sonata (unfinished); and 'So You Want to Write a Fugue?' (various performers, 1990 recordings): *Glenn Gould: The Composer*, Sony Classical SK 47 184 (1992).

—— String Quartet, Op. 1, with the Symphonia Quartet under Gould's supervision (1960 recording); and 'So You Want to Write a Fugue?', with Elizabeth Benson-Guy, soprano, Anita Darian, mezzo-soprano, Charles Bressler, tenor, Donald Gramm, bass, and the Juilliard Quartet, conducted by Vladimir Golschmann (1963 recording): GGE viii.

GRIEG, Sonata in E minor, Op. 7 (1971 recording): GGE i.

HANDEL, Suites for Harpsichord Nos. 1 in A major, 2 in F major, 3 in D minor, and 4 in E minor (harpsichord) (1972 recordings): GGE iii.

HAYDN, Sonatas Nos. 42 in D major, 48 in C major, 49 in E flat major, 50 in C major, 51 in D major, and 52 in E flat major (1980–1 recordings): GGE v.

—— Sonata No. 49 in E flat major (1958 recording): GGE i.

HÉTU, *Variations pour piano* (1967 recording): GGE i.

HINDEMITH, Sonatas Nos. 1 in A major, 2 in G major, and 3 in B flat major (1966–73 recordings): GGE ii.

—— Sonata No. 1 in A major (1966 CBC radio): Music and Arts CD-679 (1991).

—— Sonata No. 3 in B flat major (1968 CBC radio): Music and Arts CD-659 (1991).

—— Sonatas for Trumpet and Piano, with Gilbert Johnson; Horn and Piano, with Mason Jones; Bass Tuba and Piano, with Abe Torchinsky; Alto Horn in E flat and Piano, with Mason Jones; and Trombone and Piano, with Henry Charles Smith (1975–6 recordings): GGE i.

KRENEK, Sonata No. 3, Op. 92 No. 4 (1958 recording): GGE vii.

MORAWETZ, *Fantasy in D* (1966 recording): GGE i.

MOZART, Concerto No. 24 in C minor, K. 491, with Walter Susskind conducting the CBC Symphony Orchestra (1961 recording): GGE i.

—— Fantasia in D minor, K. 397 (1972 recording): GGE vi.

—— Fantasia in C minor, K. 475 (1966 recording): GGE vi.

—— Fantasia in C minor, K. 475 (1966 CBC radio): Music and Arts CD-679 (1991).

—— Fantasia and Fugue in C major, K. 394 (1958 recording): GGE i.

—— Sonatas in C major, K. 279; F major, K. 280; B flat major, K. 281; E flat major, K. 282; G major, K. 283; D major, K. 284; C major, K. 309; A minor, K. 310; D major, K. 311; C major, K. 330; A major, K. 331; F major, K. 332; B flat major, K. 333; C minor, K. 457; F major, K. 533/K. 494; C major, K. 545; B flat major, K. 570; and D major, K. 576 (1965–74 recordings): GGE vi.

—— Sonata in D major, K. 284 (1968 CBC radio): Music and Arts CD-676 (1991).

—— Sonata in C major, K. 309 (1968 CBC radio): Music and Arts CD-676 (1991).

—— Sonata in A minor, K. 310 (1968 CBC radio): Music and Arts CD-676 (1991).

—— Sonata in C major, K. 330 (1958 recording): GGE i.

—— Sonata in C major, K. 330 (1959 Salzburg concert): Sony Classical *Festspieldokumente* SMK 53 474 (1994).

—— Sonata in B flat major, K. 333 (1967 CBC television): GGC ix.

—— Sonata in B flat major, K. 333 (1969 CBC radio): Music and Arts CD-680 (1991).

—— Sonata in B flat major, K. 570 (1969 CBC radio): Music and Arts CD-676 (1991).

PENTLAND, *Shadows/Ombres* (1967 recording): GGE i.

PROKOFIEV, Sonata No. 7 in B flat major, Op. 83 (1962 CBC television): GGC vii.

—— Sonata No. 7 in B flat major, Op. 83 (1967 recording): GGE vii.

—— *Visions fugitives*, Op. 22 No. 2 (1975 CBC television): GGC vii; GGE vii.

RAVEL, *La Valse* (piano transcription by Ravel, revised by Gould) (1975 CBC television): GGC x; GGE vii.

SCARLATTI, Sonata in D minor, L. 413 (1968 recording): GGE viii.

—— Sonata in D major, L. 463 (1968 recording): GGE viii.

—— Sonata in D major, L. 463 (1968 CBC radio): Music and Arts CD-663 (1991).

—— Sonata in G major, L. 486 (1968 recording): GGE viii.

—— Sonata in G major, L. 486 (1968 CBC radio): Music and Arts CD-663 (1991).

SCHOENBERG, Lieder, Opp. 1, 2, 3, 6, 12, 14, 15, 48, and posth., with Ellen Faull, soprano, Helen Vanni, mezzo-soprano, Cornelis Opthof, baritone, and Donald Gramm, bass-baritone (1964–71 recordings): GGE vii.

—— Suite, Op. 25 (1952 CBC radio): CBC Records PSCD 2008 (1995).

—— Suite, Op. 25 (1959 Salzburg concert): Sony Classical *Festspieldokumente* SMK 53 474 (1994).

—— Suite, Op. 25 (1964 recording): GGE vi.

—— Suite, Op. 25/Intermezzo (1974 film): Monsaingeon, *Chemins de la musique*, i.

—— Suite, Op. 25/Intermezzo (1975 CBC television): GGC xvi.

SCRIABIN, *Feuillet d'album*, Op. 58 (1974 CBC television): GGE vii.

—— Prelude in C major, Op. 33 No. 3 (1974 CBC television): GGC vii; GGE vii.

—— Prelude in F major, Op. 45 No. 3 (1974 CBC television): GGC vii; GGE vii.

—— Prelude in E flat major, Op. 49 No. 2 (1974 CBC television): GGC xi; GGE vii.

—— Sonata No. 3 in F sharp minor, Op. 23 (1968 recording): GGE vii.

—— Sonata No. 3 in F sharp minor, Op. 23 (1968 CBC radio): Music and Arts CD-663 (1991).

—— Sonata No. 5, Op. 53 (1969 CBC radio): Music and Arts CD-683 (1991).

—— Sonata No. 5, Op. 53 (1970 recording): GGE vii.

—— *Two Pieces*, Op. 57 ('Désir' and 'Caresse dansée') (1972 recording): GGC xvi.

—— *Two Pieces*, Op. 57 ('Désir' and 'Caresse dansée') (1974 CBC television): GGC xvi.

—— *Two Pieces*, Op. 57 ('Désir' and 'Caresse dansée') (1974 film): Monsaingeon, *Chemins de la musique*, ii.

SIBELIUS, *Kyllikki*, Three Lyric Pieces for Piano, Op. 41 (1977 recording): GGE i.

—— Sonatines, Op. 67 (Nos. 1 in F sharp minor, 2 in E major, and 3 in B flat minor) (1976–7 recording): GGE i.

STRAUSS, *Burleske* for piano and orchestra, with Peter H. Adler conducting the Baltimore Symphony Orchestra (1962 Baltimore concert): Music and Arts CD-297 (1989).

—— *Burleske* for piano and orchestra, with Vladimir Golschmann conducting the Toronto Symphony Orchestra (1967 CBC television): GGC ix; GGE vii.

—— *Enoch Arden*, Op. 38, with Claude Rains, speaker (1961 recording): GGE i.

—— Five Piano Pieces, Op. 3 (1979 recording): GGE i.

—— Sonata in B minor, Op. 5 (1982 recording): GGE i.

SWEELINCK, 'Fitzwilliam' Fantasia in G (1959 Salzburg concert): Sony Classical *Festspieldokumente* SMK 53 474 (1994).

—— 'Fitzwilliam' Fantasia in G (1964 CBC television): GGC iii; GGE iii.

VALEN, Sonata No. 2, Op. 38 (1972 CBC radio): GGE i.

WAGNER, *Götterdämmerung*/Prologue, 'Dawn' and 'Siegfried's Rhine Journey' (piano transcription by Gould) (1973 recording): GGE v.

—— *Die Meistersinger von Nürnberg*/Act I, *Vorspiel* (piano transcription by Gould) (1973 recording): GGE v.

—— *Siegfried Idyll* (piano transcription by Gould) (1973 recording): GGE v.

—— *Siegfried Idyll* (chamber-orchestra version), with Gould conducting members of the Toronto Symphony Orchestra (1982 recording): GGE v.

WEBERN, *Variations*, Op. 27 (1954 CBC radio): CBC Records PSCD 2008 (1995).

—— *Variations*, Op. 27 (1957 Moscow concert): Harmonia Mundi France/Le Chant du Monde LDC 278 799 (1983).

—— *Variations*, Op. 27 (1964 CBC television): GGC viii; GGE vii.

—— *Variations*, Op. 27 (1974 film): Monsaingeon, *Chemins de la musique*, iii.

BIBLIOGRAPHY

ADORNO, THEODOR W., *Philosophy of Modern Music*, trans. Anne G. Mitchell and Wesley V. Blomster (New York: Seabury Press, 1973).

—— *Prisms*, trans. Samuel and Shierry Weber (Studies in Contemporary German Social Thought; Cambridge, Mass.: MIT Press, 1982).

—— *Quasi una Fantasia: Essays on Modern Music*, trans. Rodney Livingstone (London and New York: Verso, 1992).

AIDE, WILLIAM, 'Fact & Freudian Fable: William Aide on Gould & Guerrero', *The Idler*, 38 (Summer 1993), 59–61.

AIKIN, JIM, 'Glenn Gould', *Contemporary Keyboard*, 6/8 (Aug. 1980), 24–8, 30–2, 36.

ANGILETTE, ELIZABETH, *Philosopher at the Keyboard: Glenn Gould* (Metuchen, NJ: Scarecrow Press, 1992).

ASBELL, BERNARD, 'Glenn Gould', *Horizon*, 4/3 (Jan. 1962), 88–93.

BACH, CARL PHILIPP EMANUEL, *Essay on the True Art of Playing Keyboard Instruments*, trans. and ed. William J. Mitchell, 2nd edn. (London: Cassell, 1951).

BACHMANN, PLINIO, and ZWEIFEL, STEFAN, 'Die Wahrheit und andere Lügen: Auf Gouldsuche in Kanada', *Du*, no. 4 (Apr. 1990), 32–51.

BADURA-SKODA, PAUL, *Interpreting Bach at the Keyboard*, trans. Alfred Clayton (Oxford: Clarendon Press, 1993).

BARTH, GEORGE, *The Pianist as Orator: Beethoven and the Transformation of Keyboard Style* (Ithaca, NY: Cornell University Press, 1992).

BARTHES, ROLAND, *S/Z*, trans. Richard Miller (New York: Hill & Wang, 1974).

—— *Criticism and Truth*, trans. and ed. Katrine Pilcher Keuneman (Minneapolis: University of Minnesota Press, 1987).

—— *The Rustle of Language*, trans. Richard Howard (Berkeley and Los Angeles: University of California Press, 1989).

BECKWITH, JOHN, 'Shattering a Few Myths', in *Glenn Gould: Variations*, ed. John McGreevy (Toronto: Doubleday, 1983), 65–74.

—— 'Glenn Gould, the Early Years: Addenda and Corrigenda', *GlennGould*, 2 (1996), 56–65.

—— 'Master Glen Gold', *GlennGould*, 3 (1997), 14–16.

BENJAMIN, WALTER, *Illuminations*, ed. Hannah Arendt, trans. Harry Zohn (New York: Harcourt, Brace & World, 1968).

BERGSON, HENRI, *Laughter: An Essay on the Meaning of the Comic*, trans. Cloudesley Brereton and Fred Rothwell (London: Macmillan, 1911).

BERLEANT, ARNOLD, 'Music as Sound and Idea', *Current Musicology*, 6 (1968), 95–100.

BERNSTEIN, LEONARD, 'The Truth About a Legend', in *Glenn Gould: Variations*, ed. John McGreevy (Toronto: Doubleday, 1983), 17–22.

BERRY, WALLACE, *Musical Structure and Performance* (New Haven: Yale University Press, 1989).

BESTER, ALFRED, 'The Zany Genius of Glenn Gould', *Holiday*, 35/4 (Apr. 1964), 149–56.

BEYSCHLAG, ADOLF, *Die Ornamentik der Musik* (Leipzig: Breitkopf & Härtel, 1908).

BILSON, MALCOLM, 'The Viennese Fortepiano of the Late 18th Century', *Early Music*, 8 (1980), 158–62.

BLACK, WILLIAM, 'A Matter of Ifs', *The Piano Quarterly*, no. 143 (Fall 1988), 62–3.

BLUME, FRIEDRICH, *Two Centuries of Bach: An Account of Changing Taste*, trans. Stanley Godman (Da Capo Press Music Reprint Series; New York: Da Capo Press, 1978).

BODKY, ERWIN, *The Interpretation of Bach's Keyboard Works* (Cambridge, Mass.: Harvard University Press, 1960).

BOYDEN, DAVID D., 'Dynamics in Seventeenth- and Eighteenth-Century Music', in *Essays on Music in Honor of Archibald Thompson Davison by his Associates* (Cambridge, Mass.: Department of Music, Harvard University, 1957), 185–93.

BRAITHWAITE, DENNIS, 'I'm a Child of Nature—Glenn Gould', *Toronto Daily Star*, 28 Mar. 1959, 21, 28.

BROYLES, MICHAEL, 'Organic Form and the Binary Repeat', *Musical Quarterly*, 66 (1980), 339–60.

BURKHART, CHARLES, 'Schenker's Theory of Levels and Musical Performance', in *Aspects of Schenkerian Theory*, ed. David Beach (New Haven: Yale University Press, 1983), 95–112.

BURTON, HUMPHREY, *Conversations with Glenn Gould* [series of four television programmes] (BBC, 1966): i, 'Bach and Recording' (15 Mar.); ii, 'Beethoven' (22 Mar.); iii, 'Strauss' (5 Apr.); iv, 'Schoenberg' (19 Apr.).

CANNING, NANCY, *A Glenn Gould Catalog* (Discographies, 50; Westport, Conn.: Greenwood Press, 1992).

CARPENTER, PATRICIA, 'The Musical Object', *Current Musicology*, 5 (1967), 56–87.

CARROLL, JOCK, ' "I don't think I'm at all eccentric," says Glenn Gould', *Weekend Magazine*, 6/27 (7 July 1956).

CARRUTHERS, GLEN BLAINE, 'Bach and the Piano: Editions, Arrangements and Transcriptions from Czerny to Rachmaninov', Ph.D. thesis (University of Victoria, 1986).

COLGRASS, ULLA, 'Glenn Gould', *Music Magazine*, 4/1 (Jan.–Feb. 1981), 6–11.

COLLINGWOOD, R. G., *The Principles of Art* (Oxford: Clarendon Press, 1938).

CONE, EDWARD T., *Musical Form and Musical Performance* (New York: W. W. Norton 1968).

COOK, NICHOLAS, *Music, Imagination, and Culture* (Oxford: Clarendon Press, 1990).

COTT, JONATHAN, *Conversations with Glenn Gould* (Boston and Toronto: Little, Brown & Co., 1984).

COX, RENÉE, 'Are Musical Works Discovered?', *The Journal of Aesthetics and Art Criticism*, 43/4 (Summer 1985), 367–74.

—— 'A Defence of Musical Idealism', *British Journal of Aesthetics*, 26 (1986), 133–42.

CRAIG, EDWARD GORDON, *On the Art of the Theatre* (London: Heinemann 1956).

CROCE, BENEDETTO, *Aesthetic as Science of Expression and General Linguistic*, trans. Douglas Ainslie (New York: Noonday Press, 1955).

CROSS, CHARLOTTE M., 'Three Levels of "Idea" in Schoenberg's Thought and Writings', *Current Musicology*, 30 (1980), 24–36.

CRUTCHFIELD, WILL, 'Fashion, Conviction, and Performance Style in an Age of Revivals', in *Authenticity and Early Music: A Symposium*, ed. Nicholas Kenyon (Oxford: Oxford University Press, 1988), 19–26.

CULLER, JONATHAN, *On Deconstruction: Theory and Criticism after Structuralism* (Ithaca, NY: Cornell University Press, 1982).

—— 'In Defence of Overinterpretation', in Umberto Eco, *et al.*, *Interpretation and Overinterpretation*, ed. Stefan Collini (Cambridge: Cambridge University Press, 1992), 109–23.

CZACZKES, LUDWIG, *Bachs Chromatische Fantasie und Fuge: Form und Aufbau die Arpeggienausführung* (Vienna: Österreichischer Bundesverlag für Unterricht, Wissenschaft und Kunst, 1971).

DAHLHAUS, CARL, *Schoenberg and the New Music*, trans. Derrick Puffett and Alfred Clayton (Cambridge: Cambridge University Press, 1987).

—— *The Idea of Absolute Music*, trans. Roger Lustig (Chicago: University of Chicago Press, 1989).

—— *Ludwig van Beethoven: Approaches to his Music*, trans. Mary Whittall (Oxford: Clarendon Press, 1991).

DANUSER, HERMANN, 'Einleitung', in *Musikalische Interpretation*, ed. Hermann Danuser (Neues Handbuch der Musikwissenschaft, 11; Laaber: Laaber-Verlag, 1992), 1–72.

DAVID, HANS, 'Die Gestalt von Bachs Chromatischer Fantasie', *Bach-Jahrbuch*, 23, ed. Arnold Schering (Leipzig: Breitkopf & Härtel, 1926), 23–67 and *Anhang*, 1–24.

DAVID, HANS T., and MENDEL, ARTHUR eds., *The Bach Reader: A Life of Johann Sebastian Bach in Letters and Documents*, rev. edn. (New York: W. W. Norton, 1966).

DAVIES, STEPHEN, 'Authenticity in Musical Performance', *British Journal of Aesthetics*, 27 (1987), 39–50.

—— 'Transcription, Authenticity and Performance', *British Journal of Aesthetics*, 28 (1988), 216–27.

DAVIS, CURTIS, 'The Well-Tempered Listener', in *Glenn Gould: Variations*, ed. John McGreevy (Toronto: Doubleday Canada Limited, 1983), 275–94. [Text drawn from *The Well-Tempered Listener*, television programme conceived and developed by Glenn Gould, in conversation with Curtis W. Davis (CBC, 18 Feb. 1970).]

DIPERT, RANDALL R., 'The Composer's Intentions: An Examination of their Relevance for Performance', *Musical Quarterly*, 66 (1980), 205–18.

DOLMETSCH, ARNOLD, *The Interpretation of the Music of the XVII and XVIII Centuries, Revealed by Contemporary Evidence*, rev. edn. (Handbooks for Musicians; London: Novello and Oxford University Press, 1946).

DREYFUS, LAURENCE, 'Early Music Defended against its Devotees: A Theory of Historical Performance in the Twentieth Century', *Musical Quarterly*, 69 (1983), 297–322.

DRILLON, JACQUES, 'Gould Myths and Gould Facts: Two Articles by Jacques Drillon' ('Glenn Gould and Franz Liszt: The Piano Above All', and 'Gould's Gould Cult: Jacques Drillon Interviews Jacques Drillon. Old Truths and a Few New Mystifications'), *GlennGould*, 2 (1996), 73–80.

DUBAL, DAVID, *Reflections from the Keyboard: The World of the Concert Pianist* (New York: Summit Books, 1984).

DUNSBY, JONATHAN, 'Guest Editorial: Performance and Analysis of Music', *Music Analysis*, 8 (1989), 5–20.

DUTTON, DENIS, review of Geoffrey Payzant, *Glenn Gould: Music and Mind*, *Journal of Aesthetics and Art Criticism*, 37/4 (Summer 1979), 513–14.

ECO, UMBERTO, *The Open Work*, trans. Anna Cancogni (Cambridge, Mass.: Harvard University Press, 1989).

—— *The Limits of Interpretation* (Advances in Semiotics; Bloomington and Indianapolis: Indiana University Press, 1990).

—— with RORTY, RICHARD, CULLER, JONATHAN, and BROOKE-ROSE, CHRISTINE, *Interpretation and Overinterpretation*, ed. Stefan Collini (Cambridge: Cambridge University Press, 1992).

EISENBERG, EVAN, 'Glenn Gould', in *The Recording Angel: Explorations in Phonography* (New York: McGraw-Hill, 1987), 101–8.

ELLIOTT, ROBIN, 'Glenn Gould and the Canadian Composer', *Notations* [Newsletter of the Canadian Music Centre's Ontario Region], 4 (1992), 1, 4–5, 12.

—— '"So You Want to Write a String Quartet?": Glenn Gould's Opus 1', *GlennGould*, 3 (1997), 17–20.

EPSTEIN, DAVID, *Shaping Time: Music, the Brain, and Performance* (New York: Schirmer Books, 1995).

FISH, STANLEY, *Is There a Text in This Class?: The Authority of Interpretive Communities* (Cambridge, Mass.: Harvard University Press, 1980).

FORFIA, KEN, 'Rerecording the Goldberg Variations–Glenn Gould's Workshop', *Piano and Keyboard*, no. 176 (Sept.–Oct. 1995), 34–8.

FRIEDRICH, OTTO, *Glenn Gould: A Life and Variations* (New York: Random House, 1989).

FRYE, NORTHROP, *Anatomy of Criticism: Four Essays* (Princeton: Princeton University Press, 1957).

FULFORD, ROBERT, 'Ladies and Gentlemen . . . Glenn Gould Has Left the Building', *Saturday Night*, 107/7 (Sept. 1992), 46–50, 71–3.

FURTWÄNGLER, WILHELM, *Furtwängler on Music: Essays and Addresses*, ed. and trans. Ronald Taylor (Aldershot, Hants: Scolar Press, 1991).

GODDARD, PETER, 'Glenn Gould is a Conjurer', *The Canadian Composer*, 68 (Mar. 1972), 24, 26, 28.

GODDEN, REGINALD, and CLARKSON, AUSTIN *Reginald Godden Plays: The Musical Adventures of a Canadian Pianist* (Toronto: Soundway Press, 1990).

GODLOVITCH, STAN, 'Authentic Performance', *The Monist*, 71 (1988), 258–77.

—— 'The Integrity of Musical Performance', *Journal of Aesthetics and Art Criticism*, 51 (1993) 573–87.

GOEHR, LYDIA, *The Imaginary Museum of Musical Works: An Essay in the Philosophy of Music* (Oxford: Clarendon Press, 1992).

GOLDSMITH, HARRIS, 'Glenn Gould: An Appraisal', *High Fidelity*, 33/2 (Feb. 1983), 54–5.

GOODMAN, NELSON, *Languages of Art: An Approach to a Theory of Symbols*, 2nd edn. (Indianapolis: Hackett, 1976).

GOULD, GLENN, 'Glenn Gould's CBC Questionnaire from 1952', *GlennGould*, 3 (1997), 4–5.

—— 'A Consideration of Anton Webern' [1954], *GlennGould*, 1 (1995), 4–8.

—— NLC 31/5/21. [Letter to Vladimir Golschmann; 20 Mar. 1958; unpublished.]

—— 'A Piano Lesson with Glenn Gould', NLC 17/4/2. [Undated; unpublished; text for a lecture-recital delivered to an audience of children at the Vancouver International Festival, 7 Aug. 1961.]

—— 'Forgery and Imitation in the Creative Process' [1963], *GlennGould*, 2 (1996), 4–9.

—— 'Piano Sonata—Draft 3', NLC 2/35. [Undated; unpublished; draft for the second in the two-part lecture series 'The History of the Piano Sonata', Jan.–Mar. 1964.]

—— NLC 18/5. [Headed 'Part 4—Draft 1'; undated; unpublished; possibly commentary for the CBC television programme 'Concert for Four Wednesdays', in the *Festival* series, 17 June 1964.]

—— 'Anthology of Variation/Draft 1—Part 1', NLC 18/1/1. [Undated; unpublished; probably commentary for the CBC television programme 'Concert for Four Wednesdays', in the *Festival* series, 17 June 1964.]

—— NLC 2/58. [Interview with Leon Fleischer; undated; unpublished; commentary for 'Dialogues on the Prospects of Recording'.]

—— 'Dialogues on the Prospects of Recording', CBC radio programme in the series *CBC Sunday Night*, 10 January 1965. [Unpublished.]

—— 'The Art of Glenn Gould—Programme No. 13/Draft II (Final)', NLC 4/19. [Dated 5 Nov. 1966; unpublished; commentary for the CBC radio programme 'On Records and Recording', in the series *The Art of Glenn Gould*, 13 Nov. 1966.]

—— commentary for the CBC radio programme 'Glenn Gould in Recital', in the series *CBC Tuesday Night*, 29 Nov. 1966. [Unpublished; cassette copy from a private source.]

—— 'Draft II (The Art of Glenn Gould)/Part III/*String Quartet*', NLC 4/49. [Dated 25 Feb. 1967; unpublished; commentary for the CBC radio series *The Art of Glenn Gould*, 12 Mar. 1967.]

—— 'How Mozart Became a Bad Composer/(Part 1, Draft 4)' and 'How Mozart Became a Bad Composer/(Part II, Draft 5)', NLC 18/23 and NLC 18/27, respectively. [Undated; published; commentary for a CBC television programme, 1968.]

—— 'TV Intro No. 7/Abduction from the Seraglio/Draft 2', NLC 5/63. [Undated; unpublished; commentary for the CBC television series *World of Music*, 17 Mar. 1968.]

—— 'The Art of Glenn Gould: Take 1', NLC 6/38. [Undated; unpublished; commentary for 'Take One' in the CBC radio series *The Art of Glenn Gould*, 20 May 1969.]

—— 'The Art of Glenn Gould: Take 5', NLC 6/45. [Undated; unpublished; commentary for 'Take Five' in the CBC radio series *The Art of Glenn Gould*, 17 June 1969.]

—— 'Take 16', NLC 6/73. [Undated; unpublished; commentary for 'Take Sixteen' in the CBC radio series *The Art of Glenn Gould*, 2 September 1969.]

—— commentary for the CBC radio programme 'Glenn Gould in Recital', in the series *CBC Tuesday Night*, 23 July 1970. [Unpublished; cassette copy from a private source.]

—— NLC 32/47/20. [Draft of a letter to Libby Wilson; undated (*c*.1971); unpublished.]

—— commentary for an untitled programme in the CBC radio series *The Scene*, 7 Oct. 1972. [Unpublished; cassette copy from the NLC.]

—— 'Transcribing Wagner' [1973], *GlennGould*, 2 (1996), 51–5.

—— 'Arts National No. 3/Draft 2', NLC 12/29. [Dated 27 July 1977; unpublished; commentary for programme no. 3 in the CBC radio series *August Arts National*, 24 Aug. 1977.]

—— 'CBC Radio Script from 1978', *GlennGould*, 2 (1996), 10–16.

—— 'Sviatoslav Richter' [1978], *GlennGould*, 1 (1995), 12–13.

—— 'Bach Series/Program 1/Draft 2', NLC 15/85. [Dated 6 Nov. 1979; unpublished; draft of commentary for Bruno Monsaingeon's film *The Question of Instrument* (*Glenn Gould Plays Bach*, 1).]

—— *A Glenn Gould Fantasy* [recorded documentary programme in a conversation format, scripted by Gould], in *The Glenn Gould Silver Jubilee Album*, CBS M2X 35914, 1980.

—— '"Mostly Music"—A Conversation with Barclay McMillan/Draft 2—Final', NLC 16/29. [Dated Oct. 1980; unpublished; commentary for the CBC radio series *Mostly Music*, 23 Oct. 1980.]

—— 'What the Recording Process Means to Me' [1982], *Bulletin of the Glenn Gould Society*, 3/1 (no. 5, Mar. 1986), 35–7.

—— *Le dernier puritain: Écrits (Tome I)*, ed. and trans. Bruno Monsaingeon (Paris: Fayard, 1983).

—— *The Glenn Gould Reader*, ed. Tim Page (Toronto: Lester & Orpen Dennys, 1984).

Contrepoint à la ligne: Écrits (Tome II), ed. and trans. Bruno Monsaingeon (Paris: Fayard, 1985).

—— *Non, je ne suis pas du tout un excentrique*, ed. and trans. Bruno Monsaingeon (Paris: Fayard, 1986).

—— *Glenn Gould: Selected Letters*, ed. John P. L. Roberts and Ghyslaine Guertin (Toronto: Oxford University Press, 1992).

—— and MENUHIN, YEHUDI, commentary for the CBC television programme 'Duo', in the *Festival* series, 18 May 1966. [Video release: Sony Classical, GGC ii, 1992.]

—— *et al.*, *Glenn Gould: Variations*, ed. John McGreevy (Toronto: Doubleday, 1983).

GUERTIN, GHYSLAINE, 'A propos de "Glenn Gould et les Variations Goldberg": une approche sémiologique de l'interprétation', *Analyse musicale*, 7 (Apr. 1987), 16–19.

GUILLARD, GEORGES, 'Glenn Gould, organiste paradoxal', in *Glenn Gould, pluriel*, ed. Ghyslaine Guertin (Verdun, Quebec: Louise Courteau, éditrice, 1988), 137–54.

HAGESTEDT, JENS, *Wie spielt Glenn Gould?: Zu einer Theorie der Interpretation* (Munich: P. Kirchheim, 1991).

HANSLICK, EDUARD, *On the Musically Beautiful: A Contribution towards the Revision of the Aesthetics of Music*, trans. and ed. Geoffrey Payzant (Indianapolis: Hackett, 1986).

HARRIS, DALE, 'Private performer: Glenn Gould Talks to Dale Harris', *Performance Magazine* (Dec. 1981), 51–4.

HASKELL, HARRY, *The Early Music Revival: A History* (London: Thames & Hudson, 1988).

HEFLING, STEPHEN E., *Rhythmic Alteration in Seventeenth- and Eighteenth-Century Music: Notes Inégales and Overdotting* (New York: Schirmer Books, 1993).

HERMERÉN, GÖRAN, 'The Full Voic'd Quire: Types of Interpretations of Music', in *The Interpretation of Music: Philosophical Essays*, ed. Michael Krausz (Oxford: Clarendon Press, 1993), 9–31.

Hétu, Jacques, 'Variations and Variants', *GlennGould*, 1 (1995), 24–5.

Hill, Robert, '"Overcoming Romanticism": On the Modernization of Twentieth-Century Performance Practice', in *Music and Performance during the Weimar Republic*, ed. Bryan Gilliam (Cambridge Studies in Performance Practice, 3; Cambridge: Cambridge University Press, 1994), 37–58.

Hirsch, E. D., Jr., *Validity in Interpretation* (New Haven and London: Yale University Press, 1967).

Horowitz, Joseph, *The Post-Classical Predicament: Essays on Music and Society* (Boston: Northeastern University Press, 1995).

Hulme, T. E., *Speculations: Essays on Humanism and the Philosophy of Art*, ed. Herbert Read, 2nd edn. (London: Routledge & Kegan Paul, 1936).

Ingarden, Roman, *The Work of Music and the Problem of Its Identity*, trans. Adam Czerniawski, ed. Jean G. Harrell (Berkeley and Los Angeles: University of California Press, 1986).

Innes, Dale, 'Glenn Gould: The Goldberg Variations', MA thesis (York University, 1990).

Ives, Charles E., 'Essays before a Sonata', in *Three Classics in the Aesthetic of Music* (New York: Dover, 1962), 103–85.

Jander, Owen, 'Rhythmic Symmetry in the *Goldberg Variations*', *Musical Quarterly*, 52 (1966), 204–8.

Johnson, David, 'Bach's Keyboard Partitas: A Conversation with Glenn Gould' [liner notes to Bach's Partitas (complete)], Columbia M2S 693/M2L 293, 1963. [Scripted by Gould; 'David Johnson' is fictitious.]

Kallmann, Helmut, review of recordings by Glenn Gould (Bach, Clavier Concerto No. 5 in F minor; Beethoven, Concerto No. 1 in C major), *Canadian Music Journal*, 3/4 (Summer 1959), 51–3.

Kaussler, Ingrid, and Kaussler, Helmut, *Die Goldberg-Variationen von J. S. Bach* (Stuttgart: Verlag Freies Geistesleben, 1985).

Kazdin, Andrew, *Glenn Gould at Work: Creative Lying* (New York: E. P. Dutton, 1989).

Kent, James, 'Glenn Gould & Wolfgang Amadeus Mozart', *Canadian Composer*, 38 (Mar. 1969), 39–41.

Kenyon, Nicholas, 'Introduction. Authenticity and Early Music: Some Issues and Questions', *Authenticity and Early Music: A Symposium*, ed. Nicholas Kenyon (Oxford: Oxford University Press, 1988), 1–18.

Kerman, Joseph, *Contemplating Music: Challenges to Musicology* (Cambridge, Mass.: Harvard University Press, 1985).

Kind, Sylvia, 'Glenn Gould, the Man', *Bulletin of the Glenn Gould Society*, 5/2 (no. 10, Oct. 1988), 46–64.

Kirkpatrick, Ralph, 'Preface', in J. S. Bach, *The 'Goldberg' Variations*, ed. Ralph Kirkpatrick (New York: G. Schirmer, 1938), vii–xxviii.

Kivy, Peter, *Music Alone: Philosophical Reflections on the Purely Musical Experience* (Ithaca, NY: Cornell University Press, 1990).

—— *The Fine Art of Repetition: Essays in the Philosophy of Music* (Cambridge: Cambridge University Press, 1993).

KOSTELANETZ, RICHARD, 'Glenn Gould: Bach in the Electronic Age', in *Glenn Gould: Variations*, ed. John McGreevy (Toronto: Doubleday, 1983), 125–41.

KOTT, JAN, *Shakespeare Our Contemporary*, trans. Boleslaw Taborski (Garden City, NY: Doubleday, 1964).

KREBS, HARALD, 'Some Extensions of the Concepts of Metrical Consonance and Dissonance', *Journal of Music Theory*, 31 (1987), 99–120.

KRENEK, ERNST, *Exploring Music*, trans. Margaret Shenfield and Geoffrey Skelton (New York: October House, 1966).

—— 'Glenn Gould', *Bulletin of the Glenn Gould Society*, 3/2 (no. 6, Oct. 1986), 52.

LANDOWSKA, WANDA, *Landowska on Music*, ed. and trans. Denise Restout, with Robert Hawkins (New York: Stein & Day, 1964).

LEECH-WILKINSON, DANIEL, 'What we are doing with early music is genuinely authentic to such a small degree that the word loses most of its intended meaning', in 'The Limits of Authenticity: A Discussion', *Early Music*, 12 (1984), 13–15.

LELIE, CHRISTO, 'Was Gould a Disciple of Rosalyn Tureck?', *Bulletin of the Glenn Gould Society*, 3/2 (no. 6, Oct. 1986), 29–39.

LE MOYNE, JEAN, *Convergence: Essays from Quebec*, trans. Philip Stratford (Toronto: Ryerson Press, 1966).

LEONHARDT, GUSTAV M., *The Art of Fugue, Bach's Last Harpsichord Work: An Argument* (The Hague: Martinus Nijhoff, 1952).

LESTER, JOEL, 'Performance and Analysis: Interaction and Interpretation', in *The Practice of Performance: Studies in Musical Interpretation*, ed. John Rink (Cambridge: Cambridge University Press, 1995), 197–216.

LEVINSON, JERROLD, *Music, Art, and Metaphysics: Essays in Philosophical Aesthetics* (Ithaca, NY: Cornell University Press, 1990).

—— 'Performative vs. Critical Interpretation in Music', in *The Interpretation of Music: Philosophical Essays*, ed. Michael Krausz (Oxford: Clarendon Press, 1993), 33–60.

LEVY, JANET M, ' "Something Mechanical Encrusted on the Living": A Source of Musical Wit and Humor', in *Convention in Eighteenth- and Nineteenth-Century Music: Essays in Honor of Leonard G. Ratner*, ed. Wye J. Allanbrook, Janet M. Levy, and William P. Mahrt (Festschrift Series, 10; Stuyvesant, NY: Pendragon Press, 1992), 225–56.

LIPMAN, SAMUEL, *The House of Music: Art in an Era of Institutions* (Boston: David R. Godine, 1984).

LYOTARD, JEAN-FRANÇOIS, *The Postmodern Condition: A Report on Knowledge*, trans. Geoff Bennington and Brian Massumi (Theory and History of Literature, 10; Minneapolis: University of Minnesota Press, 1984).

McCLURE, JOHN, *Glenn Gould: Concert Dropout* [recorded interview], Columbia BS 15 [bonus LP released with Columbia MS 7095 (Beethoven-Liszt Symphony No. 5)], 1968 [CD release: CBS/Sony (Japan) XBDC 91002, 1986].

McLUHAN, MARSHALL, *Understanding Media: The Extensions of Man*, 2nd edn. (New York: New American Library, 1964).

—— *The Gutenberg Galaxy: The Making of Typographic Man* (New York: New American Library, 1969).

MACH, ELYSE, *Great Pianists Speak for Themselves* (New York: Dodd, Mead, 1980).

MACHOVER, TOD, 'Technology and the Redirection of Music', lecture delivered at the Glenn Gould Conference, Toronto, 26 Sept. 1992; typescript.

MANTEL, GEORG, 'Zur Ausführung der Arpeggien in J.S. Bachs "Chromatischer Phantasie"', *Bach-Jahrbuch* 26, ed. Arnold Schering (Leipzig: Breitkopf & Härtel, 1929), 142–52.

MATHEIS, WERA, *Glenn Gould: Der Unheilige am Klavier* (Scanegs kleine Kultur Splitter, 1; Munich: Scaneg, 1987).

MAUK, FRED, 'Resurrection and Insurrection: Conflicting Metaphors for Musical Performance', *Journal of Aesthetics and Art Criticism*, 45/2 (Winter 1986), 139–45.

MENDELSSOHN, FELIX, *Letters of Felix Mendelssohn Bartholdy, from 1833 to 1847*, ed. Paul Mendelssohn Bartholdy and Carl Mendelssohn Bartholdy, trans. Lady Wallace (London: Longman, Green, Longman, Roberts, & Green, 1863).

MENUHIN, YEHUDI, and CURTIS W., DAVIS, *The Music of Man* (Toronto: Methuen, 1979), 290–5.

METHUEN-CAMPBELL, JAMES, *Chopin Playing: From the Composer to the Present Day* (London: Victor Gollancz, 1981).

MEYER, LEONARD B., *Emotion and Meaning in Music* (Chicago: University of Chicago Press, 1956).

—— *Music, the Arts, and Ideas: Patterns and Predictions in Twentieth-Century Culture* (Chicago: University of Chicago Press, 1967).

—— *Explaining Music: Essays and Explorations* (Berkeley and Los Angeles: University of California Press, 1973).

MEYER, MARTIN, 'Das Sprechklavier: Glenn Gould und die Dekonstruktion', *Du*, no. 4 (Apr. 1990), 58–61, 96, 101–2.

—— 'Interview: Glenn Gould, ". . . the inner movement of music . . ." ', *GlennGould*, 1 (1995), 16–20.

MONSAINGEON, BRUNO, *Chemins de la musique* [series of four films] (ORTF, 1974): i, 'Glenn Gould: La Retraite' (30 Nov.); ii, 'Glenn Gould: L'Alchimiste' (7 Dec.); iii, 'Glenn Gould: 1974' (14 Dec.); iv, 'Glenn Gould: Sixième Partita de Jean-Sébastien Bach' (21 Dec.). [Video release: INA/Éditions du Léonard]

—— *The Question of Instrument* [film] (*Glenn Gould Plays Bach*, 1; CBC-Clasart co-production, 1979). [Video release: Sony Classical, GGC xiv, 1994.]

—— *An Art of the Fugue* [film] (*Glenn Gould Plays Bach*, 2; CBC-Clasart co-production, 1980). [Video release: Sony Classical, GGC xv, 1994.]

—— *The Goldberg Variations* [film] (*Glenn Gould Plays Bach*, 3; CBC-Clasart co-production, 1981). [Video release: Sony Classical, GGC xiii, 1994.]

MOORE, PAT, 'Interview with Glenn Gould, the Pianist', NLC 2/50. [Dated 15 Dec. 1964; unpublished; recorded for CBC radio but never aired.]

MOREY, CARL, 'Editing Glenn Gould', *GlennGould*, 1 (1995), 21–3.

MORGAN, ROBERT P., 'Glenn Gould, Extraordinary Harpsichordist', *High Fidelity*, 23/2 (Feb. 1973), 84.

—— 'Tradition, Anxiety, and the Current Musical Scene', in *Authenticity and Early Music: A Symposium*, ed. Nicholas Kenyon (Oxford: Oxford University Press, 1988), 57–82.

NARMOUR, EUGENE, 'On the Relationship of Analytical Theory to Performance and Interpretation', in *Explorations in Music, the Arts, and Ideas: Essays in Honor of Leonard B. Meyer*, ed. Eugene Narmour and Ruth A. Solie (Festschrift Series, 7; Stuyvesant, NY: Pendragon Press, 1988), 317–40.

NATIONAL FILM BOARD OF CANADA, *Glenn Gould: Off the Record* and *Glenn Gould: On the Record* [series of two films] (1959). [Video release: National Film Board of Canada B 0159 158, 1994.]

NATIONAL LIBRARY OF CANADA, *Descriptive Catalogue of The Glenn Gould Papers*, ed. Ruth Pincoe and Stephen C. Willis, 2 vols. (Ottawa: National Library of Canada, 1992).

NATTIEZ, JEAN-JACQUES, 'Gould singulier: Structure et atemporalité dans la pensée gouldienne', in *Glenn Gould, pluriel*, ed. Ghyslaine Guertin (Verdun, Quebec: Louise Courteau, éditrice, 1988), 57–82.

—— *Music and Discourse: Toward a Semiology of Music*, trans. Carolyn Abbate (Princeton: Princeton University Press, 1990).

—— ' "Fidelity" to Wagner: Reflections on the Centenary *Ring*', in *Wagner in Performance*, ed. Barry Millington and Stewart Spencer (New Haven: Yale University Press, 1992), 75–98.

—— 'The Language of Music in the Twenty-First Century: Gould as Precursor of Postmodernism?', *GlennGould*, 2 (1996), 28–35.

NEUMANN, FREDERICK, 'Couperin and the Downbeat Doctrine for Appoggiaturas', *Acta Musicologica*, 41 (1969), 71–85.

—— *Ornamentation in Baroque and Post-Baroque Music, with Special Emphasis on J. S. Bach* (Princeton: Princeton University Press, 1978).

—— *Essays in Performance Practice* (Studies in Musicology, 58; Ann Arbor: UMI Research Press, 1982).

NEWLIN, DIKA, *Schoenberg Remembered: Diaries and Recollections (1938–76)* (New York: Pendragon Press, 1980).

ORTEGA Y GASSET, JOSÉ, *The Dehumanization of Art and Other Essays on Art, Culture, and Literature*, trans. Helene Weyl (Princeton: Princeton University Press, 1968).

ORTMANN, OTTO, *The Physiological Mechanics of Piano Technique: An Experimental Study of the Nature of Muscular Action As Used in Piano Playing, and the Effects Thereof upon the Piano Key and Piano Tone* (London: Kegan Paul, Trench, Trübner and Co., 1929).

OSTWALD, PETER, *Glenn Gould: The Ecstasy and Tragedy of Genius* (New York and London: W. W. Norton, 1997).

PACSU, MARGARET, SCHAFER, R. MURRAY, TOVELL, VINCENT and ROBERTS, JOHN, 'Gould, the Communicator: Panel discussion held at The National Library of Canada, Ottawa, Wednesday, May 25, 1988', *Bulletin of the Glenn Gould Society* 6/1–2 (no. 11–12, Oct. 1989), 35–64.

PAGE, TIM, recorded interview with Glenn Gould, Aug. 1982 [bonus LP released with CBS M3X 38610 (*Glenn Gould: Bach, Volume 1*, containing the 1955 and 1981 recordings of the Goldberg Variations), 1984].

PAYZANT, GEOFFREY, 'Hanslick, Sams, Gay, and "*Tönend Bewegte Formen*"', *Journal of Aesthetics and Art Criticism*, 40/1 (Fall 1981), 41–8.

—— *Glenn Gould: Music and Mind,* rev. edn. (Toronto: Key Porter Books, 1984).

—— 'The Glenn Gould Outtakes', in *Musical Canada: Words and Music Honouring Helmut Kallmann,* ed. John Beckwith and Frederick A. Hall (Toronto: University of Toronto Press, 1988), 298–313.

—— BECKWITH, JOHN, and BAZZANA, KEVIN, 'Gould, Glenn (Herbert)', in *Encyclopedia of Music in Canada,* ed. Helmut Kallmann, Gilles Potvin, and Kenneth Winters; 2nd edn. ed. Helmut Kallmann and Gilles Potvin, with Robin Elliott and Mark Miller (Toronto, Buffalo, and London: University of Toronto Press, 1992), 540–5.

PERRY, ROSALIE SANDRA, *Charles Ives and the American Mind* ([n.p.]: Kent State University Press, 1974).

P. G. D. [PETER G. DAVIS], 'Glenn Gould Allows a Guest', *High Fidelity,* 17/8 (Aug. 1967), 22.

PHILIP, ROBERT, *Early Recordings and Musical Style: Changing Tastes in Instrumental Performance, 1900–1950* (Cambridge: Cambridge University Press, 1992).

RATTALINO, PIERO, *Da Clementi a Pollini: Duecento anni con i grandi pianisti* (Florence: Ricordi/Giunti Martello, 1983).

RINK, JOHN, review of Wallace Berry, *Musical Structure and Performance, Music Analysis,* 9 (1990), 319–38.

RIVEST, JOHANNE, 'L'Interprétation musicale chez Glenn Gould', MA thesis (University of Montreal, 1987).

RODDY, JOSEPH, 'Apollonian', in *Glenn Gould: Variations,* ed. John McGreevy (Toronto: Doubleday Canada Limited, 1983), 95–123.

ROSEN, CHARLES, 'Should Music Be Played "Wrong"?', *High Fidelity,* 21/5 (May 1971), 54–8.

—— *The Classical Style: Haydn, Mozart, Beethoven* (New York and London: W. W. Norton & Company, 1972).

—— *The Romantic Generation* (Cambridge, Mass.: Harvard University Press, 1995).

ROTHSTEIN, WILLIAM, 'Heinrich Schenker as an Interpreter of Beethoven's Piano Sonatas', *19th-Century Music,* 8/1 (Summer 1984), 3–28.

SAID, EDWARD W., 'The Music Itself: Glenn Gould's Contrapuntal Vision', in *Glenn Gould: Variations,* ed. John McGreevy (Toronto: Doubleday, 1983), 45–54.

—— *Musical Elaborations* (Wellek Library Lectures at the University of California, Irvine; New York: Columbia University Press, 1991).

SAMAROTTO, FRANK, 'Strange Dimensions: Regularity and Irregularity in Deep Levels of Rhythmic Reduction', paper delivered at the Second International Schenker Symposium, New York, Mar. 1992.

SCHAFER, MURRAY, review of recordings by Glenn Gould (Bach, Partitas Nos. 5 in G major and 6 in E minor), *Canadian Music Journal,* 3/1 (Autumn 1958), 58–9.

SCHENKER, HEINRICH, *J. S. Bach's Chromatic Fantasy and Fugue: Critical Edition with Commentary,* trans. and ed. Hedi Siegel (Longman Music Series; New York: Longman, 1984).

SCHENKMAN, WALTER, 'The Establishment of Tempo in Bach's *Goldberg Variations', Bach,* 6/3 (July 1975), 3–10.

SCHOENBERG, ARNOLD, *Style and Idea: Selected Writings of Arnold Schoenberg*, ed. Leonard Stein, trans. Leo Black (New York: St Martins Press, 1975).

SCHONBERG, HAROLD C., *The Great Pianists*, rev. edn. (New York: Simon & Schuster, 1987).

SCHOPENHAUER, ARTHUR, *The World as Will and Representation*, trans. E. F. J. Payne, 2 vols. (Keystone Series; Indian Hills, Colo.: Falcon's Wing Press, 1958).

SCHWEITZER, ALBERT, *J. S. Bach*, trans. Ernest Newman, 2 vols. (New York: Dover Publications, 1966).

SCOTT, HOWARD H., FROST, THOMAS, MYERS, PAUL, KAZDIN, ANDREW, and CARTER, SAMUEL H., 'Recording Gould: A Retake Here, a Splice There, a Myth Everywhere', *High Fidelity*, 33/2 (Feb. 1983), 55–6, 80.

SIEPMANN, JEREMY, 'Glenn Gould and the Interpreter's Prerogative', *The Musical Times*, 131, no. 1763 (Jan. 1990), 25–7.

SILVERMAN, ROBERT J., 'Memories: Glenn Gould 1932–1982', in *Glenn Gould: Variations*, ed. John McGreevy (Toronto: Doubleday, 1983), 143–9.

SKELTON, ROBERT A., 'Weinzweig, Gould, Schafer: Three Canadian String Quartets', D.Mus. thesis (Indiana University, 1976).

SLOBODA, JOHN A., *The Musical Mind: The Cognitive Psychology of Music* (Oxford Psychology Series, 5; Oxford: Clarendon Press, 1985).

SPICE, NICHOLAS, 'How to Play the Piano', *London Review of Books*, 14/6 (26 Mar. 1992), 3–9.

STEGEMANN, MICHAEL, *Glenn Gould: Leben und Werk* (Munich: Piper, 1992).

STEWART, JOHN L., *Ernst Krenek: The Man and His Music* (Berkeley and Los Angeles: University of California Press, 1991).

STRAUS, JOSEPH N., *Remaking the Past: Musical Modernism and the Influence of the Tonal Tradition* (Cambridge, Mass.: Harvard University Press, 1990).

STRAVINSKY, IGOR, *Poetics of Music in the Form of Six Lessons*, trans. Arthur Knodel and Ingolf Dahl (New York: Vintage Books, 1960).

STRUNK, OLIVER, *Source Readings in Music History: The Renaissance* (New York: W. W. Norton, 1965).

SULEIMAN, SUSAN R., 'Introduction: Varieties of Audience-Oriented Criticism', in *The Reader in the Text: Essays on Audience and Interpretation*, ed. Susan R. Suleiman and Inge Crosman (Princeton: Princeton University Press, 1980), 3–45.

TARUSKIN, RICHARD, *Text and Act: Essays on Music and Performance* (New York: Oxford University Press, 1995).

THÉBERGE, PAUL, 'Counterpoint: Glenn Gould & Marshall McLuhan', *Bulletin of the Glenn Gould Society*, 4/1–2 (nos. 7–8, Oct. 1987), 9–33.

THOMSON, VIRGIL, *A Virgil Thomson Reader* (New York: E. P. Dutton, 1984).

TOVELL, VINCENT, 'At Home With Glenn Gould' [recorded interview], programme in the CBC radio series *Project 60*, 4 December 1959. [CD release: Sony CDNK 1190, for the Glenn Gould Foundation's Friends of Glenn Gould society, 1996.]

TOVEY, DONALD FRANCIS, 'Aria with Thirty Variations (The "Goldberg" Variations)', in *Essays in Musical Analysis: Chamber Music* (London: Oxford University Press, 1944), 28–75.

TROEGER, RICHARD, *Technique and Interpretation on the Harpsichord and Clavichord* (Bloomington and Indianapolis: Indiana University Press, 1987).

TURECK, ROSALYN, *An Introduction to the Performance of Bach: A Progressive Anthology of Keyboard Music Edited, with Introductory Essays,* 3 vols. (London: Oxford University Press, 1960).

—— 'Bach in the Twentieth Century', *The Musical Times,* 103/1428 (Feb. 1962), 92–4.

TÜRK, DANIEL GOTTLOB, *Klavierschule* [facsimile of the 1st ed., 1789], ed. Erwin R. Jacobi (Documenta Musicologica, 1st ser.: Druckschriften-Faksimiles, 23; Kassel: Bärenreiter, 1962).

UUSITALO, JYRKI, 'The Recurring Postmodern: Notes on the Constitution of Musical Artworks', in *Essays on the Philosophy of Music,* ed. Veikko Rantala, Lewis Rowell, and Eero Tarasti (Acta Philosophica Fennica, 43; Helsinki: Societas Philosophica Fennica, 1988), 257–77.

WAGNER, RICHARD, 'About Conducting', in *Richard Wagner's Prose Works,* iv. *Art and Politics,* trans. William Ashton Ellis (London: Kegan Paul, Trench, Trübner & Co., 1895), 289–364.

WEBERN, ANTON VON, analysis of String Quartet, Op. 28, trans. and ed. Zoltan Roman, in Hans Moldenhauer and Rosaleen Moldenhauer, *Anton von Webern: A Chronicle of His Life and Work* (New York: Alfred A. Knopf, 1979), 751–6.

WILSON, MILTON, review of recordings by Glenn Gould (Haydn, Sonata No. 49 in E flat major; Mozart, Sonata in C major, K. 330; Mozart, Fantasia and Fugue in C major, K. 394), *The Canadian Music Journal* 3/2 (Winter 1959), 58–9.

WIMSATT, W. K., JR., and BEARDSLEY, M. C., 'The Intentional Fallacy', *The Sewanee Review,* 54 (1946), 468–88.

WINTER, ROBERT S., 'Orthodoxies, Paradoxes, and Contradictions', in *Nineteenth-Century Piano Music,* ed. R. Larry Todd (New York: Schirmer Books, 1990), 16–54.

WOLFF, CHRISTOPH, *Bach: Essays on His Life and Music* (Cambridge, Mass.: Harvard University Press, 1991).

WOLFF, HELLMUTH CHRISTIAN, 'Der Rhythmus bei Johann Sebastian Bach', *Bach-Jahrbuch,* 37, ed. Max Schneider (Leipzig: Breitkopf & Härtel, 1948), 83–121.

WOLFF, KONRAD, *Schnabel's Interpretation of Piano Music,* 2nd edn. (New York: W. W. Norton, 1979).

—— *Masters of the Keyboard: Individual Style Elements in the Piano Music of Bach, Haydn, Mozart, Beethoven, Schubert, Chopin, and Brahms,* rev. edn. (Bloomington and Indianapolis: Indiana University Press, 1990).

ZIMMERMAN, JÖRG, 'Bach as a Paradigm in Aesthetic Discourse', in *Essays on the Philosophy of Music,* ed. Veikko Rantala, Lewis Rowell, and Eero Tarasti (Acta Philosophica Fennica, 43; Helsinki: Societas Philosophica Fennica, 1988), 343–61.

INDEX

Note: Italics denote references to musical examples, figures, and plates; references to tables are treated as text and given in roman type. References to CD tracks are also included.